Black, Brown, & Beige

THE SURREALIST REVOLUTION SERIES
Franklin Rosemont, Editor

A renowned current in poetry and the
arts, surrealism has also influenced
psychoanalysis, anthropology, critical
theory, politics, humor, popular culture,
and everyday life. Illuminating its
diversity and actuality, the Surrealist
Revolution Series focuses on translations
of original writings by participants in
the international surrealist movement
and on critical studies of unexamined
aspects of its development.

Black, Brown, & Beige

SURREALIST WRITINGS FROM
AFRICA AND THE DIASPORA

Edited by Franklin Rosemont
and Robin D. G. Kelley

 University of Texas Press   Austin

Dedicated to Aimé Césaire, Ted Joans, & Franklin Rosemont

© 2009 University of Texas Press
All rights reserved
Printed in the United States of America
First edition, 2009

Requests for permission to reproduce material from
this work should be sent to:
Permissions
University of Texas Press
P.O. Box 7819
Austin, TX 78713-7819
www.utexas.edu/utpress/about/bpermission.html

Library of Congress Cataloging-in-Publication Data

Black, brown, & beige : surrealist writings from
    Africa and the diaspora / edited by Franklin
    Rosemont and Robin D. G. Kelley. — 1st ed.
        p. cm. — (The surrealist revolution series)
    Includes bibliographical references and index.
    ISBN 978-0-292-72581-2
        1. Surrealism (Literature) 2. Surrealism.
    3. Literature—Black authors. I. Rosemont,
    Franklin. II. Kelley, Robin D. G. III. Title: Black,
    brown, and beige.
    PN6071.S915B63 2009
    809′.91163—dc22   2009006978

Contents

2. *Tropiques: Surrealism in the Caribbean*   61

4. *Africa* 135

7. Surrealism, Black Power, Black Arts   237

8. Toward the New Millennium: The Mid-1970s through the 1990s   285

9. *Looking Ahead: Surrealism Today and Tomorrow*   315

This metal sculpture by Gabriel
Bien-Aime was shown in the
World Surrealist Exhibition held
in Chicago in 1976.

List of Illustrations

Tyree Guyton's art was a center of controversy in Detroit where he transformed abandoned houses into surrealist objects. In 1992 the surrealists issued a statement in his defense. (Photo by Maurice Greenia, Jr.)

Acknowledgments

Thanks above all to Penelope Rosemont, whose *Surrealist Women: An International Anthology* was not only the first book in this series, but also provides the model for the present volume.

To my surrealist friends in Paris, Amsterdam, Prague, Madrid, Leeds, London, São Paulo, Chicago, and other places, for thoughtfully sending publications and information.

And to the many translators: Myrna Bell Rochester, Marjolijn de Jager, Celia Cymbalista, Guy Ducornet, Judy Cumberbatch, Rachel Blackwell, Connie Rosemont, Cynthia Hahn, Robert Launay, Melanie Kemp, Danielle Jouët-Pastre, Neil Pischer, Jennifer Bean, Nancy Joyce Peters, Philip Lamantia, Laura Corsiglia, Gay Rawson, Marcus Salgado, Natalia Segarra, Wingo Smith, Dale Tomich, and Alex Wilder.

To longtime friends John Bracey, Dennis Brutus, Jayne Cortez, Don LaCoss, David Roediger, Tamara Smith, Gibbsy Tarnaud, Joseph Jablonski, and others, for sharing ideas and information.

Due to limitations of space and time, many of the texts represented are excerpted from a longer original.

Franklin Rosemont, Chicago

Lindsay Park (photomontage, 1999) by Patrick Turner, surrealist artist and blues musician.

Invisible Surrealists

> Only poets, since they must excavate and recreate history,
> have ever learned anything from it.
> —James Baldwin

In the vast critical literature on surrealism, all but a few black surrealists have been invisible. Despite mounting studies of Aimé Césaire, Wifredo Lam, Ted Joans, and, more recently, Jayne Cortez, academic histories and anthologies typically, but very wrongly, persist in conveying surrealism as an all-white movement, like other "artistic schools" of European origin. Occasional token mentions aside, people of color—and more particularly those from Africa or the Diaspora—have been excluded from most of the so-called standard works on the subject.[1]

In glaring contrast, the many publications of the international surrealist movement—periodicals, books, pamphlets, exhibition catalogs, and anthologies produced by the surrealists themselves—regularly feature texts and reproductions of works by black comrades from Martinique, Haiti, Cuba, Puerto Rico, South America, Africa, the United States, and other lands. These publications, moreover, are readily available to researchers at numerous libraries. Inaccessibility, therefore, is not a legitimate excuse for exclusion.

It is the aim of this book to introduce readers to the black surrealists of the world; to provide sketches of their lives and deeds as well as their important place in history, especially the history of surrealism; and, not least, to present a selection of their writings and art.

*   *   *

The surrealist movement began as a spontaneous association, based on elective affinities, and that is what it has always been and still is. Abjuring, on principle, all proselytizing and recruitment, it has never entertained the aim of being a mass movement. Indeed, surrealism has always been determinedly minoritary: French poet André Breton—its cofounder, author of the *Surrealist Manifestoes*, and first major theorist—described surrealism as a minority always "tending toward greater human emancipation," and went on to add that it is "ceaselessly renewable" and "acts as a lever."[2]

Surrealism's worldwide membership has rarely if ever exceeded two hundred at any given time. As the present volume demonstrates, well over fifty individuals of African descent, from the early 1930s on, have participated actively, at one time or another, in what its adherents often call the Surrealist International. These individuals not only have considered themselves surrealists, but also have regularly taken part in Surrealist Group discussions and other collective activities such as collaborating on surrealist books and periodicals, planning surrealist exhibitions, and in any number of ways publicly affirming their involvement in surrealism and their support for its aims and principles. A large majority, moreover, have proved to be truly distinguished figures, noted for their originality and expansion of the surrealist cause. Within the ranks of the international movement, surrealists black, brown, and beige have long been recognized as outstanding poets, theorists, critics, spokespersons, painters, sculptors, collagists, story writers, filmmakers, playwrights, dancers, and all-around agitators.

In addition to these fifty-plus participants in surrealism as an international movement, the present anthology also includes a number of surrealism's black forerunners as well as close allies, among them freelance writers and independent scholars, some with university connections. Aware that insight and imagination are not anyone's private property, surrealists over the years have readily welcomed many thoughtful and sympathetic associates who, often without even knowing it, have helped surrealism move in new directions.

A third category, also represented in this volume, includes individuals who, though neither adherents of the surrealist movement nor formally allied with it, have nonetheless proved by their exemplary attitude and activity—as poets, writers, artists, or activists—that they have fully qualified as objectively surrealist.

THE OPPOSITE OF A BUREAUCRACY

> Poetry has an aim: absolute human freedom.
> —Malcolm de Chazal

In the spirit of first things first, this is probably the place to tackle the question, "What *is* surrealism?"

Early on, surrealist painter André Masson called it "the collective experience of individualism," and poet Antonin Artaud, "a new kind of magic."[3] Such playful definitions still ring bells today. As a movement, however—and one still very much in motion—surrealism has always resisted the efforts of critics to confine it to *any* static definition. Surrealists themselves have always preferred to speak of surrealism in terms of dynamics, dialectics, goals, and struggles. One of the clearest and most succinct presentations of its fundamental aims was provided by David Gascoyne, the sixteen-year-old cofounder of the Surrealist Group in England in 1936: "It is the avowed aim of the surrealist movement to reduce and finally to dispose altogether of the flagrant contradictions that exist between dream and waking life, the 'unreal' and the 'real,' the unconscious and the conscious, and thus to make what has hitherto been regarded as the special domain of poets, the acknowledged common property of all."[4]

It cannot be emphasized too strongly that surrealism is not and never has been a school or a style or an ideology but, rather, "a community of ethical views," as the Czech surrealist painter Toyen called it in the early 1950s.[5] The spirit of solidarity is its essence. The opposite of a bureaucracy, surrealism involves no forms to fill out, no pledges, no membership cards to sign. Unlike so many artistic or literary cliques or political sects, whose narrow-minded dogmas are reflected in a stifling organizational conformity, surrealist groups have always encouraged and exemplified the widest diversity and open-endedness, not only in their collective interventions in the larger society, but also and especially in their internal affairs. In a 2005 talk at Loyola University in Chicago, poet Jayne Cortez remarked that "surrealists, even those who haven't met before, always tend to recognize each other."[6]

Above all, hack journalists notwithstanding, surrealism does not signify unreality, antireality, the nonsensical, or the absurd. On the contrary, surrealism—an *open* realism—signifies *more* reality, and an expanded *awareness* of reality, including aspects and elements of the real that are ordinarily overlooked, dismissed, excluded, hidden, shunned, suppressed, ignored, forgotten, or otherwise neglected.

Surrealism from the start differed radically from the many "avant-gardes" that preceded it. Post-Impressionism, Futurism, Cubism, Fauvism, and Dada were focused almost exclusively on art—or, as in Dada, art and antiart—and to a lesser extent on literature. These avant-gardes were not only white and European, but also, with the partial exception of Dada, openly Eurocentric. Surrealists, however, even before the publication of André Breton's first *Surrealist Manifesto* in 1924, were emphatically *anti*-Eurocentric.[7] Even during their brief period as Dadaists (roughly 1919–1922), they were calling everything European and American into question, including Dada. They openly scorned white supremacy, patriotism, religion, colonialism, prudish morality, and respect for the law. For the pious bourgeois artists and intellectuals most promoted by the commercial press, they had nothing but contempt.

In the same rebellious spirit, the contemporaries they most admired were noted for their fierce repudiation of the commercialism and conformism that sustained Euro-American values: Jacques Vaché, "past master in the art of attaching little or no importance to everything," and Arthur Cravan, the "deserter of seventeen nations." The humorous 1929 "Surrealist Map of the World"—drawn by artist Yves Tanguy—omits almost all of Europe (except Paris) and leaves out the entire United States as well.[8] All of this was part of what filmmaker Luis Buñuel called the surrealists' "obstinate dedication to fight everything repressive in the conventional wisdom."[9]

Surrealism's emancipatory, direct-action approach was emphasized by French surrealist Alain Joubert in 1969: "The essential of the surrealist project is to dismantle all sclerotic categories and inhibiting authority, all forms of alienation (internal as well as social), and to open—largely, definitively, and for all—the field of the possible."[10]

Anyone who takes the trouble to study the aesthetic avant-gardes prior to surrealism will soon recognize that the surrealists' concerns are incomparably broader, audaciously ranging far beyond traditional literary and artistic categories. Surrealists were—and still are!—interested in philosophy, magic, myth, history, heresy, the exploration of objective chance, sleep and dream, the interplay of dialectics and analogy. In their search for ways to liberate the unconscious, they practice hypnosis and dream interpretation as well as automatic writing and drawing. They have discovered new techniques, from frottage and collage to cubomania and prehensilhouette, and have invented games that result in collective poetry. "Drawing correspondences between our real and imaginative experiences"—in the words of poet and anthropologist Ayana Karanja—helps resolve the contradictions between dreaming and waking, subjective and objective.[11]

Rejecting all forms of domination and the dichotomous ideologies that go with them—intolerance, exploitation, bigotry, exclusiveness, white supremacy, and all race prejudice—surrealists make the resolution of contradictions a high priority. In surrealist games, for example, play is regarded not as a matter of power, winning, and losing, but, rather, as a joyful collective dialogue and a source of insight, discovery, beauty, and laughter. Passionate defenders of the Marvelous, the unfettered imagination, poetry as a way of life, mad love, long walks, a revolution of the mind—and indeed, *world* revolution, the surrealists' basic platform may be summed up in a few words: creation of a truly free society and the realization of Lautréamont's watchword, "Poetry must be made by all!"[12]

Again in contrast to the older avant-gardes, most of which faded away in less than a decade, surrealism not only has endured for eighty-plus years, but also happens to be enjoying a global resurgence in the new millennium. Surrealism today—in poetry, theory, art, and action—offers an unparalleled panorama. Long-established and highly productive groups in Paris, Prague, Amsterdam, Chicago, Madrid, London, Leeds, Stockholm, and São Paulo are still going strong, and several more recently formed groups—in Athens, Lisbon, Santiago de Chile, and Buenos Aires, as well as Portland, Oregon, and St. Louis, Missouri—are quite active. In addition, important surrealist nuclei exist in New York, Baltimore, Detroit, Harrisburg, Vancouver, Brussels, Berlin, Düsseldorf, Belgrade, Bucharest, and Tunis.[13]

Far from "art for art's sake" and the "art market," surrealists—now as always—champion freedom, revolt, love, humor, play, creativity, nonconformity, and wild nature. André Breton and his comrades inherited and expanded the revolutionary Romantic disdain for Progress, Modernity, and the ecocidal technological devastation that smugly persists in calling itself "development." Surrealists have always been unrelenting critics of late capitalism, its mind-numbing consumer culture, and its systematized misery, exemplified by the military, prison, and advertising industries as well as the billionaires' meretricious media. It was certainly not by accident that the first surrealist journal, started in 1924, was titled *La Révolution Surréaliste.*

One of the key elements of surrealist methodology, inherited from the nineteenth-century French utopian socialist Charles Fourier, is Absolute Divergence—divergence above all from the dominant ways of thinking and behaving. Indeed, the radical utopian tradition, from the seventeenth-century Port-Royalists to such nineteenth-century figures as Enfantin, Flora Tristan, and Saint-Yves d'Alveydre, has left a strong impact on the surrealist outlook. Combining utopian, revolutionary, and poetic thought, André Breton's mature views on social betterment—as expressed in *Arcane 17,* for example—correspond closely to some of the key ideas of the pioneering African American feminist Anna Julia Cooper, who, in her 1892 book, *A Voice from the South,* calls for nothing less than the collective creation of a true democracy founded in universal reciprocity.

Breton's agreement with Cooper on such an essential issue reminds us that surrealism's anti-Eurocentrism also involves a vigorous opposition to all masculinist ideology. Women have been active in surrealism from the movement's earliest days, and their activity has increased greatly over the years. From the start, too, surrealists attacked the institutions of patriarchal oppression: church, state, capital, the fatherland, the military, and all authoritarianism. In addition to challenging gender stereotypes and rejecting the prevailing models of maleness (soldier, cop, boss, hoodlum, officeholder, and bureaucrat), they denounced such masculinist preoccupations as punishment, imprisonment, and conquering nature.

A later surrealist concept—miserabilism—is also crucial, for it gives a name to the ruling ideologies of our own time, as epitomized in the New World Order, the World Trade Organization, and all the McMiseries of globalization. In a 1956 essay, "Away with Miserabilism!" Breton defines this new plague as "the depreciation of reality instead of its exaltation" and links it historically to the combined toxic legacies of fascism and Stalinism. As "the rationalization of the unlivable," miserabilism is the major enemy of the Marvelous.[14]

FORWARD TO AFRICA

> Africa challenges the West in a way that the West has not been challenged before.
> —Richard Wright

Surrealism's solid grounding in poetry—in the *practice* of poetry as a way of life and, indeed, a social force—is directly related to its openly revolutionary position. And that in turn is directly related to the crucial but rarely acknowledged fact that surrealism is the only major modern cultural movement of European origin in which men and women of African descent have long participated as equals, and in considerable numbers.

African influence on the founders of surrealism was evident even before they called themselves surrealists—that is, before the formation of the movement in 1924. As early as 1919 the appearance of African American jazz in France was a notable historic event for André Breton and his friends and was duly recalled as such thirty-one years later in the group's *Surrealist Almanac* (1950).[15] The works of Alexandre Dumas were also important. Dumas is not only France's best-known author of African descent, but also France's best-known author, period. Breton, Louis Aragon, Philippe Soupault, and Jacques Vaché—major players in the formation of the movement—were known for a time as the Three Musketeers (in Dumas' novel the trio was also in fact a quartet).[16] Significant, too, was Dumas' *Count of Monte Cristo*. As a story of escape, struggle against injustice, and ultimate revenge, it has never been surpassed.

Victor Hugo was another influence on the first surrealist generation—especially Hugo the poet and Romantic radical. A militant abolitionist, outspoken admirer of John Brown, and the only prominent European writer to defend the 1859 attack on Harper's Ferry, Hugo was an early source of the Surrealist Group's vehement opposition to white supremacy. "If insurrection be ever a sacred duty," he wrote in 1860, "it is against slavery."[17]

The French revolutionary Jacobin tradition also had its impact. Saint-Just and Marat, vigorous opponents of the slave trade, were early surrealist heroes and remained so through the years. Marat's December 1791 declaration defending the right of slaves to revolt in the colonies was reprinted in the summer 1959 issue of the Milanese surrealist journal *Front Unique* (United front), at the height of France's war in Algeria.[18] A Chicago Surrealist Group tract issued on Bastille Day 1989 celebrates the French Revolution's bicentennial and denounces the increasingly bloated U.S. prison industry.[19]

The surrealists' first *black* hero was undoubtedly Toussaint L'Ouverture, the liberator of Haiti. He was an especially important figure for André Breton. In his first New York interview as a refugee from Nazism in 1941, Breton told of a dream in which he was Zapata, "making ready with my army to receive Toussaint L'Ouverture the following day and to render him the honors to which he was entitled."[20]

Closer still to the specifically surrealist project and, indeed, one of its major inspirers, was the poet Arthur Rimbaud (1854–1891), whose militant scorn for European values and institutions the founders of surrealism heartily adopted. Rimbaud's defiant dissociation from the authoritarianism and hypocrisy of white society—as evidenced by his bold cry, "Je suis nègre!" (I am a Negro!)—made a deep impression on the nascent surrealist group, as it would a few years later on Aimé Césaire and his comrades from Martinique, Guyana, and Senegal.[21] Even stronger was the impact of Uruguayan-born Isidore Ducasse, who called himself the Comte de Lautréamont. His astonishing book, *Les chants de Maldoror* (Songs of Maldoror, 1869), is poetry at its most luminous and ferocious—and at the same time a merciless indictment of Western civilization's "legislators of stupid institutions" and "narrow morality."[22]

Other important precursors of surrealism are Francis Viélé-Griffin and Stuart Merrill, brilliant U.S.-born French Symbolist poets. The former, son of a Union Army general during the Civil War, frequented the anarchist milieu in 1890s Paris. Merrill, a revolutionary socialist, was the author in 1905 of a series of articles entitled "The Black Question in the United States" in the newspaper *L'Européen.*[23]

Because organized surrealism began in France, its initial adherents in other countries tended to be French-speaking artists and intellectuals. At that early stage, only scattered attention was given to forerunners of surrealism whose native language was not French. Breton's *Surrealist Manifesto*, for example, simply lists Shakespeare ("in his finer moments"), Edward Young, Jonathan Swift, and Edgar Allan Poe. By the mid-1930s, however, a sizeable Surrealist Group had formed in London, and several of its most active collaborators—including David Gascoyne, Hugh Sykes Davies, and Herbert Read—had begun to study the movement's English precursors. Their tentative quest, and its later in-depth pursuit by surrealists in the United States, greatly expanded our knowledge of surrealism's historical roots.

It is surely no mere coincidence, for example, that John Milton—widely recognized as the Western world's first all-around revolutionary intellectual, second to none in his outspoken ardor for human freedom—also bestowed upon us the splendid expression "unpremeditated verse," that is, a spontaneous and wholehearted eruption of the imaginary, clearly prefiguring the practice of surrealist automatism.

Indeed, all the poets and writers of the past that the surrealists have come to recognize as the movement's specifically English-language precursors—including Cowper, Blake, Burns, Wordsworth, Shelley, Byron, Keats, Emily Brönte, Emerson, Thoreau, Margaret Fuller, and the whole transcendentalist gang—Whitman, Melville, Hardy, Sterling Brown—are, like their French equivalents, characterized by their passion for freedom, their vehement opposition to slavery, and their rebellion against all forms of oppressive authority and conformity.

As the direct and living heir of the revolutionary traditions in poetry, surrealism has also been—and remains to this day—attuned to what the Sicilian American surrealist Philip Lamantia calls a "surrealist Afrocentrism": a more or less "underground" tradition that extends back to the Gnostics and alchemists and includes Renaissance mages Pico della Mirandola and John Dee, as well as such later figures as Martínez Pasqualis, Louis Claude de Saint-Martin, and philologist Fabre d'Olivet (whose play, *Idamore, or the African Prince*, has been described as a severe critique of colonialism and slavery).[24] Their collective effort was not merely to deemphasize the mainstream Enlightenment obsession with Greco-Roman civilization, but also and especially to revalorize the wisdom of ancient Egypt. In their various ways, the Polish revolutionary romantic Hoene-Wronski, French occultist Eliphas Lévi, and the African American Paschal B. Randolph also participated in this project. Among the surrealists, André Breton, Jorge Camacho, Ithell Colquhoun, Élie-Charles Flamand, Joseph Jablonski, Gérard Legrand, Pierre Mabille, and Kurt Seligmann have written extensively on various aspects of this heterodox tradition.[25]

African art also had a strong impact on emerging surrealism. Surrealists were in fact among the first to defend tribal sculptures, not in traditional aesthetic terms—that is, not as merely decorative commodities suitable for display in museums or other "Art Detention Centers"[26] (in Ishmael Reed's apt expression)—but rather as manifestations of visible poetry, objects imbued with spiritual energy and therefore vital elements in daily life. Rejecting also the ethnologists' bad habit of categorizing such works as mere artifacts, Breton and his friends went as far as to hail this art as an active and creative force in the development of a new and revolutionary sensibility. In the so-called primitive art of Africa, Oceania, and the Americas surrealists recognized a new kind of beauty, which Breton later called "convulsive": a subversive, liberating beauty — the beauty announced by Lautréamont, free of the aesthetic inhibitions of the West.[27]

"TRAITORS TO EVERYTHING THAT IS NOT FREEDOM"

Passionately attracted to Africa though they were, few of the young men and women who took part in the early years of the world's first Surrealist Group had more than a very modest knowledge of Africa and Africans. The sole exception seems to have been Maurice Heine, who lived in Algeria for six years. A forceful critic of colonialism, he was editor-in-chief of *La France Islamique*, a regular collaborator on other Franco-Arabic papers, and an ardent defender of the rights of the indigenous population.[28]

The first surrealists' strong pro-Africanism, accompanied by denunciation of European and U.S. imperialist politics and pretensions, made it clear that the new movement's "race politics" were unequivocally on the side of people of color. As Paul Éluard puts it in "La suppression de l'ésclavage": "The supremacy of Europe is based only on militarism and the cross — the cross in the service of militarism. . . . The white man is nothing but a corpse — a corpse who dumps his garbage under the natives' noses."[29] Addressing students in Madrid that same month (April 1925), Louis Aragon emphasized that surrealists not only supported colonial insurrections, but also recognized their own role, as surrealists, in this world revolution: "First of all we shall ruin this civilization . . . in which you [bourgeois students] are molded like fossils in shale. Western world, you are condemned to death. We are the defeatists of Europe, so take care — or, rather, laugh at us. We shall make a pact with all your enemies."[30] In short, surrealists openly defined themselves as "traitors to everything that is not freedom."[31]

The impressive extent to which surrealist eyes and ears were drawn toward Africa in this early period is most dramatically demonstrated by their enthusiasm for the revolt of And El-Krim and the Rif tribespeople of Morocco in the summer of 1925.[32] In a July 15 statement they declared their solidarity with the Riffians and affirmed "the right of peoples, of *all* peoples, of whatever race" to self-determination. This statement was followed a few weeks later by the collective tract "Revolution Now and Forever!" — the Surrealist Group's first important political declaration, in which members elaborated not only their attitude toward the war in North Africa, but also their critique of Western civilization and their growing awareness of themselves as traitors to the white race and avowed enemies of Eurocentrism: "We want to proclaim our total detachment from, in a sense our uncontamination by, the ideas at the basis of a still-real European civilization. . . . Wherever western civilization is dominant, all human contact has disappeared, except contact from which money can be made. . . . The stereotyped gestures, acts, and lies of Europe have gone through their whole disgusting cycle."[33]

In the steadily burgeoning critical and historical literature on surrealism in recent years, too little has been made of the striking fact that it was an *African* revolt that precipitated the Surrealist Group into revolutionary politics. Important, too, is the fact that the surrealists' anti-imperialism never wavered. More than five thousand copies of their vehement denunciation of the 1931 Colonial Exhibition were distributed in Paris, mostly in working-class areas.[34] Simultaneously, in collaboration with Vietnamese students, the Surrealist Group organized a well-attended anti-colonialist exhibition titled "The Truth about the Colonies."[35] In 1932 Jacques Viot, a former collaborator on *La Révolution Surréaliste* who still had close ties to the Surrealist Group, published a novel, *Déposition du blanc* (White man's deposition), a scathing exposé of the sinister role played by missionaries in dominating colonized populations.[36]

Surrealists in France were also active in garnering support for the U.S. Scottsboro defendants.[37] And in 1934 the group's "Appeal to Struggle" sounded the tocsin against the first fascist provocations in Paris.[38]

The surrealists' reading of Hegel and Marx had hastened them toward an antidogmatic, open-ended Marxism, rather like that of Walter Benjamin, Herbert Marcuse, and others of the Frankfort School. Never Stalinist, the Surrealist Group was in fact severely critical of Soviet Marxism and especially of the French Communists' vacillating policies.[39] They strongly opposed, for example, the unprincipled political blunder known as the "Popular Front."[40]

In the United States today this lamentable maneuver is scarcely remembered, except for the laughable slogan "Communism Is Twentieth Century Americanism," but the disastrous politics involved left Africa—and embattled colonies everywhere—more vulnerable than ever to European exploitation. The Surrealist Group tract *Neither Your War Nor Your Peace!*, issued at the time of the Munich talks (September 1938), rightly accuses the imperialist democracies and their staunch ally, Stalin's Soviet Union, of having "permitted Italy to annihilate Ethiopia, notably because any successful resistance to the white invader would encourage the colonial peoples to free themselves from the grip of imperialism."[41]

In their vehement opposition to white supremacy, the surrealists were in fact far to the left of the Socialist and Communist parties, in France and elsewhere, most of which regarded the issue of race as decidedly less important than that of class. In the collective statements quoted above, the Surrealist Group was very much at odds with those parties but in close agreement with such renowned black revolutionary internationalists as George Padmore, Garan Kouyaté, and C.L.R. James.

In an insightful essay, historian Sidra Stich has described surrealism as "a rebellion against . . . racist attitudes" and further explains that this rebellion, from the beginning,

> adamantly disputed an exclusionist conception of culture that took Western civilization as the preeminent model and set it above and apart from all others. Not only did they [surrealists] reject certain aspects of Western civilization, but they also recognized that its rigid, often elitist conceptions tended to obscure or deny both critical similarities with and significant differences from other civilizations. Their interest in African, Oceanic, North American, Asian, and prehistoric cultures asserted a will to expand beyond the confines and closure of Western culture while revealing the flux and variety of human expression.[42]

All through the 1920s and 1930s, French newspapers and other periodicals routinely printed malicious caricatures of Africans and Asians. A major offender in this regard was the journal *Documents* (not to be confused with the later Belgian publication of the same name). Edited by Georges Bataille, the French *Documents* was basically an academic review with a strong anti-Marxist, antisurrealist slant. In regard to jazz, its favorites included Paul Whiteman and other white imitators of the genre. Much worse, however, each issue featured a large, highly offensive smiling "Sambo" advertisement.

In contrast, the surrealists in their journals ran images and texts ridiculing white pomposity, including photographs of the French bourgeoisie, generals, clergy, and colonial agents—all accompanied by mercilessly mocking headlines or captions. In articles, too, and their "Review of the Press," and even in their poetry, games, and tales, surrealist disdain for white supremacy was loud and clear.

In the surrealist game Exquisite Corpse, each player writes a word or phrase and then folds the paper so that the next player cannot see what has been written so far. The results, always surprising, sometimes hilarious, were often printed in *La Révolution Surréaliste.* Here is one from the October 1927 issue: "The oyster from Senegal shall eat the tricolored bread."[43] Surrealist automatic writing also produced more than a few passages with comparable antiestablishment overtones. In Benjamin Péret's 1920s tale, "In a Clinch," we are told of "a host of little pigs similar to the flag of the United States"[44]—an image that suggests, some forty years early, the work of artist and cartoonist Emory Douglas in the 1960s *Black Panther* newspaper.

The barbed and bitter humor directed by surrealists against white supremacy and the entire "white mystique" surely must be recognized as part of the broader project of revalorizing blackness that Breton and his friends shared with the protagonists of Pan-Africanism and Negritude. What the surrealists in the 1930s began to call black humor—a direct descendent of Hegel's objective humor—was precisely defined as "the highest revolt of the mind and spirit," always and everywhere regarded as an unequivocally *liberating* factor. It is not by chance that the *Dictionnaire du surréalisme et ses environs* (1982)—by far the best reference work on the subject—asserts, in the entry for "noir," that "black has always been the color of surrealism."[45]

It is only fair to add that Georges Bataille not long afterward mended his ways and indeed, by mid-decade had joined André Breton and the surrealists in the formation of an explicitly revolutionary group, Counter-Attack.[46]

SURREALISM AND PSYCHOANALYSIS

> Think of the things you could be by now if Sigmund Freud's wife was your mother.
> —Charles Mingus

Surrealists shared with their Marxist and anarchist friends an abiding interest in social issues and supported collective action—and for that matter, class action—to change society. Unlike most Marxists and anarchists, however, surrealists were also passionately concerned with the individual, the inner self, the life of the mind, the world of dreams, and chance encounters. Such, indeed, was the terrain of much of the most fruitful surrealist research. What Ayana Karanja has called "the efficacy of dreams as a credible epistemological apparatus" extends back to surrealism's very beginnings, and beyond.[47]

The surrealists early on took a serious interest in the theories of Freud and his coworkers regarding internal reality: the unconscious, libido, dreams, daydreams, slips of the tongue, and so on. They were attracted to psychoanalytic inquiry not as therapy, but, rather, as a subversive activity, a form of criticism, and an aid to humankind's liberation from repression. They were also impressed by the applications of psychoanalysis to folklore, jokes, the arts, and the whole field of culture.

Here, too, as with Marxism, the surrealists' attitude was antidogmatic and open-ended. While defending Freud against reactionary criticism, Breton nonetheless points out that surrealists "reject the greater part of Freudian philosophy as metaphysics."[48]

Despite Freud's own unsympathetic view of surrealism, and an even greater hostility on the part of the psychoanalytic establishment, most surrealists considered their encounters with Freudian thought—and with the work of such thinkers as Sandor Ferenczi, Otto Fenichel, Edward Glover, Edith Jacobson, and Geza Röheim—to be provocative, stimulating, and beneficial.

Many surrealist writers—Breton, Benayoun, Calas, Crevel, Effenberger, Garon, Luca, Mabille, Pailthorpe, Seligmann, and Teige, to name a few—have drawn fruitfully on psychoanalytic insights in various articles and books.

SURREALISM'S ENEMIES

> Wherever you find injustice, the proper form of politeness is attack.
>
> —T-Bone Slim

Like all revolutionary movements, surrealism from the start had enemies, and the fulminations of these enemies are often revealing. Journalists, militarists, clergy, *litterateurs*, and other upholders of the nation's "glory" were especially hostile. In the 1920s the racist and proto-fascist paper *Action Française* frantically implored the French press never even to mention the Surrealist Group or any individual surrealists.[49] In that same decade, in a book on contemporary Paris life, a gossip columnist chose to ignore the surrealists' aims, principles, and accomplishments and instead portrayed the group as a rowdy street gang "violently opposed to bourgeois conceptions. . . . They are aggressive. They are as ready to express their dislikes with fists as with words. Their manifestoes always create an uproar. Their magazine announced [itself] as 'the most scandalous review in the world.' [Frequently, in the course of their demonstrations] the police were called in. It is dangerous to offend the surrealists. They are hysterically explosive against their age."[50]

Such simple-minded blatherings may seem little more than amusing, but other enemies of surrealism had ways of enforcing their bigotry. In Hitler's Germany, for example, surrealism in painting and poetry was reviled as degenerate art and officially forbidden, as it was in Franco's Spain and Hirohito's Japan. The Soviet Union under Stalin took a similar view. Years later, under Khrushchev, a 1961 *Dictionary of Terms Used in the Plastic Arts* still defined surrealism as a "reactionary tendency in the art of contemporary capitalist countries," and went on to state that "the perverted imagination of the surrealists concerns itself only with the world of dreams denuded of all sense. . . . The surrealists combine allusions to real forms in the ugliest succession, with the aim of destroying logic and healthy human perception."[51] Clearly, surrealism's self-declared enemies also tended to be supporters of colonialism, imperialism, white supremacy, and other forms of chauvinism, racism, and reaction.

In an interview in *New Directions 1940* the Greek surrealist Nicolas Calas sums up the surrealists' attitude toward their critics:

> The aggressiveness of surrealism, like all movements that are in pursuit of definite objects (realizations of desires) *must* lead to attack. . . . The anti-conventional attitude of surrealism breaks through all manner of good taste and prudery. Surrealism after all is shocking for the people who are shocked by dreams. . . . The poet fights for surprise. . . . Surrealism looks for a transformation of the world. . . . Poetry is the antithesis of prayer. Poetry is an exigency and leads to revolution, which is a concrete force by means of which obstacles are overturned, further desires set free.[52]

AFRICAN AMERICANS IN PARIS

> There is more freedom in a square mile of Paris than in the entire United States.
> —Richard Wright

Surrealism in the 1920s and early 1930s was much in the news, not only in Paris but worldwide. The group's many insulting letters to bourgeois celebrities, its numerous militant tracts (such as "Open the Prisons! Disband the Army!" and "Hands Off Love!") and direct action—"The Truth about Colonies," for example, and many other boisterous disruptions of official literary and political affairs—scandalized the philistines but also, and more important, attracted the interest of rebellious youth all over the globe. Surrealist groups, modeled on the Paris original, blossomed in Argentina, Belgium, Czechoslovakia, Japan, Yugoslavia, and eventually in many other lands.

The first black encounters with surrealism in Paris tended to involve African Americans seeking respite from U.S. racism. Most of these meetings were casual, brief, and—as the saying goes—without conclusion. Henry Ossawa Tanner, the preeminent African American artist in Paris from the 1910s until his death in 1937, had met Picasso and admired some of his work, but does not seem to have had any association with the surrealists. His preference for biblical themes would not in fact have attracted the vehemently atheist surrealists, but many of his works are very striking. This is true especially of the series inspired by a trip to North Africa, and those in which the predominant element is a bright, shimmering glow—a strange light from outside—suggesting what his son called Tanner's mystical fourth dimension.

Tanner's influence on young black artists was considerable. His studio on the Boulevard Saint-Jacques was something of a shrine for visiting African Americans, and he is known to have encouraged the artists among them, including the modernists.[53]

The great painter Archibald Motley, from Chicago, spent much of 1929–1930 in Paris on a Guggenheim Fellowship. Some of his finest works—bright portrayals of Paris jazz nightspots and cabarets—were painted at that time. Although not a surrealist painter, strictly speaking, Motley's passionate, warm color, combined with the vital rhythm of his lights and shadows and his lyrical, indeed musical, intensity—as in his marvelous *Blues* of 1929, and *Casey and Mae in the Street* (1940)—radiates a hauntingly beautiful African American surrealist atmosphere.[54]

Among the early expatriates was Anita Thompson, described as "a pretty, young Harlem socialite" who had left the United States "to enjoy the social freedom of life" in Paris, and who was for a time the companion of the Dutch surrealist painter Kristians Tonny.[55] Writers, artists, and other participants in the Harlem Renaissance, including the Jamaican Claude McKay, the Puerto Rican scholar and book collector Arthur Schomburg, and African Americans Countee Cullen, Jessie Fauset, Gwendolyn Bennet, Nella Larsen, Alain Locke, Jean Toomer, and Langston Hughes also visited Paris. Hughes became a good friend of Louis Aragon and probably met other surrealists at demonstrations, cafes, and parties. Surrealist Georges Limbour was one of the first to translate Hughes' poems into French.[56]

Paris-based African American entertainers, most notably the eccentric dancer Josephine Baker and the singer and nightclub operator Ada "Bricktop" Smith, counted more than a few surrealists among their friends. Georgia-born jazz pianist Henry Crowder, for several years the companion of Nancy Cunard, not only frequented the surrealist milieu, but also had the pleasure of having a book of his jazz compositions published by The Hours Press, with front and back cover designs by surrealist photographer Man Ray.[57]

Such encounters may suggest a curiosity about surrealism rather than a serious interest, but they surely helped spread the word that an exciting new radical force—rooted in poetry and revolt—was in the wind. Surrealists, at the same time, learned of the new dynamism and rebellion in black America.

A decisive forward leap was made in 1932: year one of black surrealism.

Notes

1. The following books, listed in chronological order, were well reviewed, widely circulated, and for many years regarded as key works on surrealism; none of them, however, mention any black surrealists: Georges Lemaître, *From Cubism to Surrealism in French Literature;* Anna Balakian, *Surrealism;* Matthew Josephson, *Life among the Surrealists;* Lucy Lippard, ed., *Surrealists on Art;* Mary Ann Caws, *The Poetry of Dada and Surrealism;* Wayne Andrews, *The Surrealist Parade;* Ruth Brandon: *Surreal Lives.* Examples of tokenism include Wallace Fowlie, *Age of Surrealism,* with one passing reference to Aimé Césaire; Patrick Waldberg, *Surrealism;* Herbert Gershman, *The Surrealist Revolution in France,* with a short paragraph on Wifredo Lam; Roger Cardinal and Robert Short, eds., *Surrealism,* three brief mentions of Lam and one of Joyce Mansour; Susan Suleiman: *Subversive Intent,* with brief mentions of Mansour; Dickran Tashjian, *A Boatload of Madmen,* one passing reference to Aimé Césaire; and Jack J. Spector, *Surrealist Art & Writing, 1919–1939,* two passing references to Aimé Césaire and a footnote mentioning Ted Joans.

2. André Breton, "Prolegomena to a Third Manifesto of Surrealism or Not," 282.

3. Masson, quoted in Robert Short, "The Politics of Surrealism," 33; Antonin Artaud, *A la grand nuit ou le bluff surréaliste,* 368.

4. Gascoyne, viii.

5. Toyen, in *Médium: Communication Surréaliste* 4 (1955), quoted in Penelope Rosemont, ed., *Surrealist Women,* 81.

6. "An Evening with Poet Jayne Cortez," April 7, 2005.

7. On surrealism's anti-Eurocentrism, see Sidra Stich's introduction to *Anxious Visions,* and the special "Surrealism: Revolution against Whiteness" issue of the journal *Race Traitor,* no. 9 (Summer 1998).

8. See David Roediger's essay "Plotting against Eurocentrism," 169–176. An earlier, shorter version appeared in the journal *Race Traitor,* no. 9 (Summer 1998).

9. Luis Buñuel, *My Last Sigh,* 123.

10. Alain Joubert, *Le mouvement des surréalistes,* 172.

11. Ayana I. Karanja, *Zora Neale Hurston,* 7.

12. Lautréamont, *Poèsies*, vol. 2.

13. On surrealism in the 2000s, see Ron Sakolsky, ed., *Surrealist Subversions*.

14. Breton's "Away with Miserabilism!" is included in his *Surrealism and Painting*, 347–348. See also David Roediger, *History against Misery*.

15. The almanac, originally a special issue of the journal *La Nef*, nos. 63–64 (1950), was reissued in book form by Éditions Plasma, 1978. The reference to jazz appears on p. 215.

16. On the Three Musketeers, see Breton's *Entrétiens*, 35–46.

17. In James Redpath, *Echoes of Harper's Ferry*, 99.

18. Marat, "Du droit qu'ont nos colonies de secouer le joug tyranique de la métropole," 15.

19. "It Is Time to Destroy All the Bastilles in the World," a two-sided tract, July 14, 1969.

20. Interview with André Breton, *View Magazine*, nos. 7–8 (October–November 1941).

21. A. James Arnold, *Modernism and Negritude*, 42–43.

22. Lautréamont, *Les chants de Maldoror*, 194.

23. See Reinhard Kuhn, *The Return to Reality*; Marjorie Louise Henry, *Stuart Merrill*.

24. Fabre d'Olivet's *Idamore* is reprinted in *Miscellanea Fabre d'Olivet*.

25. André Breton and Gérard Legrand, *L'Art magique*; Pierre Mabille, *Egrégores, ou la vie des civilisations*; idem, *Le miroir du merveilleux*; Ithell Colquhoun: *Goose of Hermogenes*; Kurt Seligmann, *The History of Magic*; Gérard Legrand, *Préface au système de l'eternité*; Élie-Charles Flamand, "Introduction"; Joseph Jablonski, "Millennial Soundings"; Bernard Roger, *A la découverte de l'alchimie*; Sarane Alexandrian, *Histoire de la philosophie occulte*; Jorge Camacho, *Le mythe d'Isis et d'Osiris*; and Philip Lamantia, *Bed of Sphinxes*. On the impact of this tradition in the United States, see Franklin Rosemont, foreword, in John Patrick Deveney, *Paschal Beverly Randolph*.

26. Ishmael Reed, *Mumbo Jumbo*. In an early and too rarely discussed essay ("Distances," 142–147), Breton reflects on the problems artists have in bringing their work to the attention of the public. Highly critical of the fact that art had fallen "under the control of businessmen," he goes on to denounce those "bad places" called "galleries."

27. In *Nadja* (1928), Breton had written: "Beauty will be convulsive or will not be at all." The concept was also developed in his *L'Amour fou* (1937) and *Le surréalisme et la peinture* (definitive edition, 1965).

28. See Gérard Legrand's entry on Maurice Heine in Adam Biro and René Passeron, *Dictionnaire général du surréalisme*, 203-204.

29. *La Revolution Surréaliste*, no. 3 (1925), 19.

30. Louis Aragon, "Fragments d'une conférence," 23-24.

31. Breton, "Revolution Now and Forever," 424.

32. For background on the Rif war, see David S. Woolman, *Rebels in the Rif*.

33. Breton, "Revolution Now and Forever," 423.

34. Surrealist documents on the Colonial Exhibition and extensive commentary are included in José Pierre, ed., *Tracts surréalistes et déclarations collectives (1922-1939)*. For further background, see also Herman Lebovics, *True France*. Erik Orsenna's novel, *L'Exposition coloniale*, was awarded that year's Prix Goncourt.

35. On the anticolonial exhibition, in addition to the references cited in the preceding note, see André Thirion, *Revolutionaries without Revolution*, 289-290.

36. On Jacques Viot, see Patrice Allain's introduction to Viot's *Poèmes de guerre*.

37. The Scottsboro case is noted by Breton and Péret in "Revue de la presse," 24; by Etienne Léro in *Légitime défense;* and in other surrealist writings. Nancy Cunard was especially energetic in the campaign and devotes much space to it in the *Negro Anthology*.

38. The "Appeal to Struggle" is included in Pierre, *Tracts surréalistes*, 263-264.

39. As early as October 1927, Breton roundly criticized the French Communist Party and one of its central figures, Henri Barbusse, in the pamphlet *Légitime défense*. (Note: The title of this pamphlet was adopted by Etienne Léro and his Martinican friends for their one-shot journal in 1932.)

40. See Breton's "Sur l'échec du front populaire," 1259-1260.

41. "Neither Your War Nor Your Peace!" is included in Breton, *What Is Surrealism?*, 446-447.

42. Stich, *Anxious Visions*, 15.

43. From issue no. 9–10, p. 11

44. Péret, in Eugene Jolas, ed., *Transition Workshop*, 368.

45. Biro and Passeron, *Dictionnaire*, 301.

46. The relevant documents on Counter-Attack are included, with commentary, in Pierre, *Tracts surréalistes*. See also Robert Stuart Short, "Contre-attaque," 144–176.

47. Karanja, *Zora Neale Hurston*, 10.

48. Breton, *What Is Surrealism?*, 23.

49. *Action Française* (July 6, 1925). See Maurice Nadeau, *The History of Surrealism*, 114.

50. Sisley Huddleston, *Paris Salons, Cafes, Studios*, 228–229.

51. From a *Dictionary of Terms Used in the Plastic Arts* (Moscow, 1961), printed in Russian and French translation in *L'Écart absolu*, catalog of the 1965–1966 International Surrealist Exhibition (Paris, 1965). The English translation is quoted in full in *Arsenal/Surrealist Subversion*, no. 1 (1970), 20.

52. Calas, *New Directions 1940*, 390, 392.

53. Wayne Cooper, *Claude McKay*, 254, 273–277.

54. Faith Berry, *Légitime Défense before and beyond Harlem*, 190.

55. Cooper, *Claude McKay*.

56. See, for example, "Guitare," in *Bifur*, no. 6 (July 1930), 59.

57. Henry Crowder and Hugo Speck, *As Wonderful As All That?*, 11–12.

LÉGITIME DÉFENSE

Textes de :

étienne léro
rené ménil
jules-marcel monnerot
maurice-sabas quitman
simone yoyotte

In 1932, Etienne Léro, a young Martinican poet and philosophy student with eight fellow students—all between twenty and twenty-five years old—formed a group called Légitime Défense (Self-Defense), and published a journal of that name.

1. The First Black Surrealists

I do not believe poetry is on the decline. I cannot think that money-getting is the whole business of man. Rather am I convinced that the world is approaching a poetical revolution.

—Albery A. Whitman

In 1932, from his small apartment on the Rue Tournon in Paris, Etienne Léro, a young Martinican poet and philosophy student, planned a revolution. He began by rallying eight of his fellow scholarship students—all between twenty and twenty-five years old—into a group called Légitime Défense (Self-defense) and kept things moving by immediately starting a journal of that name. Whole-heartedly surrealist from cover to cover, with a strong backup of Far Left Marx-ism, *Légitime Défense* sounded a lot of unheard-of new notes, and even a whole new tone, in Caribbean literature and thought.[1] Not in the least parochial, its twenty-four pages covered an astonishing range of material: a hot mix of sur-realist manifesto, poetry, revolutionary theory, and sharp criticism of the Antil-lean bourgeoisie, its docile politics and complacent culture.

According to some accounts, the journal was banned by the authorities in Martinique. The details of the suppression are not clear, but René Ménil, in his preface to the 1979 reprint, points out that the journal provoked an angry response from the petit-bourgeoisie and the government and was largely unknown on the island for four decades.[2] A second, much larger, issue was planned, but never appeared.

As Cameroonian scholar Lilyan Kesteloot was the first to emphasize, *Légi-time Défense* was notable for its refreshing youthfulness, originality, and daring—qualities that René Ménil later summed up as "the sensual joy of writing."[3] The group further distinguished itself with its bold internationalism. Proclaiming their admiration for Hegel, Marx, Lautréamont, and Freud, as well as Breton, Crevel, Péret, Tristan Tzara, and other surrealists, Léro and his comrades also hailed "the rising wind from America" (the poetry of Langston Hughes and Claude McKay), published a long excerpt from McKay's controversial novel *Banjo*, and expected great things from the younger generation of poets in Haiti. Social revolution was very much on the minds of these young poets. As

Ménil recalled many years later, they thought of themselves as the "intellectual spokespersons of the West Indian working class."[4]

Enthusiastic and full of fire, the Légitime Défense group created a stir entirely out of proportion to its size. Despite the fact that the journal's press run did not exceed five hundred copies, and may have been as small as three hundred—the red-and-black-covered journal is now known to have exerted an influence far greater than most historians have been willing to concede. In the 1960s, looking back on those days, Léon-Gontran Damas called *Légitime Défense* "the most insurrectional document ever signed by people of color."[5] In much the same spirit, an aging René Ménil called it "Fanonist"—hinting, perhaps, at its unexpected realization half a century later.[6]

Not least, the Légitime Défense group scandalized plenty of French colonial administrators and journalists. More significant in the long run, the group and its journal reinforced and expanded surrealism's revolutionary project and drove home the crucial point that surrealism, far from being a mere art or literary current, was in truth a movement concerned above all with freedom, equality, and revolutionary transformation. Most important, Etienne Léro and the others inspired a whole generation of young blacks from Martinique, Guyana, Senegal, and no doubt many other places on the black world map.

According to Henri Pastoureau, in those years a young French surrealist who was also a close friend and schoolmate of Léro and his group, the immediate periphery of Légitime Défense also included fellow philosophy student Raymond Tchang (b. Beijing, 1912), the first surrealist of Chinese descent, and the noted historian of West Indian slavery, Leonard Sainville.[7] Another friend and fellow student of Pastoureau's—the Algerian Jewish painter and poet Jean-Michel Atlan—was also acquainted with at least some members of the Léro group.[8]

As André Breton told Lilyan Kesteloot in a 1960 interview, the Légitime Défense Group—as an autonomous entity with its own Martinique-oriented agenda—was warmly welcomed by the Paris surrealists as a parallel movement and ally.[9] It so happened, however, that most of those who were involved in Légitime Défense were also active in the Surrealist Group. Despite rigorous school schedules they frequently attended the surrealists' daily café meetings, where they discussed vital issues of the day, played surrealist games, and helped plan the contents of Surrealist Group publications. Léro and his friends also went to gatherings at Breton's apartment at 42 Rue Fontaine. At Breton's, the discussions often focused on the relationship between politics and art and on the general problem of anticolonialism.[10]

Alas, the whole Légitime Défense saga is not easily told, for much of the basic data appears to be wanting and may even be irremediably lost. Manuscripts, correspondence, minutes of meetings, photographs, interviews, diaries, memoirs—all kinds of documentation needed to detail the internal history of a group—are, for now at least, beyond our reach. Fortunately, we have *Légitime Défense* itself, as well as a good number of other articles and poems by Légitime Défense members—including Léro, Ménil, Jules Monnerot, Pierre Yoyotte, and Simone Yoyotte—that appeared in *Le Surréalisme au Service de la Révolution*, the Belgian *Documents*, and *Minotaure*.

A crucial link between the Nardal sisters' eclectic *Revue du Monde Noir* (1931–1932) and *L'Étudiant Noir* (1935–1936), which in turn helped stimulate the great *Tropiques* (1941–1945), the almost subterranean *Légitime Défense* played a part in promoting the new tremors in the black intellectual atmosphere. It challenged the colonialist status quo, provoked thought, fomented dreams, and liberated the imagination. By no means least, it inspired—via poetry as well as polemic—the spirit of refusal and active revolt. In the history of the Negritude movement no less than in the history of surrealism, this little magazine marks an epoch.

Léro himself was an important and fascinating character. Léon Damas described him as a man who deftly combined the spirit of poetry and the critical spirit. The sheer scope of Léro's interests is impressive. Author of a scholarly essay entitled "The Bourgeois Family in the Work of Balzac," he has also been proclaimed (by Damas) "the first to give a surreal form to creole poetry."[11] Incredibly, no one has yet attempted to write his biography. Apart from Lilyan Kesteloot's pioneering study, most academic books and articles on surrealism, Negritude, Marxism, modern poetry, and race politics barely mention him.

Léro's legacy, however, was never forgotten. Damas and Senghor—who knew him well—both featured Léro prominently in their anthologies of black poetry. Damas and Léopold Senghor disagreed on many matters, but both regarded Léro as a major historical figure, a great innovator in Caribbean culture, a true genius. Decades later, the African American surrealist poet Ted Joans—who knew the founder of *Légitime Défense* only by word of mouth and his published work—proudly counted Léro among his heroes and devoted a splendid poem ("Smoke Sleep") to his memory. First published in the journal *Présence Africaine* in the 1960s, it was reprinted in his 1999 *Teducation*.[12]

Poet, revolutionary, theorist, organizer, editor, critic, and ardent jazz enthusiast, Etienne Léro, the first black surrealist, was a many-sided man. A figure of great courage, boldness, insight, and imagination, it was he—more than anyone else of his time—who related surrealism and its revolutionary program to the different but not-so-very-unrelated ideas of such varied thinkers as W.E.B. Du Bois, Claude McKay, Marcus Garvey, Langston Hughes, Katherine Dunham, Zora Neale Hurston, Sterling Brown, and C.L.R. James.

The decisive new awareness that *Légitime Défense* exemplified was, indeed, one of the central elements that united—at least in spirit—Léro's group with the far-flung Harlem Renaissance, Cuban Afro-Negrism, and the chaotic H-Group (el Grupo H, also in Cuba), as well as the diverse Indigènes ferment in Haiti, which included individuals as different as Jacques Roumain and Clément Magloire-Saint-Aude. While old-line Marxists persisted in the belief that "the Revolution" somehow involved a choice between poetry or politics, social or cultural change, Légitime Défense rejected that dreary dichotomy and dialectically demanded poetry *and* politics, social *and* cultural revolution.

SIMONE YOYOTTE AND HER BROTHER PIERRE

> The murmuring makes me change place and ink to my own measure.
> —Simone Yoyotte

Léro was the organizer, but the entire Légitime Defense Group was remarkable. Simone Yoyotte, for example, was by all standards a strikingly original figure. Her poems, included by Léro in *Légitime Défense* and by André Breton in *Le Surréalisme au Service de la Révolution*, reflect the density of hurricanes and gleam with a dark charm all their own.[13] What critic Régis Antoine has called her "hyper-individualistic lyricism" distinguishes her poems not only from Martinique's legion of sentimental versifiers, but also from the much larger legion of Europe's wannabe "modernists" of those years.[14] At once energetic and subversive, her colorful antirational imagery gives her work a unique and disturbing quality, radically unlike any other Francophone Caribbean poetry of the time. Only the very small number of her surviving poems, and her early death (probably in 1933) can explain the fact that Simone Yoyotte has remained so little known.

No less original was her brother Pierre, tireless in his devotion to surrealist research, particularly games and inquiries. His highly imaginative excursions into the realm of critical analysis—in *Le Surréalisme au Service de la Révolution*, *Documents 34*, and *Minotaure*—significantly enrich the corpus of surrealist theory. His best-known essay—on the significance of surrealism in the struggle against fascism—is comparable in many respects to the work of maverick psychoanalyst Wilhelm Reich (then unknown in France).

Surrealist criticism, especially of culture (in the largest sense of the term) was also the specialty of René Ménil, whose essays in the 1930s, and later in *Tropiques*, were much admired by Breton.

Of the eight individuals in Léro's 1932 group, the most prolific writer—and the one who eventually became by far the best known—was Jules Monnerot. A valued collaborator on surrealist publications and, later on many others, including several *anti*-surrealist publications, Monnerot became a distinguished and well-respected intellectual in France. Unfortunately, his militant participation in surrealism did not extend beyond 1935. The following year he co-edited, with Aragon and Tzara, the Communist Party journal *Inquisitions*, and in 1938 cofounded with Georges Bataille, Roger Caillois, Michel Leiris, and others the short-lived College of Sociology, a collective focused largely on religion. Although scholars have minimized his role in the College, Monnerot always claimed to have been its true originator, adding that he had "conceived the idea, found its participants, [and] named the project."[15]

After the war, however, Monnerot's book *La poésie moderne et la sacré* (Modern poetry and the sacred, 1945)—a study of surrealism and its relationship to "primitive" thought and Gnosticism—was welcomed by the surrealists as a significant work; Breton called it "absolutely convincing."[16] Two years later Monnerot contributed an interesting essay on the imaginary to the exhibition catalog *Le surréalisme en 1947.*

Monnerot's dismaying move to the Far Right, as evidenced in his *Sociology of Communism*, inevitably alienated him from surrealism. In his later years he often rudely dismissed students and researchers who were interested in his surrealist days.

However disappointing Monnerot turned out to be in the end (he was for several years a vigorous supporter of neofascist National Front leader Jean-Marie Le Pen), the fact remains that his early contributions to surrealism were by no means negligible, and indeed are his best work.

JUAN BREÁ AND MARY LOW: A SURREALIST DUO ON THE GO

In 1933-1934, sometime between the unexpected appearance of *Légitime Défense* and the equally sudden advent of *L'Étudiant Noir,* yet another important manifestation of surrealism and black insurgency burst on the Paris scene with the arrival of Cuban poet and revolutionary Juan Breá and his Australian companion, Mary Low.

In the late 1920s Juan Ramón Breá (whose nationality he specified as Siboney) had been a key figure in Cuba's first poetic avant-garde, the H-Group. Severely critical of the island's retrograde literary and artistic scene, the H-Group had more than a little in common with surrealism. While its poetry challenged an entrenched academic complacency and scandalized a conservative public, its disruptive "actions"—sometimes involving vandalism—brought the group to the attention of the police. Nonconformist to the hilt, members favored their own special blend of poetic and political radicalism, welcoming all kinds of prankishness, innovation, and audacity.[17]

The H-Group, however, was only one of Breá's many spheres of activity. He also played an important role in the 1933 overthrow of dictator Antonio Machado in Cuba and cofounded the Cuban Trotskyist movement. In Mexico he conferred with Nicaraguan anti-imperialist guerrilla fighter Augusto César Sandino.

In Paris, Breá and Low quickly found their way to the Surrealist Group, and in no time their good friends included André Breton, Benjamin Péret, Marcelle Ferry, Jacques Herold, Meret Oppenheim, Yves Tanguy, and Óscar Domín-guez. Somewhat later in the 1930s they met Wifredo Lam (also from Cuba), who became a particularly close comrade. It would seem likely that they were also acquainted with Etienne Léro and his friends, but details are lacking. This surely merits further research, especially in view of Régis Antoine's argument that Légitime Défense was actually closer, in spirit and program, to 1930s Cuban Negrismo than to what later became known as Negritude.[18] As it is, however, Breá's biography, and especially data on his acquaintances, is very sketchy. In a 1990s interview Mary Low recalled that she met Aimé Césaire only "much later," probably in the mid- or late 1940s.[19]

One of surrealism's great couples, the multilingual Breá and Low were a dy-namic force, well known and admired throughout the movement for their in-spired combination of poetry and action, their fearless nomadism, and their ex-traordinarily broad culture, which embraced a thorough grasp of Marxism and psychoanalysis along with a profound knowledge of the history of philosophy, world literature, and the arts. Their boundless enthusiasm, energy, and bold-ness in developing new ideas had a lasting impact not only on the Paris Group but also in many of the movement's other vital centers. They visited the Sur-realist Group in Brussels, where their dearest comrade was poet and collagist E.L.T. Mesens, who would later play an important role in surrealism in England. In Bucharest, the couple were welcomed by Victor Brauner; his brother, Harry (a folklorist and musicologist); Gherasim Luca; Antonia Rasicovici; and Jules Perahim; and took part in the Romanian group's activities, poetic and political. Decades later Rasicovici vividly recalled that Breá, a serious student of lan-guages, was especially impressed by the Bucharest ghetto, whose inhabitants spoke a Spanish/Jewish dialect virtually unchanged since the sixteenth century. An elated Breá declared: "This is the language of Cervantes!"[20]

Their eight months in Prague in 1939 were especially fruitful, for they en-joyed almost daily rendezvous with Karel Teige, Toyen, Jindrich Heisler, Bohu-slav Brouk, and others in the Prague Surrealist Group. The couple also managed to publish a booklet of their own poems in Prague—*La saison des flûtes* (The flute season)—under the Éditions Surréalistes imprint.

Spain in 1936 found the intrepid twosome on the front lines of the Revolu-

tion, as members of the Partido Obrero e Unificación Marxista (Party of Marxist Unification, POUM). Breá served in the workers' militia; Low helped organize the women's militia, edited the POUM's English-language paper, *Spanish
Revolution*, and gave regular broadcasts on Radio POUM. The POUM's broad
educational program featured several of Breá's and Low's public lectures on
surrealism. They were pleased to meet several surrealist comrades in Spain,
most notably Benjamin Péret, a fellow militiaman. They also met several American radicals who became their good friends, including Charles and Lois Orr,
Russell Blackwell, Leon Green, and Hugo Oehler.

With the defeat of the Spanish Revolution by Franco's fascist Falange—
aided and abetted by Stalin's counter-revolutionary political police—Breá and
Low sought refuge in Paris and began writing their *Red Spanish Notebook: The First
Six Months of the Revolution and the Civil War*. Published in London in 1937, with an
introduction by C.L.R. James, the book was hailed in *Time and Tide* by George
Orwell, whose own book on Spain, *Homage to Catalonia*, appeared a year later.
Despite virulent attacks by Stalinists, Social-Democrats, and the Far Right—
not to mention a voluminous bourgeois critical literature over the past seventy
years—*Red Spanish Notebook* is still regarded by experts as one of the best eye-
witness accounts of one of the twentieth century's greatest struggles to create
a truly free society.[21]

Breá and Low remained active in the surrealist and Trotskyist movements all
through the late 1930s and into the 1940s, notably in Paris, London, New York,
and Havana.

In April 1941 Breá died suddenly, at the age of thirty-five. In a letter to André
Breton, Mary Low wrote:

> You were acquainted with him. You know what a living miracle he was.
> Surely few men as brilliant have had his depth and solidity of thought.
> Surely also few men as capable of understanding historical materialism,
> and of applying the Marxist methodology, have known the inspired
> bursts of lyricism that characterized him. . . . You know that in an inner
> landscape such as his, filled with abruptnesses, the slopes must have
> been steep and dangerous. But you know also that his heart was laid on
> springs of steel, and that his courage had no frontier. . . . To tell you the
> whole truth, I had never envisaged the possibility that my life with Breá
> would come to an end.[22]

Low later prepared a collection of their surrealist and Marxist essays, *La
verdad contemporánea* (Contemporary truth, Havana, 1943). The 107-page book,
with a preface by Benjamin Péret, includes "The Social Function of Reproduc-
tion and Nutrition" and "The Economic Causes of Humor."

A later book of Mary Low's, *Alquimia del recuerdo* (Alchemical remembrance) assembles poems inspired by memories of her great companion. Published in Havana in 1946, it features a cover and illustrations by Wifredo Lam.

Lam and Low were, indeed, the mainstays of surrealism in Havana during and after the war. In a 1990s interview, Low recalled that "Lam dropped by at least once a week for years." Although they had many friends who assisted in various collective activities—most notably, folklorist Lydia Cabrera—there was no organized Surrealist Group in Cuba. Low's residences, however, and Lam's studio, were sites of numerous rendezvous of friends from all over. Breton, Péret, Aimé Césaire, and Pierre Mabille were just a few of their visitors.

In the 1950s Low was closely linked to the underground 26th of July movement and helped in the overthrow of dictator Batista. She remained active in surrealism in later years and was especially close to old and new friends in Paris and the group in Chicago.

THE TRIUMVIRATE OF NEGRITUDE AND *L'ÉTUDIANT NOIR*

> Sorcerer, release the dreams born here.
> —Anne Spencer

Among the most attentive readers of *Légitime Défense* in Paris were the students Aimé Césaire from Martinique, Léon-Gontran Damas from Guyana, and the Senegalese Léopold Sédar Senghor. They may not have agreed with every detail of Léro's program—especially his particular version of Freudian/Leninist Marxism—but they could hardly have failed to discuss his critical reflections on current race matters. All three, moreover, were poets and shared Léro's interest in surrealism. As residents of the Latin Quarter, they frequently ran into Robert Desnos, René Crevel, Paul Éluard, Michel Leiris, Benjamin Péret, Tristan Tzara, and other surrealists in the course of everyday life.

It was this remarkable trio—Césaire, Damas, and Senghor—who in March 1936 started the paper *L'Étudiant Noir*, long renowned as one of the monuments in the history of Negritude. Indeed, it was in the pages of *L'Étudiant Noir* that the word "Negritude" (coined by Césaire) first appeared in print. The paper's aim was not only to bring students from Martinique, Guadeloupe, other Caribbean islands, and Africa under one banner, but also to provide the entire youthful black community in Paris an open forum for discussion and debate on race-related issues. As Damas commented years later, "*L'Étudiant Noir* saw itself both as a fighting and as a unifying body," and he went on to point out that the group was significantly helped by such French friends as Breton, Desnos, and Leiris.[23]

Not Césaire nor Damas nor Senghor—nor, for that matter, Birago Diop or Aristide Maugée, who also collaborated on the paper—became members of the Paris Surrealist Group, but they were all friendly toward it, kept abreast of surrealist activities and publications, and were avid readers of the works of surrealism's precursors—Rimbaud and Lautréamont above all. In their very different ways, all three could be said to have carried on Léro's surrealist race-rebel legacy.

Alas, the story of *L'Étudiant Noir* is even more obscure than that of *Légitime Défense*. Although five or six issues are known to have been published during the second half of the 1930s, only one copy seems to have survived—discovered in the 1970s by U.S. historian Dale Tomich in an old police file at the Bibliothèque Nationale in Paris.[24]

What happened to the other issues?

When Franklin and Penelope Rosemont visited Aimé Césaire at the *Présence Africaine* bookstore in Paris during the fall of 1970, this very question came up. In reply, Césaire shrugged, shook his head, and said he had no idea where they might find a full set. His own copies, he explained, had been borrowed a few years earlier by a researcher who had never returned them.

JAMAICAN INTERLUDE

Much admired by Léro and his comrades, and a notable influence on Césaire, Damas, and Senghor, the Jamaican poet and novelist Claude McKay seems to have had no direct association with the Paris surrealists. Neither surrealism nor the aforementioned admirers appear in his autobiography, *A Long Way from Home* (1937), and his biographer, Wayne Cooper, ignores surrealism entirely, mentioning Léro and the others only in passing.

It is hard to believe that the aggressively antirational McKay—as described by Joseph Freeman—was really indifferent or hostile to a group of poets whose principal aims included the total freedom of the imagination and "poetry made by all." McKay was, after all, a friend and admirer of one of New York's most notorious eccentrics, the German Baroness Elsa von Freytag-Loringhoven, militant Dadaist poet, artist, and comrade-in-arms of Marcel Duchamp and Man Ray. Indeed, it was thanks to McKay that her poems had appeared in *The Liberator* in the early 1920s. It would seem likely that anyone attracted to the wildly nonconformist poetry of the baroness would also take the trouble to see what the surrealists were doing.

Ironically, it appears to have been politics that led the author of *Banjo* to keep his distance from surrealism. As it happened, the Surrealist Group's relatively brief combat alliance with the Communist Party coincided with Mc-

Kay's rapidly growing disillusionment with it. His own experience with the freewheeling leftist bohemianism of *The Masses* and its successor, *The Liberator* (of which he was associate editor) was perhaps a factor here, for it turned out badly in the end, with manipulative Communists firmly in control.

Like the surrealists, but unlike many other writers and painters of the time, McKay instinctively rejected the Stalinist notion of "socialist realism." What is more, he insisted—again like the surrealists—that true art had to be wholly free of any sort of political directives.[25]

Many readers today may find much of McKay's poetry old-fashioned, too restricted by the sonnet form. In his best work, however, the old form gives way to the poet's boisterously adventurous imagination, offering us a defiant and colorful collage, not unlike the art of his close friends Romare Bearden and Jacob Lawrence. In *Harlem Shadows* (1922), the recurring themes include a romantic mistrust of "Progress," fiery anger at injustice, love of wild nature, and uncompromising devotion to freedom, no matter what.

NEGRO ANTHOLOGY

The mid-1930s also brought forth that monumental book *Negro Anthology*, edited by Nancy Cunard. Praised by her friend Marcus Garvey as one who "thinks sympathetically black," Cunard had been deeply involved in surrealism since the mid-1920s; many surrealist gatherings were held at her apartment.[26] Several years in the making, *Negro Anthology* is a massive volume of 864 large and profusely illustrated pages. It brings together a stunning array of black poets, writers, and thinkers: Zora Neale Hurston, Sterling Brown, Henry Crowder (to whom the book is dedicated), W.E.B. Du Bois, Langston Hughes, Arna Bontemps, Alain Locke, George Padmore, and Jacques Roumain, to name a few— and surrealists, including René Crevel, Raymond Michelet (Cunard's chief collaborator on the book), Benjamin Péret, the Belgians Ernst Moerman and Raoul Ubac, and British painter John Banting, who would soon become an important figure in the Surrealist Group in London.

Cunard's central aims were to right the record on black history and to celebrate the creative richness and diversity of black culture around the world. Cunard also devoted much space to articles condemning white supremacy, imperialism, and racial discrimination in all its forms. Particularly important in this regard is the surrealist tract "Murderous Humanitarianism," signed by the entire Paris Surrealist Group, including the Martinicans Jules Monnerot and Pierre Yoyotte. *Negro Anthology* is also notable for its abundance of original material on the West Indies, with features on Jamaica, Haiti, Cuba, Barbados, Trinidad, Grenada, and Puerto Rico.

No publisher would accept the book, so Cunard had it printed at her own expense. Considering the magnitude and quality of the project, it received astonishingly little attention by reviewers in England or the United States. It was favorably noticed in the British *Daily Worker*, but boycotted by Stalinists in the United States, where its most important review appeared in the *Amsterdam News*. One of the few significant English reviews was written by Herbert Read, a cofounder of the Surrealist Group in London.

WIFREDO LAM

> They erupt and swirl like baby tornadoes. . . . They merge and melt into other forms.
>
> —Jayne Cortez

Another profoundly energizing development in surrealism during the second half of the 1930s was the advent of the brilliant young Cuban painter Wifredo Lam, who had come to Madrid to further his study of painting. Initially attracted by the seventeenth-century Spanish baroque painters, in the late 1920s he discovered Cubism, and particularly Picasso. Other significant influences included the work of Gauguin, Matisse, and the first generation of surrealists. Firmly rejecting the "social realism" then in vogue, he was passionately devoted to an imaginative and revolutionary art.[27]

Like Breá and Low, Lam served in the workers' militia against Franco's Falange and as a militiaman had met Eugenio F. Granell in Madrid. In Paris in 1938 he met Picasso, who not only facilitated his acquaintance with the Surrealist Group, but also became one of Lam's best friends and most ardent champions. The strong African elements in Lam's work, already evident in the 1930s, are sometimes credited to Picasso's influence, but in truth they owe more to his own Afro-Cuban upbringing. In any event, much of Picasso's work was inspired by African sculpture.

In 1940 the enthusiastic newcomer joined André Breton and most of the Surrealist Group in Marseilles, where they had gathered as refugees from the Nazi invasion. Immediately recognized as an outstanding painter and surrealist comrade, Lam readily took part in the group's games and discussions at the Chateau Air-Bel in Marseilles. While waiting for a ship to take him and his friends to the New World, he helped invent a new surrealist game—known as the Marseilles Game—which involved the creation of a new deck of cards. Lam designed two of the cards (Alice in Wonderland and Lautréamont) and also provided a series of splendid ink drawings for Breton's long poem *Fata Morgana*, which was promptly banned by the Vichy government's censor. It was later published in

Spanish in Buenos Aires. An English translation by Clark Mills first appeared in *New Directions 1941.*[28] Over the years Lam also illustrated books by many other surrealists, including Aimé Césaire, René Char, Alain Jouffroy, Gherasim Luca, Pierre Mabille, Clément Magloire-Saint-Aude, Claude Tarnaud, and François Valorbe.

Lam and his wife, Helena, sailed on the *Pierre Lemerle* with Jacqueline and André Breton and their young daughter, Aube. Also aboard were Victor Serge, his son, Vladi, and Claude Lévi-Strauss. After a mutually stimulating encounter with Aimé Césaire and the *Tropiques* group in Martinique, Lam spent the war years in Cuba. At war's end, in the company of André Breton and Pierre Mabille, he visited Haiti, particularly to pursue his study of the art and lore of voodoo.

Voodoo and its mythology had in fact long interested him in Cuba. Indeed, it has often been pointed out that Lam's family legacy—as the son of an Afro-Cuban mother and a Chinese father—prefigured the emphatically non-Western direction of his art. Such a foundation, expanded and deepened by his playful adventures with the varieties of post-Cubist painting, inspired him to develop a dramatically new creative spirit under the tropical sun. Defiantly antiexotic but pulsating with true Africanité, Lam's work—an impassioned embodiment of enchantment, revolt, and freedom—in more ways than one is a pictorial equivalent of the poetry of his contemporary, Aimé Césaire.

From the start Lam was recognized as one of surrealism's finest painters. Unfortunately, his greatness as an artist has somewhat overshadowed his appreciable stature as a writer and thinker. Although his published writings are far from bulky, they are notable for their serious commitment, philosophical depth, and poetic wisdom.

Nonsurrealist critics have also tended to slight Lam's long-standing social radicalism. He was not in fact a "joiner," but his political views were not far from the Trotskyism and other forms of Far Left Marxism espoused by his close friends Juan Breá, Mary Low, Pierre Mabille, and Benjamin Péret. As his friend Michel Leiris explains in his 1972 monograph on Lam, referring to one of the artist's most celebrated works:

> It is on several levels that we must read a painting like "The Jungle" [1943] which, set in a typical Antillean landscape, unites four figures more significant than the sugarcane harvesters they might appear to be on first sight. Giving free rein to his imagination, their creator has not only outlined the four elements of classical cosmology . . . but has shown the great source of hope that these figures incarnate in confronting the horrors of war. That source, though still incomplete, is, in the social realm, the four successive Communist Internationals.[29]

After the fall of Cuban dictator Batista in 1959, the Castro government recognized Lam as the island's national painter. He also continued to participate in international surrealist exhibitions.

Notes

1. The major sources on *Légitime Défense* remain Lilyan Kesteloot's pioneering study, *Les ecrivains noirs de langue française;* Jean-Claude Michel *Les ecrivains noirs et le surréalisme;* and Régis Antoine, *Les ecrivains français et les Antilles.* We have also drawn on various texts by René Ménil and Léon-Gontran Damas, who knew Léro well. Michael Richardson, *Refusal of the Shadow,* contains useful details.

2. Ménil, preface to the *Légitime Défense* reprint, 1979.

3. In Antoine, *Les ecrivains français et les Antilles,* 363.

4. Ibid.

5. Damas, in *Continuities* (Autumn 1974), 263. See also Daniel Racine, *Léon-Gontran Damas* (1979), 186.

6. Ménil, reprint of *Tropiques,* 1979.

7. Henri Pastoureau, letter to Franklin Rosemont, July 30, 1989.

8. Henri Pastoureau, letter to Franklin Rosemont, June 18, 1989. See also Pastoureau's *Ma vie surréaliste.*

9. Kesteloot, *Les ecrivains noirs de langue française,* 44.

10. Antoine, *Les ecrivains français et les Antilles,* 363.

11. Damas, *Continuities,* 262.

12. Ted Joans, *Teducation,* 210–211.

13. Two poems by Simone Yoyotte, with commentary on her work, are included in Penelope Rosemont, *Surrealist Women,* 66–68.

14. Antoine, *Les ecrivains français et les Antilles,* 374

15. Michel Surya, *Georges Bataille,* 536.

16. Breton, *Entrétiens,* reprint, 235.

17. Unless otherwise indicated, the information in this section on Breá, Low, and surrealism in Cuba is derived from Franklin Rosemont's inter-

views and correspondence with Mary Low, mostly in the 1980s and 1990s.

18. Antoine, *Les ecrivains français et les Antilles,* 374.

19. Mary Low, conversation with Franklin Rosemont, early 1990s.

20. Annie Rasicovici, conversation with Franklin Rosemont, Chicago, June 1993.

21. George Esenwein, "Testament of a Revolution," 176–177.

22. *View* (1941).

23. Damas, in Racine, *Léon-Gontran Damas,* 186–188.

24. In the early 1970s Dale Tomich contributed several articles on Caribbean culture and politics to the SDS (Students for a Democratic Society) journal *Radical America,* one of which ("Aimé Césaire and Negritude") is reprinted in Ron Sakolsky's *Surrealist Subversions,* 411–414. Tomich has since published *Slavery in the Circuit of Sugar* and *Through the Prism of Slavery.*

25. In his autobiography, *A Long Way from Home,* McKay discusses his friendship with Freytag-Loringhoven as well as his growing distrust of Communists. See also Cooper, *Claude McKay,* 138, 197.

26. On Cunard's involvement in surrealism, and surrealist involvement in the *Negro Anthology,* see Penelope Rosemont, *Surrealist Women,* 21–28, 61–68; and idem, *Surrealist Experiences,* 147–152.

27. On Lam, see Pierre Gaudibert and Jacques Leenhardt, *Wifredo Lam;* Leiris, *Wifredo Lam.*

28. On the Marseilles Game, see André Breton, "Le jeu de Marseilles," 66–68. For background on the surrealists in Marseilles, see Varian Fry's *Surrender on Demand,* and Bernard Noel, *Marseilles/New York.*

29. Leiris, *Wifredo Lam,* 11.

MARTINIQUE

Etienne Léro

Etienne Léro (1910–1939) was the first person of African descent to publicly identify himself as a surrealist. Born and raised in Lamentin, Martinique, and a graduate of the Lycée Schoelcher, he went to France as a young man to pursue his education. After a brief association with the Nardal sisters and their eclectic *Revue du Monde Noire,* he and several of his revolution-minded friends went on to declare their wholehearted support for surrealism and Marxism in a journal of their own, *Légitime Défense* (1932).

The chief organizer of this influential group, Léro also edited the journal. Although it was almost immediately banned in Martinique by the French colonial authorities, it circulated widely underground and even attracted a sympathetic response from South America. A second issue was planned, but never appeared.

Léro and most of his comrades were also active in the Paris Surrealist Group; collaborators on *Le Surréalisme au Service de la Révolution,* they frequently met for discussions at the home of André Breton.

Poet, theorist, and critic, Léro was a dynamic figure and a powerful inspiration to many younger black poets, artists, and radicals. His poetry was arrogantly dismissed by white critics such as Jean-Paul Sartre (in *Black Orpheus*) and Jahnheinz Jahn, but was warmly admired by poets as different as Léon-Gontran Damas, Léopold Sédar Senghor, and Ted Joans.

Severely wounded early in the war with Germany, Léro died in a French military hospital in 1939.

The texts published here open with the group's Manifesto, followed by a selection of Léro's poems and articles. "Civilization" and most of the poems are from *Légitime Défense; Le Surréalisme au Service de la Révolution,* and *Documents 34,* pages 15–18. Other sources are identified after the texts.

LÉGITIME DÉFENSE MANIFESTO

This is only a preliminary warning. We consider ourselves totally committed. We are sure that there are other young people like us who could add their signatures to ours and who—to the extent that it is compatible with remaining alive—refuse to adjust to the surrounding dishonor. And we are against all those who attempt, consciously or not, by their smiles, work, exactitude, propriety, speech, writings, actions and their very persons, to pretend that everything can continue as it is. We rise up here against all those who are not suffocated by this capitalist, Christian, bourgeois world to which, involuntarily, our protesting bodies belong.

In every country the Communist Party (Third International) is in the process of playing the decisive card of the Spirit—in the Hegelian sense of the word. Its defeat, impossible as we think it to be, would be for us the definitive *Je ne peux plus*. We believe unreservedly in its triumph because we accept the dialectical materialism of Marx, freed of all misleading interpretation and victoriously put to the test of experience by Lenin. We are ready, on this plane, to submit to the discipline that such convictions demand.

On the concrete plane of modes of human expression, we equally and unreservedly accept surrealism to which, in 1932, we relate our becoming. We refer our readers to the two *Manifestoes* of André Breton, to the complete works of Aragon, André Breton, René Crevel, Salvador Dali, Paul Éluard, Benjamin Péret and Tristan Tzara. It must be said that it is one of the disgraces of our time that these works are not better known everywhere that French is read. And in the works of Sade, Hegel, Lautréamont, Rimbaud—to mention only a few—we seek everything surrealism has taught us to find. As for Freud, we are ready to utilize the immense machine that he set in motion to dissolve the bourgeois family. We are moving with sincerity at a furious pace. We want to see clearly into our dreams and we listen to their voices. And our dreams permit us to see clearly into the life that has been imposed on us for so long.

Among the filthy bourgeois conventions, we despise above all the humanitarian hypocrisy, this stinking emanation of Christian decay. We loathe pity. We don't give a damn about sentiment. We intend to shed light on human psychic concretions—a light related to that which illuminates Salvador Dali's splendid, convulsive, plastic works, where it seems sometimes, suddenly, that love-birds could be ink-bottles or shoes or little bits of bread, taking wing from assassinated conventions.

If this little journal, a temporary instrument, breaks down, we shall find other instruments. We accept with indifference the conditions of time and space which, by defining us in 1932 as people of the French West Indies, have thus settled our boundaries without at all limiting our field of action. This first collection of texts is particularly devoted to the West Indian question as it appears to us. (The following issues, without abandoning this matter, will take up many others.) And if, by its content, this collection is addressed primarily to *young* French West Indians, it is because we think it is a good idea that our first effort finds its way to people whose capacity for revolt we are far from underestimating. And if it is aimed especially at young *blacks*, this is because we believe that they especially have had to suffer from capitalism (outside Africa, witness Scottsboro) and that they seem to offer, in that they have a materially determined ethnic personality, a generally higher potential for revolt and for joy. For want of a black proletariat, to whom international capitalism has not given the means to understand us, we speak to the children of the black bourgeoisie; we speak to those who are not already killed established fucked-up academic successful decorated decayed endowed decorative prudish decided opportunist; we speak to those who can still accept life with some appearance of truthfulness.

Having decided to be as objective as possible, we know nothing of each other's personal lives. We want to go a long way, and if we expect much from psychoanalytic investigation, we do not underestimate (from those acquainted with psychoanalytic theory) pure and simple psychological confessions which, provided that the obstacles of social conventions are removed, can tell us a great deal. We do not admit that one can be ashamed of what he suffers. The Useful—social convention—constitutes the backbone of the bourgeois "reality" that we want to break. In the realm of intellectual investigation, we pit against this "reality" the sincerity that allows man to disclose in his love, for example, the ambivalence which permits the elimination of the contradiction decreed by logic. According to logic, once an object with an affective value appears, we must respond to it either with the feeling called love or with the feeling called hate. Contradiction is a function of the Useful. It does not exist in love. It does not exist in the dream. And it is only by horribly gritting our teeth that we are able to endure the abominable system of constraints and restrictions, the extermination of love and the limitation of the dream, generally known by the name of western civilization.

Emerging from the French black bourgeoisie, which is one of the saddest things on this earth, we declare—and we shall not go back on this declaration—that we are opposed to all the corpses: administrative, governmental, parliamentary, industrial, commercial and all the others. We intend, as traitors to this class, to take the path of treason as far as it will go. We spit on everything that they love and venerate, especially those things that give them sustenance and joy.

And all those who adopt the same attitude as we, no matter where they come from, will be welcome among us.*

Etienne LÉRO, Thélus LÉRO, René MÉNIL, Jules-Marcel MONNEROT, Michel
    PILOTIN, Maurice-Sabas QUITMAN, Auguste THÉSÉE, Pierre YOYOTTE.
    1932
First published in English in 1973; translated by Alex Wilder

CIVILIZATION

The most developed of all so-called civilized countries, the United States, is getting ready to murder eight young blacks who are accused, contrary to all evidence, of raping two white prostitutes. The French press—with the exception of *Humanité*—is unanimous in maintaining a significant silence. The colored press in America, in the pay of the whites and prisoner of its class interests and political dealings, has played down the affair. The Association for the Advancement of Colored People, tiptoeing around American capitalism's criminal justice system, admits that it is unable to assume the victims' defense. The local branch of the International Red Aid has taken up the cause of the accused, and has proved quite successful in rousing world opinion against the sadism of Alabama's executioner-judges.

Will the voices of the adolescents they want to burn on the other side of the Atlantic, in spite of everything, break through the European nations' web of selfishness and prejudice? Until now, only the working class has cried out its indignation at its meetings. The blacks of the whole world owe it to themselves to be in the forefront of the struggle in favor of their brothers who are unjustly menaced with the electric chair by Yankee sexual neurosis.

When will American blacks recognize in an effective way that the only way out of the American hell lies in communism?

Légitime Défense (1932); translated by Alex Wilder

---

* If our critique is purely negative here, if we do not propose any positive
efforts in place of that which we mercilessly condemn, we excuse ourselves on the grounds that it was necessary to begin—a necessity which
did not enable us to await the full development of our ideas. In our next
issue, we hope to develop our ideology of revolt.

AND THE RAMPS

And the ramps of imprisoned flesh
The obsequious chance of honey's own saddlebows
In a morning devoured by sweat
I have lost only my feet useless for traveling
In the wind's railroad stations
The gloved shell of a ship without sails
And I speak with your voice
At the hour when all sand-paths block their own way
At the hour indicated by burned sycamore lighthouses
In the humid wound of a wingless bird
The summer breaker of shipwrecks takes a plunge

Translated by Alex Wilder

ABANDON

Abandon to electrical dentitions
Our hands and the birds
The elevator carries off
The trees and the photographs
The river keeps our heads of hair
The night strangles itself to the banging of doors
and you begin the adventure again.

Translated by Alex Wilder

PUT

Put the earrings under the chair
and the flowers of the carpet
and all the old woman's bouquets
so that the sweat of the breezes
may survive at the precipice.

Translated by Alex Wilder

Simone Yoyotte

Simone Yoyotte (ca. 1910–1933), the first black woman surrealist, was born and grew up in Martinique. Next to nothing is known of her life. The only woman in the Légitime Défense Group, she was also active in the Surrealist Group in Paris and contributed poetry to the group's journal, *Le Surréalisme au Service de la Révolution*. In Paris she married Jules Monnerot, but died after only a few months.

Her surviving poems, though few in number, mark a significant turning point in Francophone West Indian literature.

An example of automatic writing arranged as a poem, "Pyjama-Speed" was published in *Légitime Défense*. Note: "Bois-Colombes," in the first line, refers to the county seat of the Haute-de-Seine district, in the northwest Paris suburbs. Literally it means "doves' wood."

PYJAMA-SPEED

My pyjamas gilt with azure and Bois-Colombes
Tranquil atmospheres—and dance
The pavane of silence and Jew. — I am moved
—so be it—but no and if I departed softly
and the river country of my self lightly
and I smile. — My pyjamas gilt and embroidered
with myself (spear) and worst of all gilt with azure
my pyjamas balsam hammer gilt with azure
so-called Bois Colombes and Jew and you've made it.

Translated by Myrna Bell Rochester

Pierre Yoyotte

Unlike his sister, Simone, Pierre Yoyotte (19??–1940) did not contribute a text to *Légitime Défense*, but the articles he published elsewhere assured him a significant place in the history of surrealism. His delirious "Theory of the Fountain" in *Le Surréalisme au Service de la Révolution*, no. 5 (1933), is a wild phenomenological analysis, similar in many respects to

Salvador Dalí's paranoiac-critical method (interestingly, Yoyotte around that time frequented a Dalinian faction within the Surrealist Group). In contrast, his essay on surrealism's antifascist significance (in the "Intervention Surréaliste" issue of *Documents* 34) is rigorously Marxist as well as Freudian and is generally regarded as his most important article. Finally, his brief response to the inquiry on encounters in *Minotaure* 3-4 (December 1933)—however different from his other writings in style and tone—nonetheless conveys the author's serious approach to surrealist research.

Yoyotte's biography remains a mystery. Even Henri Pastoureau, a close friend in the Paris Surrealist Group, did not know exactly where or when he was born.

A French army volunteer (1939), Yoyotte became a corporal in the colonial infantry. He was killed in May 1940 during a reconnaissance mission in the war with Germany.

THEORY OF THE FOUNTAIN

The fountain constitutes a sexual provocation of a very simple type, when the water or the liquid that this fountain procures flows brusquely in small quantities, I would say gurgling, as if by a submerged trigger provoking the impression that the water which is generally hard, is at that moment soft, it is a question of tin or silver foil which generally share the same physical nature, dissolved in liquefied ambrosia. The water is limpid metallic, it is soft, mingling within itself not through currents but through textures a smiling bond of mercury and gelatin, all marinated in the silver elixir provoked by alchemists' boiling: it is a beverage.

A simple and easily observable phenomenon can illustrate by example what I say: faucet poorly turned off, mysterious and brutal outpouring of a latecoming body of water.

On the other hand, the fountain is the mouth: the fountain following like the body of an automobile in the hollow of the hand, from the basin its tow arms joined, falling in silence, you have only to convince yourself to place your two hands under the faucet and to observe the ebullition of the water. *Fountain closed mouths fountain*

You will find the man, his arms bare up to the elbow, washing himself in blood. He will have discovered, in one of the corners opposite the daylight, two or three paralyzed rats, hanging by their tails.

Surréalisme ASDLR (1933); translated by Robert Launay

ANTIFASCIST SIGNIFICANCE OF SURREALISM

1. Psychological Consequences of Capitalism among the "Middle Classes."

In order to do justice to capitalism, it is urgent to insist on the economic poverty produced by it, as well as its other consequence—a psychological misery that must be differentiated from the first in its essence, as well as in its processes.

Capitalism has received and maintained the poverty that Christian feudalism knowingly sustained and transmitted. That is the antagonism between the suppressed human emotions of ego-based materialistic desires—sexual love, desire for supremacy, etc.—and idealized collective emotions such as group "attachments"—family or fatherland, and abstract passions—religion or art. Nothing was changed here, the financiers succeeded the nobles. Wherever a minority seizes the upper hand in the satisfaction of its own desires, psychological constraints are imposed to moderate the desires of the majority of individuals.

And not only the majority because under the watchful eye of the powerful but oppressed majority, the advantages gained by oppressors such as the nobility, the clergy or the bourgeoisie, can only be preserved in relative secrecy; this requires a modicum of self-restraint. Sometimes consciously, and more often simply objectively, a hypocrisy both painful and degrading imposes itself on the suplus-value profiteers, and the repression of *desires* by psychological constraints creates an equally shared emotional misery in capitalist society.

In the higher classes, however, wealth offers desire such abundant opportunities that it often overrides constraints. . . . But below a certain level, one not easy to define, at the level of those whose "small properties" distinguish them from the pure proletarians, the *misery of desire* is usually greater than economic poverty.

For each individual, in capitalist society, the elaboration of *misery of desire* is established by an instrument that is the brilliant legacy of Christian feudalism and which characterizes its civilization—the family.

What results is the original and paradoxical contradiction of capitalism—a form that, on the one hand, develops sublime sentiments and on the other, represses and irritates them, thus preparing a *psychological misery* as intense as the *misery of desire.*

Except within the proletarian class where both are separated from economic misery since for the average individual, they are luxuries quite out of proportion to his limited financial means.

Therefore, if the proletarian minority wants a revolution to solve the economic misery to which emotional misery is linked, the majority of the French middle classes, burdened as they are with a moral guilt—reinforced against desire *and* mocked by money—are absolutely ripe for a *counterrevolution of emo-*

*tions and ideals that is to be directed against both money and desire, a revolution in which a
few material demands will come about hypocritically hidden by repressed emotions.* Such a
counterrevolution has already occurred in two large European countries by
using effectively the local and historical aggravations of psychological misery.
This is what I was driving at. Naturally, I am speaking of fascism.

2. *Fascism.*

When these sentiments were provoked by military defeat, they produced a
national inferiority complex, and the beginnings of a proletarian movement.

The only way out was satisfaction. But compared to material satisfactions,
the emotional or mystical ones (or those of the horde) have the advantage of
a long history. Their infantile victories over primary desires endow them (as in
war) with the appearance of a paradise. *This is how, through such a displacement, they
have managed to contain all the affective aspirations of successive generations.* This was the
invention of Hitlerism and Mussolinian fascism—it was just a matter of masks
to forget the money battles after the kisses, and to hide—as if it was dirty—the
necessity of love and pleasure. Emotions survive on masks, not realities. What
Hitler and Mussolini gave in terms of material satisfactions amounts to very
little, but that is exactly the point. Capitalist inequality is in reality not the
enemy of the hysterical exaltation of the hordes in black and brown shirts.
The young fascists find it exciting to despise easy living—at the same time, the
easy life of the bosses, their parasites and their inheritors continues in broad
daylight.

If fascism is not an economic revolution, the fact is that the essentially emotional and ideational revolution it represents *prevents* the coming of the economic revolution, that was seemingly imminent because of the material situation of the masses, the petit bourgeoisie, the peasantry and the proletariat—the
majority, that is! The great discovery and the essential originality of fascism is
its utilization of the *irrational* as autonomous and important factors in the political domain.

What must also be admitted is that communist propaganda, exclusively
based on Marxist teachings, has failed to understand, to denounce and to attack
the political importance of collective emotions. Marxism only fights against the
domination of money in material and definitive ways. The communists have
always been officially (and obtusely) suspicious of the discoveries of psychoanalysis that would have helped them fight knowledgeably against the irrational processes of family, religion, fatherland, etc.

Fundamentally, the communists never really fought against emotional repressions for two reasons (which are but one): the first one is subjective: it was

considered only a matter of secondary importance, tightly dependent upon the economic regime; the second was objective: for the proletarian thinking that is responsible for the orientation of the Marxist intellectual stream, problems of emotional repression were really secondary in view of the proletariat's material situation. For those of us who must prevent that salvation, the task is clear.

3. *Antifascism.*

It is extremely significant that during the myth-building post–WWI period, while the fascist hordes were forming, a group of young men got together in France in order to *systematize* the poetic tradition of revolt—which also happens to be a moral one—one that was handed down from the previous century by the few rebels who objected to the monstrous invasion of money. If these few cases seem "limited," they are by no means exceptional, as the success of surrealism tends to demonstrate. Starting with emotional repression (still poignantly part of today's reality), the surrealists immediately addressed themselves to the defense of desire, to individual inspiration, to solutions that were diametrically opposed to the Mussolinian or racist militarization of their time.

When fascism was still very far from its present hyper-actuality, these men born in the bourgeoisie were amazingly flouting their moral revolt, contrary to the fascist ideals. Their joining the communist revolutionary action has put an end to it, as has the intellectual recognition of psychoanalysis and historical materialism. This is revealed in André Breton's *Communicating Vessels.* A specifically surrealist ethical position was formulated—to discredit all ideals and reveal the material reality of desire behind their appearances.

The united antifascist action in France depends upon a wide moral unity. The program of action will proceed from it.

The concept of the destruction of ideals should be intelligently understood—it is contradictory for a society to be without any collective exaltation. As a revolutionary, I like the idea of creating a tolerable society. The ethics of the future will not consist of suppressing the irrational emotions; instead we shall master them and subordinate them to desire.

In the face of a generalized deficiency of ideas, the attitude of the surrealists and a few others represents the beginning of what must be done.

Documents 1934; translated by Guy Ducornet (original emphasis)

Maurice-Sabas Quitman

The author of this informative article is one of the less-well-known figures of the *Légitime Défense* Group, and this text may well be his only published work. In any case, unlike Léro, Ménil, Monnerot, Pierre Yoyotte
and his sister Simone, Quitman was not active in surrealism after 1932.

PARADISE ON EARTH

Anyone interested in current affairs will agree that it is just as difficult to manage seven or twelve francs as it is to manage a billion. Obviously the burden is
not heavy enough. The "Negro" does not kill himself. Such is Langston Hughes'
"Beggar Boy":

> And yet he plays upon his flute a wild free tune
> As if fate had not bled him with her knife!

What is the upshot of this situation? The worker in the fields, "that wretched
lump of black clay with breath of life," is barely able to feed himself on his
"wages." He does not, however, wander around naked. Clothes? Sure, but
not from clothing stores. Their European style notwithstanding, the worker's
clothes are cut from stolen guano sacks; in some places their hemp bears the
name "Aubery khaki."

Without overlooking this economic situation, let us take into account the
case of the worker who establishes a family. Life becomes even harder. The parents increase their sacrifices until the day comes when the children reach the
age of six or eight and can join the struggle for existence. They are hired, without sexual distinction, into the job category known officially as "little workers,"
and collectively as the "little gang," adding a few more francs to the family's
"wages."

And here is the reason: The Negro works while the white man gets rich at
his expense—rich to the extent that he can easily deposit a million in the near-
est bank when "Mlle. His Daughter" is born. Who is to blame?

"The Governor!"

"No," as one of them—a passenger from the *Lamotte-Picquet*, author of *Civilian
among Sailors*—said to his hosts: "Their certainty of not staying in the colony
means that they are not inclined to govern."

The blame lies with those who, refusing to regard these outcasts as compatriots, should at least regard them as human beings. The blame lies with those

who put their intelligence at the service of the factory owners, skillful exploiters of their false pride, which consists in denying their origins and deprecating "blacks" who, despite them, are nonetheless their compatriots.

The remedy, therefore, does not require the creation of primary schools in the rural areas. They are already there. What is necessary is to make it possible for the poor to attend these schools, and that means improving working people's situation. Three-quarters of the island belongs to five or six families of factory owners whose cupidity is equaled only by their workers' patience. However, this patience should not be counted on. A people cannot remain oppressed forever. No government, even of the "left," has ever limited feudal power through laws concerning the relations between owners and workers, or has had the power to even *supervise the application of those laws.*

In the absence of such an intervention, the day will come when the workers will revolt. And the doctors whom Chance has not classified among the ranks of the "lazy and uncultivated" will perhaps attempt—in imitation of those French doctors examining some trivial problem—to explain this revolt as the triumph of some "medullary automatism" over the will.

Légitime Défense, translated by Franklin Rosemont (original emphasis)

Jules Monnerot

Born in Fort-de-France, Martinique, Monnerot (1909–1995) went to Paris to pursue his education. Unlike his father, Jules Senior—the principal founder of the island's Communist Party—the son lived most of his life in Paris. A cofounder of the Légitime Défense Group, he contributed texts and poems to its journal and, like his comrades, went on to take part in the activities of the Paris Surrealist Group. Monnerot's article "On Certain Traits Particular to the Civilized Mentality" demonstrates his competence as a surrealist theorist. His involvement in the movement, however, proved sporadic. In 1938, he was briefly associated with Georges Bataille, Roger Caillois, and other former surrealists in the ill-fated College of Sociology.

Monnerot's best and most influential book, *La poésie moderne et le sacré* (1945), in large part a study of the parallels between surrealism, Gnosticism, and "primitive" thought, was much admired by André Breton and others in the Surrealist Group.

Most of Monnerot's later books have little to do with surrealism, but at least two of them—*Les faits sociaux ne sont pas des choses* (1946) and even *Inquisitions* (1974), with its remarkable critique, "Television: Birth of a Power"—include deeply interesting material. His contribution to the exhibition catalog *Le surréalisme en 1947* was his last direct participation in surrealism.

ON CERTAIN TRAITS PARTICULAR TO THE CIVILIZED MENTALITY

What I especially can't stand are things that are half-dead but still living, such as current fads that are the backbone of everyone's thinking—all that is disgusting—those things that I just glance at during an easy, but distant stroll through their slip-shod constructions, fields of rust, the cancerous vegetation of "collective consciousness" (at least we can stop worrying about the end; the rear exit actually does open to the Outside).

That capitalism finds certain ways of thinking or not thinking necessarily complementary to itself, ways of thinking that by definition are likely to assure its effective survival, is an odd idea that is understood by us only in the few moments of our lives in which we are awake. Conventional thinking corrodes slowly even the most rigorous concepts circulating like blood, and thanks to this the poison of conventional thinking becomes permanent and definite; this is the immobilizing environment where the minds of those concerned with spirituality flounder.

These specialists in morality, like everyone else, maintain constantly a fundamental dichotomy between their official self and their actual self—obviously, they would be struck with a fatal case of vertigo if they tried to picture themselves outside these necessary conventions—largely professional, military, family—connections that are the coat-hangers they use to hang up their selves every night before they go to sleep. It will truly not be easy to take these "selves" away from a considerable number of people. Worse yet, their "real lives" are just as phony as their "selves" are. Their positivism, a submission to what existed before they were born, is a trick of ideology that the bourgeoisie uses to keep itself in power. Positivism sees facts as given, discarding the dialectical law of their development—the only way that they can actually acquire meaning. The denial of this "reality" is a denial of the development of society by active negation and becomes likewise a denial of the reality which it claims to oppose. Civilized thinking, when it applies its own standards to itself and sees itself in its own notorious "facts" comes upon a vicious circle. Truly, positivism nurses an infant covered with pox, one that would be better to beat to death—that is, realistic art which consists solely of "what one sees" and which will never be able to contribute to any real progress, because there can never be any true discoveries unless they are antithetical to this world.

If one shakes the main principles of bourgeois morality, they jingle like money. I state flatly that every word that expresses these principles has or has had a financial or business-related meaning. If one gives even the most flimsy consideration to the meaning of these words, the "moral" fraud becomes clear instantly. Duty means Debt, a clearly Christian idea of a loan that one has not yet finished repaying. This duty, which benefits those who hold the loans in the first place is called Obligation. Its repayment, according to books on morals, confer value on the subject. (The word "value" is found more often in that kind of literature than the word "good.") The slickest "philosophers" manage to disguise these ideas only imperfectly; they visibly remain in the service of monstrous military and industrial exploitation.

In the Civilized Mind the basic idea of value or wealth, i.e. property, sup-poses the correspondingly basic idea of a person or persons who own that value or wealth. In France, for instance, there is absolutely nothing in existence about which one cannot ask the question (at the same time indispensable, ignoble, and sacred): "Who owns it?" Not even consciousness itself can be conceived of except as a property of the subject. Publications and books of all types discuss always the ideas of Mr. So-and-so or the thought or spirituality of this or that individual, state, business, family, or countryside.

Surrealism, a dialectical continuation of Dada, brought poetry to such levels that it no longer belonged to literature. Situated at the far limits of the poem, poetry now only needs to make a leap. But even today its form in literature can only be explained by social conditions which are the antithesis of poetry and which will not be destroyed until a while after the victory of workers' revolution on a world scale.

How we will gain possession of the controls that govern the changes of State, we do not know. One can only affirm the dialectical necessity of finding them—the dialectical progression of surrealism consists in closing the gap that separates the word from the prime matter it represents. This means a dialectical reinvention of magic. The poet will see himself as a technician of this transition from word to world. But don't rest assured by these thoughts on poetry; the surrealists are devoting the greater part of their time to the most practical of thoughts—revolutionary theory and propaganda—so much for now. What was once the poet, will then become the magician who will liberate the dream, the magician in a world in which bad faith's moral conscience has necessarily been abolished, in which the pleasure principle is identical to the reality principle, the unreal to the real, united in an alchemical marriage. Morality devours psy-chology, poetry devours verse, actions devour individuals, humankind devours the I, the world devours all things. But the clear streams carry forward their ever-changing diamonds.

Le Surréalisme au Service de la Révolution 5 (1933); translated by Rachel Blackwell

INDISPENSABLE POETRY: RESPONSE TO AN INQUIRY

Amoebalike, poetry invades us from every direction. It is life itself. It is present in the secrets of a coolie suffering from elephantiasis at the foot of Mont-Pelé. In egotistical movies where the urge to climb the social ladder, to descend or to re-situate oneself is fulfilled at any cost. In certain so-called detective novels. In the slander, calumny and defamation, at times brilliant, of so many concierges and non-combatants. In the luminous and subtle homage Parisian dressmakers offer up to vanished civilizations, to outdated feelings, and to colonial races, while exploiting the curves of the female body. In the daily grind of delirious justifications and absurd claims. Socialization of the marvelous slowly consumes itself under our eyes. Man, whether in his cathedrals, his bistros, or his Paramounts, is clearly an animal in which the need for poetry exists naturally.

Cahiers G.L.M. (March 1939); translated by Myrna Bell Rochester

Yva Léro

Most academic studies of the Negritude movement have surprisingly little to say about Yva Léro. A direct descendant of Michel de Montaigne, she was married to Etienne Léro's brother, Thélus (a mathematician by profession and a cosigner of the 1932 *Légitime Défense* manifesto). Yva and Thélus Léro and Suzanne and Aimé Césaire lived in Paris at the same time and were often together; in later years, too, back in Martinique, Yva and Suzanne remained close friends. Although Yva did not contribute to *Tropiques* or take part in surrealist activity as such, she did write poetry of striking originality, such as the examples published here, from her chapbook, *Peau d'ébène* (1979).

LITTLE BLACK DIVERS

There were six little divers
six lively little divers
six undersized little divers . . .

Whenever a boat came into view,
on the blue waves of the Caribbean,
tossing off their games and their rags
offering their naked bodies to the sun
they leapt in, splashing each other
fighting for first place.
And the blue waves took them in . . .

But just like corks
they popped up, disappeared
reappearing, jostling each other
in a sometimes violent struggle
ignorant of reefs and sharks
each had a single goal . . . just one
to get closer to the big boat.

Their empty bellies urged them on
whispered touching words to them,
words that opened purses . . .
And all the curious passengers
ventured one coin and even two . . .
he really did deserve all those bravos
the winning little diver!

They lusted after the shining coin
ignoring reefs and sharks . . .
for they had but a single goal . . . just one,
to possess that coin
And without so much as suspecting the danger
threatening the little divers
the passengers had fun watching . . .

There were six little divers
six lively little divers
six undersized little divers . . .

Translated by Myrna Bell Rochester

Aimé Césaire

Martinique-born Aimé Césaire (1913–2008) is beyond question the most world renowned black surrealist. His poetry and plays as well as his theoretical and polemical works have been translated into many languages and have inspired a large critical literature.

After graduating from the Lycée Schoelcher in Fort-de-France in 1931, Césaire studied in Paris, notably at the École Normal Superieure, an advanced training school for teachers. In Paris, with his childhood friend Léon Damas and the Senegalese Léopold Senghor, Césaire studied African history, read *Légitime Défense*, and immersed himself in the writings of the surrealist poets and their precursors (especially Rimbaud and Lautréamont). With Damas, Senghor, and others, he also started the newspaper *L'Étudiant Noir* and cofounded the Negritude movement, which exerted a strong influence throughout the black world.

As a teacher in Martinique in the 1940s, Césaire—with his wife, Suzanne, and a former coeditor of *Légitime Défense*, René Ménil—founded the journal *Tropiques*, a special blend of Negritude and surrealism that continued publication for five years. Throughout the war years, *Tropiques* was recognized as international surrealism's principal vehicle.

At war's end, Césaire was elected mayor of Fort-de-France and deputy to the French National Assembly. Often called the "surrealist mayor," he continued to participate in surrealist activity, particularly during the 1947 International Surrealist Exhibition in Paris. Politically, he focused on the central problems of colonialism and racism. His *Discourse on Colonialism* (1955) had a worldwide impact. Momentous, too, was his intervention at the First International Congress of Negro Writers and Artists (1956) in which he calls for the revolutionary overthrow of colonialism and the creation of a new culture.

Césaire's interviews from the 1960s and later show that his identification with surrealism, and his admiration for André Breton, remained intact, along with his anticolonialism. In 2006, at the age of ninety-three, he publicly rebuked the French minister of culture, who had proposed that Martinican textbooks feature a less critical view of colonialism and slavery.

NÉGRERIES: BLACK YOUTH AND ASSIMILATION

What is difficult is not to ascend, but in ascending to remain oneself.
—Michelet

One day, the Black seized hold of the White's neck-tie, grabbed a bowler hat, dressed up in them, and left laughing . . .

It was only a game, but the Black did not let himself take it as a game. He became so accustomed to the neck-tie and the bowler hat that he ended up believing he had always worn them. He made fun of those who didn't wear them at all and disowned his father whose name is Spirit of the Bush . . . This is a bit of the history of the pre-war Negro, who is only the Negro before reason. He sits down at the school of the Whites. He wants to be "assimilated."

I would gladly say that it is madness, if I didn't remember that, in a certain sense, the madman is always "the man who has faith in himself," and because of that saves himself from madness.

If assimilation is not madness, it is certainly foolishness. To want to be assimilated is to forget that nothing can change animal nature. It is to misunderstand "otherness," which is a law of Nature.

This is so true that the People, elder brothers of Nature, warn us of it every day: A decree says to the Blacks: "You are similar to the Whites. You are assimilated."

The People, wiser than the decree because they follow Nature, shout to us:

"Begone! You are different than us! You are only aliens and negroes." They deride the "Black man with a bowler," bully the "poorly whitened," and bludgeon the "negro."

I confess that it is justice, though unfortunate for the one who needs to be convinced by means of a cudgel that he can only be himself.

Moreover, it is enough to reflect on the notion of assimilation to see that it is a dangerous business for the colonizer as well as the colonized.

The colonizing nation that "assimilates" another quickly becomes disgusted with its own work. Copies only being copies, the prototypes have the contempt for them that one has for apes and parrots. For if man is afraid of "the other," he also has an aversion for the similar. It is the same for the colonized. Once similar to the one who has molded him, he no longer understands the contempt of the latter, and he hates him. In a like manner, I have heard it said that some disciples hate the master because he still wants to remain the master when the disciple has ceased being a disciple.

Thus it is true that assimilation, born of fear and timidity, always ends in contempt and hatred. It carries within it the germs of struggle. The struggle of self against self, that is to say, the worst of struggles.

For this reason, Black youth turns its back on the tribe of the Old.

The tribe of the Old says, "assimilation." We respond, resurrection!

Black youth of today want neither enslavement nor assimilation. They want emancipation.

They will be called "men," because only man walks without a tutor on the great roads of thought. Enslavement and assimilation resemble one another. Both are forms of passivity.

During these first two periods, the Negro has been equally sterile.

Emancipation, on the other hand, is action and creation.

Black youth want to act and create. It wants to have its poets and its novelists who will speak to it. It wants to have its misfortunes and its greatness. It wants to contribute to universal life, to the humanization of humanity. For that, it must preserve itself or find itself once again. It is the primacy of the self.

But to be oneself, it is necessary to struggle. First struggle against the misguided brothers who are afraid of being themselves, the senile mob of the assimilated.

Then struggle against those who want to inflate their egos, the legion of the assimilators.

Finally, to be oneself, it is necessary to struggle against oneself. It is necessary to destroy indifference, extirpate obscurantism, strike sentimentalism at its root, and Meredith tells us what, above all, must be cut:

Black Youth, it is hair that keeps you from acting. It is the desire to conform, and it is you that carry it.

Crop your hair close so that this desire may escape.

Cut your hair.

It is the first condition of action and creation.

A long head of hair is an affliction.

L'Étudiant Noir, no. 1 (March 1935); translated by Dale Tomich

JAMAICA

Claude McKay

Although McKay (1890–1948) took no part in surrealist activity, his influence on the movement was both significant and enduring. Jamaica-born, he had already published two books of poems when he left for the United States in 1912. Settling down in New York a few years later, he quickly became a forceful presence in the city's radical cultural and political scene, and particularly in what would later be called the Harlem Renaissance. A member of the Industrial Workers of the World and coeditor of *The Liberator,* he was also well known as a poet.

In Paris in the 1930s he was something of a liaison between the Harlem poets, the Martinican Nardal sisters (who published his poems in their *Revue du Monde Noir*), and other poets from Africa and the Caribbean. His poetry was much admired, but it was his explosive 1929 novel *Banjo: A Story without a Plot,* that made everybody sit up and take notice. A realistic novel of blues-loving working-class black dockworkers, largely set in Marseilles, the book was as much a scandal to the "respectable" as it was a joy and revelation to young black radicals looking for answers. *Banjo* was a decisive inspiration for Césaire, Damas, and Senghor. (Interviewed by Senegalese scholar Lilyan Kesteloot in the 1960s, all three were still able to "cite entire chapters" of the book.) Most significantly, in regard to surrealism, the journal *Légitime Défense*—as an act of defiance—published a long excerpt from the book, reprinted here.

DOWN TO THE ROOTS

"I believe in a racial renaissance," said the student, "but not in going back to savagery."

"Getting down to our native roots and building up from our own people," said Ray, "is not savagery. It is culture."

"I can't see that," said the student.

"You are like many Negro intellectuals who are bellyaching about race," said Ray. "What's wrong with you-all is your education. You get a white man's education and learn to despise your own people. You read biased history of the whites conquering the colored and primitive peoples, and it thrills you just as it does a white boy belonging to a great white nation.

"Then when you come to maturity you realize with a shock that you don't and can't belong to the white race. All your education and achievements cannot put you in the intimate circles of the whites and give you a white man's full opportunity. However advanced, clever, and cultivated you are, you will have the distinguishing adjective of colored before your name. And instead of accepting it proudly and manfully, most of you are soured and bitter about it, especially you mixed-bloods.

"You're a lost crowd, you educated Negroes, and you will only find yourself in the roots of your own people. You can't choose as your models the haughty-minded educated white youths of a society living solid on its imperial conquests. Such pampered youths can afford to despise the sweating white brutes of the lower orders.

"If you were sincere in your feelings about racial advancement, you would turn for example to whites of a different type. You would study the Irish cultural and social movement. You would turn your back on all these tiresome clever European novels and read about the Russian peasants, the story and struggle of their lowly, patient, hard-driven life, and the great Russian novelists who described it up to the time of the Russian Revolution. You would learn all you can about Gandhi and what he is doing for the common hordes of India. You would be interested in the native African dialects and, though you don't understand, be humble before their simple beauty instead of despising them."

The mulatto student was not moved in his determination not to go to the African Bar, and so Ray went alone.

CUBA

Juan Breá

More or less simultaneously the Havana-born Juan Breá (1905–1941) was an important figure in the 1933 Cuban Revolution, cofounder of the Cuban Trotskyist organization, and a major player in the island's first surrealist-oriented cultural current, the H-Group. In Paris in 1933 he met Mary Low, an English-born poet of Australian parents, and the couple soon joined the Surrealist Group. During the next eight years they were international surrealism's most notable nomads, active in the Surrealist Groups of Paris, Brussels, Bucharest, and Prague. In 1936 the indomitable pair went to Spain to fight for the revolution as members of the workers' militia and also aided the cause with radio broadcasts and by editing the English-language paper *Spanish Revolution*. Their record of that struggle, *Red Spanish Notebook* (1937), was praised by George Orwell and is considered a classic. Their chapbook of poems, *La saison des flûtes*, appeared under the Éditions Surréalistes imprint in 1938, and a collection of their theoretical essays and lectures on surrealism and politics, *La verdad contemporánea*, was published in Havana in 1943.

MY LIFE IS A SUNDAY

My life is a Sunday,
a Sunday when one doesn't work
or play,
when one is merely tired.
A Sunday just as stupid
And as strange
As a statue of Jesus walking on the sea.

I still have
a little lustful horse-power left,
and ten calories in my heart—
in this heart that dreams
of a soft, sweet, cowardly death,
like all those who haven't the courage to meet it face to face.

He who has not enough courage to live on the edge of the law
has always enough cowardice to live
on the other side of life.

Already the heat is going away
in the short skirts it wears on summer nights;
but I don't want to die in winter—
not because it would be very cold,
but because it would be very soon.

O the sweet cowardice of dying
just a little!

In every afternoon that rains,
In every love that ends,
To die a little, in every being and in every thing.

La saison des flûtes (1937); translated by Mary Low

THOUGHTS

The only sacrifice of individual freedom that society has a right to demand
of the individual is courtesy.

*   *   *

Throughout written history, all the prejudices that accompany thought—
be it scientific, political, or philosophical—are the same as private
property: an original sin that has merely been altered.

*   *   *

In the final analysis, the concept of quality is nothing but the
divinization of human behavior at the expense of the broad dehumanization
      of
other behaviors. What is deemed great and what is deemed small in no way
implies goodness or badness: the first is a size, the second a bias.

*   *   *

Civilization, culture, progress. These are no more than the written history
of manual labor.

*   *   *

Laws are no more than the portion of the truth that suits us.

*   *   *

The age-old error of philosophy—the error that explains its only reason
for being—consists of having taken as absolute or eternal a relative or
temporal truth: the existence of private property, the expression of a type
of production and mother of all the philosophical "isms": unanism, dualism,
egotism, etc.

*   *   *

Poetry is above all a great premonition, hence, its supernatural tone. When this poetic value begins to be or ends up being understood by everyone, the poem loses its very essence: its prophetic power. Poetry ends when it stops being a hypothesis; from then on its life consists precisely of that lapse in hypothetical reality; and finally, truth transforms it either into an axiom or into the absurd.

All from *La saison des flûtes* (1937); translated by Myrna Bell Rochester

Juan Breá and Mary Low

NOTES ON THE ECONOMIC CAUSES OF HUMOR

But first, what *is* humor, in general? No one up till now has been capable of replying satisfactorily to this question. But if we cannot offer a concrete definition, why not try for an *impression* of what humor is? This is the modest pretension that has brought us to write these lines.

One aspect of this sentiment is a certain sense of judgment, a *critical* tendency which humor expresses more or less openly. We might define its general function as a regulator between the exaggerated and the average, between the ideal and the everyday. Humor would therefore be the psychological expression of the essential reality of a specific epoch or people.

Reduced to its simplest terms, we see that humor has a vital critical function. In its best form, and apparently its most disinterested form—the non-tendentious joke—it seems rather like a spontaneous judgment, disinterested and without reservations. This kind of joke, devoid of personal motives, resentment, or envy, resembles a critical judgment motivated by a noble and natural manifestation of the spirit of justice.

Developing its role as critic, humor exercises a constructive influence. As a form of criticism, it is a creative activity; its nature is to restrict and comment, and in this there is a humanizing factor. Why is there laughter when the fat and self-important Colonel slips on a banana-peel in the street? And why don't we laugh when a working-girl opens a torn umbrella? Humor embodies an equalizing influence, and in this—as in its unconscious rebellion—it reveals its revolutionary role.

La verdad contemporánea (1943); translated by Mary Low

TRINIDAD

C. L. R. James

"Renaissance man" though he was, James (1901–1989) somehow never got around to participating in surrealism, and indeed, despite the interests he and the surrealists shared—Hegel, Marx, Melville, Freud, Wilson Harris, poetry, anti-imperialism, and social revolution, to name a few— he does not seem to have made a special study of the movement's aims, principles, and achievements. However, as a revolutionary interested in culture, he inevitably encountered people active in surrealism, such as Pierre Naville in 1930s Paris (a decade later Naville translated James' *The Black Jacobins* into French), and André Breton in 1938 in Mexico, where Breton, James, and Diego Rivera cofounded the International Federation of Independent Revolutionary Art (Fédération Internationale de l'Art Revolutionnaire Independent, FIARI). These were mostly fugitive meetings in any case, and surrealism was rarely the main topic of discussion.

As it happens, James' closest direct link to surrealism in those years was his short introduction to the book *Red Spanish Notebook*, a firsthand account by two young surrealists, Juan Breá and Mary Low, published in London in 1937.

In later years, it is true (from the mid-1960s on), many individuals associated with the international surrealist movement—including Ted Joans, Jayne Cortez, Paul Buhle, David Roediger, Dale Tomich, and Franklin Rosemont—met or corresponded with James and sometimes brought up the subject of surrealism. Significantly, James' 1962 appendix to *The Black Jacobins* devotes several beautiful pages to Aimé Césaire's *Return to My Native Land*, excerpted here from *Red Spanish Notebook*. And in the 1980s he contributed a number of articles to Paul Buhle's surrealist-oriented *Cultural Correspondence* and to *Free Spirits: Annals of the Insurgent Imagination*.

INTRODUCTION TO *RED SPANISH NOTEBOOK*

When the bourgeois parties with this powerful aid had strangled the first phase of the socialist revolution, Breá and Mary Low left Barcelona. And yet this is not a depressing book. Far from it. Catalonia leads Spain, and for some few months at least the workers and peasants of Catalonia, politically inexperienced, thought that the new world had come. The flame has been lit and Fascism can pour on it the blood of thousands of workers, can stamp upon it, and even stifle it for a time. But it will burn underground, is imperishable, and will blaze again. For Breá and Mary Low, despite their eye for picturesque personalities, are proletarian revolutionaries, and their little book shows us the awakening of a people.

The bootblack who good-humoredly but firmly refuses a tip, showing his union-card; the peasant who will not be kept waiting as of old because equality exists now; the hundreds of women stealing away from their husbands to join the women's militia and attend Marxist classes, throwing off the degrading subservience of centuries and grasping with both hands at the new life: They will conquer. They must. If not today, then tomorrow, by whatever tortuous and broken roads, despite the stumblings and the falls. There is no room for the democratic republic in Spain today. Either Spain must go back to a nightmare of reaction infinitely worse than the old feudalism, or on to the social revolution. And the guarantee of their victory is that for the eager thousands who march through these pages, smashing up the old and tumultuously beginning the new, workers' power emerged half-way from books, became something that they could touch and see, a concrete alternative to the old slavery.

2. _Tropiques:_ Surrealism in the Caribbean

CUBA, MARTINIQUE, HAITI, DOMINICAN REPUBLIC, TRINIDAD, PUERTO RICO

Everywhere—in New York, in Brazil, in Mexico, in Argentina, in Cuba, in Canada, in Algiers—voices echo that would not be what they are . . . without surrealism.

—Suzanne Césaire

MARTINIQUE

Did you know that Martinique fully qualifies as one of the vital centers of the surrealist universe? It is not exactly common knowledge, but in the eighty-odd-year history of surrealism, this tiny volcanic island has played—again and again—a hugely volcanic role. Etienne Léro and his _Légitime Défense_ comrades were Martinicans one and all, and although most of them settled in Paris, it is obvious from their writings that their homeland remained very much in their hearts and minds. In 1939 appeared one of the greatest, most volcanic, and most internationally celebrated surrealist poems: Aimé Césaire's _Return to My Native Land,_ largely inspired by the island. André Breton himself, deeply moved by his three-week visit with Suzanne and Aimé Césaire in the spring of 1941, wrote one of the most beautiful and enchanting surrealist books of the 1940s— _Martinique: Snake Charmer,_ supplemented with texts and illustrations by André Masson.

Especially impressive was the indigenous surrealist activity in Martinique during the Second World War. In 1941, nine years after _Légitime Défense_ appeared, Martinicans Suzanne and Aimé Césaire, together with former _Légitime Défense_ collaborator René Ménil, began publication of a new periodical— _Tropiques_ —on the island itself.[1]

A shoestring operation from start to finish, _Tropiques_ was initially presented as a modest and eclectic journal of culture. From its third issue on, however, it was unequivocally surrealist. Indeed, André Breton and others regarded _Tropiques_ as the movement's best, most exciting, and most relevant vehicle during the war years. Nazi invasion had made it impossible for the Surrealist Groups in Paris, Prague, Bucharest, Brussels, and Copenhagen to function openly, and most European surrealists sought refuge in New York, London, Havana, Buenos Aires, or Mexico.

For five long years, then, 1941–1945, Fort-de-France—the capital of Martinique—was recognized as one of the liveliest points on the world surrealist map. As the Greek surrealist Nicolas Calas noted in *View* magazine (October–November issue) in New York in 1941:

> When the detestable writings of so many famous authors of our day
> will have been forgotten and when critics and poets will begin to look
> for the creative writing of the war period, they will then dig out and
> reprint, with all the honors due to them, the early numbers of *Tropiques*.
> I know of no review which can boast of the high quality of this small
> quarterly French review of Martinique. The fact that such a review can
> be published is enough to put to shame those artists and poets who
> today feel discouraged and abandon all struggle, either because the
> public is not interested in their work, or because they are afraid of the
> political consequences of their efforts. It is difficult to imagine that
> conditions anywhere outside nazi-dominated Europe could be worse
> than they are in the Vichy colony of Martinique; as to the cultural
> conditions of a colony that France has always neglected, from all one
> hears they are abominable. Yet, Aristide Maugée does not hesitate to
> defend in *Tropiques* the case of obscurity in poetry, in an article which
> we hope some day to see published in English. René Ménil writes about
> "Directions in Poetry," a most inspired and inspiring article, while Aimé
> Césaire published a fragment of an admirable poem.

A striking fact about the *Tropiques* Group—rarely noted in the critical literature—is that nearly all of its adherents, including the Césaires, were of working-class background. Indeed, most of them—again including the Césaires—were employed as schoolteachers. Their work on *Tropiques* was a spare-time volunteer activity, and very much a labor of love.

The journal's increasingly surrealist character was doubtless influenced by the visits to the island by Breton, his wife, Jacqueline, and the painters André Masson and Wifredo Lam. Its surrealist inclinations, however, were evident from the beginning. The debut issue—the one Breton found by chance at the Fort-de-France variety store—already radiated a surrealist sensibility and a surrealist tone, in Aimé Césaire's two-and-a-half-page "Presentation," for example, and René Ménil's "Birth of Our Art."

That sensibility and tone were sustained and amplified in issue after issue, for five years. Sad to say, we know next to nothing about the *Tropiques* Group's internal workings—its meetings, for example. We do not even know how often the group met, or where, or how many attended. Everything leads us to believe, however, that these were lively occasions for discussion and debate—full of ideas, criticism, creativity, humor, inspiration, and play. Looking through the journal itself and noting its broad range of topics and lack of repetition, it is clear that the *Tropiques* writers, each in his or her own way, gladly and boldly took up the defense and illustration of surrealism's emancipatory project.

Suzanne Césaire's texts are particularly outstanding in this regard—not only her deeply moving commentary on André Breton's poetry, but also her hard-hitting critique of Martinique's bourgeois literature, and above all her "1943: Surrealism and Us," a veritable manifesto on surrealism in the service of international black revolution. A brilliant writer with a strong grasp of theory and an audacious imagination, Suzanne Césaire was one of the major surrealist thinkers and dreamers of her time.[2] Her assessment of Leo Frobenius' work on Africa is likely to strike current-day readers as overly generous, but in truth it reflects the paucity of sources available in those days, and in any case represents a view shared by more than a few others at that time. Decades later, indeed, readers—especially young readers looking for answers—continue to be thrilled by Suzanne Césaire's still-up-to-the-minute revolutionary insights and exhortations.

Aimé Césaire's wonderful poems—featured in almost every issue of *Tropiques*—are enhanced and expanded by his trenchant surrealist essays: on poetry and knowledge, on African American poetry, and on Lautréamont. René Ménil's many contributions—his "Introduction to the Marvelous," for example, and his essay on humor, in which he notes the affinities between Duke Ellington's music and Benjamin Péret's surrealist tales—added appreciably to the movement's already incredibly wide-ranging perspectives.

And so it was with the others involved in *Tropiques*: Georgette Anderson on the Marvelous; Aristide Maugée on the practice of poetry; Georges Gratiant on dreams; and S. Jean-Alexis on chance: each and all were determined to do their part to illuminate aspects of surrealism's ongoing quest, and thereby to illuminate the actuality of surrealist revolution in Caribbean life.

Tropiques made no secret of its surrealism, and its editors and writers were passionately internationalist. But it is also important to emphasize that its surrealism was decidedly Martinican. Its Martinique-centeredness was in fact one of its most glorious features. In the midst of a world war, with much of Europe overrun by fascism and in utter disarray, here was an inspired group on a tiny island in the Caribbean, bravely upholding life's true priorities: poetry, freedom, and the Marvelous.

Far from being an import, therefore, the surrealism of *Tropiques* was plainly an indigenous cultural eruption. The journal's fourteen issues include a total of seventeen texts by surrealists from other lands: Breton, Pierre Mabille, Jeanne Megnen, and Charles Duits from France; the Romanian Victor Brauner; and the Chilean poet Jorge Cáceres. The great majority of the content, however— well over sixty texts—was authored by the *Tropiques* group: the Césaires, Ménil, Lucie Thésée, Aristide Maugée, Georges Gratiant, and Georgette Anderson. The journal also featured many reprints: several texts by and about the nineteenth-century French abolitionist Victor Schoelcher; excerpts from Lautréamont, Villiers de l'Isle-Adam, Mallarmé, and Lafcadio Hearn; a tale by Lydia Cabrera; and some scholarly essays on Martinican flora, fauna, and folklore. A two-page presentation of surrealist games, a collective project, was a highlight of the fifth issue.

The reciprocal influences of André Breton and Aimé Césaire have been exhaustively debated by critics, and there is no reason to reopen the debate here except to note that, in the heat of argument, the reciprocity has been too often overlooked.[3] It is obvious and beyond argument that Breton's impact on the Césaires was significant and lasting, as they readily and repeatedly acknowledged, but it is also evident that the impact of the Césaires—Aimé's *and* Suzanne's—on Breton was (as *he* acknowledged) at least as great, and in certain respects even greater.

For Breton, and by extension for other European surrealists, his encounter with the Césaires and their friends was a profound educational experience. The author of *The Communicating Vessels* no doubt had learned much from Etienne Léro and others in the Légitime Défense Group about the "Negro Question" (as it was then called in leftist circles) and, more generally, about "life in the colonies." His sojourn in Martinique, however, involved the direct and intense experience of a black community and its repressive colonial context. After disembarking, he was immediately put in a concentration camp, and throughout his stay on the island he was under constant police surveillance. One Vichy official even warned him that Martinique had no need for surrealism!

Thanks to the comradeliness and hospitality of the *Tropiques* Group, with whom he enjoyed many long walks and discussions—supplemented by serious study on his own (he is known to have read, while in Martinique, a two-volume economic history of the island)—André Breton's awareness of black history, politics, and culture expanded immeasurably.

Although it has received almost no attention from critics, one of the many consequences of Breton's 1941 visit to Martinique had an immediate practical effect: in the surrealist spirit of mutual aid, he introduced the Césaires and their friends to the international surrealist network. Prior to Breton's visit, Aimé Césaire had bemoaned the fact that Martinique was completely cut off from the world. *Tropiques* at first had a small, almost entirely local circulation, with little prospect of expansion. Breton changed that. Soon, the poetry of Aimé Césaire, writings by Suzanne Césaire, reproductions of works by Wifredo Lam, and significant notices of *Tropiques* began to appear in surrealist publications in such faraway places as New York, London, Santiago de Chile, Havana, Cairo, and eventually in many other surrealist outposts.

As *Tropiques* became more surrealist, surrealism in effect became more black.

Although the Martinique Group, as such, broke up after 1945, its five years of activity left strong traces on the history of the island, on Francophone litera-ture, and on the history of surrealism. Later generations of creative Martinicans have drawn of course, in various ways, on this rich tradition. Those who, with-out having actually taken an active part in the surrealist movement, nonetheless have shared some of the mood and spirit of *Tropiques,* include Aimé Césaire's brilliant student, Frantz Fanon, poet, critic, and theorist Édouard Glissant, and filmmaker Euzhan Palcy, to whom we owe the admirable documentary *Aimé Cé-saire: A Voice for History.*

HAITI

> The greatest effects are often caused by the smallest causes.
>
> —Lautréamont

The world's first black republic—independent since 1804—has played a con-siderable role in the history of surrealism. Although plagued by a succession of dictators and numerous military coups, including a couple of uninvited and extended U.S. occupations, the second-largest island in the Caribbean has re-tained its just renown as a vibrant, passionate, freedom-loving land, celebrated for its art, poetry, music, and dance.

André Breton regarded Haiti as one of those "privileged places" that are at once "a permanent temptation" and a "resting-place for poetic thought."[4] His 1945 visit there, however, allowed him little time for rest. His modest yet significant role in bringing down the dictatorship was surely a mighty event for all who happened to be on the scene. A French journalist asked him in an interview: "It appears that you played a role in the Haitian revolution. Could you comment on precisely what took place there?" And Breton replied:

> Let us exaggerate nothing. Toward the end of 1945, the poverty—and therefore the patience—of the Haitian people had reached their limit. Bear in mind that, on the large island of Gonova on the Haitian coast, men received less than an American cent for a full day's work. Even the

more conservative newspapers readily acknowledged that children on
the outskirts of Port-au-Prince lived on tadpoles scooped from sewers.

The situation is all the more poignant in view of the fact that the
Haitian spirit, more than any other, miraculously continues to draw its
strength from the French Revolution, and that Haitian history shows us
some of humankind's most moving struggles to abolish slavery and to
attain freedom.

In an initial lecture on "Surrealism and Haiti" I tried—not only for
clarity's sake, but also out of deference to the underlying spirit of the
island's history—to align surrealism's aims with the centuries-old goals
of the Haitian peasantry. In conclusion, I felt obliged to condemn "the
imperialism that the war's end not by any means averted, as well as
the ruthlessly maintained game of cat and mouse between proclaimed
ideals and endless egotisms," and to reaffirm my trust in the motto on
the Haitian flag: "Union Makes Us Strong." The newspaper *La Ruche*
[The hive], the voice of the younger generation, which dedicated the
next day's issue to me, declared my words electrifying, and decided to
adopt an insurrectionary tone. The paper's immediate confiscation and
suspension led to a student strike, followed within forty-eight hours by
a general strike. A few days later, the government was held hostage. [In
the turmoil, dictator Lescot fled the island—Ed.] Unions were being
organized everywhere, and free elections were promised. Even without
yet knowing the final results—for the outcome of the Haitian revolution has been heatedly debated—I would add that I expect real benefit
to come of it, particularly since the learned ethnologist, Dr. Price-
Mars—one of the most respected men, intellectually and morally—has
been elected to a key post in the new government.[5]

In the course of his meetings with René Bélance, René Dépestre, Paul
Laraque, and others, Breton discovered that Haiti's young poets not only were
generally receptive to surrealism, but to a large extent had already received it
and made it their own. Jacqueline Leiner, in her entry on Haiti in the *Dictionnaire
general du surréalisme*, mentions René Philoctete, Francketienne, Anthony Phelps,
Jacqueline Bauge, Jean-Richard Laforest, "and others" in this regard.[6]

None of these poets, however, with the partial and very brief exceptions of
Bélance, Dépestre, and Laraque, ever involved themselves in surrealism as an
organized movement. Few of them, in any case, seemed to agree with any of the
others on important matters, and the island's political chaos exacerbated their
disagreements. Several, for example—notably Dépestre and Laraque—opted
for Stalinism, at least for a time.

Two major developments for surrealism did occur in Haiti during the immediate postwar years. In poetic matters the big news was the surrealists' discovery of Clément Magloire-Saint-Aude, who was promptly hailed by Breton and the Surrealist Group as one of the greatest surrealist poets.[7]

And in painting, the big news was Hector Hyppolite, a self-taught artist immersed in the lore of *vodun*, whose works were prominently featured at the 1947 International Surrealist Exhibition in Paris.[8]

Later Haitian participants in surrealism include the painter and poet Hervé Télémaque, active in the Paris group in the 1960s, and the poet Gérard Janvier, in Chicago.

DOMINICAN REPUBLIC

In the Dominican Republic during the 1940s, the group around the periodical *La Poesía Sorprendida* (Surprising poetry) included several individuals who were strongly oriented toward surrealism. In truth, *La Poesía Sorprendida* was probably as close as one could get to a surrealist publication under a regime such as Trujillo's. Exemplifying the importance of this small but passionate and persistent group, Alberto Baeza Flores, in his authoritative 748-page *La poesía dominicana en el siglo XX*, devotes 217 pages to *La Poesía Sorprendida* and its contributors.[9]

Receptive to diverse currents of poetry, and opposed to all orthodoxy, the group was emphatically international minded and published numerous translations from French, English, German, Catalan, Egyptian, and Chinese. Especially prolific were translations of surrealist poems: from the French of Artaud, Baron, Breton, Crevel, Desnos, Magloire-Saint-Aude, and Mesens; from the English of Toni del Renzio; and from the Turkish of Feyyez Fergar, who for a time was associated with the Surrealist Group in London. *La Poesía Sorprendida* maintained particularly close relations with Jorge Cáceres and the Surrealist Group in Santiago de Chile.

Poets from foreign lands were always welcome. Surrealist painter and writer Eugenio Fernández Granell, a refugee from Francoist Spain, served for four years as one of the periodical's directors and editors. A refugee from Nazi Germany, Erwin Walter Palm, from Frankfort, was well known as the German translator of Federico García Lorca. In 1946 André Breton's visit concluded with a big *La Poesía Sorprendida* celebration at Granell's home.

Multicultural long before the term was coined, *La Poesía Sorprendida* was also resolutely multiracial. Several of its "militants" were of African descent, including Aída Cartagena Portalatín, Manuel Llanes, Manuel Valerio, and J. M. Glass Mejía, who also happen to have been among the group's most zealous champions of surrealism.

This portrait sketch of Clément Magloire-Saint-Aude by Milo Rigaud appears on the cover of Magloire-Saint-Aude's *Veillée*.

Not surprisingly, the group led a precarious existence. While upholders of the oppressive dictatorship suspected the group of harboring "intolerable rebels," Stalinists denounced it as "bourgeois," "an evasion of Dominican reality," and even—shockingly!—"transcendentalist evasion."

Between October 1943 and May 1947, sixteen issues of *La Poesía Sorprendida* were published. André Breton hailed the "noble quality" of this modest publication, which, in exceptionally grim and difficult conditions, defiantly kept the promise of poetry "alive and kicking."

PUERTO RICO

Despite a rich heritage of anarchism, syndicalism, feminism, and other revolutionary currents—and a rich poetic tradition as well—surrealism in Puerto Rico has been sporadic.

The Spanish surrealist painter Eugenio F. Granell, a refugee from Franco's fascism and from Stalinism in Guatemala, settled in Puerto Rico in 1950. Welcomed as professor of art and painting to the faculty of the university in Río Piedras, he met many colleagues in exile, including Juan Ramón Jiménez, and Federico de Onís, Manuel García Pelaya, and collaborated on the magazine *Universidad*. During his eight years on the island, Granell met many young Puerto Rican painters and writers, several of whom shared his deep commitment to surrealism. Together, in mid-decade, they formed a surrealist group called El Mirador Azul (the blue bay window), which organized a large and important exhibition in 1956, as well as several smaller solo shows. The group, however, had only a brief existence. When Granell departed for New York in 1957, organized surrealism in Puerto Rico virtually disintegrated.

The best known of the Mirador Azul surrealists was Luis A. Maisonet, a painter and art teacher whose instructors' manual, *Art for Elementary School*, was for many years the standard work on the subject throughout the island.[10]

In the early 1990s a young Puerto Rican poet, collagist, and photographer, Daniel del Valle Hernández, started a surrealist bulletin, *Lagarto Verde* (Green lizard). Five issues appeared, along with a couple of chapbooks of poems. Interestingly, *Lagarto Verde's* only collaborator was the British writer Louise Cripps, who was then living on the island. Cripps, who had been a close friend and coworker of C.L.R. James' during the 1930s, was the author of more than a dozen books, including a study of James' life and work and several on Puerto Rico and its struggle for independence.[11]

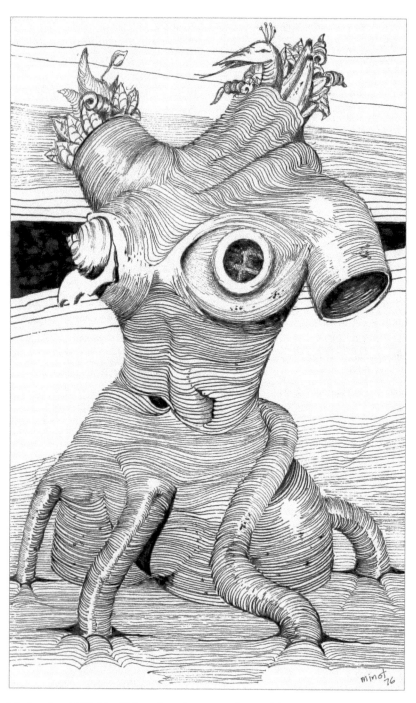

Ink drawing (1970s) by Cuban American artist Jacinto Minot.

This drawing from the surrealist journal *Arsenal* (vol. 4 [1989]) is a good example of Jacinto Minot's humorous style.

TRINIDAD

One of the more deplorable afflictions of large countries, and especially those that consider themselves "superpowers," is their ignorance of, and indifference to, the histories and cultures of "small" countries and islands. Such ignorance and indifference is evident not only among the general population, but also, and more glaringly, among the ruling elite, including the "intelligentsia."

Those whose "knowledge" of Trinidad is limited to exotic tourist propaganda are only cheating themselves, for the island has a fabulous history. Indeed, Trinidad is particularly interesting for its long and valorous political and cultural resistance to oppression. From the 1881 Amboulay Riots—a pitched battle between police and Carnival masqueraders involving entire communities—to the General Strike of 1970, a veritable insurrection against capitalism and the state, the working people of this small island have again and again offered the world object lessons in mass direct action and collective defiance of the status quo. Anyone interested in mass uprisings and other forms of social upheaval would do well to study these historic events.

Doubtless in large part precisely because of this heritage of radicalism and internationalism, Trinidad is also renowned for its rich intellectual tradition: "That Trinidad has produced a disproportionate number of unusual men [and women, we might add—Ed.] is a truism; that so many of them have been forgotten is a scandal." Thus spake J. R. Hooker, biographer of the great Trinidadian Sylvester Williams, "the Father of Pan-Africanism."[12]

The list is indeed impressive, including, among many others, the following:

Maxwell Philip, attorney and novelist, whose *Emmanuel Appadocca, or, Blighted Life: A Tale of the Buccaneers*, was provoked in large part by the passage of the 1851 Fugitive Slave Law in the United States;

Eugene Chen, who served as minister of foreign affairs in Sun-Yat-Sen's government in China;

Novelist Vidia Naipaul;

Ornithologist Antoine Leotaud;

Elma François, a leader of the Negro Welfare Association, and an important figure in the 1937 General Strike and Insurrection;

George Weekes, the island's major independent radical labor leader from the 1960s through the 1980s;

George Padmore, Pan-Africanist and prolific writer;

Marxist theorist and journalist Claudia Jones;

Eric Williams, historian and premier;

Oliver Cromwell Cox, whose *Caste, Class and Race* has long been recognized as a Marxist classic;

Susan Craig, historian, author of *Smiles and Blood: The Ruling Class Response to the Workers' Rebellion in Trinidad and Tobago*;

And on and on, into the night.

Also in this grand tradition are the four Trinidadians represented in this section:

John Jacob Thomas, a nineteenth-century forerunner whose work anticipated the surrealist exploration of folklore and, more generally, popular culture;

C.L.R. James, the great Marxist thinker who prefaced the *Red Spanish Notebook* by Juan Breá and Mary Low, associated with surrealists in the FIARI, and later wrote movingly on the poetry of Aimé Césaire;

John La Rose, poet, bookseller, and activist, who always recognized surrealism as a significant force in radical social and cultural change and was a longtime friend of the Chicago Surrealist Group;

Anthony Joseph, author of two volumes of poetry, *Desafinado* and *Teragaton*, poet, theorist, activist, teacher, a longtime friend of Ted Joans. Joseph—currently active in the Surrealist Group in London—is one of the quickening forces in international surrealism today.

Notes

1. "Interview with Aimé Césaire," by Jacqueline Leiner, introduction to the two-volume Éditions Jean-Michel Place reprint of *Tropiques* (Paris, 1978).

2. For further details on Suzanne Césaire, and a selection of her writings, see Penelope Rosemont, *Surrealist Women*, 126–137.

3. Robin D. G. Kelley, *Freedom Dreams*, 166–170.

4. "Interview with René Bélance" and "Speech to Young Haitian Poets," in Breton, *What Is Surrealism?*, 335–342.

5. Breton, "Interview with Jean Duché, *Entrétiens*, 343–347.

6. Jacqueline Leiner, "Haiti," in Biro and Passeron, *Dictionnaire*, 198.

7. Breton's tribute to Magloire-Saint-Aude is included in his *La clé des champs*, 131–132. See also François Leperlier, "La solution poétique."

8. Breton, "Hector Hyppolite," in *Surrealism and Painting*, 308–312.

9. For the chapters on *La Poesía Sorprendida* and "*suprarealismo*," see 441–748. Breton's praise of *La Poesía Sorprendida* is noted in E. F. Granell, "La aventura surrealista en las Antiles," 95–100.

10. Thanks to Natalia Fernández Segarra for details on Luis Maisonet and surrealism in Puerto Rico in the 1950s.

11. Louise Cripps' work includes *Puerto Rico* and *C.L.R. James*.

12. On Trinidad, we have relied chiefly on conversations with John La Rose in London, 1970; correspondence with Anthony Joseph in the 2000s; and on the following printed sources: the two introductions to the New Beacon reprint of John Jacob Thomas' *Froudacity* (Donald Wood's biographical sketch and C.L.R. James' essay "The West Indian Intellectual"); James Millette's essay, "The Black Revolution in the Caribbean"; and scattered issues of Millette's newspaper, *Moko*.

MARTINIQUE

Aimé Césaire

PANORAMA

This land is suffering from a repressed revolution. Our revolution has been stolen from us.

The worst mistake would be to believe that the West Indies devoid of strong political parties are devoid of powerful will. We know very well what we want.

Liberty, dignity, justice, Christmas torched.

What has the youth been offered during these last fifty years? Positions. Trades. Words. Nothing. Not one idea.

If the great and healthy anger of the people does not (as it did a century ago) stand in its way, we will march straight ahead to the logical conclusion of three centuries of Caribbean history: the triumph of total flunkeyism.

When the essential problems (the weight of facts) discourage the mind's elation, a society is at a pre-revolutionary stage.

The Martiniquan revolution will be made in the name of bread, of course; but also in the name of fresh air and poetry (which comes to the same thing).

I tell you we are choking.

The principle of a healthy Caribbean politics: open the windows. More air. More air.

Thus I condemn any idea of Caribbean independence.

. . . But this is not in order to bark with the dogs.

. . . But this is not so as to cast my pearls before swine. Martiniquan dependency—willed, calculated, reasoned as much as sentimental—will be neither dis-grace nor sub-grace.

I only know one France. That of the Revolution. That of Toussaint L'Ouverture. Too bad for the gothic cathedral.

We want to be able to live passionately.

And in the last resort the resolution will come from the blood of this land. And this blood has its tolerances and its intolerances, its patiences and its impatiences, its resignations and its brutalities, its whims and its forbearances, its stillnesses and its tempests, its calms and its whirlwinds.

And this is what, in the end, will act.

This kind of blood doesn't cast votes.
This kind of blood reinvigorates or strangles.

Tropiques, no. 1 (April 1941); translated by Alex Wilder

INTRODUCTION TO BLACK AMERICAN POETRY

We recognize man by his cry. By the cry that is life's eldest son, or rather life itself embodied without any let-up, without wavering, in the immediacy of the voice in a free and unforeseen movement. Here is the black poet crying out:

We cry among the skyscrapers
As our ancestors
Cried among the African palm trees,
For we are alone
And we are afraid.

It means that the primary feeling of the black poet is a feeling of uneasiness, better yet, of intolerance. Intolerance of the real because it is sordid; of the world because it holds him caged up; of life because he is robbed of it on the highway of the sun:
"I speak in the name of the black millions."
And against the harsh background of anguish, of returning disgrace, of despair long unvoiced, a rage rises and shrieks here, and America, on the bed unhinged by its conformities, is anxious to know of what atrocious hatred this cry is the deliverance:
"I speak in the name of the black millions."
The black waiting room has risen. All that was here of humanity suffering in the slums of Harlem, the cornfields of Maryland, the cotton plantations of the Carolinas. And helter-skelter they file by, men, women, and children, and the stubborn dirt of wretchedness and hunger clings to their ankles. There are those who belong to the chain gang, there are the embittered, the optimists, the resourceful, the fools, those who come from Mississippi, from New Orleans, and from Atlanta; musicians with their syncopated rhythms, barefoot urchins, prostitutes with their rouge-embellished chocolate complexion; epileptic trombone players, jazz musicians who throw their drumsticks at the moon. An entire horde passes, cries, sings, gesticulates, and dies.
Another humility of the black poet is equally precious to us, that of fidelity. How many opportunities to escape! He has been given access to the civilized world with a thousand exits, and these exits are called science, morality, culture. He refuses them all. And he accepts religion itself only when it is demoted from

the rank of subject to the rank of attribute: an attribute of the only subject around which the world henceforth gravitates: mankind.

He makes a hero of the ordinary black man, the everyday black man, about whom an entire literature has set itself the task to unearth the grotesque or the exotic; he depicts him seriously, passionately, and through the miracle of love the limited power of his art succeeds, his art to which more bountiful means have been denied, even one might suggest—the personal strengths that control destiny.

Is it a small thing to create a world? To make a world emerge where the exotic inhumanity of a junk shop was displayed; where we were only drawing forth the vision of grotesque puppets, gathering a new way to suffer, die, become resigned, in a word to bear a certain human load?

Tropiques, no. 2 (1941); translated by Marjolijn de Jager

IN THE GUISE OF A LITERARY MANIFESTO

For André Breton

Let us count:
the madness remembering
the madness howling
the madness seeing,
the madness unleashed

Who and what are we? Admirable question! Haters. Builders. Traitors.
    Hougans. Especially hougans. For we want all the demons
Those of yesterday, those of today
Those of the yoke, those of the hoe
Those of the forbidden, of prohibition, of marronnage

and we mustn't forget those of the slave trader . . .
And so we sing.

We sing of poisonous flowers bursting across furious prairies; skies of love
    slashed with embolism; epileptic mornings; the white blazing of abyssal
    sands, the descent of wreckage in the course of nights struck by wild
    scents.

What can I do about it?

You must begin.

Begin what?

The only thing in the world worth beginning.

The End of the world, my God!

Make room for me. I will not get out of your way.

Sometimes I am seen, in a grand toss of the hat, to snatch an overly red cloud,
    or a caress of rain, or a prelude of wind,

don't sedate yourselves too much:

I force open the yolk sac keeping me from myself.
I force open the great waters which gird me with blood

I, only I check my place on the last train of the last surge of the tidal wave,

I, only I

take up the tongue in the final anguish

I, oh! only I
ensure that I receive from the straw

for you who one morning will hoard my words in your beggar's pouch and
    will take, as the children of fear while they sleep,

the oblique path of flights and monsters.

Tropiques, no. 5 (April 1942); translated by Cynthia Hahn

KEEPING POETRY ALIVE

Protect yourself from the social world by the creation of a zone of incandescence. It is here, inside this zone, wherein flourishes in a terrible security the unprecedented flower of "I"; scrutinize all of material existence in silence and in tall fires frozen with humor; let this be by the creation of a zone of fire; let this be by the creation of a zone of icy silence, conquering by revolt the frank portion where one incites oneself, wholly; such are some of the demands which for nearly a century have aimed to impose themselves upon all poets.

As a result of an implacable evolution, which henceforth we shall call poetry, this strength, ready-made and obvious in nature and in the individual, opposes the just-so-ness of life and of the person. Or again, put more analytically, it is the generalized system of maladjustment which tends to substitute hallucination for sensation, illogic for logic, an image for argument, the arbitrary for the proven, the discontinuity of present moments for the continuity of blind memory.

Here, poetry equals insurrection.
It is Baudelaire.
It is Rimbaud, vagrant and visionary.
It is our great André Breton.

Damned poetry.
This thing is the command.

Damned, because it is knowledge and no longer entertainment. Damned because of the caravan of far-off interiors. Damned because of the lifting of the ban of black seas. Damned in the wake of Prometheus the thief, Oedipus the assassin. Damned in the wake of world discoverers. Damned, because in the ears of the poet is re-attempted the same voice which haunted Columbus: "I will found a new heaven and a new earth so wonderful that one will no longer think of who is to be first."

And we listen faithfully to poetry, keeping it alive; like an ulcer, like a panic, like images of catastrophes, liberty, the fall and deliverance, consuming without end the liver of the world.

Tropiques, no. 8–9 (October 1943); translated by Connie Rosemont

ISIDORE DUCASSE, "COMTE DE LAUTRÉAMONT"

The poetry of Lautréamont, beautiful as a decree of expropriation.

He invented modern mythology.

He discovered the hysterical freezing power of Parody.

He delivered logic from the absurd, and the grotesque from logic.

He is the first to have understood that poetry begins with excess and
    extravagance.

He set poetry back on its feet. "Poetry must have practical truth for its aim."

Humor is a liberating force.

This literary Flamel resolves the delicate problem
    of the transmutation of metals.

He replaces the dictatorship of the object with the dictatorship of the spirit.

By means of the image, we reach the infinite.

Tropiques (February 1943); translated by Laura Corsiglia

Suzanne Césaire

An important surrealist theorist and polemicist, Jeanne Aimée Marie Suzanne Roussy was born in Trois-Islets, Martinique, in 1913. In the 1930s she studied philosophy at the Lycée Henri IV in Paris under the then-famous Émile Chartier, known as Alain, the subject of one of her *Tropiques* articles. Employed in the bookbinding department of a small private press, Harrison of Paris, Roussy was also active in the early Negritude milieu, which included Léon Damas, René Ménil, Yva Léro, and Aimé Césaire, whom she married in 1937.

Back in Martinique in 1941, Suzanne Césaire with her husband and René Ménil constituted the editorial triumvirate of *Tropiques*. One of the most influential West Indian periodicals of all time, *Tropiques* was also a major voice of the international surrealist movement.

POVERTY OF A POETRY

Martinican Bards.
Talent? Of course, for those who are interested in that sort of thing.
But what a pity!
They pass by. They look. But they don't see.
It occurs to them to pity the Negro. But they do not know the Negro soul.
They evoke the bluffs.
But the *marvelous* bluffs?
Their sorcerous, malignant aura?
Their courageous promise? Their dynamite?
Instead of all that, they give us swooning, nuances, style, words, sentiment,
      the color blue, shades of gold, pink.
It's pretty, and nice, and overdone.
Is it literature? Oh yes! Literature of the hammock.
Literature of sugar and vanilla.
Literary tourism. The Blue Guide.
Poetry? Not a bit of it!
Enough! Poetry is elsewhere!
Far from rhymes, complaints, trade-winds, and parakeets.
Martinican literature will be cannibalistic or will not be at all!

Tropiques, no. 4 (January 1942); translated by Alex Wilder

Aimé Césaire, Suzanne Césaire et al.

VOICE OF THE ORACLE: SURREALIST GAME, APRIL 1942

Do you want to hear the great voice of the oracle? The explosive voice of life?

Sit down around a table. Take a sheet of paper and boldly write down what it is you want to know. Fold the paper, pass it to your neighbor who will write an answer without reading your question. And so on.

Open the paper and read. You will hear echoes that come from very far away, farther than yourself; and you will finally have the most beautiful conversation you have ever had with anyone and with yourself.

Take a look.

What

Q: What is night?
A: It is eternally breaking the same heart.

Q: What is hating?
A: Hiding behind one's face, very far away.

Q: What is poetry?
A: It is the bell tolled by the sky's great wind.

Q: What is being in despair?
A: It is getting out of a masterful mess.

Q: What do you desire?
A: It is to hear the romance of romance.

Q: What is death?
A: Traveling across the world with closed eyes.

Q: What is a dream?
A: A great flash of light right in the heart.

Q: What is desire?
A: An exciting catastrophe.

Q: What am I?
A: Scrupulously separating day from night.

Q: What is loving?
A: Being able to sleep peacefully.

Q: What then is thought?
A: Walking dangerously on tiptoe on the line of fire.

Q: What is boredom?
A: It is a dreadful sea monster.

Q: What is speaking?
A: It is to fly off swiftly into the great fog.

Q: What is harmony?
A: It is that which sees the eye.

Q: What is a child?
A: It is movement.

Q: What is life?
A: It is the desire that eats the world.

Etc. Etc.

Tropiques, no. 5 (April 1942); translated by Myrna Rochester

René Ménil

A professor of philosophy in his native Martinique as well as in Paris, René Ménil (1907–2004) was, next to Etienne Léro, the key figure in the Légitime Défense Group; so, too, a decade later he was Suzanne and Aimé Césaire's chief collaborator on *Tropiques*. Noted above all for his essays as theorist and polemicist—much admired by André Breton— Ménil was also a far from negligible poet. In later years, however, his persistent support for an increasingly nonrevolutionary Communist Party separated him not only from his longtime friend Aimé Césaire, but also from the international surrealist movement.

Many of Ménil's critical essays were collected in the 1981 volume *Tracées*.

INTRODUCTION TO THE MARVELOUS

> The marvelous is the image of total freedom.
> —René Ménil

History invariably transforms an era that is ending into a travesty of itself. Each event is turned into the opposite of itself, each act becomes a farce, all the lines are jokes. The spirit of life deserts the living, and the actors are no longer anything but ghosts who hang around an empty stage. And myth, the highest truth of a vital people, can't be distinguished from tidbits in the daily newspapers.

This century, selecting practical reason as its highest virtue, has been unafraid to insist that we adore merchants as heroes, soldiers of fortune as saints, and ordinary commentators on known facts as philosophers. But if we stray too far from the forces of nature in order to domesticate them, we risk missing their reality and in fact missing an aspect of our own destiny.

The truly great historical eras are not the outcome of the results of human understanding. They are gifts that are the result of mankind's reaction to the powerful shocks of life. Peoples and individuals as they merge their lives with history through their passivity to their times no longer hold back their destiny, but instead their passions and their times move together with the secret complicity of the world.

The true task of mankind consists solely in the attempt to bring the marvelous into real life, so that life can become more encompassing. So long as the mythic imagination is not able to overcome each and every boring mediocrity, human life will amount to nothing but useless, dull experiences, just killing time, as they say. Humanity, to be worthy of its name, must not accept such complacency.

Tropiques, no. 3 (October 1941); translated by Rachel Blackwell

THE ORIENTATION OF POETRY

The imagination though an abstraction is *what* becomes real or is in some way realized.

The experience of objective reality would only be hypothetical if it wasn't necessary to resort to illusion just to continue *to be*. It is impossible for human beings to experience reality directly.

When the awful stark power of the real world reveals itself to us (a bolt of lightning, perhaps) we feel the powerlessness and precariousness that is an instinct to all living beings. The touch of fear, the touch of death. We cannot exist in such a hostile environment.

All reality as it is experienced is so distilled that it comes to us transformed, masked or embellished, its very strength is proportional to our capacities for passion and dream.

As we live we elaborate the capacity of the world, the power of our imaginations.

Nothing is more real than the imaginary especially when it is considered only imaginary.

Reality and the imagination are not opposites the way that *being* and *nothingness* are, but rather the way *being* and what *will be* are.

Of our dreams we ask questions, to their answers we listen, and we act in the light of their advice.

On this motionless voyage, that we call dreamlike, we are the movers at the center of the world but it is life itself that will feel the footprints of our imagination.

A strange luminescence is emitted by the poetic image that is difficult to resist. So long as it continues, the mind's activity delights in disrupting the everyday sense that is simply utilitarian.

We are released from the domination of objects and able to create true goals for life; the pursuit of this truth is no longer to be laughed at.

That moment is the moment of the mind's liberation.

Tropiques (July 1941); translated by Juliet Pétremont

WHAT DOES AFRICA MEAN TO US?

We are at the crossing. The crossing of races and cultures.

It is obvious that all our conscious reactions are determined by European culture, arts, sciences, technical methods. And we have indeed decided to make use of these precision armaments with their latest improvements. But in our veins flows a blood that demands from us an original stance in the face of life. Under penalty of failure (let the word be understood in a non-commercial sense), we must respond to the poet, more than to any other, regarding the special dynamics of our complex biological reality. Moving back across one of our lines of force, we encounter this immensity—Africa. Africa with its unique poetic gifts, its unique artistic and above all sculptural production. Africa and its noble abandonment to life, contemptuous of learned industrial robbery.

An essential work, of the great European ethnographer Leo Frobenius, will permit the reader, if he is not lazy, to understand the unprecedented cultural richness that will result for us from the comprehension of African reality. Is it not our task to attain our total humanity? We believe that we can attain it—

imbeciles and cowards should expect no concession on this from us—only through the expression, made possible thanks to valuable European techniques, of all that is asked of us concerning our Negritude.

Tropiques, no. 5 (April 1942); translated by Melom Peacock

POETRY, JAZZ & FREEDOM

It is the existence in itself of jazz, of major importance to us, that has more than any critical thinking caused us to understand the stylistic character and content of a work in its historic context and even its limitations and to grant the value of spontaneity to these works only.

In its essence jazz is improvisation. If one created a theory of esthetics using jazz as a basis, it would mean creating it using as a means the invention of the marvelous as one went along. Because jazz itself is the result of a process using the very contradictions of being and its style consists of forming by means of music or any other means (note this also applies to poetry)—emotions and images in progression, as they occur in the mind's eye. Any blockage, any laziness, any rigidification of life threatens the true development of this delicate crystallization.

No rhythm is set before beginning.

No meaning is conceived before hand.

No rhythm, no meaning except a passion for being—a being dedicated to a desire that demands its realization–or its substitution in the sublimation of "song."

The musician doesn't know, cannot know, what his next note will be, nor will he know his next phrase, or the next possible adventure.

But he leaps like a rope-dancer on the tight-rope of chance.

A work of beauty is a work of chance.

However, how many agree with Goethe when he says that the only works of lasting value are works of chance?

At this point our existence is drugged by the poison of eternity. Jazz is one of the best antidotes to that poison, creating in us the feeling of the moment, of transition.

For us, we do not hesitate to view the moment, whatever it is called, as the arena where all the problems that are common to humankind must be resolved from the world of music or any other. In the moment is found all the previous instants to a particular action in the process of becoming—since, in any thing that exists "that which has been superceded [*sic*] is at the same time also preserved, and in losing its immediate and apparent existence, is not destroyed." (Hegel)

The moment of being exists in the present, however, the present itself exists in a particular existence that is the outcome of its extension through duration in time.

Thus, for things that exist, there is no contradiction that cannot be reconciled between the past and the present except the one that exists in the minds of those who attempt to abstract its essence. Likewise in society there is no contradiction between the creations that are contemporary and those that are past, between new works (not yet accepted) and the existing culture; the new creation although it may not be "valued" or regarded presently as valuable—combines all the resources of that particular social group that is being considered.

A poet is not contemporary because he is familiar with the past or has rejected it, but because he exists as a dialectical outcome of those stages of past existence. Thus at the same time, he is a living negation and a living preservation of all the old cultural forms. His contemporary aspect will be broader and of greater value because of the fact that it is a totality formed of the past.

Cultural traditions that are reflected by the poet cannot serve as a model, there is no model for what has not yet come into existence. It will exist, however, as a pillar of the past and thus situates the poet in his time inflexibly; it makes him a poet who is modern in a time that is modern.

So much for the freedom of poetry: before us the future, yet unformed.

Tropiques, no. 11 (1944); translated by Juliet Pétremont

Lucie Thésée

Thésée was an important participant in the *Tropiques* Group from the spring of 1942 on, but historians and memoirists of the period have, strangely, ignored her. It has been impossible to locate even basic biographical information about her. This neglect is all the more curious in that Léon Damas, in his *Poètes d'expression française* (1947), highlights Thésée's critical importance in *Tropiques* (no. 10) and more particularly hailed the abundance and excellence of her poetic imagery.

PREFERENCE

An obsessive sound of steps behind the screen, an obsessive sound of steps inside the screen: the viewers shiver in the half light. An obsessive sound of steps before the screen, the obsessive steps descend into the entrails of the mute crowd, pressing in on the old wide-lathed barricade displayed by the barely lit screen . . . The obscure ambience chirps with inaudible, tufted sounds while the obsessive step materializes further: two long legs covered in grey wool crossed the full width of the screen, and probably walked all around the barricade for they wandered over, among the crowd, the shadow, hardening space, is far too opaque to let them be counted . . .

The two legs stop into two wide sawteeth, halfway up to the thigh. Upright in the valley, they spell out a name _____. She rises, stretches, and goes out quietly. She's a young dark-haired woman whose aerial gait heralds beauty.

Outside, the chilly breeze smells of dried sap, the bright moon climbs, climbs as far as the eye can see.

The dark-haired woman pregnant with the name revealed at the show stops at the seashore: the sea glistens like a painting, garfish leaping here and there . . .

". . . later, you know, he touched my throat for a moment with his hand, his open hand."

"All right. This morning in the foliage a joyful face smiled, with flashing teeth and prodigiously sparkling eyes."

The dark-haired woman continues calmly, "However, I would have preferred him to give me my blood."

"Didn't the milk dry up?" the other woman answers languidly.

Our December's breeze has incrusted the green leaf cut and broiled by the sun within their sensitized beings.

Still facing the sea, they inch forward toward a gate, leaving behind the bulky white building on their left.

Dull sounding male voices burst forth, . . . the gate suddenly opens. The woman from the show goes through the door, stretching her long neck: "It's not that I'm curious, I could have already gone to look."

"It's two players, they're still attached, they've already played a great deal tonight and their shirts are still totally white," says the other woman.

Suddenly the screen's step, the obsessive step plunged into its tongue, appears, first at a distance and from the side, way beyond the players . . . He draws near and the dark-haired woman points him out. The two legs become whole: "It is he . . . he's become terribly elongated," she avidly extends her index finger towards his head, "just look how purple his face is!" she observes.

Angrily he rushes toward her, the long barrel of a strange weapon on the dark-haired woman's index finger.

"You robbed me!" he says. Shaking her head no over and over, she answers, "No, I didn't steal." . . . and then continues, "Why are you aiming exactly at the tip of my index finger?"

He pursues this thought with a ferocious muttering, "So that the bullet will slip into your heart.". . . "I want it completely broiled, woman of my blood." Her only reply to him, a brilliant smile.

The other woman remains at the shore, her glance stubbornly turned toward the sea, sadly objects, "but . . . the whole house was dusted this morning."

Tropiques, no. 10 (February 1944); translated by Myrna Bell Rochester

Georges Gratiant

Born into a mulatto family in Martinique, Gratiant (1907–1992) attended the Lycée Schoelcher, received a bachelor's degree, and then went to Paris to study law. Returning to Martinique, he opened a law office in Fort-de-France. A militant communist, in the early 1930s he founded the short-lived Common Front group with René Ménil and Thélus Léro (Etienne's brother). In the years 1941–1943, he helped the Césaires and Ménil edit *Tropiques* and contributed several texts of his own.

As it turned out, his active involvement in cultural matters did not last long. After the Liberation (1946), he was elected the first president of the General Council of the new Department of Martinique, a term lasting one year. Later, for thirty years (1959–1989), he was mayor of Lamentin, the island's "second city."

EXTINCT VOLCANO

Flamboyant's vomits
Carrousel of the red border at the Great Copper Palace
The cassia fleuzals of reddish-brown honey give rise to the long black
    silhouettes of opiated molasses
White laurels facing the sea
Mottled hooves of glowing din
hooves of fire and of blood

shreds of fire that descend
into the ruined flanks full of blood that descends
and that flows and that rolls
ball of fire
black sparkling hoof
ball of fire and of black clotted blood
And the cassias crumbling with golden honey run along the long burned flesh

From the marine cup abruptly overturned from the din of thunder
here it is recreated
Son of molasses brown flesh father of this molasses with the grains of gold
    dust
gilded grains whose eyes shine
from this molasses that grabs your throat
thirst for milk gorged with alcohol
from this molasses that grabs your gut
Gastralgic nights to dreams of silvered belladonna
And from the blisters on fire runs your living flesh
And from your exacerbated plant grinds the young turf of varied locusts.
Youth gilded with gilded edges
of smoke and of ashes
Youth of blue wreaths of extinct trails
of dead ashes
Mortals and crucibles under your ebony heel
where to the four winds the indolent white latex throws
terrifying exudation to the October sun
flamboyant tempest of the eruptive snows
crimson Euphorbia crackle with anger
And everywhere
and always
in the blood in the turf
the heavy noise of the heel full of mud full of turf
the deaf noise of heels in the turf that ends.

Tropiques, no. 8-9 (October 1943); translated by Gay Rawson

Aristide Maugée

A collaborator on *L'Étudiant Noir* in mid-1930s Paris, Maugée went on to assist the Césaires in the publication of *Tropiques* in 1940s Martinique. Albeit few in number, his contributions to the journal reveal a lively critical intelligence. The text reprinted here is surely one of the earliest appreciations of Césaire's great work. Regrettably, little is known about Maugée beyond the fact that he married Césaire's sister, Mireille, an English teacher.

AIMÉ CÉSAIRE, POET

The poet is really stealing fire if what he brings from there has shape, he gives shape, if it is shapeless, he gives shapelessness.
—Rimbaud

*   *   *

A poet is born to us. After a century of conformity and poetic nothingness. So much for those who could not perceive the change as we passed from countless rhapsodies to authentic poetry.

Modern poetry, starting with Rimbaud, locates the secret of creation in the dream. Triumph of the Marvelous: the poet is seer, the poet is prophet.

Aimé Césaire is the heir to such poetry. An irresistible burst of inspiration, anxious to express feeling in its infinite complexity, to measure the Unfathomable, and impatient to seize the Absolute.

For him, the word is both object and sign. In other words, the poet cares less about communicating his ideas than about creating an atmosphere. An environment, an unreal setting in which, strangely but certainly, we can feel the poignant drama of Man alone; terrifyingly alone, standing up against the world and the prohibitions of his Destiny.

Poet of the highest, most dizzying metaphysics. But also a Negro poet. A Negro poet, though not in the manner of a Toomer or Hughes or Johnson, whose lyrical qualities are simpler and more direct. Here Césaire reveals another depth, a different formal richness, the expression of an effortlessly flaming art.

Not that he chooses the image for image's sake, or music for music's sake. His work is decanted in the crucible of the unconscious. Rather, it is a prodigious force of enchantment, the magic of sound, which compels the poet and embodies his soul.

More variety too, in the rhythm.

Rhythm—a Negro element *par excellence*!

Rhythm of the tom-tom, in the enchantment of the forest, magic incantations to the God of Death.

An orchestra where bright sounds alternate with flat sounds, like trumpets and cymbals, and the melody is kept up by the airy sweetness of liquids.

Césaire is a Negro poet also in terms of feeling: Love of his race. Love without treason or weakness, doubtless and limitless

Racist? Not in the least.

Neither bitterness, nor contempt of other races. Nor blindness: vices, defects, he sees it all. He knows his race to be "riddled with stains," "which no ablution of hyssop and lilies combined could purify."

He surveys the whole spectrum of mean, cowardly and perfidious acts. And yet, what pride! Sublime hope. Confidence in the future: such is the meaning of this prophetic song. Now is the time to turn the soil in order to fertilize it. Now is the time for sowing. Do you hear this invitation?

*   *   *

One man has stood up to say *no*.

Yes, there is one poet able to discover a true humanity, on our beautiful island of torment.

Poetry of vertigo and love, of blood and courage.

Aimé Césaire is at the point of a new dawn.

Tropiques, no. 5 (April 1942); translated by Jeanne Hageman

REVIEW OF REVIEWS

"No city. No art. No Poetry. Not a germ, or even a sprout. Or else the hideous leprosy of counterfeits. In truth, a land sterile and mute."

Thus *Tropiques* saw the West Indies in 1941. No longer is it a question of "folding arms, in the sterile attitude of a spectator," but rather of modifying our destiny. Our mission? To participate—yes, we too—in the concert of the world.

We do not want to be the Saprophytes of culture.

The welcome *Tropiques* has received has not surprised us. Not believing in immediate conversions, we expect nothing from docile shadows.

In the meantime, our voice has not remained without echo. Seeing hope reborn in the youth brings forward the promise of new beginnings.

And seeing that *Tropiques* has received from strangers an even larger audience than it has in the islands.

And seeing that great and friendly voices from afar have assured us of their affection and their sympathy, beyond the Caribbean Sea: in Cuba, Curaçao, Mexico, New York.

*   *   *

Mexico: Benjamin Péret is preparing an anthology of myths, legends, and popular tales from the Americas, a project deserving of the greatest interest. It is myth that explains humankind. And legend is the mysterious thread that leads us, by means of the imagination and fantasy, to the very heart of the Marvelous.

Cuba: From Cuba we are informed of the imminent publication of Aimé Césaire's poem, *Notebook of a Return to My Native Land,* translated into Spanish by Lydia Cabrera, illustrated by Wifredo Lam, and preceded by a preface by Benjamin Péret.

New York: Last October, the New York exhibition of *gouaches* by Wifredo Lam had the great success that it deserved.

New York: A magnificent realization: the new journal directed by André Breton. And Breton's capital article: "Prolegomena to a Third Manifesto of Surrealism or Not." A doubly important article because of the author, and because of the new horizons now opening for surrealism.

After the present cataclysm, the value of traditional knowledge must be reexamined in the light of a new day.

Tropiques, no. 6-7 (February 1943); translated by Franklin Rosemont

Georgette Anderson

Many of the contributors to *Tropiques*—like the Césaires and René Ménil—were teachers by profession, and this was probably also true of Georgette Anderson. In the vast literature on Negritude and Aimé Césaire, Anderson is rarely more than mentioned. Her study of Mallarmé and Debussy appeared in the debut issue of *Tropiques* (April 1941), and the text published here in the third issue.

SYMBOLISM, MAETERLINCK & THE MARVELOUS

We will not hide here the weaknesses of symbolism, its puerility, its tics, its taste for refined sentences but also, what witnesses for its defense! And if, from among these, one should retain only the *marvelous*, the position of Mallarmé, and his group, it would still remain one of the key literary movements.

Let us pass over the great masters and let us stop at Maeterlinck. And more precisely at *Pelléas and Mélisande.*

Finally, the *orchestration*. Is it a question here of introducing destiny's precursors? Debussy conveys the theme with a whole subtle mixture of superimposed melodic fragments, underpinned by a cello pattern, which give a sad color to the simple air heard previously.

But then how is it that we resist Maeterlinck?

Because it's true that we resist him.

The reason, the main reason, can be found in the author of Pelléas' pessimism.

How can one be pessimistic when the revenge of the *marvelous* on the world remains?

But then Maeterlinck is a pessimist.

We remember the words of Pelléas:

"I played like a child with a thing I did not suspect. . . . I played in my dreams with destiny's traps."

Traps. Why traps? Fate, adventure, and dreams which set traps for you on the road of life?

Let us reread Giraudoux's *Intermezzo:*

"That which we call human knowledge is at best human religion, and it is a terrible selfishness.

Its dogma is to make every relationship with anyone else but humans impossible or sterile, to unlearn all the languages a child already knows, except for human language. With this false modesty . . . what marvelous overtures from all stages of the world, from all its kingdoms have we not rejected?"

All the languages. Those that the child inevitably knows. All the roads. All the entrances.

But woe to the one who, before giving it a try, does not get rid of his heavy mind. Maeterlinck is one of them.

Tropiques, no. 3 (October 1941); translated by Marjolijn de Jager

Stéphane Jean-Alexis

Tropiques, no. 8–9 (October 1943), features an interesting article by Sté-
phane Jean-Alexis on chance, concluding with André Breton's definition
of "objective chance." The question arises: Who is (was) S. Jean-Alexis,
who made no other contributions to *Tropiques* and does not figure in
scholarly studies or memoirs of Negritude? Was the name perhaps an
early nom de plume for Jacques Stephen Alexis, who in 1945 was editor
of the Haitian paper *La Ruche* (The roach) when the students in Port-
au-Prince — and *La Ruche* itself — welcomed Breton to Haiti? In view of
the fact that Jacques Stephen Alexis was later a well-known Communist
politician and novelist — indeed, a hard-line Stalinist — he would seem
an unlikely suspect as author of a text sympathetic to the fiercely anti-
Stalinist Breton. In the present state of our knowledge, the identity of
"S. Jean-Alexis" remains unknown.

A NOTE ON CHANCE

While the world seen through causality or through finality appears to us to be
a lucid system, the world seen through luck appears as an inextricable chaos
where events are produced according to their whims, and before these the only
attitudes possible are waiting, self-abandonment to the forces about which it is
impossible to have more than a vague intuition, and of which it is not possible
to modify the outcome.

We must, however, note that a coincidence cannot take on the value of a
stroke of luck if it is not endowed, at least in our eyes, with a certain importance, or else if it cannot be considered the possible end of a series of final
causes.

Thus, eventually one finds included in the notion of chance, this idea that
what appears in the form of a mechanical necessity, is, in reality, the manifestation of an intelligent will, a will that would overturn happiness, bad luck or the
surprising in circumstances that we find troubling. Doesn't one see the athlete,
just after winning, prepared to thank his luck? That is his good luck, as if it was
a question of an intelligent power that had intentionally favored him.

Which explains the halo of wonder that encircles manifestations of luck. To
say that something happens by luck is to lend it attributes that only belong to
mankind or to regret not finding these attributes. It unconsciously affirms this
idea that "all that is within us, is as all that is outside of us and constitute a single
reality."

In reality, the determining factor is not in things, it is in us that it lives—in us the anxieties, in us the desires, in us the aspirations. It is here that the Kantian term *end in itself* has all of its value.

For all these reasons, we believe that the most acceptable definition of chance is the one that André Breton proposes in *L'Amour Fou*—the meeting of an internal necessity and an external end, or "the manifested form of an exterior necessity that clears a path in the unconscious."

Translated by Wingo Smith (original emphasis)

CUBA

Wifredo Lam

Universally recognized as one of the greatest surrealist painters, Lam (1902–1982) was born in Sagua la Grande, Cuba, of an Afro-Cuban mother and Chinese father. In 1924, after studying painting at the School of Fine Arts in Havana, he left for Madrid, where he immersed himself in the spirit of Spanish baroque and studied "primitive" art. In Spain, too, he came in contact for the first time with surrealists, most notably Eugenio F. Granell, who, like Lam, was a combatant in the revolutionary war against Francoist fascism.

With the defeat of the Revolution, Lam went to Paris, where he met Picasso, an ardent admirer of Lam's work, and soon also met André Breton and others in the Surrealist Group. Faced with the threat of the Nazi occupation of Paris, Lam joined the surrealists in Marseilles, helped invent the Marseilles Game (a surrealist card game), illustrated Breton's long poem *Fata Morgana*, and took part in other surrealist activities. Lam joined Elisa and André Breton (as well as anthropologist Claude Lévi-Strauss) on a ship for Martinique, where they met Suzanne and Aimé Césaire and others of the *Tropiques* Group. Lam soon went on to Cuba. One of his closest friends in Havana was Juan Breá's widow, Mary Low; in 1946 he illustrated her volume of poems, *Alquimia del recuerdo*. In 1945 he visited Haiti and studied the rituals and symbols of *vaudou*. Lam left Cuba in 1952 and spent the next several years in New York, Paris, and Albisola Mare, Italy, where he established a studio.

Cover drawing by Wifredo Lam for the French surrealist journal *Médium* (New Series, January 1955).

Lam's work was featured in every international surrealist exhibition from the 1942 New York show through the 1976 show in Chicago and was reproduced in numerous surrealist journals, including *Minotaure, London Bulletin, VVV, Médium, Le Surréalisme, même, BIEF, La Brèche, Brumes Blondes, L'Archibras, A Phala, Analogon, Dies und Das,* and *Arsenal/Surrealist Subversion.*

PICASSO

Everybody felt this influence, for Picasso was the master of our times. Even Picasso was influenced by Picasso! But when I first painted bulls in Spain, I had not seen his bulls. And I had done my own paintings in a synthetic style, in an attempt to simplify my forms, before discovering his. Our plastic interpretations simply coincided. I already knew the Spanish temperament, for I had lived it, suffered it, in the country itself. Rather than an influence, we might call it a *pervasion of the spirit.* There was no question of imitation, but Picasso may easily have been present in my spirit, for nothing in him was alien or strange to me. On the other hand, I derived all my confidence in what I was doing from his approval.

*   *   *

I decided that my painting would never be the equivalent of that pseudo-Cuban music for nightclubs. I refused to paint cha-cha-cha. I wanted with all my heart to paint the drama of my country, but by thoroughly expressing the negro spirit, the beauty of the plastic art of the blacks. In this way I could act as a Trojan horse that would spew forth hallucinating figures with the power to surprise, to disturb the dreams of the exploiters. I knew I was running the risk of not being understood either by the man in the street or by the others. But a true picture has the power to set the imagination to work, even if it takes time.

Max-Pol Fouchet, *Wifredo Lam*

ARROWS IN RAPID FLIGHT

Arrows in rapid flight that leave behind them the perfume of their primitive essence: Oya (goddess of dreams who dictates our destiny and watches over us in death), and that other god with hair of water, Ogue-Oriza (herb of the gods). These beliefs, similar to the fires burning in our curiosity, keep alive the idea of animated stone, Elegua in the languages of our black brotherhoods. Like wounded birds they spread across my canvases the myth forged by primitive man.

Mind, Body and Soul, by Patrick Turner, collagist. This early work was printed in the surrealist journal *Arsenal* (vol. 4 [1989]).

* * *

What's so curious is that these dramas so close to us seem like distant appari-
tions—. Knives—become in turn vigilant, disquieting, ready to open mortal
wounds. Wings of evasion, omens of birds in flight skimming the surface of our
eyes in contemplation of their fleeing, their exodus, like tongues of fire in an
anxious infinity—. Elsewhere the sound of tom-toms, in obsessive rhythm, is
materialized by light and shadow: sexes as tender or cruel as flashes of lightning, in the shape of flame, detaching their luminous appearances from the
impenetrable darkness of night in the background.

Dies und Das

Agustín Cárdenas

Widely regarded as surrealism's greatest sculptor, Cárdenas (1927–2001)
was born in Matanzas, Cuba, the son of a tailor. In 1943 he enrolled in
the San Alejandro Academy of Fine Arts and pursued his studies there
until 1949.

In 1955 he moved to Paris, settled in Montparnasse, and met André
Breton and the Surrealist Group. The following year he participated in a
Surrealist Group show, "L'Étoile Scellée" (the sealed star), at the gallery
and was later well represented in international surrealist exhibitions in
Paris (1959) and New York (1961). His work has also been featured in
dozens of solo shows and over a hundred collective exhibitions. Based
in France for years (his five sons were all born there), he also worked in
Canada, Austria, Japan, and especially Italy, where he enjoyed sculpting
in marble. After 1994 he lived mostly in Cuba.

The best literature on his sculpture was written by his surrealist
friends, including André Breton, Édouard Glissant, and José Pierre.

Well-educated and articulate, Cárdenas nonetheless appears to have
done very little if any writing. Bibliographies of the extensive literature
on his work are silent on the subject. In lieu of an article by him, or an
interview, he is represented here by a short list of some of the titles he
gave his sculptures: strong images, a true found poem.

ONE, TWO, THREE

One, two, three
The big Bird
Life and Earth
Never-ending Alliance
Column of Fire
The Music Box
Woman with Chewing-Gum
Orpheus at Rest
The Window
The Doorway
Family Jewels
Dogon
The Tortoise
Fire-Eater
My Shadow after Midnight
Indian Flower
Unknown Girl
Antillean Root
Fruit of Memory
Dialogue
Toward the Light
History Is Not Finished

Translated by Mary Low

Jacques Roumain

In his December 1945 "Speech to Young Haitian Poets"—an audience
that included René Bélance, René Depestre, Paul Laraque, and Clément Magloire-Saint-Aude, among many others—André Breton quoted
a beautiful passage from Jacques Roumain's (1907–1944) revolutionary
novel *Masters of the Dew* and concluded by saying: "I salute you, gentlemen, in the example of Jacques Roumain that stands for Haiti and the
world." These words are especially moving in view of Breton's general
dislike of novels, but of course *Masters of the Dew* was no ordinary novel,

and Roumain no ordinary novelist. On other occasions Breton also affirmed his admiration for Roumain's poetry and ethnological studies.

Poet, journalist, revolutionary, short-story writer, ethnologist, and professor, Roumain was one of the most remarkable men of the last century. Sent by his family to Switzerland for schooling, he pursued his education for the next six years in France, Germany, and Spain. Returning to Haiti, he joined the resistance movement against U.S. occupation, and was soon elected president of Haiti's Patriotic Youth League, the group that eventually forced the withdrawal of the hated troops.

In the 1920s and 1930s, he collaborated on *La Revue Indigène*, a forerunner of Negritude and noted also as the journal that introduced modern poetry into Haiti.

He died in Mexico; *Masters of the Dew* was published posthumously. An English translation of *Gouverneurs de la rosèe* by Langston Hughes and Mercer Cook was published in New York in 1947.

The poem reprinted here dates from the 1920s.

WHEN THE TOM-TOM BEATS

Your heart trembles in the shadows, like the reflection
   of a face in troubled water
The old mirage rises from the hollow of the night
You know the sweet sorcery of memory
A river carries you far from the banks,
Do you hear those voices: they're singing love's heartache
And in the mournful darkness, hear the tom-tom panting
   like a young black girl's breasts.

Your soul is the reflection in the murmuring water where your ancestors
   bent their dark faces
And the white man who made you a mulatto is this bit of sea spume cast out,
   like spit, upon the shore.

HAITI

Clément Magloire-Saint-Aude

Long regarded by surrealists as one of the movement's greatest poets,
the work of the Haitian Clément Magloire-Saint-Aude (1912–1971) is
still not well known to the larger public. Born Clément Magloire, he
adopted the name Magloire-Saint-Aude around 1940. A contributor to
the journal *Les Griots* in the 1930s, his 1941 pamphlet of poems, *Dialogue
des mes lampes*, confirmed his definitive adherence to surrealism. Asked
in a letter for his curriculum vitae, he replied, with characteristic simplicity: "Born in Port-au-Prince in 1912. No university title. No voyages.
Anticonformist. Have turned my back on society, and live — retired — in
the southern outskirts of Port-au-Prince. Have collaborated on all the
newspapers in the capital."

Although his involvement in the surrealist movement was above all
via poetry and correspondence, personal association also played a role.
In June 1944 he met Aimé Césaire, who was in Haiti for a conference,
and in December of that year and early 1945 he enjoyed several meetings with André Breton, Pierre Mabille, and Wifredo Lam.

Breton and his friends consistently proclaimed Magloire-Saint-
Aude's poetry to be one of the essential works of the twentieth century.
Here, as Breton put it, "language and the poetic attitude are constantly
brought to their supreme point."

UTTERANCES

of my lamp and my emotion
provoked along the way
and of my truth
on the surface of the cloak of mourning
and the ponderous dignified rings
of the horseman with the bell
ringing from his elbow
artful, the pastel
of sun and soot on my wall.

Paroles, translated by Franklin Rosemont

TALISMANS

To Vincent Bounoure and to Jorge Camacho

Surging hours
in a fiery façade
Sparks echo
toward the mirror of time
Little bells child's rattles
a wild mop of hair
sound a halt
to the messenger's song

Taboo, in *Dialogue de mes lampes et autres textes*, translated by Franklin Rosemont

NOT THE LEGEND

This is not the legend
Which rouses me from sluggishness
At the Chinese man's tomb

In the bard's tent
Sleeps the gold of my lamp

Weighing upon me, in this world, my grimoire
And also my old lashes

If, in a loose tone,
Longer than my shadow,
In the magician's mirrors
I confuse uproar and silence,
I am here for five
And the lure of humus
Has no hold on me

Taboo, in *Dialogue de mes lampes et autres textes*, translated by Franklin Rosemont

THREE POEMS

I

For my burned-out lights.

Safe passage, pilgrim.

II

To the weary poet's exploits,
My stained-glass window, shattered
On the melody's rails.

For my beautiful girl, ruined
Like the street urchin's harmonica.

Toward the cracked web
Of broken stanzas.

On the blind blotter
Of my extinct talents.

V

Prisoner's poem
To the tolling of remembered suns.

Rattles buried
In the pilgrim's heart.

Déchu (1956); translated by Franklin Rosemont

THE SURREALIST RECORD

To accept the easily palatable is the fate of the mob. For most people, *to be* is merely a matter of rumination. For the poet, however, to exist is to marvel. The poet is the one who pursues the strange and unfamiliar. Unwilling to surrender to mob formulas, or to seek the logic of mundane rhythmical phrases, the poet plunges into the darkest, most hidden corners of the Unconscious. The world of the Marvelous is the very source of the creations that in turn engender the unfettered images of wonder and the impossible.

Symbolists and surrealists celebrate the dream and the unconscious. Mallarmé was a "master of the dream." Saint-Pol-Roux declared: "We are the pioneers of the Beyond," and E.L.T. Mesens said: "Even when asleep we are tireless."

A counteraction to Parnassus and naturalism, Symbolism freed the possibilities of internal reality ("There was no way," wrote Jean Cassou, "to stop the spirit that had already started moving toward the dream and temptation in its construction of splendorous worlds").

"In essence," according to Pierre Montal, "surrealism is a poetry liberated from critical sense. It is a quest for freedom."

Déchu, an early book of poems by Clément Magloire-Saint-Aude, with cover illustrated by Milo Rigaud, an artist noted for his study of voodoo, was printed and published in Haiti.

Surrealism has never found any sympathy among superficial minds. It attracts rebels, Baudelaireans, those who have not been coerced into behaving themselves.

The stylistic exaggerations indulged in by surrealism's parasites do not in any way invalidate the radiance of a poetical/political current whose masters are venerated by disciples of every race.

Haiti-Journal (April 25, 1941); translated by Franklin Rosemont

ON POETRY: A 1970 INTERVIEW

Q: What made you choose surrealism?
A: Instinct.

Q: To whom did you show your first surrealist poems?
A: In the journal *Les Griots*, I published a poem in prose titled *Dialogue of My Lamps*. The same title was taken up again for my first collection of poems. Perhaps unconsciously there are some hesitations and pale reflections of the prose-poem in the collection. I have therefore published it without a specifically surrealist intention.

Q: How did the public react to this hermetic tablet?
A: At first, there was a general outcry of indignation. People were not familiar with this genre of poetry, which was a veritable revolution. *Dialogue of My Lamps* attracted partisans, adversaries, commentators. . . . They were intent on finding a meaning in the poems.

Q: How do you see the future of surrealism?
A: Jean Schuster, in the first issue of *L'Archibras: Le Surréalisme*, April 1967, has stated our position on this question.

Translated by Franklin Rosemont

René Bélance

Bélance (1915–2004) as a young man was among the group of rebel poets who welcomed André Breton to Port-au-Prince in 1945, thereby precipitating a student upheaval which in turn led to the collapse of the brutal Lescot regime. The young poet's interview with Breton appeared in the *Haiti-Journal* (December 12–13) and was reprinted in Breton's *Entrétiens.*

Bélance's volume of poems, *Épaule d'ombre*—published around the same time—was promoted in the press as a surrealist work, in part because of the author's association with Breton, but above all because of its own remarkable poetic quality. Indeed, it was for his stature as a poet that Bélance was acclaimed as the doyen of Haitian literature. Later, however, for political reasons, he had to leave Haiti. In the United States, where he found refuge, he made his living as a professor of literature.

AWARENESS

Hopelessly, I left perception behind
under a bay of rooftops
Crimson dawn no longer spreads a path
to welcome our weary footsteps
our silver voices
I hold a memory of mists, past times
torches lit our way
I drink deeply of the sands of oblivion

Chemins critiques (1989); translated by Rachel Blackwell

NOISE

What's right, what's wrong, I don't know
they're just wavering mysteries
I swell with the ocean swell, open to desire
all day long I disdain the ordinary
I despise the church's threats and punishments
because I want beautiful Sundays
and celebrations instead of smoothed-over fears.

Chemins critiques (1989); translated by Rachel Blackwell

ENCOUNTER WITH LIFE

I started to be labeled a surrealist after the publication of *Luminaires* in 1942. At that time I didn't know anything about surrealism. In school, I had read

Rimbaud, Verlaine, and a few modern poets. I think it was with Rimbaud that I started orienting my style without knowing it toward what they call surrealism. In other words, I started writing a kind of poetry which was not romantic or purely symbolic. I started entering into myself and expressing the inner world I could contemplate. That inner world was directly linked to my personal experience, to my encounter with life, and with other people and with myself. I wrote about what I felt and how I reacted.

The poet for me is a man of the world. He/She is a witness, someone who partakes in the human experience and has a vision he/she tries to communicate to the world. The poet is comparable to Moses leading a whole tribe to the promised land. He/She is someone who is going to try at some point to find a way of abandoning the corpse he/she is imprisoned in, so as to go farther, so as to go higher, in order to see more than the others could see and to reveal the voice he heard indicating the way to paradise for the other men to hear.

Aimé Césaire puts it better when he says: "Make me the voice of those who have no voice." That's what the poet is for me: he who speaks for those who can't speak; he who expresses the dream that the others fail to express; he who encourages people to go beyond themselves in order to bring some kind of relief to human suffering; he who lives in his flesh all human sufferings and is ready to give his life and energy to change the world.

Callaloo 15, no. 3 (Summer 1992)

Hervé Télémaque

Born and raised in Port-au-Prince, Télémaque (1937–) studied with painter Julien Lévi at the Art Students League in New York, 1957–1960. After moving to Paris in 1961 he met the surrealists and was soon attending their daily meetings and other events. The first reproductions of his works appeared in the fifth issue (October 1963) of the Surrealist Group's *La Brèche* (The breach)—the same issue that introduced Ted Joans (writing from Timbuktu) and the nascent Surrealist Group in Chicago. He also collaborated on such later surrealist periodicals as *L'Archibras* and the *Bulletin de Liaison Surréaliste*. His paintings have been featured in individual and group shows all over the world, including three international surrealist exhibitions: Paris, 1965; São Paulo, 1967; and Prague, 1968. He has illustrated books by Clément Magloire-Saint-Aude and Gérard Legrand.

WHY ARE YOU PERFORMING, JEAN?

A hand slipped through the window frame, grasping the plant with its long, slightly malleable leaves that resembled those of the leek.

"Stop thief!" the muffled voice of the sleeping man cried out.

"Why are you performing, Jean?"

Jean began to laugh; he knew he was going to answer in that emphatic tone so characteristic of black intellectuals in radio interviews.

He was overcome by a frightening doubt. Everything evened out. The honest man started to look like a bastard, intelligence was becoming systemic. Everything always had to start over again; ideas disintegrate as they are used and man presents man. Accepting the movement of things, placing one's note with the required distance. But to do so, should one have to enter the fight again, take sides, and in the end come back to one's doubt?

You were invited here to attend a birth rather than a death, in such a way that the "obstacle-casing" can be thrown to the wolves with the ambiguous indulgence of the other budding mariners.

The jar of white paint ejaculated as an ink stain on the painter's fly!

L'Archibras 2 (October 1967); translated by Marjolijn de Jager

DOMINICAN REPUBLIC

Aída Cartagena Portalatín

Poet, novelist, critic, scholar, and teacher—a major figure in the literature of the Dominican Republic—Aída Cartagena Portalatín (1918–1994) was a regular contributor to the island's most renowned surrealist-oriented periodical, *La Poesía Sorprendida* (1943–1945), a mimeographed review edited by the exiled Spanish surrealist poet and artist Eugenio F. Granell.

Resolute in her surrealist solidarity—she was one of the group that welcomed Elisa and André Breton to the island in 1945—Portalatín was very much a militant in poetic matters as well as social issues. A radical feminist, she was outspoken in her opposition to all exploitation, oppression, and injustice. She was also a lifelong supporter of Negritude in the *Tropiques* tradition, to the end deeply interested in Africa, Africans, and their struggles. The last book published in her lifetime was *Culturas africanas: Rebeldes con causa* (African cultures: Rebels with a cause, 1986).

Portalatín was the author of more than twenty books. Apart from *Yania Tierra,* however—her 1982 documentary poem—almost none of her work has appeared in English translation.

MOON AND MARBLE

Sadness will roll over the violated light
of metals.
A channel of expectations trails behind this song.
A tear dropped from the moon
Let us seek a new understanding.

Burn night, make ash of the sky
Strip naked moon, abandon your green body.
Let us silence your silence!

Marbles are dreamless;
I shall race ages
to give them my song.
Speak tongueless shadow this night of space;
I wait for the new dawn awakening fields of grain.

La Poesía Sorprendida (1943); translated by Myrna Bell Rochester

TRINIDAD

John Jacob Thomas

Born in Trinidad two years after the abolition of slavery, Thomas (1840–1889) was a major nineteenth-century Caribbean intellectual whose works are still influential. A schoolteacher who became secretary of the Board of Education, he was first and foremost a philologist, noted for his pioneering study, *The Theory and Practice of Creole Grammar* (1869). In 1873 he read a paper on the subject before the Philological Society in London and was later elected a member, thereby receiving the recognition of the most eminent body in his field in the English-speaking world. His later volume, *Froudacity*, is an example of merciless criticism at its most powerful: a point-by-point refutation of the misunderstandings, distortions, and outright lies written by the British racist and apologist for imperialism, James Anthony Froude.

Thomas' status as a precursor of surrealism rests primarily on his deep interest in—and his superb collection of—Creole proverbs. He was influenced by Jean Price Mars in Haiti and Fernando Ortiz in Cuba. An offshoot of his philological research, these folkloric treasures, in his view, were valuable not only as expressions of human wisdom, but also and above all because among them were beautiful sayings that ornament African discourse. As the examples here amply demonstrate, surrealist imagery, proletarian humor, and a strong awareness of the Marvelous are at the core of these wonders of oral literature. When *Froudacity* was reissued in 1969, C.L.R. James declared that "Thomas is more important [now] than he was in his own time."

CREOLE PROVERBS

Conversation is the food of the ear.

Every glow-worm sheds light for its soul.

The ox is never weary of carrying his horns.

You have not yet crossed the river; do not curse the crocodile's mother.

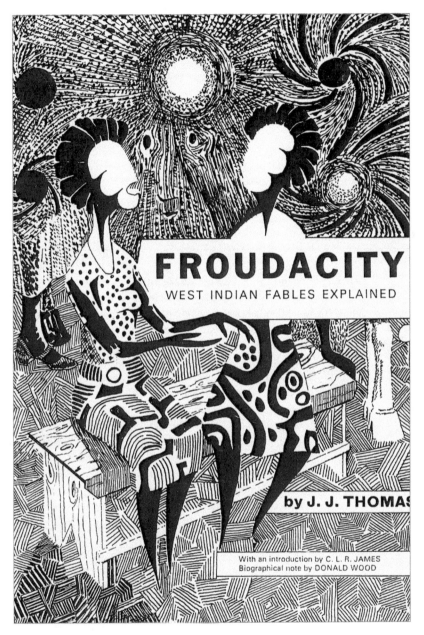

FROUDACITY
WEST INDIAN FABLES EXPLAINED

by J. J. THOMAS

With an introduction by C. L. R. JAMES
Biographical note by DONALD WOOD

Froudacity: West Indian Fables Explained, by J. J. Thomas, is a classic originally published in 1869. This edition was published in 1969 by London's famous Caribbean publisher, New Beacon Press, with an introduction by scholar and political theorist C.L.R. James.

Teeth never laugh at things that are good.

You shall bite finger when it is too late.

Ox never tells the pasture, "thank you."

What business have eggs in the dance of stones?

Sleep *your* sleep.

John La Rose

Trinidad-born and raised, La Rose (1927–2006) was a schoolteacher, journalist, essayist, poet, filmmaker, publisher, and labor activist. In the late 1950s he settled in London, where he soon became a central figure in the black community. In 1966, with Sarah White, he established New Beacon Books, a bookstore and publishing house specializing in West Indian and Pan-African literature. New Beacon reprinted such classics as C.L.R. James' 1936 novel, *Minty Alley* and J. J. Thomas' *Creole Grammar* and *Froudacity.* It also brought out many new titles, such as Susan Craig's important monograph on the Trinidad workers' insurrection of 1934.

La Rose was a cofounder of both the Caribbean Artists movement and the International Book Fair of Radical Black and Third World Books. Secretary of the West Indian Independence Party in Trinidad in the 1950s, he later became the European representative of the Trinidad Oilfield Workers Trade Union.

La Rose's surrealist connections began in 1967, when he encountered surrealists from Paris at the Cultural Congress of Havana. Three years later his meeting with surrealists from Chicago, and his reading of the special "surrealist issue" of the American Students for a Democratic Society journal *Radical America,* greatly expanded his interest. Thereafter, New Beacon was among the few London bookshops to stock surrealist publications.

The poem reprinted here is from *Foundations.*

CONNECTING LINK

The lineal connection
Between space and time
Tangles like ship's rope

No coils unwind
But stretch their stench
To unobtained oblivion

Torment,
Twined in an underbrush
Of corroding custom,
Unwinds itself in inky blood lettings
Unstatisticated.

Memory
Mounts its past
In muddled pride

PUERTO RICO

Luis A. Maisonet

Born and raised in Hatillo, Puerto Rico, Luis Maisonet (1924–) in the early 1950s met the Spanish surrealist painter, poet, and writer Eugenio Granell, a refugee from Franco's Spain who was teaching on the island at the time. Maisonet became Granell's student and good friend, and a member of the Surrealist Group in Puerto Rico, El Mirador Azul. He took part in the group's solo and collective shows and helped organize the 1956 surrealist exhibition on the island, for which André Breton wrote a comradely salutation.

Following his studies at the University of Puerto Rico and later in Mexico, Maisonet returned to Puerto Rico and became well known as a painter, photographer, filmmaker, and teacher. His best-known film, the strongly feminist *Modesta* (1956), won first prize for the Best Short Film at the Venice Film Festival. Maisonet also wrote a textbook, *Arte para la escuela elemental* (Art for elementary school, 1953), introduced by Granell, who praised it highly: "I believe this book will prove to be very useful. . . . Its value lies above all in the author's basic aim: to 'exalt the purity and freedom of the child's rich expressive essence.'" The brief text published here is excerpted from that book.

FREEDOM OF EXPRESSION FOR YOUNG CHILDREN

This freedom of expression allows children to explore the profundities of their existence, their experience, real or imaginary, and whatever else they wish to express, no matter where it comes from—school, the street, the home or the countryside. When I speak of this freedom, I mean that children should be granted the privilege to express that which they consider significant and of the highest interest. This freedom is what is called Dewey self-expression, that is to say, a type of expression able to enlighten the highest ideals of integrity and sincerity.

At times, the exercise of this freedom is so abundant and enthusiastic that to the careless observer, it can appear to be child's play. That which seems like a game or folly is, at its root, work, concentration, reflection, the capacity to overcome the impossible and arrive at a new beginning, with a new determination that satisfies the desperate need to surpass that which is insecure and incoherent in their world.

Translated by Alex Wilder

3. South America

BRAZIL, GUYANA, COLOMBIA

All the revolutions in the world succeed chiefly by the message of the poets.

—Léon-Gontran Damas

BRAZIL

As this section should make plain, contemporary surrealism in Brazil has a long and impressive ancestry, especially among poets of African descent.[1] At odds with the trendy nationalist "modernisms" of their time, brave poets such as João da Cruz e Souza in the late 1800s, Rosário Fusco and Sosígenes Costa in the 1920s, and Fernando Mendes de Almeida in the 1930s pursued distinctive and solitary paths of their own. Today they are recognized by the Surrealist Group in São Paulo as their principal forerunners.

Yet another facet of surrealist prehistory in Brazil revolves around the French surrealist poet Benjamin Péret, who, as a militant in the Brazilian Trotskyist movement, lived in Rio de Janeiro in the years 1929–1931. Péret's wife, Elsie Houston, regarded as one of Brazil's all-time greatest singers, also figures prominently in the story.

As an organized movement, however, surrealism in Brazil began in 1967, with the formation of a Surrealist Group in São Paulo. In the mid-1960s, the poet, collagist, and theorist Sérgio Lima had visited Paris, where he met with André Breton and the younger generation of surrealists in France. Inspired by the Paris Group's diverse activities as well as its camaraderie and encouragement, Lima returned to São Paulo and, with the assistance of Leila Ferraz, Raul Fiker, Paulo de Paranagua, and others, immediately set about organizing a group.

This first step was soon followed by the publication of a hefty 150-page lavishly illustrated journal, A Phala (The lighthouse), with contributions not only by Brazilians but also by Robert Benayoun, Jean Benoît, Aimé Césaire, Alain Joubert, Annie Le Brun, Artur do Cruzeiro Seixas, Wifredo Lam, Joyce Mansour, Mimi Parent, and others from the Paris Group and elsewhere.

A large part of A Phala served as the catalog for yet another manifestation of the young Surrealist Group in Brazil: an international surrealist exhibition, featuring a wide selection of works by many surrealist painters, sculptors, collagists, and photographers, plus a showing of Paulo de Paranagua's film *Nadja*.

A *Phala* also published the Brazilian surrealists' first collective declaration, which reads in part:

> Throughout its historic evolution, surrealism has been and continues to be the most acute point of the Marvelous in the human world. . . .
> The nocturnal trajectory of the erotic and the magical join together, with sudden splendor, the reality of Poetry in all its works. . . .
> In the majestic breach of the future, surrealism is the rising flower.

The Surrealist Group has remained active through the years and has produced a large number of important books and pamphlets of surrealist poetry and theory, as well as occasional bulletins and tracts. One of international surrealism's outstanding poets, Sérgio Lima, is also the author of *A aventura surrealista* (The surrealist adventure), in four volumes of 500-plus pages each, surely one of the most massive, insightful, and detailed studies of surrealism in any language. Lima is also the author of other important works in the surrealist canon, including *Amore* (1963), *Collage* (1974), and *O corpo significa* (1976).

Other participants in the São Paulo Group have also published books or contributed widely to periodicals. Michael Löwy, a major figure in the Paris Surrealist Group today—and author of many outstanding books on surrealism, philosophy, and politics—is of Brazilian origin and in close communication with the São Paulo comrades.

In the late 1990s and early 2000s, the Brazilian group had the distinction of being the only surrealist group in which women were a substantial majority.

Brazil to this day remains one of international surrealism's key places. The São Paulo Group, recently reorganized under the name Decollage, has proved to be very active. In the summer of 2006, the group issued a joint statement with the surrealists in Portugal and announced plans for other events and publications.

COLOMBIA

An academic writer in Bogotá once remarked that the word "surrealism" was as infrequently heard in Colombia as the word "Assyriology," and that no surrealist movement existed—or had ever existed—in that country. There was, however, he continued, a Nadaista movement, indigenous to Colombia, in the 1950s and 1960s. Nadaistas considered themselves an offshoot of Dada and surrealism, but were more negativistic, as the term *"nada"* (nothing) implies. Evidently, the

Nadaistas produced several books and many pamphlets, which are almost impossible to find today.

In 1970 a lone Nadaista, Armando Romero, visited the Chicago Surrealist Group. He explained that the movement in Colombia, after many police battles, had practically disbanded. One member was said to be in prison in Nebraska for trafficking in cocaine.

Two Colombian poets in the earlier part of the twentieth century appear to have had a strong "passional attraction" (to use Charles Fourier's expression) for surrealism: Luis Vidales, author of *Suenan timbres* (Reverberating ringing, 1926); and Andrés Holguín, whose work includes many translations of surrealist poetry.[2]

Vastly more important, however, not only in regard to the cultural life of Colombia, but more particularly in the recent history of surrealism, was the explosive 1960s arrival on the world scene of the great Afro-Colombian painter Heriberto Cogollo. Immediately and enthusiastically welcomed by surrealist writers—including Ted Joans, José Pierre, and Joyce Mansour—Cogollo was soon recognized throughout the world as one of the important artists of our time.

Fortunately for us all, he is still very active. May his magical and magisterial work long continue to make our world a better and more enchanting place!

GUYANA

Several Guyanese poets and writers, starting as long ago as the 1930s with Léon-Gontran Damas, have had a strong and enduring impact on the surrealist movement.

Damas was a schoolboy chum of Aimé Césaire in Martinique, and later a comrade and admirer of Etienne Léro in Paris. Other Paris friends included several Harlem Renaissance poets, especially Langston Hughes, and the surrealists. A coeditor of *L'Étudiant Noir*, Damas was a lively presence in the black and surrealist milieux of 1930s Paris. As raconteur and "man about town," he seems to have known everybody and to have been everywhere—rather like Ted Joans a generation and a half later.

Above all Damas was a first-rate poet, indeed, one of the major poets of his generation. Mallarmé was an early influence, but Damas' discovery of Baudelaire (and particularly his translations of Poe) had a much greater impact and in turn led him to the works of Rimbaud, Lautréamont, and the surrealists. Another major influence was the poetry of Sterling Brown, whose *Southern Road* (1932) was an illuminating force in the lives and thought of the entire Negritude movement.

Notably, among the original triumvirate of Negritude—Césaire, Senghor, Damas—it was Damas who first readied a book for publication (*Pigments*, 1937), with a preface by French surrealist poet Robert Desnos. Two years later, following long and grueling interrogations by the French police, the book was banned by the government.

Damas was well known as a lifelong surrealist sympathizer, but he was also something more: an ardent defender of surrealism's revolutionary aims and principles. In his later years his friendship with (and influence on) younger black poets and artists was an important part of their development, as Ted Joans, Jayne Cortez, and Mel Edwards have not hesitated to affirm.[3]

Walter Rodney also influenced surrealism, quite possibly without knowing it (he was assassinated in 1980). His pamphlet, *The Groundings with My Brothers*, was early on an important text for the Chicago Surrealist Group and was quoted, significantly, in what became one of the most frequently reprinted and translated U.S. surrealist tracts of later years: *Three Days That Shook the New World Order: The Los Angeles Rebellion of 1992*. And in a 1994 minimanifesto, "Sure, Really We Are," Ted Joans urged that "all young and youthful-thinking surrealists should read Walter Rodney's book, *How Europe Underdeveloped Africa*."

The first issue of the journal *Arsenal/Surrealist Subversion* (Chicago, 1970) salutes "the demoniacal, compelling lyricism of the Guyanese writer Wilson Harris," and from *The Palace of the Peacock* on, surrealists have followed his novels and critical essays with the greatest interest. Here again John La Rose's wonderful London bookshop has proved to be an invaluable source. In 1982 texts by Harris and by C.L.R. James appeared in the surrealist publication *Free Spirits: Annals of the Insurgent Imagination*. And in 2000, thanks largely to James scholars Paul Buhle, Selwyn Cudjoe, and Paget Henry, some of the writings by James on Harris, and by Harris on James, were brought to wider attention in a special issue of *The C.L.R. James Journal* (Winter 1999–2000).

The works of Jan Carew—poet, novelist, playwright, and historian—have also been important for surrealism, and especially for the Chicago Group. In 1985, during the prolonged Free Nelson Mandela and Divest Now demonstrations at Northwestern University in Evanston, Illinois—protests in which the surrealists were very active—South African poet and activist Dennis Brutus introduced Carew to the surrealists. A lively discussion over lunch ensued, joined by Ted Joans, who had just arrived in town.

Notes

1. My principal source on surrealism in Brazil has been an extensive correspondence with Sérgio Lima, extending over a period of many years. I

also benefited from discussions with Brazilian poet Robert Ponge during his 2001 visit to Chicago, and more particularly with Célia Cymbalista during her 2006 visit.

2. Letter to Franklin Rosemont from Armando Romero, February 1972. The details on Colombian poets appeared in the Chantilly-based French anarchist journal *Le Puits de l'Ermite* (The hermit's cave), in a special 1978 issue titled "La domaine poétique international du surréalisme" (Surrealism's international poetic domain).

3. On Damas, see Racine, *Léon-Gontran Damas;* Keith Q. Warner, ed., *Critical Perspectives on Léon-Gontran Damas;* and Damas' interview in the journal *Jeune Afrique,* no. 532 (March 16, 1971), 57–65.

BRAZIL

João da Cruz e Souza

Marginalized in his own time, not only for his extraordinary anticipation of Negritude but also for his unsparing protosurrealism, Cruz e Souza (today's critics often prefer to spell it "Sousa") (1861–1898) was reduced to the status of a pariah in the bourgeois "modernist" establishment of Rio de Janeiro, the literary capital of Brazil during the Belle Époque. French scholar Roger Bastide—author of important studies of Afro-Brazilian culture—scandalized this narrow-minded white intelligentsia when he declared Cruz e Souza the equal of Mallarmé. Indeed, Cruz e Souza's amazing work—above all his *Evocações* (1898), characterized above all by eroticism, the Marvelous, and its "subversive and revolutionary spirit" (Sérgio Lima)—was truly rediscovered only in the 1950s and 1960s, when the first organized Surrealist Group in Brazil was beginning to take shape.

For Sérgio Lima and his friends in the São Paulo Surrealist Group, the work of Cruz e Souza in the history of surrealism in Brazil is comparable to that of Lautréamont in France—the major precursor.

"Black Rose" and "Tenebrous" were first published in the late 1880s or early 1890s.

BLACK ROSE

Imperious, restless, flesh-devouring flower
Flower of Death's dream and shadow
Trammeled, I try to escape
Vexed by your soul's icy depths

Your night-clad byword, as good as Dante,
tragic irony drenched in Hell
And I, eye-witness of your anguish
and the ruthless torment of your heart

Delirious flower steeped in blood
erupting floodlike wave after wave
Such voluptuousness makes me dizzy
Black rose of night, flower of oblivion

offer me your acrid, incendiary kiss
which I shall cherish vastly more
than any endearment
from pallid lips

Evocações, translated by Celia Cymbalista

TENEBROUS

I wish I could possess your love—your love that must be like a leafy blood tree with tenebrous fruits. Your love of impetus of beast, in the dense woods and jungles, over the thick and granitic scars, in the caustic solarity of exotic warm weathers of races tropicalized in emotion, because you are made of burning sun and of dusky sands, of the warm soil that deserts are made . . .

I wish I could possess your love—complete, strange, eternal this love! And I wish I could—if I possessed and enjoyed it—possess and enjoy the Sea and have inside myself the curdled ocean—as my soul is curdled of dreams—ships, yachts, schooners, galleons, vessels and galleys, through a vassalizing tempest in which formidable thunders and electrical frisks of phosphorescent rays, cracking the firmament, would shake, in a harsh stormy shiver, the frizzy, tumid and wailing neck of the Waves.

I wish I could love you like that! And in this stormy Sea, under the anguishing pressure of the elements, reacting to a cabalistic sign of mine—as if absolute power had granted me the terrible and supreme God of the Earth—yachts, ships, schooners, vessels and galleys, leading the whole of humanity towards several regions of the monstrous world, would suddenly sink into the gaping gorge of the wide-open Sea, astounding, quivering . . .

I wish I could love you like that! Vibrating to the sun of your blood, burned by your flaming skin, whose most penetrating savage aroma arouses me, dazzles me, narcotizes me.

Evocações, translated by Marcus Salgado

Rosário Fusco

Although an organized surrealist movement did not develop in Brazil until the 1960s, the history of Brazilian poetry and art is rich with objective surrealists, individuals who, indifferent to the many trendy "modernisms," boldly exemplified—in their lives as well as their works—surrealism's revolutionary and emancipatory spirit.

In 1926, in the small town of Cataguazes, near São Paulo, Rosário Fusco (1910–1977) edited a one-shot poetry magazine called *Jazz-Band*, followed by an aggressively polemical journal, *Verde*, which featured some of the first explicitly surrealist texts to appear in Brazil. Modernist critics, then as now hostile to surrealism's total nonconformism, dismissed Fusco's work as mental gymnastics and accused him of introducing European irrationalism into the national literature.

The two poems translated here are from his 1928 book, *Poemas cronológicos*.

WIND IN THE WOODS

1.

The wind soothed the fountain
and the fountain in the park sang
—all night long—
the broken-glass music
on the mosaic-bottomed basin.

2.

. . . and this wind that comes from the woods in the moist night is a kiss
long and resinous fragrant of ripe fruits
suspended and swaying . . .

This wind from the woods fills our heart with wild wilderness!

This wind from the woods fills our heart with desire for the exhilaration of
    life!
All the voluptuousness pulsing in the bulging womb
of the wind from my woods

Translated by Celia Cymbalista

Sosígenes Costa

A poet completely outside Brazil's modernist mainstream, Sosígenes Costa (1901–1968) pursued an unparalleled path of his own. He had friends in the so-called Academy of Rebels in Bahia, but even they found his work too radically different to publish. He in turn rejected their nationalist regionalism and stuck to his own peculiar style. Close in spirit to Brazil's rural songsters and their improvisations, he was indeed a primitive poet, or, in the words of Sérgio Lima, a Brazilian Douanier Rousseau in poetry. His poems are an explosion of wild colors and odd words — a veritable cornucopia of the unexpected, the Marvelous, the flora and fauna of the popular imagination. He is the poet of talking animals and the world turned upside down — a world in which the Marvelous is no longer the opposite of the everyday, and in which the most ordinary objects are imbued with strangeness.

Much of his work can be described as mythic and frolicsome, but he is not a narrow or one-sided poet. Indeed, he is also the author of inspired fulminations against racism and impassioned dreams of a true social utopia of equality and freedom for all.

THE GOLDEN PAPYRUS

As a matter of fact, in the next day
the Serpent came after me

I got crazy.
Hopeless.

Sleepless
as I had never been.

I took a medicine, ingested poison,
finally fell asleep and had a dream
but alas!
I dreamed about the snake.

The snake came and pushed me
into the river,
killed the fish that wanted to see me
killed the fish-eyed sphinx

killed the fish that read a papyrus
killed a snake with a flower around its tail
hurt Osiris and Osiris died.

Suddenly the kingdom of green ooze

And the puma rubbed its tongue all over the fish
in order to check if the little fish would give the ruby.
And the Incan threw a fishnet on the lake
and the king who owned the ruby threw a fishhook,
and the sun that swam at the bottom of the lake
passed by the sleeping fish
and the fishnet fell over the sun.
The snake told me:
Our son will be Tupac-amaru,
snake of the sky
scale-mouthed snake
celestial snake that casts the ray,
and the snake opened its mouth full of scales.
I screamed and the snake got angry.
The fish woke up over the rock
and the lake that was like rainbow
now was trembling and its water muddy.

Morro do desterro, translated by Marcus Salgado

THE RED PEACOCK

Well now, happiness, this red peacock,
is presently living in my backyard.
He comes to land like a sun on my knee
When the dawn is piercing my backyard.

Scarlet morning-glory,
This red peacock
rises above the peacocks outside.
It is a party of purple and I liken him
To dawn's flaming flag.

He is the very doge looking in the mirror.
And the red color waxes sonorous
with this pompous horned peacock.

Lilac peacocks I once possessed.
After I loved this peacock,
My other peacocks went away.

Morro do desterro, translated by Danielle Jouët-Pastre and Neil Pischner

Fernando Mendes de Almeida

Another "outsider" in the history of Brazilian poetry—to this day denied
a place in the nation's official literary pantheon—Fernando Mendes
de Almeida is nonetheless a landmark figure, for his *Phantom Carrousel*
(1937) was the first book in Brazil to be identified as surrealist. Ignored
by Brazil's conservative (and nationalist) modernists, the seventy-six-
page collection of poems was praised by more perceptive readers for its
alarming originality and its revelation of a different sensibility, reflecting
the chaos that reigns in the tumultuous life of our time.

PHANTOM CARROUSEL

Let Saturn wait for me in the avenue
Oh heart wrapped in untruth!

Look at the city of the street cries!
Rita! Vessel! Victory! Shelter!

Love is a big red bread
and I had a multicolored garland for lunch

Night promises me worthless separation
From unpaired lovemaking to amazons

I feel a finger coming into my mouth
quick abyss of the body!

Oh agonies of harmful resources!
I am Narcissus yet no one understands me
And the hot afternoons wrap me with secrets,
With sports hidden by the past
Let me enter these labyrinths

I am not civilization and god already knows it
Oh, regular love does not cut away my thirst!

I want the Sea Sierra for myself!
And I feel so small what I've already done
That the pain of suicide invites me

Where is it Baghdad?

I want the tormentous Cape Horn
To kill my love.

I want the Sea Sierra!
I want the Sea Sierra!

Phantom Carrousel, translated by Celia Cymbalista

Jorge de Lima

Surrealism did not exist as an organized movement in Brazil until 1967, when Sérgio Lima and his comrades organized a major international surrealist exhibition in São Paulo and founded a dynamic group there. Earlier, however, many individual Brazilians—poets, artists, dancers— had, in varying degrees, identified themselves with surrealism's aims and principles. One of the first, in the 1930s, was Jorge de Lima (1893–1953), later hailed as one of the nation's greatest poets. He grew up in an area made famous by Zumbi, the great seventeenth-century black resistance leader who established a refuge for escaped slaves, and the legends and lore he learned as a child were decisive in shaping his life. As he recalled in 1945, it was then and there that he had first felt touched by poetry.

Jorge de Lima's career was breathtakingly diverse. Author of novels, essays, biographies, and at least one film script, he was also a noted painter, sculptor, and collagist. He was a physician by profession (with a 1914 degree in medicine from Rio de Janeiro's medical school) and deeply involved in politics, serving at different times as state deputy, director of public education, and president of the Rio de Janeiro city council.

Above all, he was a poet, and here too his diversity was notable. His work includes Parnassian sonnets, religious and regionalist verses, various forms of Brazil's highly eclectic modernism, and, in 1952, the ten-canto *Invenção de Orfeu.* His specifically surrealist moments were sporadic but powerful. In many scattered poems, and the album of collages, *A pin-tura em pânico* (Painting in a panic, 1943), the surrealist Jorge de Lima left us much of his finest work.

HOWLING DOGS

Howling dogs howl longer in a long night
And the woman turns the corners in a long night.
Lingering drunkards disperse, dizzy,
And let the long woman pass.
A solitary woman, she turns the corners.
The drunkards stop!
The howling dogs pursue her, the long solitary woman,
in the streets, as she turns the corners.
She must have phosphorescent vision.
She must have very cold hands.
She must be the muse of suicides.
Someone digs in the night. Who is digging?
The long woman turns the corners.
Someone digs in the night. What are they digging?
Too long is the dogs' howling.
The long woman turns the corners.
Do not look at her, brother poet.
The solitary woman has a mad vision.
She must be the muse of the drowned.
The long woman goes down the street.
The street is longer now,
And the dogs' howling is longer, too.
Stop, drunkards! You may come down now,
Down, oh down!

Scattered Poems, translated by Celia Cymbalista

GUYANA

Léon-Gontran Damas

"If I have become the man that I am," Léon Damas (1912–1978) said in 1973, "I owe it to surrealism." One of the major poets of Negritude, he was born into a middle-class family in Cayenne, French Guyana. His father was a mulatto of partly European ancestry, his mother, African and Native American. After attending the local school in Cayenne he enrolled in the Lycée Schoelcher in Martinique. While studying philosophy there he met Aimé Césaire, who became his lifelong friend. Later, in France, he studied law and anthropology, got involved in radical politics, and spent a lot of time with Michel Leiris and Robert Desnos. In Paris he and Césaire, together with their Senegalese friend Léopold Senghor, founded the short-lived but influential paper titled *L'Étudiant Noir*—an early voice of what soon became known as Negritude. Later he published his first book of poems, *Pigments*, with a preface by Desnos.

Damas' poetry, with its hard-driving rhythms, staccato repetition, and disquieting images, was influenced not only by surrealism but also by African song, the Harlem Renaissance poets, and Sterling Brown.

He was an important inspiration for the Black Power and Black Arts movements.

FOR SURE

For sure I'll get fed up
without even waiting
for things to ripen
like a good camembert

So until then I'll just go
and put my foot in it
or grab by the collar
everything I can't stand
In capital letters:
colonization
civilization

assimilation
and all that

Meanwhile
you'll often hear me
slam the door

Pigments, translated by Franklin Rosemont

GOOD BREEDING

Where I come from they don't yawn
the way they yawn around here
with their hand
on their mouth

I want to yawn without hubbub
my body bent over
in the aromas that torment the life
that I've made for myself
out of their ugly cur of a winter
out of their sun that couldn't even
warm up the coco juice
that bubbled in my stomach
when I woke up

Let me yawn
with my hand
right here
on my heart
obsessed as I am with all those things
that in just one day one single day
I turned away from

Pigments, translated by Franklin Rosemont

A CARIBBEAN VIEW ON STERLING A. BROWN

I should like to say that this distinguished man has done much, and was among
the first to open the road to Negro consciousness through his first book, *Southern Road,* and afterwards *Negro Caravan,* which marked the beginning of the
Negro Movement and which so greatly influenced the Negritude Movement of

the thirties. The new Negro generation should never forget, and indeed always remember the significant literary contributions and personal struggles made by their forefathers, men with such rigorous intellectual and physical stamina. . . . According to the ancient proverb which asserts that poets are born, not made, Brown and I were born with a poetic gift which is not learned, but cultivated, and favored by a predestination. Additional reasons have permitted Sterling Brown not only to develop himself and his works, but to extend his optic to embrace and treat the Black race in the United States and elsewhere.

His stature has already secured him an important place in the tragic history of our race and indeed human history, which Africans were not considered to be a part of.

Sterling Brown: A UMUN Tribute

A SINGLE INSTANT OF BELIEF

For a moment believe
in a hand without a glove
a hand luminous of springtime
naked in the birth of spring
springtime born from magic
magic of rhythm
the toothless
diseased mob
single-eyed and paranoid
cried all over
my insane heart without hate

Pigments, translated by Alex Wilder

NEGRITUDE AND SURREALISM

Startlingly, the Negritude was not conceived by Africans in the Motherland but by those influenced by the spirituals, blues and jazz of the United States of America; the sound and dance of Cubans; the *batucada, samba, frevo,* and *capoeira* of Brazil; the *merengue* and *petro* of Haiti; the *merenque* of the Dominicans and Puerto Ricans; the *calypso* of Trinidad and Jamaica; and the *casse-co* of Guyana, not to mention the *beguine* of Martinique and Guadeloupe—all of which had their origins in Africa.

Here Negritude was born—not in Africa, but in the West Indies.

It was not until the 1920s and 30s that there arose a generation of writers who, instead of voicing cries of complaint and hope, demanded justice, and were openly determined to make this known. They affirmed clearly their quality of Blackness as well as its entitlement to civil and cultural rights, as W.E.B. Du Bois defended so eloquently.

It was the birth of the Harlem Renaissance and the New Negro in whose name Langston Hughes proclaimed a manifesto:

> We younger Negro artists who create now intend to express our indi-
> vidual dark-skinned selves without fear or shame. If the white folks
> seem pleased, we are glad. If they are not, it doesn't matter. We know
> we are beautiful. Ugly too. The tom-tom cries and the tom-tom laughs.
> If colored people are pleased, we are glad. If they are not, their pleasure
> doesn't matter. We build our temples for tomorrow, strong as we know
> them, and we stand on the top of the mountain free within ourselves.

The profound sense of this manifesto was realized by the pioneers of Negritude: Césaire, Maugée, Achille, Gratiant, Senghor, Diop, myself and others. We were determined to follow in the footsteps of Langston Hughes, Countee Cullen, Jean Toomer, Sterling Brown, and Claude McKay, the author of *Banjo*, who realized in 1930 (a date to remember) a much-deserved success. Césaire, Senghor and I helped as much as we could to make all of their works well known.

The period between the 1920s and 30s was one of great fertility. The first Pan-Negro Congress, due to the initiative of Du Bois, took place in Paris. The theories of Marcus Garvey were in the air. René Maran published *Batouala*. It was the time of the Paris publication of the first Black journals: *Les Continents*, *The Paria*, *The Dépêche Africaine*, the *Revue du Monde Noire*, founded by a Haitian physician, Dr. Sajous, with the collaboration of Paulette Nardal.

The disappearance of *Revue du Monde Noire* in 1932 accelerated the historical movement leading to the birth of Negritude, with the appearance in 1934 of *L'Étudiant Noir*, a result of the initiative of Césaire, Senghor, and me.

Somewhat before this (1932) *Légitime Défense* had appeared—a *Periodical of Struggle* which survived only one issue, but was sufficiently packed with rich ideas and views to make it worthy of preservation. In *Légitime Défense*, Etienne Léro and other West Indians signed a manifesto which remains the most insurrectional document of French-speaking men of color.

For Léro, the exceptional mediocrity of French West Indian poetry was clearly related to the existing social order. The majority of the population could not read, or write, or speak French. Starting with Léro's poems, a new West

Indian poetry was born. To Léro and no other the poetry of the French West Indies owes its first new blood. It is to Léro that we owe the fact that, since 1932, French West Indian poetry has taken the path of dreams.

Continuities (Autumn 1974)

Wilson Harris

Poet, novelist, and essayist Wilson Harris (1921–) was born in Guyana (then British Guiana), but has lived most of his life in London. His first publication was a suite of audaciously experimental poems titled *Eternity to Season*, but it was his first novel, *Palace of the Peacock* (1960) that brought him wide attention. Its free-floating oneiricism and ecstatic intensity at once lead perceptive readers to compare it to Rimbaud's "Drunken Boat." Even more amazingly, the oft-abused adjective surrealist has, in this case, been rightly applied—and not only to *Palace* but also to Harris' other tales.

Much less well known are his critical essays, which are, however, every bit as imaginative and insightful as his poetry and novels. The text reprinted here, from his early collection, *Tradition: The Writer and Society*, also appeared in the surrealist journal *Free Spirits: Annals of the Insurgent Imagination* in 1982.

VOODOO, TRANCE, POETRY AND DANCE

Haitian vodun is one of the surviving primitive dances of ancient sacrifice, which, in courting a subconscious community, *sees* its own performance in literal terms—that is, with and through the eyes of space: with and through the sculpture of sleeping things which the dancer himself actually expresses and becomes. For in fact the dancer moves in a trance and the interior mode of the drama is exteriorized into a medium inseparable from his trance and invocation. He is a dramatic agent of subconsciousness. The life from within and the life from without now truly overlap. That is the intention of the dance, the riddle of the dancer.

COLOMBIA

Heriberto Cogollo

Born in Cartagena, Colombia, Cogollo (1945-) studied painting there (1957–1960) and later in Madrid. Since 1967 he has lived primarily in Paris. His work has been shown in individual and collective exhibitions in Colombia, Spain, France, Germany, and other countries. Photographic reproductions of several of his paintings illustrate Ted Joans' 1999 volume of selected poems, *Teducation*.

The artist's statement published here is taken from the exhibition catalog *Cogollo: Le monde d'un Nohor* (Galerie Suzanne Visat, Paris, 1973), which also includes a preface by Jose Pierre.

THE WORLD OF A NOHOR

In Senegal and Uganda, a Nohor is a semi-sorcerer, that is to say a sorcerer through his father; he is someone endowed with "supernatural vision," who is able to contemplate, at his leisure and in complete passivity, the viscera and entrails of his peers. He would be incapable of killing a victim to feed on its flesh, which is the prerogative of the unqualified sorcerer.

As much as I am a Nohor, it doesn't make me any less a man and my inner world is closely mingled with these projections so much so that it is sometimes difficult to make the distinction between what I see and what is actually my own.

What I do know is that I would like to be able to also show the inner world I gaze upon.

Translated by Marjolijn de Jager

4. Africa

THE SURREALIST GROUP IN CAIRO

> The door swings open and the one no one expected
> Makes his way through the costume ball
>
> —Nicole Espagnol

The mid- and late 1930s effloresence of Paris-based African and Caribbean
surrealism appreciably strengthened surrealism as an international movement,
expanding its horizons in the realms of poetry, theory, politics, and the arts.
Together with the growing number of surrealist groups in Europe and elsewhere—from Buenos Aires to Belgrade, from London to Tokyo—the Martinicans and Cubans also did much to rectify the widespread but erroneous belief
that surrealism was somehow exclusively French.

In 1937 the expansion of the Surrealist International received a major boost
from a group in Africa. The Cairo Surrealist Group, which flourished for well
over a decade, was itself international. Most of its members were Egyptian, but
it also included the Italian anarchist painter Angelo de Riz, the Armenian photographer Ida Kar, and English critic Victor Musgrave.[1]

The group's chief instigator and organizer was Georges Henein, who would
soon become one of the best-known figures in world surrealism.[2] Son of a Coptic Egyptian father and an Italian mother, Henein was a magnificent poet, perceptive critic, brilliant strategist, and born agitator. He discovered surrealism
as a student in Paris in 1934, at the age of twenty. Before becoming active in
the movement he took part in a Cairo group called Les Essayistes, which published a monthly, *Un Effort*. The February 1935 issue features his manifesto "On
Irrealism," showing that he was well on his way to surrealism: "Nothing is more
useless than the real. . . . Why seek truth where it is not, in external things,
when our internal resources have hardly been explored at all? The only true
world is the one we create within ourselves; the only sincere world the one we
create against others." This manifesto was accompanied by an example of automatic writing, an Irrealist tale titled "The Noumena Evaded and Resuscitated."
The same issue, moreover, includes Henein's merciless critique of the former

surrealist Aragon's Stalinist novel, *Les cloches de bâle* (The bells of Basil). Henein's opening line: "A literary work is not an election poster."

Thanks to Henein, the Essayistes moved steadily in the direction of pure provocation. In one of the group's fugitive publications—an antibourgeois dictionary—he offers such definitions as these:

Anarchy: Victory of the Spirit over certainty
Beauty: The power to act
Pantheon: A place for the interment of men who might otherwise be forgotten
Work: Everything that we don't want to do

Increasingly attracted to surrealism, he began a campaign to bring the new movement to wider attention. With tireless energy, he trumpeted the surrealist message all over Cairo. Always controversial, his numerous articles and debates with the Essayistes were much discussed. In October 1935 he gave a lecture on Lautréamont and published an article on the suicide of René Crevel. Two months later, having decided to join the surrealist movement, he wrote his first letter to André Breton, whom he met the following spring.

By 1937 he had not only given his first public talk on surrealism in Cairo, but had also begun organizing an Egyptian Surrealist Group, which later adopted the name Art and Freedom. Among the first adherents of the group were poet Edmond Jabes and the painters Kamel Telmisamy, Angelo de Riz (a refugee from Mussolini's Italy), and Ramses Younane. One of Henein's closest friends for many years, Younane—who came to be recognized as Egypt's foremost surrealist painter—was also an important surrealist theorist.

While planning an Egyptian surrealist publication, the question arose: Should it be published in French or Arabic? Henein's friend Benjamin Péret urged him "to make every effort" to publish it in Arabic, arguing that "however incomprehensible Arabic may be here [in France], it is always good for a little truth to burst out elsewhere. Eventually it will spread out widely."[3]

As it turned out, Henein and his friends published three journals. *Art et liberté* appeared in French and Arabic (two issues, March and May 1939), while *Al-Tattawor* (Evolution) was entirely in Arabic (eight issues in 1940). The third, *Don Quichotte* (two issues, December 1939 and March 1940) also appeared in French and Arabic.

All three of these publications were concerned with political as well as cultural matters. The high priority given to politics was not by chance. Stalinists were bitter enemies of surrealism—and of all true revolutionists—and so were the Egyptian nationalists. But Cairo's surrealists were also well aware of another impending menace: fascism. With Mussolini's troops stationed in nearby Libya and in Ethiopia, the fascist threat was very real in Egypt.

There is reason to believe—although the critical literature appears to be silent on the matter—that each of the Cairo Group's periodicals was meant to serve a different purpose and was also directed to different readers. *Art and Freedom*, which included the participation of several nonsurrealist artists and writers, was primarily a bulletin of the arts and current intellectual life, deeply concerned with pressing problems of the day and, more generally, with civil rights and free-speech issues. It was closely allied with the International Federation of Independent Revolutionary Art (FIARI), formed in 1938 by André Breton and Diego Rivera (with the support of Leon Trotsky and the additional participation of C.L.R. James) as a revolutionary alternative to the various Stalinist cultural fronts. The FIARI manifesto, *For an Independent Revolutionary Art*, signed by Breton and Rivera, demands "complete freedom for art. No authority, no dictation, not the least trace of orders from above!" Like the FIARI elsewhere, the *Art and Freedom* readership embraced socialists, Trotskyists, anarchists, syndicalists, and several artists and writers who thought of themselves as independent radicals.

Al-Tattawor, edited by Anwar Kamel, was an explicitly political and agitational organ, affiliated with the Fourth International. Aimed principally at workers and radical students, it focused on local labor news, women's struggles, and revolutionary news from around the world. Unlike most agitprop publications, however, it also featured texts on modern poetry and art.

Don Quichotte, on the contrary, emphasized high-caliber cultural criticism and polemic. Henein contributed numerous articles on a wide range of subjects: Jean Malaquais, *Alice in Wonderland*, Jacques Vaché, the painter El Telmisany. His denunciation of such "classical" French authors as La Bruyère and La Fontaine appears under the title "In Regard to Some Slovenly Characters." In short, *Don Quichotte* was a journal clearly intended for that sector of the population that Marxists liked to call advanced intellectuals.

The opening statement of the inaugural issue of *Don Quichotte* sums up the basic orientation and tone of all these journals: "We struggle against: indifference, anachronism, facility, the use that people don't make of freedom, all falsifications, and all euphemisms."

All through the late 1930s and the war years the Cairo Surrealist Group maintained an intense collective activity. In addition to its journals, books, pamphlets, tracts, lectures, and occasional radio appearances, it organized five large collective art and freedom exhibitions between 1940 and 1945, notable not only for the high quality of the work, but also for the large number of women participants. Nonsectarian, the Cairo surrealists and their friends took part in discussions and debates with other radicals, most notably at the gatherings of diverse artists and intellectuals at the home of Henein's friend Maria Cavadia. But the Cairo surrealists were also active in labor struggles, at workplaces, and in the streets.

Inevitably, Henein and his comrades had their troubles with the police, who more than once confiscated the group's tracts and other publications. At least for a time, the group was also the target of a press boycott. Persecution notwithstanding, the Cairo Group remained one of the most active and productive centers of the international surrealist movement.

THE AMAZING JOYCE MANSOUR

The most important figure in Egyptian surrealism from the late 1950s on was the great poet and fiction writer Joyce Mansour, who readily acknowledged the influence of Henein and his comrades. Mansour, a longtime militant in the Surrealist Group, lived most of her life in Paris. Her first book, *Cris* (Shrieks), was a sensation when it appeared in 1953. Its ferocious sexuality—unprecedented in French feminine literature—was a scandal to many. In Egypt, too, many readers were shocked, but few books were more widely read and discussed.

Her later poems and tales seethe with the same violent eroticism, and a savage, ready-for-anything humor. Compared to her *Jules César*, it was said, the then-notorious *Story of O* was mere rosewater. Her "women's column" in the surrealist magazine *BIEF* offered readers hilarious *détournements* (puns) of clichés from fashionable women's periodicals. An insatiable inventor of original ways of questioning *what is*, Joyce Mansour was above all a bright exemplar of poetic excess. All her writing is characterized by ardent rebelliousness, daredevil anti-conformity, and belligerent scorn for the conventional in all its forms.

André Breton called her *Les gisants satisfaits* (The satisfied effigies), the twentieth century's *Garden of Earthly Delights*. Breton, indeed, admired Mansour's work immensely and made it known that he considered her one of the finest postwar surrealist poets and writers in France.[4]

A generous supporter of surrealist painters, to whom she dedicated appreciative articles and poems, Mansour helped organize the group's many collective exhibitions. In 1960, with Robert Benayoun, Octavio Paz, and Nora Mitrani, she represented the Surrealist Group on an important BBC radio broadcast, "In Defense of Surrealism."

The cigar-smoking Mansour was also a gutsy activist; in 1967, for example, she gave the notorious Stalinist Siqueiros a swift kick in the pants at the Cultural Congress of Havana. A large supportive crowd applauded and chanted: "¡Cuba, sí! ¡Siqueiros, no!"

RAPACES

JOYCE
MANSOUR

SEGHERS

Rapaces (1960), a book of poems by Joyce Mansour, one of the most important poets of the postwar period. The cover is by Jean Benoît.

Cover of *Anthologie du nonsense,* by Robert Benayoun, 1957.

As poet, writer, spokesperson, organizer, and activist, Joyce Mansour always manifested a warm sense of international surrealist solidarity. Fluent in English, she maintained friendly ties with Ted Joans as well as the group in Chicago.

NORTH AFRICA: THE MAGHREB

The northwest region of Africa known as the Maghreb—consisting of Algeria, Tunisia, and Morocco—has been home to several active participants in the surrealist movement, and also to writers and artists friendly to it. Algiers, in particular, though never a locus of collective surrealist activity per se, nevertheless over the years served as a surrealist port of call. We know, for example, that Georges Bessière, an early Paris surrealist who collaborated on *La Révolution Surréaliste* in 1925, and then dropped out of sight, published a book of his surrealist poems, *S.O.S.*, in Algiers in 1937. A pamphlet edition of Breton's *Situation du surréalisme entre les deux guerres* appeared in the same city in 1945.

Four of the eight individuals represented in this section—Baya, Benayoun, Kréa, and Lariby—actively participated in collective surrealist activity: Baya's 1947 Paris exhibition catalog has a preface by André Breton, and Benayoun, from 1949 on, was one of the most prolific and original writers in the Paris Group. Kréa took part in the Milan Group, and Lariby in the short-lived Arab Surrealist Movement in Exile, headquartered in Paris (see below). Atlan is something of a special case. His close friends included several surrealists, but his main activity centered on the Cobra movement.

Khair-Eddine, Tengour, and Laâbi had no direct involvement in organized surrealism. In the repressive regimes they lived under, the police would not have permitted a surrealist group to exist. However, their varied works exemplify a serious commitment to surrealism as a revolutionary means of disalienation, a subversion of the language of commerce and power, and a passionate pursuit of the practice of poetry.

THE ARAB SURREALIST MOVEMENT IN EXILE

> Freedom is the most persistently lingering of desires.
>
> —Haifa Zangana

The Paris-based Arab Surrealist Movement in Exile was formed in the mid-1970s. Its principal founder and spokesperson was the Iraqi poet and agitator Abdul Kader El Janaby (born in Baghdad in 1944). Already a rebel in his teens, and constantly in trouble at school, El Janaby encountered surrealism in 1967 in a U.S. paperback. In his early twenties he translated several dozen African American poems and blues songs, which were published in various Iraqi journals. With the formation of the Arab Surrealist Movement in Exile his socialist political views evolved increasingly toward anarchism, and he developed close ties with surrealist groups in Paris and Chicago. The Arab Group's strident Manifesto—featured in English in *Arsenal*, no. 3—includes these lines:

> We practice subversion twenty-four hours a day. We liberate language from the prisons and stock markets of capitalist confusion.
>
> Our surrealism, in art as in life: permanent revolution against the world of aesthetics and other atrophied categories; the destruction and supersession of all retrograde forces and inhibitions.

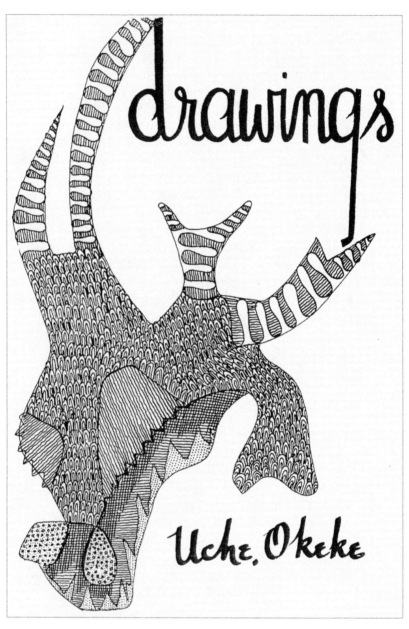

This book of drawings by Uche Okeke was published in Ibadan in 1961.

Subversion resides in surrealism the same way history resides in events.

Its signatories, in addition to El Janaby (which he later spelled Janabi), were Maroin Dib (Syria), Faroq El Juridy (Lebanon), Fadil Abas Hadi (Iraq), Farid Lariby (Algeria), and Ghazi Younes (Lebanon).

For six or seven years this group, aided by the English poet and translator Peter Wood, was a dynamic force in international surrealism. Marxist oriented at first, its decided turn toward anarchism is indicated by the title of its mimeographed magazine, *Le désir libertaire* (Libertarian desire). Political and antipolitical tracts did not, however, dominate the magazine's content. *Le désir libertaire* published poetry by most members of the group, as well as Arabic translations of poems by Joyce Mansour, Benjamin Péret, and several American surrealists. Considerable space was also given to theoretical texts. El Janaby was acquainted with Georges Henein's widow, Ikbal El Alailly, and with her help devoted a special issue to Henein's life and work. His other friends in Paris included surrealists Jean Benoit, Mimi Parent, Ted Joans, Nicole Espagnol, Alain Joubert, Édouard Jaguer, and the Tunisian Situationist Mustapha Khayati.

In addition to the signatories to the manifesto quoted above, the Arab Group attracted a number of other collaborators over the years, most notably the Iraqi writer Haifa Zangana, who was also active in surrealist activity in London. Together with the Arab Group, Zangana also took part in the 1976 World Surrealist Exhibition in Chicago. Author of a harrowing memoir, *Through the Vast Halls of Memory* (1991), she has more recently distinguished herself as an international journalist.[5]

Alas, the Arab group—always prey to bitter factionalism and schism—disintegrated in the early 1980s and completely disbanded not long afterward.

In 1998 A. K. El Janaby published a memoir in French: *Horizon vertical.* Largely devoted to his youth in Baghdad and his involvement in the London hippie scene in the 1960s, the book is sketchy about surrealism generally, and about the Arab group in particular.

NORTHEAST AFRICA: ETHIOPIA

Ethiopia is noted for its many fine painters, but the only one directly associated with surrealism was Alexander (Skunder) Boghossian (1937–2003), who also happens to have been widely celebrated as one of the greatest twentieth-century African artists. During his years in Paris (late 1950s, early 1960s) his friends included Sheikh Anta Diop, André Breton, Wifredo Lam, and Ted Joans.

In later years he taught painting at Howard University and eventually returned to Ethiopia.

SUB-SAHARAN AFRICA

Hundreds of years before the advent of modern art in early-twentieth-century Europe, Africans were making art that not only inspired but actually prefigured such European movements as Cubism, Fauvism, Dada, and Surrealism.

Fauvists and Cubists were chiefly attracted by the formal aesthetic values of African sculpture, and Dadaists by what they regarded as the weird or humorous character of certain masks. The surrealists' interest was substantially broader and deeper. Powerfully moved by the "convulsive beauty" of African art, they were also eager to know more about traditional African thought and ways of life—so very different from the ideologies and lifestyles of an increasingly decadent and imperialist-minded Europe. Above all, surrealists admired the African artists' fervent grasp of the poetic spirit, or, in other words, their impassioned sense of the Marvelous.

In view of their long traditions of stonecutting, wood carving, painting, and other arts, it should not be surprising that African artists in more recent times, and in our time, have continued to produce works in which the triumph of "convulsive beauty" and the Marvelous are very much in evidence. Nor should anyone be surprised by the fact that works by many of these artists—and also by African poets—are frequently recognized as surrealist.

For the record, the first explicitly surrealist exhibition in sub-Saharan Africa opened in Luanda, Angola, in October 1953. It was organized by the Portuguese painter and poet Artur do Cruzeiro Seixas, who lived in Africa for fourteen years. An accompanying two-sided flyer features quotations by Aimé Césaire, André Breton, Mário Cesariny, Lautréamont, Rimbaud, Heraclitus, and Blaise Pascal.

Despite geographical separation and language barriers, people find ways to communicate. Just as contemporary surrealists in Paris, Prague, São Paulo, and Chicago have been able to see and appreciate the art of contemporary Africa, so too many of today's African artists have had opportunities to see work by surrealists from all over the world. In short, the influences are more reciprocal than ever.

Humor in its most imaginative vein retains a strong place in African surrealism. Let three examples of practitioners suffice:

1. The Ghanaian coffin builders who, not so long ago, reinvented the coffin by shaping them into brightly colored automobiles, airplanes,

Drawing (1970) by Ignácio
Matsinhe.

Drawing by Cheikh Tidiane Sylla in *Arsenal* (vol. 4 [1989]).

ships, and—at least once—a giant beer bottle. Smaller models of these coffins are also made as household sculptures;[6]

2. The anonymous creators of a wonderful new literary genre, ferry boat literature: eight-page stapled pamphlets featuring wildly imaginative stories just long enough to read while crossing a river; and

3. The introduction of Bugs Bunny as a motif on dashikis displayed at Chicago's 2006 GhanaFest, as noticed by Surrealist Group member Tamara Smith.

African genius, as expressed in its boundless innovative propensities—in the visual arts as well as poetry—seems to have an intimate affinity with surrealism's quest for a social order based on poetry, love, and freedom.

Most of the poets and artists represented in this section have been directly involved in surrealism, as participants in surrealist exhibitions (Malangatana Valente, Inácio Matsinhe, Cheikh Tidiane Sylla) or collaborators on surrealist publications (Dennis Brutus). Although the South African painter and sculptor Ernest Macomba did not take part in the surrealist movement, he was a cofounder, in Paris in 1948, of the surrealist-influenced European Cobra movement—with Asger Jorn, Jean-Michel Atlan, Corneille, and others, including Macomba's Danish wife, Sonja Ferlov.

Poems by Jean-Joseph Rabéarivelo, an important African surrealist forerunner, have been included at the urging of Dennis Brutus and several surrealist friends.

Notes

1. In addition to other sources noted in this section, I have drawn appreciably on documents on surrealism in Egypt—and elsewhere in Africa—sent to me by Georges Henein's widow, Ikbal El Alailly; the Iraqi writer Abdul Kader El Janaby; Dennis Brutus of South Africa; the French poet and critic Édouard Jaguer; the English painter Conroy Maddox; the Portuguese poet and painter Arturo do Cruzeiro Seixas; and Hédi Abdul Jaouad.

2. Sarane Alexandrian, *Georges Henein*.

3. David Renton, "Georges Henein," 82–103.

4. Breton, interview with Jacqueline Piatier, *Le Monde*, January 13, 1960.

5. Haifa Zangana, *Through the Vast Halls of Memory*. Writings by Zangana, with commentary, are included in Penelope Rosemont, *Surrealist Women*, 364–367, 416–419.

6. "Artists' Killer Coffins Send Dead Out in Style," *Chicago Tribune* (May 8, 2006).

EGYPT

LONG LIVE DEGENERATE ART!

It is well known that modern society looks with aversion on any innovative creation in art and literature which threatens the cultural system on which that society is based, whether it be from the point of view of thought or of meaning.

Such feelings of repugnance are clearly visible in countries of a totalitarian nature, most particularly in Hitlerian Germany, where free art has met with extreme hostility and is now termed "Degenerate Art" by those ignoramuses. Artists from Cézanne to Picasso have been vilified, and the work that is the product of modern artistic genius with its sense of freedom, energy and humanity has been abused and trampled under foot.

We believe that the fanatical racialist, religious and nationalistic path which certain individuals wish modern art to follow is simply contemptible and ridiculous.

We think that these reactionary myths will only serve to imprison thought. Art is, by its nature, a constant intellectual and emotional exchange in which humankind as a whole participates and which cannot therefore accept such artificial limitations.

In Vienna, which has now been abandoned to the barbarians, a painting by Renoir has been torn into pieces and books by Freud have been burnt in the public squares. Works by great German artists such as Max Ernst, Paul Klee, Karl Hoffer, Oskar Kokoschka, George Grosz and Wassily Kandinsky have been confiscated and replaced by worthless National Socialist art.

Similarly in Rome, a committee has recently been formed "for the purification of literature"! It has taken up its duties and has decided to withdraw everything that is "anti-Italian, anti-racist, immoral and depressing."

Intellectuals, artists and writers: Let us stand together and accept the challenge! We must align ourselves alongside this "Degenerate Art," for in such art reposes the hopes of the future. Let us work to support it so that it will prevail against the new Middle Ages which they are trying to resurrect within the heart of Europe.

This statement has been signed by artists, writers, journalists and lawyers. Their names are as follows: Ibrahim Wassily; Ahmed Fahmy; Edouard Pollack; Edouard Levy; Armand Antebi; Albert Isra'il; Albert Cosseri; Kamel al-Telmisany; Alexandra Mitchkovski; Emil Simon; Angelo Paulo; Angelo de Riz; Anwar Kamel; Annette Fadida; A. Politis; L. Galanti; Germaine Isra'il; Georges Henein; Hassan Subhi; A. Rafu; Zakariah al-Azouni (from the Union of Law-

yers); Sami Riyadh; Sami Hanouka; Scalet; Abdul Khaliq al-Azouni; Fatima Na'amat Rashed; Fouad Kamel; Kemal Wiliam; Laurent Salinas; Marcelle Biagini; Marcel Nada; Malanos; Muhammed Saif-al-Doen; Muhammed Nur; Nadif Selair; Hassia; Henri Dumani.
Cairo, December 22, 1938

London Bulletin 13 (1939)

Georges Henein

Son of a Coptic father and an Italian mother, and French-speaking early on, Henein (1914–1973) discovered surrealism as a student in Paris in the mid-1930s. He promptly joined the group and became one of its strongest and most innovative voices. During the next two decades his poems, articles, and stories appeared in *London Bulletin, Clé, VVV, Phases, Edda,* and many other surrealist and revolutionary periodicals.

In 1937 Henein returned to Cairo and founded Art and Freedom, which included surrealists and other radical artists as well as an assortment of miscellaneous rebels and free spirits united by their militant opposition to imperialism and "traditional values." The group, an affiliate of FIARI, organized several major exhibitions featuring the most original painting and photography in Egypt at the time. An especially interesting aspect of these well-attended shows is the fact that a large number of the artists were women.

Meanwhile, Henein, together with his companion, Ikbal El Alailly, the painter Ramses Younane, and others, had also formed the Surrealist Group of Cairo and started a surrealist journal, *Le Part du Sable* (two issues were published). Art and Liberty and the Surrealist Group were also active in strikes and other workers' struggles and not infrequently involved in scrapes with the police.

In 1947 Henein, along with Sarane Alexandrian and Henri Pastoureau, became part of the secretariat of Cause, a Paris-based international bureau of surrealist information and liaison. Unfortunately, various differences with some of the French members led Henein to distance himself from the group around 1950. Even in later years, however, he remained true to his surrealist inclinations and maintained friendly contact with Breton and many others.

During the 1950s he lived mostly in Cairo; in 1960 he moved to Rome, and then went back to Paris, where he edited the magazine *Jeune Afrique* for several years.

Henein was a major inspiration for the Arab Surrealist Movement in Exile during the 1970s and early 1980s. Most of his books have been reprinted, previously unpublished writings have been issued at last, and much of his work has been translated into other languages.

MANIFESTO

I have sown dragons; I reap fleas.
—Karl Marx

At the very time when events are sanctioning the partition of the globe into two unyielding fronts, what should our position be towards Marxist doctrine, which one of these two antagonistic blocks would aim to put into practice?

Our position regarding Marxism is the inverted reflection of that adopted by Marxist groups towards the individual, freedom and the activities arising from literary or artistic creation in general. At the stage that is historically considered as that of the struggle for power, Marxists always pursue a policy of systematic opportunism that consists of taking power soon followed by a change in both tone and purpose, that assumes a character of blatant terror. Indeed, it is of primary importance for the Marxist forces, during the difficult period of struggle for supremacy, to unite the most highly developed elements, the greatest minds, and the most representative intellectuals and writers under one flag. Insidious propaganda and outrageous underhandedness have been put into effect for the sake of this plan, and it has been displayed to all that the rights of the individual, respect for mankind, and cultural heritage could be in no safer hands than that of Marxism in practice.

In short, the new society to whose edification they mean to contribute will provide ample leeway for critical judgment as well as inventiveness. Sad to say, the real facts are far from confirming such claims; indeed, they are nowhere near. Let it suffice to mention that, one century after coming into being, Marxism is the sole economic doctrine which immediately considers blasphemous any critical views or any attempt to criticize it, despite the major upheavals that have affected the face and structure of the modern world, whose interpreter Marxism would be. We do not hesitate to hold this type of "taboo," which has become the "sign of the cross" of so many revolutionaries, as responsible for the foul smell of such wretched infallibility and "infallibilism" pervading the laboratories of both the right and the left and that acts as a common denominator for both Marxist and Fascist parties. The faults of Marxism strike us as being due to a kind of mental rigidity that is unable to adjust to the shifting reality of the world in motion.

Our grievance against Marxism lies not in its leaning towards revolution, but on the contrary, to its taking a starchy, stagnant, reactionary stance towards the revolutionary growth of science and thought. Karl Marx's ideas may have enlightened the nineteenth century, but for us now, we must understand the crises of Western Civilization as a whole, and they are of no more help to us than the philosophies of Nietzsche or Spengler, to name but two of those necessary adventurers who have penetrated to the very depths of our age. And what can be said about the analysis and the forecasts that Marxists so generously conferred on us between 1920 and 1940? What can be said, indeed, other than that they are as far from our historical evolution as what Marxists in power have brought into being, a far cry from the original socialist ideal of the material and spiritual liberation of mankind.

Faced with such an aberrant state of affairs where, every day, we are mired more and more in the ways of lies and "tactics," and faced with such a huge detour from initial principles that we end up back at their beginning source and intention, we proclaim that we consider the individual as the only thing of worth, yet today, seemingly, it is under relentless fire from all sides. We declare that the individual is in possession of largely unexplored inner faculties, the most important of which is imagination armed with the most marvelous powers, an untapped force of vigor and spirit.

The individual against State-Tyranny.

Imagination against the routine of dialectical materialism.

Freedom against terror in all its forms.

"L'Enfance de la chose" (Cairo, 1945), signed Georges Henein, Hassan el
    Telmisany, Adel Amiu, Kamel Zehery, Fouad Kamel, Ramses Younane
Translated by P. Wood

ART AND FREEDOM

> We salute with the greatest sympathy the constitution of the Art and Freedom group in Egypt. Just formed, its objectives are nearly identical to ours, as the following statutes indicate.

On January 19, 1939 a group was constituted, under the name Art and Freedom. Its objectives are:

a) The affirmation of cultural and artistic freedom;

b) To promote awareness of works, individuals, and values, knowledge of which is indispensable to understand the present time;

c) To maintain a close contact between the youth of Egypt and current
literary, artistic, and social developments around the world.

Clé (February 1939); translated by Marjolijn de Jager

HOT JAZZ

Before saying what hot jazz is, we should first say what it is not. Hot jazz is
not dance music. It is not cacophony. It is not snobbery. It is not folklore.
Thus, it is not any of what people suppose it to be and in the name of which
denounce it.

To me it seems permissible to make the distinction between two kinds of
musical creation. An arrested creation, a continuous creation.

There is "arrested" creation when a composer finishes a given work that is to
remain immutable within the established course.

The composer's work then begins to live according to his will and his will
only. The performer or the orchestra that plays it does not interpret it but re-
constructs it the way its author thought of it. We are in the presence of a single
creation, frozen in time at the moment that the composer finishes his work, and
respected from that moment on.

In contrast, let us imagine a given musical theme. The theme itself already
constitutes a first creation. Then an artist arrives who, instead of faithfully keeping it as is, distorts, folds, multiplies, and improvises on it in such a way that
he fuses his own active personality to that of the composer. Here we have a
continuous creation. Continuous because the score, which is an order, sees
itself replaced by the freedom to improvise, that is to say the freedom to create
as often as the different sensitivities, originalities, in a word, different tempera-
ments require it.

Hot jazz is actually a direct assault that engages your senses and pulls them
into an exquisite and furious embrace with the sound. It is a shortcut. We are
left with the memory of an irresistible aggression after listening to Louis Armstrong's "Tiger Rag," whose final chorus consists of a single plaintive note, alter-
nately repeated by the brass and the saxophones in a swelling rage.

Un Effort, no. 54 (May 1935); translated by Marjolijn de Jager

BETWEEN THE EAGLE'S NEST AND THE MOUSE-TRAP

Overcoming contradictions is our perennial problem and their existence seems
precisely for the purpose of being overcome. In a time like ours which, I fear,
will remain one of stasis, one must live with contradictions. And as if contra-

dictions inherited from the past weren't enough, I'd swear main activity of our contemporaries is without purpose other than to create new ones.

To the world it seems as if "knowledge" and "freedom" were terms of opposition. The fantastic advances achieved in science and knowledge should give wings to humanity and its development, but a brief glance reveals the reverse is true and mankind is rigid, standing chained in endless unhappy rows. Ours is a strange century—part eagle's nest and part mouse-trap; in this century man has finally persuaded himself that he knows too much to be free.

Utopias wither in the shadows of manifestoes. Recall the cover of *La Révolution Surréaliste* illustrating a quote of Engels:

"What these gentlemen lack is Dialectics!"

Today, it is possible to say, Aragon and Sartre have truly abused Dialectics. The triple beat of this Hegelian waltz seems designed to bring all strong persons to the brink of catastrophe.

I have already declared and I still maintain that surrealism should withdraw onto the Aventine and leave the century's hawkers to unload their trash in the world's market.

I believe that if a true closed and secret group is not possible, a discrete society should be created, unpretentious and yet exclusive, which could forge its own desires.

Through its use of the disrupted image, the image transformed, surrealism expanded seeing: seeing beyond the immediate, beyond words, beyond the blind-alleys where mankind stands rotting. It is this ability that we must abandon or exercise without limit. So much the worse if poetry is slow to be made by all. At least, let it be lived by some!

Cairo (Winter 1957); translated by Rachel Blackwell

PERSPECTIVES

To André Breton

why not encounter a woman with cantering eyes on a footbridge suddenly cast between two catastrophes who would give you her name that is more beautiful to plunge into than a precipice cloaked in black fabrics?

why not arrange immense sunsets of multicolored hair on the always-deserted stage of the horizon?

why not enhance mountain slopes with radium-sexed creatures who would become one with the landscapes and burn them with each embrace and remain alone in a vertiginous limpidity?

why not in a single blow release the myriad of mirrors nailed to the bedside of the earth?

why not render life fit for habitation?

why not abandon customary flesh and sufficiently experienced destinies?

why not avert the eyelids from cursed roads and vanish into the most insoluble night taking along for all future time the body of an unknown woman chopped into minuscule bits by a dream to be honed without the risk of waking up?

Déraisons d'être, translated by Marjolijn de Jager

JACQUES VACHÉ—NOT A RUN-OF-THE-MILL ADJUTANT

On Monday January 6th 1919, around 6 P.M., were discovered in a room of the Hotel de France, in Nantes, the completely naked bodies of two young people. They had succumbed to toxic poisoning through having taken an overdose of opium. One of the victims was called Jacques Vaché, 23 years of age, an adjutant in the squadron of the army service corps.

This man, who has left practically no written trace of his passing on earth, who, in fact, never had the opportunity of giving his full measure, he whose personality can be imagined only in a sense beyond measure, must be held as one of the most remarkable originators of the Surrealist spirit, of a keen *humor,* the career of which is only just beginning. An unconscious originator, it goes without saying, since his death preceded by several years the publication of the *First Manifesto of Surrealism,* and since he always behaved as if nothing of himself was meant to survive and cast light. Some will speak of unpretentiousness and forget all the pride that such a difficult attitude implies.

There is in Jacques Vaché a great concern to keep himself pure while befouling the world.

There is in Jacques Vaché a grandiose contempt for self-satisfied literature and litterateurs satisfied with their literature.

There is in Jacques Vaché a taste, nurtured at great expense, for the gratuitous act, a feel for the gratuitous which leaves Lafcadio way behind in his railway carriage.

This shooting-star suddenly stopped in motion by its immense reflection in modern poetry is Jacques Vaché. This *h*-less one of pure blood superbly embodied in a single being and remaining faithful to him until his death is Jacques Vaché.

Of his *War Letters,* published by Sans Pareil in 1919 through the personal attention of his friends, must be spotlighted the admirable design for the future, which constitutes the famous letter of November 14th, 1918.

. . . I shall come out of the war slightly, or maybe quite doddering, just like those splendid village-idiots (and I do hope so) . . . or else . . . what a film I shall play in—with crazy motor-cars, you know what I mean, bridges collapsing, and outsize hands groping for I wonder which document . . . with such tragic dialogues, in evening-dress, behind the eavesdropping palm.—And then, of course, Charlie, rictussing unblinkingly. The cop hiding in the trunk, forgotten.

And further on this shimmering of un-encountered nostalgias.

I shall be just as well a trapper, or a robber, or a prospector, or a hunter, or a miner, or a driller. Arizona Bar (Whisky-Gin and Mixed?) and lovely timber-forests, and you know those lovely riding-pants with their six-shooters, going together with being well-shaved, and such lovely hands wearing diamonds. It will all end up with a fire, I tell you, or in a saloon with fortune made.

Talking of making fortunes, Jacques Vaché once had the touching cynicism of speaking to André Breton about being successful in the grocery business. But to this mock suicide, it was inevitable that he should come to prefer the real thing. His excess of *Umour*, for want of a foothold in a valid reality, could lead him nowhere else.

. . . My present dream is to wear a red sports-shirt, a red scarf, and high boots—and be a member of a Chinese secret society with no objective in Australia.

The daily spectacle of the war inspires Jacques Vaché with short, dry comments in which the richest vein of Alfred Jarry turns up once more.

I am with the English soldiers—they have advanced on the enemy staircase a great deal around here. There is a lot of noise—I am very bored behind my glass-monocle, put on khaki and hit the Germans—The brain-blowing machine cranks forward and I have, not far away, a tank-stable—quite a unique but joyless animal.

And, in conclusion, this categorical declaration:

I object to being killed in war-time.

It is not for no reason that in his "Confession of Contempt," one of the most heart-felt texts that Surrealism has ever given us, André Breton reserves for Jacques Vaché pride of place, a high-lighted place.

I owe most of all to Jacques Vaché . . . without him I should perhaps have become a poet; he thwarted in me this intrigue of dark designs which has one believe in something as absurd as a vocation. I am fortunate, in turn, in not being blind to the fact that many young writers today do not have the slightest literary ambition. They "publish" to search out others, and nothing more.

Jacques Vaché was not inexperienced in drugs. He knew full well what he was doing on the evening of January 5th, 1919, when he took forty grams of opium at one go.

And now that, on both sides of certain sign-posts, the frailty of which will eventually yield to mankind's desire for fraternity, now that men are once more beginning to serve causes they have not chosen, it is with pleasure that we hail in Jacques Vaché the paragon of the objector *per se*, the apostle of moral obstruction in a chaos, as ignoble as it is uninhabitable, — the coolest and most elegant of the terrorists of the new persuasion.
Cairo, February 1940

Don Quichotte, no. 7 (January 1940); translated by Myrna Bell Rochester (original emphasis)

THE PLAIN TRUTH

For Iqbal

I speak to you because the night
never falls all by itself
I speak to you because the night
is an object found
coins of the stars
the trapeze missed
by the acrobat in a flowered dress
a mad object at your sensible feet
the finery of the woman passerby whom the police takes away
a mouth to be fed
a mouth to be hollowed out with a cry
the black glass screen in which the painter's colors rise up
I speak to you because the night
shimmers with a thousand disregarded balconies
some located on the threshold
others beyond any possible possessions
I speak to you because the night
was created by dreams

and not just to dream
I speak to you from a booth that is deaf to all messages
the whitewashed receiver tows bedewed lianas
an existence more marvelously misunderstood than words
I speak to you because the night
is at one and the same time
the black glass screen of magic
and the finery of that woman they take along in vain
and that phantom-booth stranded in the forest
and something more
than time to be deceived
and silence up for sale.

Le signe le plus obscure; translated by Myrna Bell Rochester

A TRIBUTE TO ANDRÉ BRETON
PROSE THAT SHINES ABOVE ALL OTHERS

André Breton is dead. This poet who gave us the prose that shines above all others lived in the fragile and sorrowful intransigence of souls in love with the morning dew. He ever refused to submit to the petty dictates of society. He never settled with the forces of decomposition. He was the last Druid, emerging from the forest to declaim the brilliance of the world. In the rat's maze of our present where only the cheesy psychology of the peddlers of leisure wins out, he appeared as the provocateur of accomplishments, as one who ceaselessly demanded more; as one who tired only of slaves.

Jeune Afrique, no. 300 (October 7, 1966); translated by Myrna Bell Rochester

Ikbal El Alailly

Known as "Boula" to her intimates, Ikbal El Alailly was one of the principal figures of the Surrealist Group in Cairo. The granddaughter of Ahmad Chawki, Egypt's "Prince of Poets," she was born to Moslem parents but was already a nonconformist by her teens. Her 1939 meeting with poet Georges Henein was love at first sight. Despite the fact that their parents opposed their marriage, the couple was inseparable thereafter, though they were not legally married until 1954.

Active in the Cairo surrealists' daily meetings at Tommy's Bar, she collaborated on the group's publications and coorganized its collective exhibitions. Her best-known work is the big anthology of German Romantic and other presurrealist writings, *Vertu de l'Allemagne* (1945), to which she also contributed an important preface.

After Henein's death in 1979, Boula—then living in Paris—undertook the task of publishing his uncollected works and reprinting those that had gone out of print. She also encouraged and assisted the Paris-based Arab Surrealist Group and (via correspondence) maintained friendly relations with the surrealists in Chicago.

The text published here originally appeared in *Le Part du Sable*, published by Heinein in Cairo in February 1947.

PORTRAIT OF THE AUTHOR AS A YOUNG RABBIT

And the Bororos think they are blue macaws . . .
—L. Lévy-Bruhl

What a stupid story! The more I think about it, the more I realize how difficult it is to have a peaceful life.

Only five years ago, I was a little white bunny, sporting big whiskers and the most beautiful pair of ears you can imagine.

Only five years ago, I had a friend; he had told me he was an influential member of the animal protection society. That friend knew I was a bunny. He was so aware of it, that without him, I never would have known it myself.

It was he who taught me the proper food for bunnies. They must eat carrots, he told me one day, without elaborating further. And since I wished to reciprocate the interest he took in me, I went ahead and ate carrots, I even learned to like carrots, me who hated them so.

The next time, he summoned me for a very serious talk. I went willingly, because I liked him. Totally counter to my little bunny mentality, I abandoned a goodly number of my small pleasures to answer his summons. But that day, he used a voice I'd never heard before. It reminded me of my father's, gruffly speaking about things that didn't thrill me, but which I was obliged to face up to and to fulfill to live out my fate as a loyal little bunny. Saying, for example, "You must stop dancing, you must stop laughing, you must let things go as they may. A bunny is a bunny and if you try to explain this fact any other way, the very act turns you into a rebellious bunny."

So I obeyed and he rewarded me, caressing my whiskers, tickling my ears, and offering me a whole field of carrots.

That honeymoon didn't last long. After a few weeks of this grand bunnyness, he declared he was emperor of China. And, said he, an emperor, the emperor of China, could never compromise himself with a bunny. I absolutely had to change my skin, or else . . . woe is me!

Translated by Myrna Bell Rochester

POST-SCRIPTUM

"Once upon a time there was someone who didn't like the past and who found that once was not enough." Once there was a night. That night had strange noises. It was, perhaps, very beautiful . . . There were locusts, crickets, and the oh-so-gentle spirits that passed through, crying. A big star waited in the sky. All over the world there were also many men and many women. But those men and those women, and that night, and those crickets had stopped believing in the brilliance, that is to say, in the madness of men. And that is why they were all so sad.

They no longer wished to hear speak of Fervor, of Love, or of Truth. The Madness of God left them indifferent; moreover, they no longer believed in God. And that is why they were all so mournful.

Comfortably despairing, they had become very ugly; and as though to explain themselves, they repeated endlessly: "We are Good, we are Just . . ." and many other phrases we know too well . . . "Oh my brothers, one day someone looked into the heart of the Good and the Just, and he said: 'They are Pharisees.' But no one understood him . . . The Good have always been the beginning of the end."

God knew how to find Man's path. But Superman shut himself off from God's path. His refusal, the refusal to make himself into a man-god, is blasphemous only vis-à-vis Man, not vis-à-vis God. Exiled upon the heights of folly, Nietzsche lost his earthly portion. But the patience of the stars is infinite . . .

"And may every day one has not danced at least once be a wasted day—And may every truth that does not provoke a burst of laughter appear false."

La part du sable, translated by Myrna Bell Rochester

Anwar Kamel

An Egyptian poet active in the Trotskyist movement, Anwar Kamel (1919–1973) was one of the principal figures in the Art and Freedom group, to which all the Egyptian surrealists belonged. He was in fact the editor of the Art and Freedom newspaper, *Al-Tattawor*, which billed itself as "the premier review of art and literature in the Arab world." Emphasizing radical opposition to the "reactionary spirit," that is, opposition to fascism, Stalinism, and Arab nationalism, the paper also promoted women's rights, workers' solidarity, modern art, and the short stories of Albert Cossery, a member of the group. We know that Anwar Kamel was still issuing manifestoes in 1952, but his later activities do not seem to be chronicled.

THE PROPAGANDISTS OF REACTION AND US

This magazine has been conceived as a cradle in which the free ideas of youth and their new transformative tendencies can grow and mature and pave the way for the development of this country.

We roar in the face of those who call for a reactionary order and exploitation. We shall continue on our path without attaching any importance to the obstacles that they seek to put in our way. We are convinced that we will sweep away all that exemplifies the most abominable manifestations of exploitation and abuse.

As for those who still insist that we are corrupting people's minds through our ideas, we now announce that if liberating minds from superstition and reactionary myths is corrupt, if liberating people from bondage and slavery is corrupt, then from hereon our mission and message in life is: to corrupt the minds of men.

We desire, and we know what we desire.

Al-Tattawor, no. 5 (May 1940); translated by Judy Cumberbatch

Ramses Younane

Egypt's most renowned surrealist painter, but also an important theorist
and critic, Younane (1913-1966) from 1939 on was closely associated
with Georges Henein in the Surrealist Group in Cairo. A Trotskyist
in the early and mid-1940s, Younane edited *El Magalla El Guidda* (1943-
1945), a paper vehemently and fiercely opposed to English colonialism,
Hitler, and Stalin. In 1947 he took part in two international surrealist
exhibitions: the huge show in Paris, and the somewhat smaller version
in Prague. Although he cosigned the international statement "Rupture
Inaugurale," disagreements regarding certain positions of the French
Group led him, and others in the Cairo Group, to pursue an independent path. Returning to Cairo in 1956, Younane—long since a convinced
anarchist-individualist—found the cultural and political climate increasingly stifling. Still very much a surrealist at heart, he bravely persisted in
his defiant nonconformism in highly unfavorable circumstances.

The paintings of Younane's last decade—which have a lot in common with the work of his Danish contemporary Wilhelm Freddie—are
characterized by a nonfigurative spontaneity that Édouard Jaguer called
abstract-impressionism.

WHAT COMES AFTER THE LOGIC OF REASON?

On a cultural level, the bourgeoisie worked to replace blind faith with rational
analytical reason. But the glorification of reason, insightfulness, and commercial shrewdness molded life into a technological mechanical system that did
not allow for the caprice of imagination and the pleasure of a free spirit. Natural
instincts and deep-seated affections whose nature it was to search for pleasure
were exploited and distorted by commercial battle and competitive struggle
or through the military anthems and hysterical cries which the dictatorial and
colonial governments used to arouse their people.

Bourgeois society now faces a greater crisis than that posed by the issue of
consumption. It is not just a problem of bread, but a crisis of greedy hearts and
hungry, crazed imagination; a crisis of poetry, enjoyment and delirium; a crisis
of movement, growth and openness. A crisis of life.

The values of bourgeois rationalism are unable to rescue us from the crises of
bourgeois civilization. In order to survive and be saved, we must rebel against
these values, rebel against rationalism and go beyond it—not by returning to

servile and humble belief but rather by confirming the right of the liberated, rebellious spirit to triumph over the limits of reason and the chains of faith.

Death is better than life in a world in which work is dissociated from dreams.

Al-Tattawor, no. 5 (May 1940); translated by Judy Cumberbatch

Victor Musgrave

While stationed in Cairo during World War II, young Victor Musgrave (1919–1984) befriended Georges Henein and others in the Art and Freedom group and eventually married one of its active members, the Armenian-born surrealist photographer Ida Kar. In London after the war, he was particularly noted as an art gallery proprietor and one of the first in England to exhibit Outsider Art. This salute to the Cairo surrealists appeared in the journal *La Séance Continue.*

VOICES IN THE TWILIGHT

(A Tribute to Art and Liberty)

Something is happening in the city; there are Voices which make themselves heard above the cacophony of the crowd; they are the Voices of Ramses Younane and Fouad Kamel, green, purple and sombre.
listen: the Cairo of the bourgeois is a magic square bounded by four main streets, ten cinemas and a million vulgar expletives but this is not Egypt.

Look, the crowd continues to march towards a yawning abyss which resembles in shape the bowl of a water-closet. Slowly, unable to save themselves they slide down into its depths, filling the spongy violet air with ludicrous cries and shouts until in a few minutes they have all disappeared and nothing remains except a few hair-pins, wooden legs, pawn tickets, cinema tickets, false teeth and hair, pages from intimate diaries, photographs of sweethearts, Christmas presents and children's toys. Soon, however, these were all destroyed by an unexploded bomb which went off suddenly.

Once the crowd had disappeared it could be seen that the road they had been following was lined with huge reproductions of the works of Telmisany, Ramses Younane, Fouad Kemal. . . . etc. . . . which had offered their mute message unnoticed. Had a solitary observer remained in the absence of the crowd it must have seemed to him that their eloquence was overwhelming.

In the distance the sound of another large crowd approaching could be heard.

Albert Cossery

A member of the Art and Freedom group in Cairo, Cossery (1913–2008) cosigned the Egyptian surrealist tract "Long Live Degenerate Art!" (1938) and collaborated on the group's various journals and newspapers. After World War II he moved to Paris and began writing in French. Introduced to the English-speaking world by Henry Miller, Cossery is best known for the short stories collected in *Men God Forgot* (1946), and his novels, including *The Lazy Ones* and *The House of Certain Death*. Reprinted here is a selection from the latter book.

THE HOUSE OF CERTAIN DEATH

They disappeared in the dust, as if they had been snatched away by the hands of invisible giants. Automobiles, carriages and donkey carts sped pell-mell in every direction. People and things were urged on by a synthetic animation that pushed them toward the broad horizons of their daily misery. Kites, on the lookout for food, soared in the darkening air. A group of anemic children was playing near a grass plot which was hedged in by barbed wire. Among them was the little naked boy who had come to fetch Abdel Al, the teamster. The unlucky child did not dare to go home. Having come across some children who were playing, he joined them, waiting for nightfall. He was still terribly naked, except for a rag which he had picked up and knotted around his neck, and which somehow made him seem more respectable.

The Lazy Ones, a novel by Albert Cossery, Egyptian surrealist, was published in 1949.

Joyce Mansour

Widely renowned as the best-known woman surrealist poet, Joyce Mansour (1928–1986) is also — second only to Georges Henein — the most
celebrated surrealist of Egyptian origin. Born in England, the daughter
of Sephardic Jews, Mansour grew up in a family that spoke a mixture of
English and Judeo-Spanish dialect, with more than a touch of Arabic.
From the 1950s on she lived in France, mostly in Paris. She was a central
figure in the Surrealist Group, a prolific contributor to the group's publications, and hostess of many surrealist gatherings. Her poetic genius,
characterized by a unique erotic intensity and wild humor, was greatly
admired not only by André Breton and other surrealists, but also by
such figures as Gaston Bachelard and Henri Michaux.

FLOATING ISLANDS

Later on, towards morning, I am on a beach surrounded by persons of both
sexes. A turbulent cloud advances in the same way as a race-elephant. General
hysteria. I next find myself sitting on S.'s knee in an old black car. Very tall
car, and very black. (My grand-mother possessed a similar model, but hers
was red.) The cloud advances without ceremony on the sands and among the
dunes: "The abyss summons up the abyss," says a curious voice entwined in
the hollow of my ear. I think I see the spirit of Théophile Gautier prancing on
the shore. Someone throws a buoy or a seagull in the direction of the old machine. The cloud returns to the fore. I vainly attempt to close the rear-window
of the motor-car. I operate the pre-war window-winder, my breasts quiver and
churn butter under my blouse. S. sings a few verses of his own invention. I
operate the window-winder (S.'s member?), the window closes stiffly; S. sings
and the glass drops, leaving an aperture of approximately two inches. The cloud
comes bellying along. It invades the whole scene. To me its whiteness seems ex-
cessive, unhealthy. I try more successfully, to keep the window fastened tight. I
now realize with horror that S. is sitting on the car-roof: only his legs dangling
like ham-shanks (hams, phallic reminder) remain inside. The cloud envelops us.
It is both inside and out. The road dissolves beneath my eyes and the car-wheels
sink down in the mire. In the snot. The legs fall onto the front seat like parentheses (prostheses?). I wake up. One can say, "Open parentheses. Let's open
our legs-cum parentheses; judge the tree by its roots, the dawn rather than the
defunct day. . . ." "You sound like a prostitute," said my father.
　A year after transcribing this dream I read the following in "Le violoncelle

qui résiste," by Pierre Bourgeade. P.B.: "I am on top of a mountain. I look down at the clouds below. They rise. When they reach me, I shall die. They are not really clouds but a sort of gas. I cannot escape. They rise. They reach me. I awake." Now I remember: this fragment is part of a discussion I had with Pierre Bourgeade in 1970. It was published in the *Quinzaine littéraire,* and reappears today with twelve similar texts in book-form. I had totally forgotten the contents of the interview, the dream likewise; to the point of repeating it, image for image, without recognizing it as belonging to another. Plagiarism or pantaloonery?

Histoires nocives, translated by Peter Wood

FRESH CREAM

My mother eats me
Tortures me
And to prevent me from following her
She buries me
I eat my family
I spit on their remains
I hate their tightrope diseases
And their ear hallucinations
Be careful of toothpaste
That bleaches without destroying
It is wiser to have fun by devouring one's own people
Than to walk on all fours
To drink
Or try to please
Girls

Shrieks, translated by Peter Wood

FORTHWITH TO S

All this because I like to make love under water
Pommade my hair with fog and bile
And let myself sink deep into the couch
With a hunchbacked ostler
And a finger of wanderlust
All this because you know I was once a thief

Shrieks, translated by Peter Wood

NORTH EXPRESS

Cobra is the night image of a Chinese water-print
Cobra ignited by moonlight
Unfurls as does the sea
On beaches black with mountain ash
And oblique corridors
Eyes behind goggles
Asphalt hells
The nettlegrown quarrels of the cultural owl
Subside
Cobra swallows Cobra as desire
Desire
Far from the shallow sex of habit
Far from the empty port of mechanical rape
Through the blazing hiccups of volcanic mirth
Into the foxglove
The very heart of panic
Rides Pierre Alechinsky and his left-handed mirror
Qui vive?
Cobra

Shrieks; translated by Peter Wood

RESPONSE TO AN INQUIRY ON MAGIC ART

I. Recently it has been said that "civilization has dissipated the fiction of magic only to exalt, in art, the magic of fiction." Do you agree with this judgement?

   Response: The distinction between the fiction of magic and the magic of fiction is for me, a sophism. Art and magic are but two artificially differentiated terms, designating the same means of communication with the incommunicable. Traditional art is magic in action, and its message: the seemingly artistic expression of contemporary materialism is but the sensation of magic filtered through the artist's intellect. The difference between magician and modern artist resides in this: the former sought to accumulate external forces *en-soi* while the latter, a victim of dispersion, limits himself to "finding relief." Their main thread is well and truly the same, the search for spiritual expansion.

In André Breton, *L'Art magique;* translated by Cynthia Hahn

MOROCCO

Robert Benayoun

Benayoun (1928-1996) was born in Port Lyautey, Morocco, and met André Breton and the Surrealist Group in Paris in 1949. He remained one of the most active and productive members of the group. With the assistance of Ado Kyrou, Georges Goldfayn, and Gérard Legrand, he started (and served as editor of) *L'Âge du Cinéma*, a surrealist film magazine (six issues, 1951-1953). A regular collaborator on the group's successive journals—*Médium, Le Surréalisme, même, BIEF, La Brèche,* and *L'Archibras,* he was also the author or editor of important books, including his classic *Anthologie du nonsense* (1959), *Erotique du surréalisme* (1965; expanded 1979); a full-length study of the balloon in comic strips; and several books relating to film animation, Buster Keaton, John Huston, the Marx Brothers, Woody Allen, and Tex Avery.

His perfect command of English made him a first-rate translator of— among others—Edward Lear's poems, Charles Fort's *Book of the Damned,* and Ted Joans' *Black Power.* He was also the Surrealist Group's main correspondent with the "Anglo-Saxon" world.

As the texts translated here demonstrate, Benayoun is noted for his playfulness, sense of mystification, and lively humor.

NO RHYME FOR REASON!

In the Okefenokee Swamp an absurd poetry contest is staged between an earthworm and an alligator; a self-taught cow does not know how to moo; a dog takes himself for a cuckoo. Genus and species yield wholly to a carrousel of errors and defiances, formally contradicting Buffon at every turn.

Such is the climate of *Pogo,* written and drawn by Walt Kelly, one of the rare comic strips to win the recognition of being published in book form. Edward Lear, whose spirit pervades the series from beginning to end (preoccupied as he was, long before Magritte, by the relation of word and image), would certainly have appreciated such manifestations as these, further enhanced by a graphic sense worthy of the best nonsensical doodlers.

Médium/Informations Surréalistes, no. 8 (June 1953); translated by Myrna Bell
   Rochester

THE OBSCURE PROTESTS

The game's activity, one day we will realize it, can be a big push in the universe: it allows children to resist the corrupting reasoning of adults; it's up to the artist to suppress his artistic outbursts, up to the oppressed to fool the tyrant's watchfulness. Such are the colonized black peoples. Yesterday, Jean Rouch showed us in *Moi un noir* (Me a Black Man) and in *Les Maîtres-fous* (The Crazy Masters) how a split personality, the adoption pure and simple of a borrowed personality, either fictitious (a film star), or real (preferably from dominating categories: the governor, the police chief) could help a colonized man to get by, all the while mimicking and exorcising the wretched defects of the white man.

It is now up to Lionel Rogosin, an American filmmaker, that the honor returns to in *Come Back Africa*, a film clandestinely made in South Africa, that paraded before us the silent cortege of secret societies, false religions, spontaneous movements, fictitious cults, non-ritualistic dances, mirror games, fortune music, in short, the little voodoo of indistinct places and what he overcomes, concisely, the terrible stress of the transplanted person, bound and shamelessly exploited by an imposter of treacherous sciences.

In the enslaved there is, despite all the abuse committed on his spontaneity, a capacity for wonderful things, a gift of confidence and physical joy that will assure his final victory over the barbarous techniques, as well-proven as they are. The Schlemils' schizophrenia is not the unique privilege of the Semitics, his innocent compensations are as dark, and innocence does not exclude lucidity (assured by intuition), more than lucidity knows how to exclude anger. Let's be merciful to Rogosin: in the end he lets the anger speak, an invading anger, a dark indignation, almost sensual, one that is necessary for the revolutions of tomorrow.

Genêt, enslaved by poetry, spoke to us through his incantation of the fatal sensation of an adequate absorption of light through the obscure. But it is to Rogosin that I give credit, with an avenging satisfaction, in Sophiatown in front of Johannesburg, of an immense protest by the obscure.

BIEF, no. 10–11 (February 1960); translated by Melanie Kemp

LETTER TO CHICAGO

Paris, the 13th of February, 1963

Dear Franklin Rosemont,

André Breton asks me to answer you in his place, since his command of the English language is practically nonexistent.

Your letter was very encouraging to us, and you must excuse the delay in our answer, due to several grave affairs, which have completely engrossed us.

As you know (from J. H. Matthews's report in *Books Abroad*) we are publishing right now a review called *La Brèche*, the fourth number of which is due in the next couple of weeks. We also publish tracts and booklets, a few occasional columns in left-sided weeklies like *France-Observateur*, and hold occasional exhibitions, collective and individual.

The group includes mostly young people from nineteen to thirty-five years old, the only "elder" being Breton himself. We are about twenty "regulars," meeting every day in the same café to discuss and organize things. But we have many satellite members, like André Pieyre de Mandiargues, Julien Gracq, Matta, Man Ray, Bellmer, Octavio Paz, Leonora Carrington; friends like Arp, Miro, Lam, et al., who join us in occasional declarations, manifestoes, or exhibitions.

In England the only two surrealists left from *London Bulletin* are Jacques B. Brunius and E.L.T. Mesens. They tell us that they hope to publish a new bulletin, but it seems they have practically no support.

In the states, you should contact poet Claude Tarnaud, who's been living in New York for several years and has our total confidence (250 Riverside Drive, New York 25). Calas is our very good friend, but Tarnaud has closer contacts with us.

The political attitude of the movement is still very marked, even though we do not associate with any parties. We have been publishing a political paper called *Quatorze juillet* [July Fourteenth], which ceased to appear after the big affair of the Manifesto of the 121. We are proud to be the initiators of that very important manifesto, which indicted French torture in Algeria, advised insubordination in the army, and demanded immediate negotiations. It impressed DeGaulle so much that he smothered every act of repression against us and bowed to what amounted to be the judgment of the French intellectuals, a judgment he could not afford to neglect. We are sure that without this act of open defiance, and the acclaim it received in foreign countries, DeGaulle would have pursued the war, since he repeatedly sabotaged all peace talks.

We were at that time persecuted by the police, and received death threats from the fascist underground movement called O.A.S. Now the Gaullist government claims that he enforced peace in Algeria, which is a derision. Now that DeGaulle deals with Franco and offers to "deliver" the Spanish refugees (see the enclosed tract), we hope it will be clear that under a thin mask of liberalism, DeGaulle is still the tyrant and dictator he never ceased to be.

How far has your project gone, concerning *Arsenal?* We look forward to it, and think a renewal of the *International Bulletin* a very opportune gesture.

Right now it would be possible to promote several foreign numbers—such as English, Belgian, Italian, Mexican, and American numbers—which could be rewarding.

Breton still receives regularly letters and communications from the world over, but it is very difficult, first, to answer every one, and second, to shape all this into a meaningful panorama. Our best hope lies precisely in the organization of national centers, which would group all individual activities.

What is the extent of your Chicago group? Tell us more about your activities and orientation. Unfortunately, you will have to read our contributions in French, since practically all we do is published in Paris, and has not been translated. I will send you *La Brèche 4* and the first three numbers.

The poem you sent us received sympathetic appreciation.

We are happy to see that subversive thought keeps everywhere its power of impact.

Very fraternally yours,
Robert Benayoun

THE PHOENIX OF ANIMATION

Animation, in principle, has no other plastic imperative than movement. Stills from the most beautiful animated films are as deceptive, as little representative of the original, as are stills from a film by Resnais. When certain critics write, therefore, that the animated film is not cinema, they commit the same error as so many neophytes who imagine, once they have used an animation stand to shoot a number of free forms in the act of moving, that they have made a *film*. They treat the genre as if it were a kind of annex to the beaux-arts, an after-dinner amusement. But if an animated film is made to be projected in a hall, its images registering at 24 per second on the retina, it surely constitutes a film. An animated film made without traveling shots, without pans, without cuts or other cinematic grammar, without dramatic progression, would not only be a ludicrous anachronism but would also be as silly as those dance films which record a beautiful ballet with deadly stolidity—and in so doing betray the spirit of dance as well as that of film.

The great artists of animation seem to be distinguished very clearly from the experimenters. Art in animation begins at that moment when the "experimental" phase ends, and *freedom* ensues.

Film Quarterly (Spring 1964) (original emphasis)

TOO MUCH IS TOO MUCH

(An unperformable play)

The stage shows King Arthur's palace at Camelot as imagined by a colorblind Pygmy of the Demi-Sikkim.

Refrigerators, paper pots, and sibyls in overalls.

Enter VARECH: He is dressed in the uniform of a greedy asparagus eater but we understand at first sight that this charming young man is actually a shoe tycoon in Sunday dress at breakfast time. He sits down in a chair, making it clear that he is thinking of the future. His dog, TRICOT, played by a person with liver problems in a chimpanzee costume, crouches down beside him and cleans his nails with a conceited look.

TRICOT: May I scratch my left ear?

VARECH (nodding yes): No.

They both freeze in position, their eyes vacant. It is very obvious that VARECH has just made the irrevocable decision to cut off any support for his son RROYCE, a Cévennes landscape artist whom he adores but whose painting is annoying to TRICOT. The latter, having been hired by Metro-Goldwyn-Mayer to play the role of the *Dog of Flanders* in a production by Dreyer, obviously has not memorized his lines and is considering a nervous breakdown.

These two cerebral storms can be worked as discreet stage business that goes on for forty minutes in absolute silence, barely interrupted by the hesitant requests for explanation from a music-loving woman in the audience who thinks she is at the Salle Pleyel.

VARECH (racking his brains): Was it Crémone of Escarcelle? Calixte of Moyeu? Obole of Arlincourt? Gertrude Pronoun? Clotilde of Inverness? Bundle of Plethora? Fetters Lagrenaille? Daisy Tsé-Tsé? Giberne of Hévéa? Agnes of Babiole? Moufle Dumdum? Aumone of Muscat? Adorée Madrépore? Oeillére of Alcali?

The audience walks off with the CURTAIN.

La Brèche (December 1964); translated by Marjolijn de Jager

COMIC SOUNDS

gnook, sploop, whop, pock, pfff, ugh, humpf, kablowie, shooie, drip, aaugh, sniff, whack, augh, smooch, goo, snort, bam, berk, thud, pounce, zowie, gnish, buzz, rowf}, woof} which are synonyms, *et arf}, smack, blap, yipe, thonk, tsk, zoop, urk, ow, poof, boot, ouch, blub, snore, clink, eeeek, scoop, glomp, vop, bash, bonk, slurp, oww, vroosh, flutter, clang, chop, screech, zip, burp, zonk, boffo, glug, sob, wham, splat, pok, bawoing, koff, plomp, gasp, drool, whew, hoot, skid, blat, whiz, zak, whap, socko, ping, biff, pow, boof, bing, pant, tickle, bonk, slam, tag, aargh, shazam, pat, clomp, klunk, crack, zap, swat, va-voom, unghn, bang, vroom, swish, klunk, thwap, slobber foom*

Vroom, Tehac, Zowie

Abdellatif Laâbi

Born in Fes, Morocco, the sixth child in a family of eight, Abdellatif Laâbi (1942–) was the founder and chief editor of the Maghrebian journal *Souffles* (Breaths) in the 1960s—a publication very much in the spirit of *La Révolution Surréaliste* and its many successors. The prologue in the first issue of *Souffles* reads in part: "Something is brewing in Africa and elsewhere in the Third World. . . . No one can foresee what this ex-prelogical thought will give to the world. But when the true spokespersons of these collectivities really begin to hear their own voices, it will amount to a dynamite explosion in the old humanism's rotting mysteries." For such pronouncements, *Souffles* was banned in 1971. A year later Laâbi was arrested for "crimes of opinion" and sentenced to ten years in prison. Released in 1980—amnestied after years of international protest about his case—he now lives in exile in France.

The following text is excerpted from his novel, *Rue du Retour* (1982).

RUE DU RETOUR

A footstep behind the door. Did someone knock? A feeling of having been here before. That January dawn almost a decade ago hovered in the silence and half-shadow of the room. A menace which has been since then an integral part of your metabolism. You're so used to it you do not even react physically. But you react by shriveling inside and straining to listen. It's the same reaction as that of a wild animal who senses its lair is surrounded and whose eyes swivel around in its dark den-like sentinels.

Your eyes renew their pillaging. The ceiling of this room is no higher than that of your cell. You start to look at the patches of damp to pick out or imagine shapes, outlines, animal silhouettes or geographers' maps. There, a small poodle stands on its hind legs and here, the southern tip of Africa flanked by the island of Madagascar; further off a pattern that resembles a Rorschach test.

You are now falling back on one of the many habits you learned in prison. The prisoner and the ceiling of his cell. A silent, secret dialogue. . . .

TUNISIA

Farid Lariby

Of Algerian nationality, Farid Lariby (1937–1990) was born in La Marsa, Tunisia, and later lived in Tunis. He moved to France in 1956 and for ten years worked there as a journalist, painter, and poet. In 1973 he cofounded—with comrades from Iraq, Lebanon, and Syria—the Paris-based Arab Surrealist Movement in Exile and collaborated on its periodical, *Le Désir Libertaire*. With others in the Arab Group, he took part in the 1976 World Surrealist Exhibition in Chicago.

Two memorial pamphlets of his poems, *Hâter l'exigence* (Hasten the urgency), and *Homage a Farid Lariby* (with an introduction by Michel Lequenne) were published in 1990.

POME BRUT

Here we stand without outrage rigged up in black powers
Masters of resurrections that wriggle into the winds
Strangling your gray promenades
And the debris of the fatal poem
Here we stand without grandiloquence facing the sinuous suns
absent the guardian of symbols
We unfurl the reddest the blackest Ocean
without a flag
Daylight pause on our lips
And hyphenated flesh and world

Graduate the number of the crossed expectation
in this successive song
And prepare yourself prepare yourself for the treks
For the long treks into the surrealist void

I lean back against the forest of eyes harsh with realities
and ashes against the poem-fire-wheel torpedoing
a beam of mineral numbers in the vast night
Against the notch of history
Or nothing for an imaginary life in the routine

of refuting the last contradictory beasts
Oh my accomplices—not to prove—but to hasten
the urgency
For on the threshold of the expanse fiction is red Space radiated by the winds
    of written desire
the imprecise peace of births
the game's triumph over the road's wheel
For we will emigrate laughing souls
with the sounds of music
We will emigrate into the intense logic
of our nerves
A swarm of new stars will sparkle in the inlets
of violent nights

Hâter l'exigence, translated by Myrna Bell Rochester

ALGERIA

Henri Kréa

An Algerian poet and revolutionary, Kréa (1933-) collaborated on the
surrealist journal *Front Unique,* published in Milan in 1960. His first book
was *Liberté première* (1957). *Revolution and Poetry Are One and the Same Thing*
(1960) opens with an anticolonialist epigraph by André Breton. Two
of Kréa's other books were illustrated by the Chilean surrealist painter
Matta.

NEVER FOREVER ONCE MORE

We are immortal
We are free
We are unalterable
We are identical

We do not change
We have no reason to change
We are simultaneously
Sky and ocean
Sand and sadness
Salt and joy
We are the tree
We are the plain
We are childhood and sleep
We are immobile
We are in motion
We have multiple dimensions
We are many
We are one
We are two

Eddaz (March 1959); translated by Franklin Rosemont

OH YES

Oh yes the lovely scenery
Lofty appearances
Good breeding
Correctness
Good manners
Distinction
Just the right amount of mineral water
The cold elegance of milk
Hermetically sealed
Oh yes oh yes

Edda 2 (March 1959); translated by Franklin Rosemont

Jean~Michel Atlan

Born and raised in Algeria, the partly Jewish Atlan (1913–1960) lived most of his adult life in Paris. Though never a member of the Surrealist Group, he followed its trajectory and counted several surrealists among his friends. Henri Pastoureau, an important figure in surrealism in the 1930s and 1940s, recalls in his autobiography that it was Atlan, his fellow philosophy student and roommate, who in the early 1930s first urged him to read the *Surrealist Manifestoes.*

A Resistance fighter, Atlan at one point during the Nazi occupation of Paris had himself admitted to the Saint-Anne Hospital as a mental patient. After the war, in 1945, he was briefly associated with Arp, Brancusi, Gertrude Stein, and others in the short-lived Paris/Chicago *Continuity* Group. The following year he illustrated a French translation of Kafka's work. And shortly afterward he was an early and crucial figure in an offshoot of surrealism known as the Cobra movement. His studio on the Rue de la Grande-Chaumière was a favorite Cobra meeting place. Édouard Jaquer was a fellow member of Cobra.

In the first monograph on his work, published in 1950, Michel Ragon emphasizes that Atlan's art is above all African, but also a bold synthesis of the major movements of the first half of the twentieth century: Expressionism, surrealism, and abstraction.

Atlan's celebrated color cries and other innovations made him a major force in Cobra, and he always welcomed the most audacious experimentation, including collective improvisation. "If I get lost in the woods," he once said, "it is only to find the forest."

THE TIME HAS COME TO CALL UP A WORLD

The time has come to elaborate a new language, to invent the forms, to create the shapes, to call up a world of lines and colors with no indebtedness to literature, one which does not resemble what one calls reality, but which constitutes, by itself, a reality.

Can forms hitherto unknown be forced into being?

Is a purely plastic expression possible?

It will gradually be realized that the essential mission of the young school of painting will consist in substituting for the vision of reality the authenticity and reality of vision.

Continuity, no. 2 (1945); translated by Alex Wilder

Baya

Born in Algeria into a poor family of Algerian and Berber ancestry, Baya (1931–1998) was orphaned as a child and raised by her grandmother. She was already painting at the age of eleven, when she was adopted by a French woman. At sixteen she had her first solo exhibition in Paris at the Galerie Maeght, for which André Breton wrote an important preface for the catalog. The following year her terra-cottas attracted the interest of Picasso.

Although unable to read, she also narrated stories that were taken down by a stenographer.

Apart from a ten-year period of inactivity, she continued painting: large gouaches; arabesques in the brightest colors featuring women and children; large birds; musical instruments; and dreamlike landscapes and labyrinths strangely evoking the myths and rhythms of ancient Egypt and Sumer.

Like the story published here, her tales tend to draw on the same magical themes as her paintings.

THE BIG BIRD

Once there was a little girl, and her mother was very wicked. The girl wanted to get married and her mother wouldn't let her.

But one day, a Gentleman came along, and this girl hid him in a hole and put the *djifna* [mortar] on top.

In the evening the mother comes home and she says: "Someone came in here." "No, no mommy, no one came," says the girl.

The mother says: "I'll rub henna on everyone in the house."

Henna is brought, and the girl comes, and the little dog and the cat, the chickens, the rabbits, all the animals, but not the birds, the jars come, the *tadjin* [spoon] comes, even the pitcher and the sieve and the basket.

But the *djifna* doesn't want to move, the Gentleman is underneath. The girl says: "The *djifna* is too old, it can't walk." She took a bit of henna in her hand, and she went and put it on the *djifna* there in its corner.

Pleine Marge, no. 6 (December 1987); translated by Myrna Bell Rochester

Habib Tengour

One of the Maghreb's foremost postcolonial poets, Tengour was born in 1947 in Mostaganem, in eastern Algeria, and has lived ever since in Algeria and Paris. Educated as an anthropologist and sociologist, he has taught at universities in both countries. As his Maghrebian Surrealism manifesto amply shows, humor and playfulness are central to his work, which nonetheless reflects a larger seriousness. This manifesto, for example, subtly makes the point that surrealism—commonly considered of French origin—is in truth a recent European variant of much older Maghrebian traditions and practices.

MAGHREBIAN SURREALISM

During these past twenty years, some Maghrebians in exile have made an act of Relative Surrealism. They could hardly do otherwise: the family was an absence they mourned in front of a postal window, homeland a confiscated identity, and religion an I.O.U.

It is, after all, in Maghrebian Sufism that surrealist subversion asserts itself: pure psychic automatism, mad love, revolt, unanticipated encounters, etc. Always there is a spark of un-conscious Sufism in those Maghrebian writers who are not simply sharp operators—reread Kateb or Khair-Eddine.

Feraoun is surrealist in Si Mohand
Kateb is surrealist in tradition
Dib is surrealist in the *derive*
Senac is surrealist in the street
Khair-Eddine is surrealist in ethylic delirium
I am surrealist when I am not there
Baya is not surrealist, despite Breton's sympathy

Translated by Myrna Bell Rochester

SENEGAL

Cheikh Tidiane Sylla

Painter, poet, and, later, architect, Sylla was born in Senegal, West Africa, and came to the United States as a young man and settled in Milwaukee. Shortly after the 1976 World Surrealist Exhibition in Chicago he came into contact with the Surrealist Group in that city and immediately identified himself with it. He collaborated on the surrealist issues of Paul Buhle's *Cultural Correspondence* (1978 and 1981), *Free Spirits: Annals of the Insurgent Imagination* (1982), and the fourth issue of the Chicago Group's journal, *Arsenal/Surrealist Subversion* (1989). He also took part in the "Surrealism in 1982" group show in Chicago, and over the years has cosigned several surrealist declarations.

After acquiring a degree in architecture, Sylla later moved to Florida, where he eventually opened his own architectural firm. In part because of the press of business, but also because of his geographical distance from his surrealist comrades, he has been less involved in the day-to-day activities of the movement in recent years.

SURREALISM AND BLACK AFRICAN ART

The surrealist aspects of the African way of life, as well as the African implications of surrealism, have tended to be ignored for reasons already touched on. Instead of the alienating dualistic intellectualization that usually defines the headlines of European social practice, black Africans enjoyed the presence of the practice of poetry throughout the totality of their traditional social life. In Africa, that is, the *living experience of surreality* has since prehistoric times enjoyed supremacy over its theoretical justification. In the Western world, however, surrealism is the result of a long philosophical, political, scientific and poetic struggle to recover what the traditional African has never lost.

Against all forms of indifference and misery, surrealism and black African art remain irreducible examples in the development of the complete unfettering of the mind. Surrealism and black African art show that History's last step—the step *beyond* History—coincides with a return to *first principles*, which is also a return to primordial glory, involving nothing less than the systematic and *definitive liberation* of the whole of human society and of Nature itself.

Arsenal/Surrealist Subversion, no. 4 (1989) (original emphasis)

THE SPIRIT OF UNITY—FOR FREEDOM

As a surrealist painter, my art is first to question whatever might be related to the psychic circuit of the mind: a question whose answer is freed from any experience already lived, or any criteria conceived by the social elaboration of our existence. The priority is for a new starting point chosen out of our knowledge by any automatic impulsion to interpret the vibrations of the unconscious.

If the surrealist movement has been the victim of many dismemberments in the past, it is time now to realize the necessity and the imperative of the coherence that must animate the spirit of unity, for the freedom of the mind, and thereafter, of all societies.

Arsenal/Surrealist Subversion, no. 4 (1989)

CONGO

Tchicaya U Tam'si

In a 1970 letter from Africa to the Chicago Surrealist Group, published in the first issue of the journal *Arsenal/Surrealist Subversion*, Ted Joans emphasizes Africa's "marvelous goings-on and creativeness" and adds: "A poet like Tchicaya U Tam'si of Congo B. is just as seriously surreal as thee."

While still in his teens, in 1946 Tchicaya (1931-1988) went to Paris and Orléans to study, escorted by his father, a deputy from what was then called the Moyen Congo. His first book of poems, *Le mauvais sang* (Bad blood) appeared in Paris in 1955, followed two years later by *Feu de brosse* (Brush fire), and by many others. Early on he was identified as a surrealist in the African art and poetry magazine *Black Orpheus*. He was also active in the vibrant political life of the time; during much of 1960, for example, he edited the daily *Le Congo*.

Although his association with organized surrealism was tangential, reviewers—not surprisingly, in view of his extraordinary imagery—frequently describe his work as surrealist.

AGAINST DESTINY

I pulled up my throat with multicolored glass
I wished to kick chance in the pants
my second victory
a little pox on the brain
and I don't know how to save myself
then I dreamt of returning
to my village
with eyes behind dark glasses
and I had to fear my sorcerer

I leaped the sea
with my sensual insomnia

salt fills my head

I must arm my people
against their destiny tonight
in order to name it later
in golden figures
he earned his death
long live love

Selected Poems

MOZAMBIQUE

Inácio Matsinhe

A sheepherder in his native Mozambique, Matsinhe (1945-) took up
painting while still quite young.
    Befriended by the leading figures of the Surrealist Group of Lis-
bon—Artur do Cruzeiro Seixas, Mário Cesariny, Isabel Meyrelles—he
also became well known in Portugal and began exhibiting with the
surrealists. Active in several antiapartheid exhibitions as well as festivals

supporting African liberation movements, he went on to show his work in Holland, Italy, Venezuela, and England. A participant in the 1976 World Surrealist Exhibition in Chicago—where, in addition to his own work, he also showed some pieces done in collaboration with the Lisbon Group—Matsinhe entered into correspondence with the Chicago Surrealist Group and soon was promoting the group's journal, *Arsenal/ Surrealist Subversion* on an extended speaking tour of Africa.

PAINTING AS A CONTRIBUTION TO CONSCIOUSNESS

Macumba, which also lives in my paintings, is a mysterious world inherited by the blacks from their ancestors. It has been passed down from generation to generation, although missionaries and other agents of Portuguese domination have tried to destroy it, along with other rituals of my people. Sexual initiation and education, and much else, have been repressed and subjected to contempt by the white Portuguese colonialists.

I shall continue to paint—as a protest, and as a contribution to the rising consciousness of a people.

Inácio Matsinhe

I BECAME A TORTOISE TO RESIST TORTURE

I paint for my people, but of course these are problems that the world should know about. So I also paint for the world, so they may know the problems of my people.

I am making a political portrait of the suffering of the people in Mozambique, Angola and Guinea: the people oppressed by the Portuguese. I chose this form because I believe this is a form in which I can tell other people of this suffering. I utilize symbols to mark the rage that lives within me.
I have used the tortoise to symbolize the resistance that people have to have to face suffering and the conditions of their lives. In order to resist the oppression they have to become like tortoises, protected by those very big shells.

Marvelous Freedom/Vigilance of Desire, catalog of the 1976 World Surrealist Exhibition

THE SNAKE (A STORY)

On that morning, Thursday, in Xipamanine, a snake was found inside a small barrel of *maheu*.

A porter was going to order the aforementioned drink. "I want a mug of *mahev*, but well-stirred," he said. He stirred. But only pretended. The porter seemed to have some knowledge of the drink. He yelled, "Stir well, mamana." He stirred, but hesitantly. By accident, he touched the snake at the bottom of the barrel that was casting a spell to entice the client and to have the drink filled up more. It appeared at the surface of the drink. The porter screamed: "Snake! Snake! Snake in the *mahev* . . ." The snake fled. And it was disgraced. Everyone who spends the whole morning in Xipamanine drinking *xicajú*, every cocuana who has fun the entire morning selling *nhagane* or whatever, every mamana who crowds Xipamanine buying things, and every molwênes who spends the day picking bananas, robbing the vendor women and picking oranges and rotten mangoes, encircled the snake and filled the place with plaintive screams against its witch-owner. They lambasted it, beat it, threw rocks, sand, in short anything that was handy. But the snake came back after having performed many miracles, such as turning into rectangular objects, hiding in the *mboa, nhagane* leaves, etc.

After these miracles, it returned to its owner and hid inside her blouse.

Noticias L.M. (1963); translated by Danielle Jouët-Pastre and Neil Pischner

ANGOLA

Malangatana Valente Ngwenya

Born in southern Mozambique, where his father was a migratory miner and his mother a tattooist who also sold beads and filled teeth, Ngwenya (1936–) had little schooling as a child. At twelve he left home to seek work in Maputo. While working there as a ball boy at a tennis club, he attended night school and began painting "furiously," as he put it.

In 1963 the Portuguese surrealist poet and painter Artur do Cruzeiro Seixas, then employed at the Museum of Angola, exhibited a large canvas by Ngwenya at the museum. This provocative gesture resulted in Seixas' interrogation by the Salazarist police, but it also brought Ngwenya's work to wide attention. The following year, however, Ngwenya was accused of being associated with the revolutionary

Drawing (1970s) by Malangatana
Valente Ngwenya.

movement FRELIMO (Frente de Libertação de Moçambique; Front for
Liberation of Mozambique) and imprisoned by the colonial police for
two years. After independence he served for four years as a FRELIMO
deputy and later as a member of the Maputo Municipal Assembly.
Around this time his poetry began to appear in *Black Orpheus* and other
periodicals.

Cofounder of the Mozambique peace movement as well as the National Museum of Art, he also initiated an important cultural center in
his native village, Matalana. He has long been recognized as one of
Africa's greatest artists. His paintings, drawings, watercolors, prints,
ceramics, tapestry, and sculpture are included in museum collections
throughout the world. He has also exhibited in numerous gallery shows.
In 1976 he took part in the huge World Surrealist Exhibition at the Gallery Black Swan in Chicago. The poem reprinted here appeared in that
show's catalog, *Marvelous Freedom/Vigilance of Desire.*

SURVIVOR AMONG MILLIONS

I am the survivor among millions
dead from lack of pure air
they were not used to air conditioning
or to the mine that caved in.

They died, died without saying goodbye
buried in this mine
where there is no cackling of hens
where there is nothing but men

The lantern that blew out
left us in the dark
when the mine exploded
and the gods took advantage of us
and demanded some glass beads from us

And since we had no glass beads
we are dead dead dead.
And me I sounded the alarm. I survived
I raised my hands without weeping
or crying for help
and because they were my friends
they let me survive.

Translated by Mary Hardy

Amílcar Cabral

Of the great world revolutionists and strategists of guerrilla warfare in
the 1950s and 1960s, few if any were more deeply affected by poetry
than Cabral (1924–1973), the leader of the movement to liberate Africa's
Guinea-Bissau and the Cape Verde Islands from Salazarist Portugal's
fascist colonialism. A student in the 1940s, Cabral was an impassioned
reader of the works of Aimé Césaire and of Léopold Senghor's anthology of the new black poetry: "Things I had not even dreamed of,
marvelous poetry written by blacks from all parts of the French world,
poetry that speaks of Africa, slaves, men, life and human hopes . . . Sublime . . . infinitely human . . . The book brings me much [including] the
certainty that the black man is in the process of awakening throughout
the world" (Cabral, *Unity and Struggle*).

A poet himself—one who, indeed, identified his very being with
poetry, Cabral affirmed the practice of poetry as an essential part of
what he called the re-Africanization of the mind. Only by freeing the
colonized peoples from imperialist domination, he argued, could they
re-become Africans.

An agronomist by profession, Cabral also developed a profound and radical ecological perspective, rare among the Marxists of his time (or ours).

NATIONAL LIBERATION AND CULTURE

History teaches us that, in certain circumstances, it is very easy for the foreigner to impose his domination on a people. But it likewise teaches us that, whatever the material aspects of this domination, it can be maintained only by the permanent and organized repression of the cultural life of the people concerned. Implantation of domination can be ensured definitively only by physical elimination of a significant part of the dominated population.

In fact, to take up arms to dominate a people is, above all, to take up arms to destroy, or at least to neutralize and to paralyze their cultural life. For as long as part of that people can have a cultural life, foreign domination cannot be sure of its perpetuation. At a given moment, depending on internal and external factors determining the evolution of the society in question, cultural resistance (indestructible) may take on new (political, economic, and armed) forms, in order fully to contest foreign domination. . . .

Study of the history of liberation struggles shows that they have generally been preceded by an upsurge of cultural manifestations, which progressively harden into an attempt, successful or not, to assert the cultural personality of the dominated people by an act of denial of the culture of the oppressor. Whatever the conditions of subjection of a people to foreign domination and the influence of economic, political and social factors in the exercise of this domination, it is generally within the cultural factor that we find the germ of challenge which leads to the structuring and development of the liberation movement.

Unity and Struggle

Antonio Domingues

Antonio Domingues was a good friend of the Surrealist Group in Portugal, and especially of the great painter and poet Artur do Cruzeiro Seixas. Because he was also closely associated with Amílcar Cabral and other radical African students, Domingues in effect served as an informal liaison between the two groups.

THE INFLUENCE OF AIMÉ CÉSAIRE IN
PORTUGUESE-SPEAKING AFRICA

Lisbon, 24 February 1999

Dear Franklin Rosemont,

Through our common friend Artur do Cruzeiro Seixas I acknowledge your letter of 12th January last, and by the means I have, it is with all pleasure that I am going to try to answer your questions.

Aimé Césaire was one of the most important points of reference for some African people during the 1940s and 50s, such as: Amílcar Cabral (Guine); Agostinho Neto (Angola); Mário Pinto de Andrade (Angola); Francisco José Tenreiro (S. Tomé e Príncipe); Alda Espírito Santo (S. Tomé e Príncipe); Noêmia de Sousa (Mozambique); Antonio Domingues (Portugal).

Aimé Césaire's work (*Discourse on Colonialism*) was translated into Portuguese around 1950 by the poet Noêmia de Sousa, with introductory remarks by Mário de Andrade.

I am Antonio Domingues (painter/poet) and I was deeply attached to the African milieu in Lisbon since the 1940s, having lived together and taken part in many activities with all the persons mentioned above, including Amílcar Cabral, whose portrait I painted in 1952.

Apologizing for my poor English, and hoping that it is at least enough to be understood, I am at your disposal for any further questions.

With my best regards,
Antonio Domingues
Lisbon

MADAGASCAR

Jean-Joseph Rabéarivelo

Rabéarivelo (1901-1937), who lived his entire life on the island of Madagascar, belongs to the "accursed" tradition of Baudelaire, Rimbaud, and Jean-Pierre Duprey. In the course of a short and tragic life dominated by myriad so-called practical failures, large and small, poetry was—in his view—all that really mattered. Unfortunately, his seven books of poems provided little income for his far-from-prosperous family. Indeed, Rabéarivelo, a victim of colonialist prejudice, never came even close to finding a way of making a living that met his hopes and expectations. Instead, he devoted his idleness to the pursuit of dreams, reveries, and reckless experiments with narcotics. At the time of his suicide, he was employed as a proofreader.

His poems, however—especially those translated from the night—are a great legacy. Fittingly, he is to this day recognized as Madagascar's finest poet.

A PURPLE STAR

A purple star
evolved in the depth of the sky—
a flower of blood unfolding on the prairie of night
Evolve, evolve.
You see nothing of her but her myriads of eyes
her triangular reptile eyes,
that open one by one
among celestial lianas.

24 Poems

SOUTH AFRICA

Dennis Brutus

Born in Rhodesia of mixed parents who soon moved to Port Elizabeth, South Africa, Brutus' (1924–) irregular education included extensive reading of the English poets. With a B.A. from Fort Hare University, he taught for fourteen years in South African high schools. His antiapartheid agitation led to his dismissal as a teacher in 1962, and his arrest in Johannesburg the following year.

The years 1963–1966 involved more agitation and more police persecution—including getting shot in the back and eighteen months' imprisonment. Finally, in 1966 he sought exile briefly in England, but soon moved to the United States, where he has lived, taught, and agitated ever since.

His surrealist connections are long-standing. Shortly after settling in Chicago he attended the 1976 World Surrealist Exhibition, which he subsequently described to Franklin Rosemont as "the single greatest cultural event" during his stay in the city. He collaborated on the surrealist journal, *Free Spirits: Annals of the Insurgent Imagination* (1982), as well as the special "Surrealism: Revolution against Whiteness" issue of the journal *Race Traitor* (1998), and cosigned such surrealist declaration as "Poetry Matters: On the Media Persecution of Amir Baraka" in 2003.

During the mid-1980s' agitation to free Nelson Mandela—agitation in which the Surrealist Group was very active—Brutus in an impromptu speech at Northwestern University to antiapartheid students awaiting trial urged them to support the Surrealist Movement.

THE SUN ON THIS RUBBLE

The sun on this rubble after rain

Bruised though we must be
some easement we require
unarguably, though we argue against desire.

Under jackboots our bones and spirits crunch
forced into sweat-tear-sodden slush
—now glow lipped by this sudden touch

—sun stripped perhaps, our bones may later sing
or spell out some malignant nemesis
Sharpevilled to spearpoints for revenging

but now our pride-dumbed mouths are wide
in wordless supplication
—are grateful for the least relief from pain
—like the sun on this debris after rain.

Stubborn Hope

POET AGAINST APARTHEID

All artists have an important contribution to make in assertion of humanity and humane values. It seems to me that the mere act of creation, the creative process, is itself an assertion of our human worth, our human dignity. And so we should be conscious of our responsibilities as people who are able to make that statement on behalf of all humanity.

I harbor the conviction that all human beings have creative ability, that the creative spark exists in all of us. It takes different forms; it must be nurtured and developed, but no one of us is incapable of a creative act.

In the apartheid society, blacks are told that they must know their place, that they are less than human, are subhuman. Told they must accept certain limited horizons and cannot rise above them. The notion of African people ultimately determining their own destiny, governing their own society, achieving full stature as human beings—this is not admitted. In that context therefore, a simple assertion of humanity by an artist is made in defiance of a total denial of that humanity.

Perhaps the most positive thing people can do is a negative thing, and that is to ensure that the racism of South Africa does not penetrate to other parts of the world. It must be stopped.

Buhle et al., *Free Spirits*

The Early Strips   1911-1912

George Herriman created the complex character Krazy Kat, a true classic of American literature. This early strip is from 1911.

5. Surrealist Beginnings in the United States, 1930s–1950s

> The marvelous represents the triumph of the human spirit over chaos.
> —Ralph Ellison

Apart from Man Ray, American involvement in organized surrealism in the 1920s and early 1930s was far from impressive. Man Ray, of course, was no run-of-the-mill exception. Photographer, painter, filmmaker, writer, and a veteran of New York Dada, he moved to Paris in 1921. Arriving on Bastille Day, he was warmly welcomed by the Paris Dadaists, who were soon to declare themselves surrealists. Cited in Breton's first *Manifesto* (1924) and included in the first surrealist exhibition the following year, Man Ray was recognized as the first (and for several years the only) U.S. surrealist. A devout Parisian most of his life—apart from the Second World War years, which he spent in Los Angeles—he remained active in the movement well into the 1960s.

Joseph Cornell never joined the surrealist movement, preferring an isolated independence that he maintained throughout his life. His object boxes, however, as well as his collages and film scenarios, were much admired by Breton and other surrealists and frequently included in surrealist exhibitions and reproduced in surrealist publications. Of Cornell it can truly be said that he was, despite himself, *objectively* surrealist.

Other Americans of the 1920s–1940s who are sometimes misidentified as surrealists—I am thinking particularly of such writers as Evan Shipman, Matthew Josephson, and Wayne Andrews—were, truth to tell, little more than tourists or dabblers, or both. They may have met one or more surrealists or attended a few parties, but their understanding of what was at stake in the surrealist quest and their actual participation in the movement, were, in a word, *nil*.[1]

Most published writings on surrealism in the United States in those years—by literary folk, newspaper critics, and academics—tend to be of little or no help. Articles from that period by Kenneth Burke, Malcolm Cowley, Ezra Pound, Herbert Muller, Mike Gold, Samuel Putnam, and a host of others are notable not only for their superciliousness, but also and above all for their superficiality.

Meanwhile, several African American writers seem to have given surrealism at least half a try even as they consciously avoided the word. At their best, the surrealist sparks in Fenton Johnson's poetry bring to mind the imagery of his out-of-the-mainstream contemporaries Samuel Greenberg and Mina Loy, and that is not small praise. Jean Toomer, in his early 1930s Chicago days—years after the success of his phenomenal *Cane*—had what might be called an authentic surrealist moment, to which he gave strong expression in his little book *Essentials* (1931). Privately printed in a limited edition, the book was unfortunately almost unknown to readers for seven decades.

George Herriman is a special case. In *Krazy Kat*, a marvelous world of his own creation, he left us an unsurpassed verbal circus—much better than most poetry of the time—enhanced by his supreme mastery of the comic strip as an art form. A unique multimedia vernacular surrealism, Herriman's *Kat* saga is also one of the true classics of American literature.[2]

And then there was Zora Neale Hurston. Not many people seem to know it, but the great folklorist, anthropologist, and novelist was a writer with strong albeit unavowed surrealist tendencies. French surrealist Guy Ducornet, in his study of surrealism in the United States, was quite right to cite her as an important inspirer and precursor.[3] In the early 1930s she contributed six brilliant articles to Nancy Cunard's surrealist-influenced *Negro Anthology*. These texts— including "Characteristics of Negro Expression," "Visions," and "Shouting"— abound with the insight, imagination, originality, vivacity, and humor that characterize her later folkloric studies: *Mules and Men* (1935) and *Tell My Horse* (1938), the latter focused on voodoo practices in Jamaica and Haiti. Even in childhood, as she notes in her autobiography, *Dust Tracks on a Road* (1942), that loneliness was a constant shadow, suggesting that her rebellious self-consciousness and curiosity regarding "otherness" started early.

Far more than any other ethnographer of her time, she was acutely sensitive to what Pierre Mabille calls the mirror of the Marvelous. For her, as Larry Neal once observed, fieldwork involved above all the sensibility of the artist. Passionately attracted to all manifestations of the imaginary—dreams, visions, trance, magic, the wonders of everyday life, and wild nature—she also embodied a flamboyant but deeply serious black feminism. In retrospect, it is clear that what has subsequently been called Hurston's visionary anthropology closely resembles the nonconformist poetry-inspired anthropology developed by the surrealists at the same time.

As it happened, the first really serious and in-depth inquiry into surrealism in the United States was the work of another African American: a former porter, messenger, postal worker, and ditchdigger, better known as the author of *Uncle Tom's Children, Native Son,* and *Twelve Million Black Voices.*

RICHARD WRIGHT AND HIS GRANDMOTHER

In 1936-1937 an immense exhibition called "Fantastic Art, Dada and Surrealism" opened at the New York Museum of Modern Art. Despite its eclecticism, the show gave the U.S. public its first chance to see the new art that was provoking so much controversy. More than a few of its many thousands of visitors came to laugh or express their scorn, but some were unafraid to admit that the show had, in various ways, significantly changed their lives. For painter Arshile Gorky, an Armenian immigrant whose earlier work was largely derivative of early Picasso, the surrealists' paintings provided a decisive turning point; his later works would be recognized as some of surrealism's finest masterpieces. For Dorothea Tanning, a young art student from Galesburg, Illinois, the New York show made her realize that she herself, lo and behold, was a surrealist.

Poetically and philosophically, however, it is doubtful that anyone was more affected by this gigantic surrealist manifestation than Richard Wright. The exhibition's nearly seven hundred works, and its catalog — especially the second edition (1937), with essays on surrealist history and theory — had an impact on him that lasted the rest of his life.[4]

In 1937, when he moved to New York, Wright was still in his twenties, fresh from Chicago, and, as always, on the lookout for anything new and daring and liberating. His response to surrealism was deep, spontaneous, and, characteristically, his own. First and foremost, he recognized surrealism as a creative process which helped him clarify a double mystery: the mystery of his grandmother's unusual use of language, and the mystery of blues singers' song-composition. Wright was struck by his stern grandmother's religion-saturated folk speech, full of disconnected sentences and fragmented images, and the blues singers' freewheeling lyrics, with their lack of narrative sequence and juxtaposition of discordant elements. Likening both to surrealist collage, he went on to explore the affinities between surrealism and jazz, more particularly, between surrealist automatism (in writing and drawing) and jazz improvisation.

Wright's surrealist adventure reveals his profound grasp of fundamentals. In contrast to most Left art critics and *litterateurs* of the time, including the Trotskyist intellectuals around *Partisan Review*, Wright recognized surrealism as a revolutionary method of learning, a means of resolving immobilizing contradictions, a way of seeing things whole and thereby changing the world.

His 1940-1941 essay "Memories of My Grandmother" is surely the most insightful and original text concerning surrealism written in the United States up to that time. By relating surrealism to African American folk expression, and to his own life, Richard Wright accomplished more — much more — than most Americans who had, to one degree or another, expressed interest in surrealism.

Wright was not simply interested; he was *fascinated*. He read Freud and Ferenczi and dared to explore the world of dreams. Listening to what Breton called the surrealist voice, he immersed himself in the surrealist *experience* and applied surrealist methods to the problems that troubled him. Indeed, his surrealist research was so full of new ideas that it could easily have expanded the movement's perspectives in many directions. Unfortunately, Wright seems to have kept his surrealist explorations all to himself. "Memories of My Grandmother" was not published, or even completed.

In his books, however—novels, short stories, essays—the light of surrealism burns brightly. Surrealism early on reinforced his break with so-called pro-letarian literature and, more broadly, with all "closed" realism. Radical open-endedness and free-spirited imagination are the heart and nervous system of *Twelve Million Black Voices* (1941) as well as such 1940s tales as "The Man Who Lived Underground" and "The Man Who Came to Chicago." Not until Ralph Ellison's *Invisible Man* (1952) would American fiction include such large doses of concrete irrationality and outrageous humor. Ellison was no disciple of Wright, but in his best-known novel, and in many of his essays as well—on jazz, for example, and on the collage art of Romare Bearden—he, more than anyone else of his time, seems to have picked up hints and flashes of Wright's surrealism.

In "Harlem Is Nowhere" Ellison evokes a social reality that Wright surely would have recognized: "a world so fluid and shifting that often within the mind the real and the unreal merge, and the marvelous beckons from behind the same sordid reality that denies its existence. Hence the most surreal fantasies are acted out in the streets of Harlem. . . . For this is a world in which the major energy of the imagination goes not into creating works of art, but to overcome the frustrations of social discrimination."[5]

Although some critics have found Wright guilty of existentialism, the tag fits only a few of his tales, and even then only slightly. The real hallmark of Wright's work (and Ellison's) is not Sartre's dreary absence of exits, but, rather, a powerful poetic refusal—a refusal of *misery* or, in more positive terms, a search for an exalting and liberating Marvelous. From his 1940s "Memories" through *The Long Dream* and his late experiments with haiku, he pursued this passionate quest.

Wright's sojourn in surrealism was first brought to wide notice by the scholar and critic Eugene Miller in his pathbreaking *Voice of a Native Son*. Few commentators, however, have been willing to pursue the topic. Regrettably, too, no one seems to have bothered to correct Miller's mistaken assertion that Wright made no attempt to meet André Breton or any of the surrealists, in New York or in Paris.

It is not certain that Wright encountered any of the European surrealist refugees from Nazi-occupied France during World War II. However, when one considers the number and variety of situations in which such encounters might have occurred—cafes, bookstores, jazz clubs, exhibition openings, film showings, neighborhood bars, and parties—it is risky to insist that no such meetings did in fact take place. In any event, Wright in 1944 is known to have been in touch with at least one frequenter of the New York surrealist milieu: the great photographer Helen Levitt, a collaborator on the surrealist journal *VVV.*

After 1946, however, when Wright himself—as a refugee from U.S. racism— resettled in Paris (where he remained until his death in 1960), his encounters with Breton and others from the surrealist milieu were not only numerous but are also well documented. Interestingly, several of these meetings occurred in the course of protest actions. In May 1948, at the opening session of the United Nations in Paris, a former U.S. bomber pilot named Garry Davis tore up his passport, denounced the inherent militarism of nation-states, and proclaimed himself a "citizen of the world," a gesture followed by his arrest. Among the first to rally to his support were André Breton and the Surrealist Group. According to the newspaper *Combat* (October 26), Breton and Wright were present at Davis' press conference, and—with Albert Camus, Jean-Paul Sartre, and a few other writers—served as members of his Solidarity Committee.

Wright and Breton met again in December 1948, at the historic Writers' Congress sponsored by the Rassemblement Democratique Révolutionnaire (Revolutionary Democratic Assembly, RDR), a New Left group. On this occasion Wright also met Gerard Rosenthal, who presided at the meeting and as Francis Gerard Rosenthal had directed the Bureau of Surrealist Research back in 1924–1925 and later served as Leon Trotsky's French lawyer.[6] At least twice in public speeches during this period, Breton significantly mentioned Wright.[7]

In his Paris years Wright met many others who, at one time or another, were involved in surrealism. They include Marcel Duhamel (who translated *Black Boy*), Maurice Nadeau (author of the first history of surrealism), essayist and critic Roger Caillois, poet Jacques Prévert, novelist Raymond Queneau, poet and short story writer Lise Deharmé, and Madeleine Rousseau of the Chicago/ Paris *Continuity* Group, whose members included Jean Arp and Jean-Michel Atlan.[8] Wright is also known to have contributed one of his manuscripts to a fund-raising auction for the ailing and indigent surrealist poet and playwright Antonin Artaud.

In connection with the founding of the journal *Présence Africaine*, Wright met Aimé Césaire, Léon Damas, Frantz Fanon (a student of Césaire's), and Léopold Senghor. On the same occasion he met two more surrealist pioneers: Michel Leiris, who had become a distinguished Africanist; and Pierre Naville, who had coedited with Benjamin Péret the first surrealist journal, *La Révolution Surréaliste,* in 1924–1925. Naville in 1949 translated and introduced the French edition of C.L.R. James' *The Black Jacobins*.

To sum up: very few Americans of his time came even close to having as wide an acquaintance with past and present participants in surrealism as Richard Wright.

THE SURREALIST DIASPORA

New York, 1940–1945: The Harlem Connection

> The modulations we manufactured were the weirdest.
>
> —Dizzy Gillespie

When Nazi military invasion in effect shut down public surrealist activity—and all forms of free speech and assembly—in France and many other European countries, the "surrealist diaspora" began. Most of the Paris surrealists, after a brief respite in Marseilles during the winter of 1940–1941, left for New York. Others fled to Argentina, Mexico, or the Caribbean. Underground surrealist publications existed, notably in France and Holland, but the surrealist refugees in New York and elsewhere did not see them until the war was over.

Even in New York the status of refugees left much to be desired. André Breton and Luis Buñuel, to name only two, were granted asylum in the United States on the condition that they avoid political activity of any kind. Both were kept under close FBI and police surveillance throughout the war.[9] Despite such restrictive circumstances, however, a Surrealist Group in exile carried on as best it could.

International communication was severely hampered. Inhabitants of the overrun countries of Europe could neither send mail to the United States nor receive mail from it. The once-flourishing Surrealist Group in Tokyo had been outlawed and most of its members jailed or placed under house arrest for the duration.[10] Only in Egypt, England, Martinique, Chile—and New York—were Surrealist Groups openly and uninterruptedly active during this period.

Fortunately, a number of Americans rallied to the surrealist cause in New York. Among them were the young painters William Baziotes, Gerome Kamrowski, and Jackson Pollock; sculptor David Hare and his poet wife, Susanna; friendly critics such as Harold Rosenberg and Meyer Schapiro; photographers Clarence John Laughlin, Helen Levitt, Frederick Sommer; and—of special importance—the young Sicilian American poet Philip Lamantia, whose poetry Breton greatly admired.

The fact that the group's meetings were mostly conducted in French caused some difficulty, for few of the Americans were fluent in that language, and few of the refugees spoke English. More peripherally associated were Paul Goodman and his circle of anarchist friends, and a more working-class anarchist group around the Italian Carlo Tresca. The two latter groups did not in fact take part in Surrealist Group meetings, but now and then encountered Breton and his friends at exhibition openings and eating places.

In February 1942 an "Open Letter to the President of Mexico" protesting Stalinist persecution of antifascist refugees in that country appeared in *Partisan Review*, which was then in its most radical period. The signatories included— among many others—André Breton, Anita Brenner, civil-libertarian Roger Baldwin, novelist James T. Farrell, Lyle Lane (of the *Harlem Age*), Adam Clayton Powell, A. Philip Randolph, Carlo Tresca, and Edmund Wilson.[11]

At least once in 1945 Suzanne and Aimé Césaire came to New York, met with Breton, and attended Surrealist Group gatherings. Wifredo Lam also visited the city in connection with his 1941 solo exhibition, and later to attend other shows. To what extent the Césaires or Lam also visited African American acquaintances during their New York stays does not seem to be recorded. African American interaction with the surrealist refugees from Europe is also poorly documented.

Interestingly, however, at least two Euro-Americans associated with the Surrealist Group in New York authored notable books on African American history. In 1937 Robert Allerton Parker published a scholarly study of the evangelist sect Peace Mission, run by Father Divine (George Baker) in Harlem, and nine years later Brion Gysin brought out *To Master: A Long Goodnight* (1946), a somewhat fictionalized biography of Josiah Henson, the escaped slave who is believed to have been the model for the title character in Harriet Beecher Stowe's *Uncle Tom's Cabin*. In addition to its historical dimension, Gysin's book also included a strong attack on U.S. racism, 1940s style.

Parker's book, incidentally, seems to have had a modest influence on the 1942 New York International Surrealist Exhibition. The catalog, titled *First Papers of Surrealism*, features Breton's album, "On the Survival of Certain Myths and on Some Other Myths in Growth or Formation." Halfway through, Breton inserted a photograph of Father Divine as an example of a "modern Messiah."

Neither Parker nor Gysin was a surrealist, but both felt attracted to the movement, and both collaborated (Parker prolifically) on *VVV*. Also attracted to surrealism in those days was Gysin's friend Herbert Hill, who years later became a noted civil rights attorney and historian of black labor. In the 1940s Hill was a young Trotskyist, still in his teens. Interviewed in the 1990s, he recalled Gysin's telling him about "surrealist expeditions to Harlem to hear the new jazz" back in the Forties. That this was no mere rumor is confirmed by

surrealist painter Gerome Kamrowski, who, also in a 1990s interview, emphasized that "going to Harlem was certainly part of the surrealist scene in those
days."[12] Matta, Frederick Kiesler, William Baziotes, Nicolas Calas, David Hare,
and Robert Motherwell were among the names Kamrowski mentioned in this
regard. Kamrowski himself was particularly fond of the Stuyvesant Ballroom,
where Bunk Johnson's band played, but he also enjoyed going to the Savoy
Ballroom and the Apollo Theatre.

It is not clear, from the recollections of Herbert Hill or Gerome Kamrowski,
that any of the surrealists from Europe managed to visit Minton's Playhouse,
where, mostly in the wee hours, the newest jazz—bebop—was being collectively created by such geniuses as Charlie "Bird" Parker, Dizzy Gillespie, Max
Roach, Thelonious Monk, and other young and adventurous musicians.

Whether they actually heard bop live or not, the influence of the Harlem
experience on the surrealist refugees is evident in their writings. In *New Directions 1940* Nicolas Calas comments on the phenomenon of objective chance,
pointing out that "everything from deep-sea life to the dance at the Savoy in
Harlem can be poetic." And in his *Confound the Wise*, reflecting on the most vital
forces in America, he affirms that Harlem's Savoy and its ferocious rhythms
were vastly preferable, from the surrealist point of view, to the Ballet Russe.[13]

Harlem jazz was especially significant for André Breton. The first surrealist generation, in 1920s Paris, included many jazz enthusiasts—Jacques Baron,
René Crevel, Robert Desnos, Michel Leiris, Jacques Rigaut, and others—who
frequented a black jazz nightspot, the Tempo Club, on the Rue Fontaine in
Pigalle. (Man Ray did a painting of it.) Many also frequented the Bal Nègre on
the Rue Blomet, in the heart of the Paris Caribbean community; André Masson
and Joan Miró lived next door. Breton, for his part, was tone deaf and for a long
time shared Georgio de Chirico's indifference to music. Kamrowski recalled
that in the early 1940s he had heard John Cage remark that Breton considered
music "escapist."

According to Elisa Breton, however, her husband's attitude toward music
changed dramatically in mid-decade. As she explained to Chicago surrealist
Paul Garon in 1973, Breton—at her request, circa 1944–1945—took her to
Harlem to hear a jazz band. As had been the case with several refugee friends,
Elisa was deeply impressed, and so was André. Not long afterward, in his sole
article on the subject of music, he reflected, in Hegelian terms, on the fusion of
music and poetry and looked forward to a potential reunification of hearing.[14]

No one knows for sure, but it may well have been the Chilean painter
Roberto Matta who, by bringing his large collection of records from New York
to Paris, introduced the newer bop to the suddenly burgeoning postwar Paris
surrealist milieu. In no time at all, it seems, Victor Brauner, Claude Tarnaud,

Stanislas Rodanski, Georges Goldfayn, and Gérard Legrand had formed what Robert Benayoun later called a Thelonious Monk cult within the Surrealist Group.[15]

Matta's special favorite among musicians was Cab Calloway, but his taste in jazz was all-embracing and enthusiastic to the point of fanaticism. He sums it up in 1984 in his response to Ted Joans' surrealism/jazz inquiry in the German one-shot surrealist publication *Dies und Das*, which Joans coedited with poet Richard Anders in Berlin: "Jazz is a word of revolt, pleasure and justice."[16]

In any event, by 1947 at the latest, the black music known as jazz had become, incontestably, not only the "crazy music" that a large part of the public identified with surrealism, but also the music with which surrealists themselves identified. Make no mistake: the younger French and other European surrealists' chance encounter with the "hip" international African American subculture added up to a high-powered new tremor in the intellectual atmosphere.

Harlem, then—like Martinique, Cuba, and Haiti—left a strong impact on postwar surrealism. The new black jazz, no doubt about it, was a prime inspiration for free spirits in Paris, London, Brussels, Cairo, Lisbon, Amsterdam, Santiago, Bucharest, and wherever else surrealism was in flower. The impact, moreover, was lasting and assumed many forms. Postwar surrealist exhibition openings, for example, especially in the 1950s, often featured jazz, and appreciations of the new music increasingly appeared in the movement's publications. Such surrealist works as the jazz poems of Claude Tarnaud, Gérard Legrand's *Puissances du jazz*, and François Valorbe's *Carte noir*—a suite of poems celebrating black musicians—amplified the fact that African American jazz was *the* music of choice for surrealists.

As Legrand puts it in *Puissances du jazz*, the essence of black music is poetry and the spirit it radiates. In other words, jazz was regarded as a crucial part of the surrealist project. *Arsenal/Surrealist Subversion*, no. 3 (1976) is no less explicit: "Surrealists recognize in black music, and especially in the recent evolution of jazz, not only an ally and a fraternal tendency, but also an irreplaceable constituent element of the surrealist revolution."[17]

Down through the years, love of black music has in fact remained one of the constants of surrealism. The movement's publications have now and then included appreciations of other kinds of music—Kurt Weill, Harry Partch, Balinese Gamelan music, and Spike Jones' comic "music depreciation"—but these are rare compared to the voluminous surrealist literature on African American blues and jazz. Black surrealists—René Ménil, Ted Joans, Jayne Cortez, Cheikh Tidiane Sylla, Robin D. G. Kelley, and Anthony Joseph, to name just a few—have written widely on the subject, but so have writers of European or Euro-American descent: Claude Tarnaud, Hilary Booth, Carmen Bruna, Jorge

Camacho, Paul Garon, Georges Goldfayn, Joseph Jablonski, Georges Gronier, Jaroslav Jezek, Jean-Jacques Lebel, Gellu Naum, Artur do Cruzeiro Seixas, Charles Radcliffe, Anthony Redmond, Michael Vandelaar, and many others.

Special credit here belongs to Paul Garon, who has unquestionably written more on black music than any other surrealist—or any other *ten* surrealists. For nearly forty years, he has written inspiredly and prolifically on blues and bluespeople, affirming and exploring their manifold affinities with surrealism via poetry, humor, dream, imagination, freedom, love, revolt, and social transformation. *The Devil's Son-in-Law* (1971; revised 2003); *Blues and the Poetic Spirit* (1975; revised 1996); *Woman with Guitar: Memphis Minnie's Blues* (with Beth Garon, 1992); and *What's the Use of Walking If There's a Freight Train Going Your Way* (2006)—are indispensable to researchers and regarded as classics. He has also contributed dozens of blues-related articles to scholarly and popular journals as well as encyclopedias, other reference works, and—of course—surrealist publications.

NEW PATHS FOR SURREALISM

> The only way out is inward and forward.
> —Hilary Booth

Despite intrusions by FBI and other police snoopers, New York's surrealist refugees—with the help of their U.S. allies—accomplished a lot during their five years in the New World. They produced three large issues of a wonderful journal called *VVV*—Triple-V, a name clearly inspired by the African American Double-V movement (victory over fascism but also over U.S. racism). The three issues total 314 pages.

In addition to numerous smaller shows, New York's surrealist refugees organized the comprehensive International Surrealist Exhibition in 1942, featuring more than fifty artists. The catalog includes a brief preface by Breton focused on the urgency of poetry: "The surrealist cause, in art as in life, is the cause of freedom itself. Today more than ever, to speak abstractly in the name of freedom or to praise it in empty terms, is to serve it ill. To light the world, freedom must become flesh, and to this end must always be reflected and recreated in the *word*." They also published books—quite a few for impecunious refugees. Among them was the first English translation of Aimé Césaire's *Return to My Native Land*. Breton was able to bring out an expanded edition of *Le surréalisme et la peinture*; a volume of poems, *Young Cherry Trees Secured against Hares*; a monograph on artist Yves Tanguy; and *Arcane 17*. André Masson published *Anatomy of My Universe* and *Nocturnal Notebook*, and Nicolas Calas, a collection of essays, *Confound the Wise*.

They also made effective use of sympathetic U.S. periodicals. Calas' 200-page surrealist anthology in the *New Directions 1940* annual was a real break-through—an unprecedentedly extensive collection of surrealist writings in English. *New Directions 1941* featured Clark Mills' translation of Breton's long poem, *Fata Morgana*, illustrated by Wifredo Lam.[18]

The art and literary magazine *View* was especially receptive to surrealist collaboration. Its early newspaper format series included a special Surrealist Number, and surrealists remained prominent in subsequent issues. A glorious hodgepodge of surprises, *View* published letters from Antonin Artaud, Suzanne Césaire, and Toni del Renzio; poems by André Breton, Philip Lamantia, and Juan Breá; a fantastic novella, "Dark Sugar," by black outsider artist Paul Childs; drawings by Wifredo Lam (who did the cover for the special May 1945 "Tropics" issue); articles by Nicolas Calas, Benjamin Péret, Paul Nougé, Man Ray, and Mina Loy; a review of Richard Wright's *Black Boy;* and even one of Lydia Cabrera's Afro-Cuban folktales, translated by Mary Low.

Also largely devoted to surrealism was the double "Tropics" issue (no. 2-3) of Yvan Goll's magazine, *Hemispheres* (Fall/Winter, 1943-1944), featuring Breton's tribute to Césaire, "A Great Black Poet," four pages of Césaire's poetry, and some of Breton's Martinique-inspired prose poems, including his salute to Suzanne Césaire, as well as drawings and a text by Masson. The issue offered readers several more pages of poems by Césaire, together with a full-page drawing by Lam.

As the preceding paragraphs suggest, surrealists of African descent were increasingly in the forefront of the movement's expanding activity throughout this period. Well represented in every issue of *VVV*, which also included a display ad for *Tropiques*, Aimé Césaire's poetry was simultaneously appearing in other languages in other lands. Wifredo Lam's paintings—full-page features in *VVV*—also proved to be a sensation wherever they were shown. In the 1940s alone, four surrealists—Breton, Calas, Aimé Césaire, and Mabille, plus surrealist sympathizer Pierre Loeb—wrote major articles on Lam. (Breton, Calas, and Césaire in fact wrote two articles each.)

In the December 1945 "Speech to Young Haitian Poets," Breton, noting that "people of color have always enjoyed exceptional favor and prestige in surrealism," went on to emphasize that "it is therefore no accident, but a *sign of the times,* that the greatest impulses toward new paths for surrealism have been furnished, during the war just ended, by my greatest 'colored' friends—Aimé Césaire in poetry, Wifredo Lam in painting—and that I find myself among you in Haiti in preference to any other place in the world."[19]

Strikingly, on that very trip to Haiti, in that same tumultuous December, Breton encountered yet another black Caribbean genius, Clément Magloire-Saint-Aude, whose extraordinary poetic work—at that time scarcely known outside Haiti—added a wildly new dimension to an already amazingly multi-dimensional surrealism. Almost haikulike in its uncompromising simplicity, his poetry is not only "entirely free of the picturesque" (as Gérard Legrand notes),[20] but also electrifyingly spontaneous, smoldering with a disquieting hermetic humor.

DISSOLUTION OF THE NEW YORK GROUP

Surrealism in New York during the first half of the 1940s had many bright moments as well as some lasting achievements. The movement's very presence, moreover, as a multiracial revolutionary poetic force, had a vivifying effect on young artists, poets, and other assorted malcontents throughout the country. But it did not last.

In 1945-1946, when Breton and most of the other European surrealists in exile returned to their homes across the sea, the Surrealist Group in New York ceased to exist. Its concluding collective effort was the "Bloodflames 1947" exhibition at the Hugo Gallery. Organized by Nicolas Calas, it featured new work by David Hare, Arshile Gorky, Gerome Kamrowski, Wifredo Lam, Roberto Matta, Isamu Noguchi, Helen Phillips, and Jeanne Raynal. An important manifestation, it might have sparked a renewal of New York surrealist activity, but no one came forward to maintain the momentum. Discouragement was very much in the air.

With the effective dissolution of the New York Group, the individuals who had been active in it went their own ways. Max Ernst and Dorothea Tanning moved to Arizona. Painter and poet Sonia Sekula, who had lived in the United States since 1936, had a nervous breakdown and returned to her native Switzerland. Interestingly, there she became good friends with another refugee from the "American way of life," the blues singer and pianist Champion Jack Dupree.[21]

Several of the Americans were especially hard hit by the New York breakup. Kamrowski, who abhorred the New York art scene's antisurrealist xenophobia, jealousy, and commercialism, fled halfway across the country to Ann Arbor, Michigan, where he remained the rest of his life, surrealist to the end. Clarence John Laughlin went back to New Orleans, also to stay; he, too, remained firmly committed to surrealism's ideals.

A disconsolate Philip Lamantia returned to San Francisco, where an attempt to form a local Surrealist Group with the painters Charles Howard and Jean Varda proved a flash in the pan. More enduringly, in 1947—aided by conscientious objector Robert Stock and other rebel Bay Area poets—Lamantia helped start *The Ark*, an anarchist journal with surrealist leanings, now well respected by scholars as a significant link between the New York surrealist refugees and the later Beat Generation. Soon, however, Lamantia began nearly a decade and a half of wandering: to France, Italy, Spain, North Africa, and Mexico.[22]

Ironically, as the New York surrealists dispersed to the four winds, new-comers began to show up, and more than a few of them were black. From Cleveland, the indefatigable experimenter Russell Atkins in 1947 sent a poem to *View* magazine, which published it. Two years later, Oliver Pitcher's poems appeared in another surrealism-friendly journal, *Tiger's Eye*, published in the wilds of Westport, Connecticut. Meanwhile, black artists such as Romare Bear-den and Norman Lewis in New York and Hughie Lee-Smith in Detroit were producing fine work very much in the surrealist spirit.

Whether any of these poets or painters ever considered themselves sur-realists is not known, but this much is obvious: had the New York Surrealist Group held together after war's end, these and who knows how many other newcomers might have appreciably added to it or, even more important, trans-formed it into a sturdier and more effective force.

Unfortunately, that did not happen. Scattered, isolated individuals continued to uphold surrealism's aims and principles—and indeed, to lead exemplary sur-realist lives—but the spirit of collective adventure was noticeably missing.

Depressing, too, was the unmistakable rightist shift in the U.S. cultural scene. Several New York painters who had associated with the surrealist refugees, and even exhibited with them, had formed a vehemently antisurrealist clique in the postwar years, largely under the tutelage of conservative art critic Clement Greenberg, a declared enemy of surrealism. More comical—or psychopatho-logical, depending on your point of view—were the hate-filled outbursts of Congressman George A. Dondero. To this Republican we owe a long list of crackbrained declarations solemnly uttered on the floor of the House of Rep-resentatives and duly printed in the *Congressional Record*. His outbursts included such pixilated propositions as these:

All modern art is Communistic.
All these isms are of foreign origin, and truly should have no place in American art.
All are instruments and weapons of destruction.
Surrealism aims to destroy by the denial of reason.
The question is: Who has let into our homeland this horde of germ-carrying art vermin?
The evidence of evil design is everywhere.[23]

So now you know!
Meanwhile, the aforementioned potential newcomers to New York surreal-

206 *Black, Brown, & Beige*

ism were pursuing distinct paths of their own. Atkins, who opted for a poetics close to French Lettrism, rallied offbeat poets (black and white) from all over; his eclectic journal, *Free Lance,* ran from 1953 to 1976. Oliver Pitcher published a chapbook of his poems, *Dust of Silence,* in 1958, but he remained better known as an actor and playwright. Romare Bearden, Norman Lewis, and Hughie Lee-Smith eventually achieved wide recognition as important American artists.[24] For the time being, however, organized surrealism in the United States had simply faded away.

Those who lived through the 1950s in the United States tend to recall them—and particularly the decade's first half—as bleak years, with occasional and brief eruptions of nonbleakness. Fear, hopelessness, and boredom were a large part of a daily life in which the Bomb, the cold war, the Korean War, race discrimination, McCarthyism, the House Un-American Activities Committee, gray-flannel suits, and *I Led Three Lives* were always present. In such an atmosphere, intellectual and cultural life became increasingly conformist. Hard as it may be to believe today, the banalities of Arthur Schlesinger, Jr., were, circa 1954, praised as the wisdom of a "major thinker."

Not until 1955, with the Montgomery bus boycott and the subsequent sit-ins and Freedom Rides, would a new hope—and a new Left—start up again in this country. By decade's end, a rising youthful radicalism, largely inspired by the black struggle, was everywhere in the wind. A few years later, a resurgence of surrealism in the United States would also be much in evidence.

POSTWAR PARIS

In France the surrealist resurgence started much earlier. Despite the hostility of existentialists, Stalinists, the art establishment, the Far Right, journalists, clergy, mainstream critics, and academics, the Surrealist Group from 1945 on—and especially during and after the large 1947 International Surrealist Exhibition— enjoyed a massive rejuvenation as dozens of young people from all over swelled its ranks and multiplied its activities. This renewal persisted all through the 1950s up to and including the near-revolution of May 1968, when the walls of Paris were brightened with countless surrealist graffiti.

It was during this long and productive period that the sculptor Agustín Cárdenas, from Cuba; poet Joyce Mansour, from Egypt; Robert Benayoun, from Morocco; Édouard Glissant, from Martinique; Ted Joans, from the United States; Hervé Télémaque, from Haiti; Michel Zimbacca, from Syria; Henri Kréa and Farid Lariby, from Algeria; and Alexander Boghossian, from Ethiopia, all became active in surrealism, or at least close to the group.

The exodus of black poets and intellectuals from the United States also gained momentum throughout these years, doubtless inspired at least in part by the example of Richard Wright and, later, of Ted Joans and the painter Beauford Delaney. The sensationally successful French tour of Katherine Dunham's dance troupe was also a great inspiration. Other new additions to the postwar cultural life of Paris were novelists James Baldwin, Chester Himes, and John A. Williams; cartoonist Ollie Harrington; poet Henry Bibbs; and dozens of jazz musicians, including drummer Kenny Clark and alto-saxophonist Pony Poindexter.

Interestingly, nearly all of these brief or longtime refugees from the United States had personal encounters with one or more surrealists in Paris. Several met André Breton. Robert Benayoun, Jean-Jacques Lebel, and former surrealist Marcel Duhamel gladly served as translators as well as liaisons with publishers, periodicals, and bookstores. Other surrealists invited the African American newcomers to Surrealist Group exhibition openings, rendezvous, demonstrations, and parties.

BACK IN THE "LAND OF THE DOLLAR"

In the United States, however, during the late Forties and early Fifties, public awareness of surrealism reached a low ebb. With few exceptions the media—particularly art, poetry, and intellectual magazines—ignored the subject. In earlier years, André Breton's writings regularly appeared in English translation, but this was rarely true in the Fifties. Young, upcoming surrealist artists found it harder and harder to convince galleries to exhibit their work. In most universities, the study of surrealism was actively discouraged.

A gloomy existentialism was the journalistic and academic fad of the hour. It was in the 1950s that French surrealist Alain Joubert observed that "the idea of *freedom* is hibernating in the Frigidaires of technical progress."[25] Naïve name-droppers were particularly fond of Heidegger, whose long support of Nazism was not yet well known in the United States.

The official "in" art of the Fifties was of course abstract expressionism, massively promoted by the U.S. State Department and the CIA in a 1953–1954 exhibition titled "Twelve Contemporary American Painters and Sculptors." A major maneuver in the cultural cold war, the show opened in Paris and went on to Zurich, Dusseldorf, Stockholm, Oslo, and Helsinki. As with similar exhibits that followed, it was closely linked to the so-called Congress for Cultural Freedom, a notorious CIA-managed organization with offices in thirty-five countries.[26]

Interviewed in the 1990s, Gerome Kamrowski recalled Vincent Price's 1950s remark that this new fashionable art (like the later Pop Art) was ideal for the walls of corporate headquarters, executive law offices, and deluxe hotels.[27] As Price went on to explain, surrealist paintings—or for that matter Cubist and Expressionist paintings—always had a disturbing element: they challenged, sometimes even defied the viewer. Abstract expressionism, however—occasional exceptions aside—was above all a *decorative* current, hence its wide use in full-page chic magazine advertisements for expensive gowns and other luxuries. Not too surprisingly, by the time the abstract expressionists had established their Cold War identity, they were also well known as respectable, nonradical, very much a "white" phenomenon, and *almost* all-male (Lee Krasner being the sole female exception). Needless to say, the champions of this new school regarded surrealism as old hat.

And there you have it. Disregarded and scorned by the great majority of critics, journalists, and academic poets, the surrealists were where they always are: radically *outside* and *against* the established order. Then as now, uncomprehending critics found it hard to accept the crucial fact that surrealism has *never* been chiefly concerned with art or literature, but, rather, with "the practice of poetry," human expression in its largest sense, and social and cultural revolution. As Philip Lamantia put it in a letter to André Breton, published in *VVV* in October 1943: "A true revolutionary poet can not help defying every appalling social and political instrument that has been the cause of death and exploitation in the capitalistic societies of the earth. . . . To rebel! That is the immediate object of poets! We can not wait and will not be held back by those individuals who are the prisoners of the bourgeoisie, and who have not the courage to go on fighting in the name of the 'idea'! The poetic marvelous and the 'unconscious' are the true inspirers of rebels and poets!"[28]

Ten years later, there was not a "serious" journal in the land that would print such insurrectionary sentiments. In the late 1940s and early 1950s, even the most radical Marxist or anarchist publications shied away from surrealism. Bleak years, indeed!

In revenge, however, popular culture proved much less timid. Surrealism was a recurring subtheme in paperback mysteries such as Clayton Rawson's *Footprints on the Ceiling* and his other tales featuring a magician sleuth. Surrealism also pops up in such appropriately unlikely places as Helen McCloy's *Who's Calling?*, David Goodis' *Nightfall*, and Betsy Allen's *The Secret of Black Cat Gulch*, a mystery for teenage girls. Best of all was the riotous 1948 comic book, "Captain Marvel and the Surrealist Imp," which truly bubbles over with surrealist imagery and humor. Even today it is as good as a night at the movies!

Notes

1. The widespread incomprehension of surrealism in the United States from the 1920s on is surveyed in Franklin Rosemont's foreword to M. E.

Warlick's *Max Ernst and Alchemy*. See also Guy Ducornet's *Le punching-ball & la vache lait*.

2. See Franklin Rosemont's "George Herriman (Krazy Kat)," 58–64.

3. Guy Ducornet, *Ça va chauffer!*, 98. On Hurston in a surrealist perspective, see especially Karanja, *Zora Neale Hurston*.

4. Eugene Miller, *Voice of a Native Son*, 87–93.

5. Ralph Ellison, "Harlem Is Nowhere," in *Shadow and Act*, 294–302. Guy Ducornet, a student and friend of Ellison's, informs me that *Invisible Man* was supposed to have included surrealist photographs by Gordon Parks, but that this plan was rejected by the publisher.

6. In response to a query, Rosenthal wrote me (April 9, 1991): "After the Second World War and André Breton's return to Paris, my relations with him were very friendly, indeed excellent, and above all personal. We naturally found ourselves working together on various actions, particularly matters of the moment, such as the Committee for the Truth on Stalin's Crimes, and the Garry Davis affair. I presided at the historic meeting of the Revolutionary Democratic Assembly (RDR) on December 3, 1948, at the Salle Pleyel, which brought together Camus, Breton, Sartre, Rousset, Richard Wright, Carlo Levi and others."

7. André Breton, *Oeuvres complètes*, vol. 3, 977, 1433.

8. Michel Fabre, *The Unfinished Quest of Richard Wright*.

9. In the late 1990s, under the Freedom of Information Act, Franklin Rosemont succeeded in obtaining documents indicating that Breton and Buñuel were closely watched by the FBI and immigration authorities throughout their stay in the United States.

10. On the outlawing of surrealism in Japan, see the entries "Repression" and "Japan" in Biro and Passeron, *Dictionnaire*.

11. The letter appeared in *Partisan Review* (March–April 1942), 174–176.

12. Gerome Kamrowski and Herbert Hill, telephone interviews with Franklin Rosemont, late 1990s.

13. Nicolas Calas, *Confound the Wise*, 266–267.

14. Paul Garon, conversation with Elisa Breton, Paris, 1972. Breton's article on music, "Silence Is Golden," is included in *What Is Surrealism?*, 348–353.

15. Robert Benayoun, *Le rire des surréalistes*, 104.

16. Matta, "Jazz Inquiry," *Dies und Das* (unpaginated).

17. On surrealism and jazz, see Legrand's *Puissances du jazz*, especially "Jazz et surréalisme," 189; and Paul Garon, "Surrealism and Music," in *Blues and the Poetic Spirit*, 207–216. The quotation from *Arsenal* appears on p. 18.

18. The Clark Mills translation of Breton's *Fata Morgana*, with Lam's drawings, was reissued by the Black Swan Press in 1969.

19. Breton, *What Is Surrealism?*, 341; original emphasis.

20. Gérard Legrand, "Magloire-Saint-Aude," in Biro and Passeron, *Dictionnaire*, 253.

21. Writings by Sonia Sekula, with commentary, are included in Penelope Rosemont, *Surrealist Women*, 163–165, 278–279. Her friendship with Champion Jack Dupree is noted in Dieter Schwarz, *Sonja Sekula, 1918–1963*, 257.

22. See Nancy J. Peters, "Philip Lamantia," 329–336; and Franklin Rosemont, "Surrealist, Anarchist, Afrocentrist," 124–143.

23. Frances Stonor Saunders, *Who Paid the Piper?*, 253–254.

24. Bearden and Henderson, *A History of African American Artists*, 315–327, 328–336.

25. Alain Joubert, one of the mainstays of the Paris Surrealist Group, became active in the movement in the 1950s. His contributions to surrealist periodicals are largely devoted to cultural and political "actuality." For *BIEF* and *La Brèche*, for example, he wrote excellent articles on racism, neofascism, and neo-Stalinism. His *Le mouvement des surréalistes* is the best study of surrealism in the postwar years and includes a superb critique of the 1969 split and its aftermath.

26. Saunders, *Who Paid the Piper?*,

27. In several 1990s telephone interviews, Gerome Kamrowski recalled not only Vincent Price's estimate of the new painting, but also his own recollection of the commercial exploitation of Pollock's work.

28. Philip Lamantia, letter to André Breton, *VVV*, no. 4 (1944), 18.

Fenton Johnson

One of the first African American poets to identify with a distinctly twentieth-century avant-garde, Fenton Johnson (1888–1958) was very much "on the scene" in Chicago in the 1910s and 1920s, the heyday of *The Little Review* and the free-for-all open forum known as the Dil Pickle. While still in his teens he was producing original plays at Chicago's Pekin Theatre. Kenneth Rexroth in his autobiography recalls Johnson's poetry readings at the Green Masque.

Although his early poetry drew largely on spirituals and dialect, Johnson soon found his own convention-shattering voice—a voice of radical and yet lyrical pessimism embodying, according to Sterling Brown, striking departures. The much anthologized "Tired," for example, is notable for its vehemently antisentimental and quasi-Dadaist/surrealist rejection of Western civilization and the Protestant work ethic. Though very different in tone, "The Phantom Rabbit" also sounds a new and disquieting note. A flashback to the African "Trickster" and to African American slave-era "Bre'r Rabbit" tales, it also looks ahead to the surrealist cartoon star Bugs Bunny, who would in turn, over the years, become a zoot-suiter, punk, hip-hopper, and all-around nonconformist icon.

Johnson's books include *A Little Dreaming* (1913), *Visions of the Dusk* (1915), *Songs of the Soil* (1916), and a collection of stories, *Tales of Darkest America* (1920).

THE PHANTOM RABBIT

Look, my weary brother, ere you die;
Night is here, and phantom nigh;
Soul of rabbit with the magic breath,
Soul of Life and foe of living Death.
Ere we die, my brother, ere we die.
Look, my weary sister, ere we die;
O'er the hills the phantom shadows lie;
Rabbit ghostly soothes your aching fears,
Rabbit ghostly dries your endless tears,
Ere we die, my sister, ere we die.

Songs of the Soil

TIRED

I am tired of work; I am tired of building up somebody else's civilization.
Let us take a rest, M'Lissy Jane.
I will go down to the Last Chance Saloon, drink a gallon or two of gin, shoot
    a game or two of dice and sleep the rest of the night on one of Mike's
    barrels.
You will let the old shanty go to rot, the white people's clothes turn to dust,
    and the Calvary Baptist Church sink to the bottomless pit.
You will spend your days forgetting you married me and your nights hunting
    the warm gin Mike serves the ladies in the rear of the Last Chance Saloon.
Throw the children into the river; civilization has given us too many.
It is better to die than to grow up and find that you are colored.
Pluck the stars out of the heavens. The stars mark our destiny. The stars
    marked my destiny.
I am tired of civilization.

George Herriman

Despite Ishmael Reed's noble efforts to set the record straight, most
people still do not know that the all-time greatest U.S. comic strip artist
was African American. Celebrated above all for his long-running *Krazy
Kat* saga, Herriman (1880–1944) elaborated a glorious open-ended mythology full of outrageous humor, constant surprise, philosophical insight, and plenty of poetry. With his action-packed dreamy drawing and
delirious wordplay, Herriman exemplified vernacular surrealism at its
very best. His comic tales embody the adventurous spirit and dynamism
of Alexandre Dumas, the wit and wisdom of Spinoza and Hegel, and the
fast pace of the silent film comedies he enjoyed.

Ishmael Reed, by the way, dedicated his great novel *Mumbo Jumbo* to
Herriman.

POSITIVILLY MARVILLIS

Wundafil wondafil—
There must be a catch in it
You turn off the light

an turn on the dark
You turn off the dark
an turn on the light
Positivilly MARVILLIS

Jean Toomer

"A flash bridges the gap between inner and outer, causing a momentary fusion and wholeness. Thus poetry starts." A major and much-
anthologized poet, deeply influenced by Walt Whitman, Toomer (1894–
1967) is best known for *Cane*, his Imagist- and Cubist-oriented 1923
novel, which includes many poems. A French translation of "Harvest
Song," from *Cane*, appeared in the second issue of *Tropiques* in July 1941.

An unusually complex figure, Toomer was subject to sudden, sweeping shifts in his philosophical and poetic outlook, including a six-year
stint as student of the Greek Armenian guru, Georges Gurdjieff and a
later (and longer) identification with Quakerism. In the midst of great
spiritual turmoil, in 1931 he self-published *Essentials*, a seventy-two-page
collection of highly imaginative and often cryptic aphorisms, dedicated
"to my friends in and near Chicago." Rarely discussed in the extensive
critical literature on Toomer, this small book can be considered the
poet's chief contribution to surrealism, although he does not use the
term. Not quite automatic writing but close to it, he claims he left each
line as it was formed originally, without fillers. These spontaneous jot-
tings invite comparison with the secret notebooks of such very different
writers as Pascal, Baudelaire, Lautréamont, Saint-Pol-Roux, and Georges
Henein.

ESSENTIALS

We are tired of not being intense.
Some people can endure so little so well that they appear to be
satisfied.

This is a psychological adventurer: one who, having had the stock
experiences of mankind, sets out at right angles to all previous experience
to discover new states of being.

At best, education is a means of acquiring other people's ideas and habits. At worst, it is a system of misfortunes. It is a systematic imposition of abnormalities upon normal being.

Aim to use insanity as a means of developing reason.

From dreams we talk to each other about reality. The science of life consists in deriving significance from all possibilities.

Essentials

Zora Neale Hurston

Folklorist, ethnographer, novelist, playwright, and a remarkably imaginative individualist, Zora Neale Hurston (1891–1960) has long been recognized as a central figure in everything having to do with the New Negro, the Harlem Renaissance, the Jazz Age, and—more recently—womanist literature and postmodern anthropology. She is still today very much on people's minds, and her books are acknowledged classics. Surrealists have greatly admired her poetic insight, originality, and nonconformism. As Ayana Karanja, one of her most cogent commentators, has noted, Hurston is the author whose work, more than that of any other black literary foremother, profoundly affects black women's writing today.

HOW THE GODS BEHAVE

Gods always behave like the people who make them. One can see the hand of the Haitian peasant in that boisterous God, Guedé, because he does and says the things that the peasants would like to do and say. You can see him in the market women, in the domestic servant who now and then appears before her employer "mounted" by this god who takes occasion to say many stinging things to the boss. You can see him in the field hand, and certainly in the group of women about a public well or spring, chattering, gossiping and dragging out the shortcomings of their employers and the people like him.

Nothing in Haiti is quite so obvious as that this loa is the deification of the common people of Haiti. The mulattoes give this spirit no food and pay it no attention at all. He belongs to the blacks and the uneducated blacks at that.

He is a hilarious divinity and full of the stuff of burlesque. This manifestation comes as near a social criticism of the classes by the masses as anything in all Haiti. Guedé has another distinction. It is the one loa which is entirely Haitian. There is neither European nor African background for it. It sprang up or was called up by some local need and now is firmly established among the blacks.

Tell My Horse

Richard Wright

One of the greatest U.S. novelists, Wright (1908–1960) was also among the front-ranking social critics of his time, as evidenced by such very different works as *Twelve Million Black Voices* and his introduction to St. Clair Drake and Horace R. Cayton's *Black Metropolis.* His late 1930s immersion in the surrealist adventure was not well known at the time, even by his friends, and in its most intense phase was relatively brief. As the excerpt published here demonstrates, however, surrealism marked a passionate moment and a major turning point in his life and thought. It also strongly affected his later novels, his haiku, and his ever-more-radical politics.

LAWD TODAY

"You know, the first time I ever set down beside a white man in a streetcar up North I was expecting for 'im to get up and shoot me."

"Yeah, I remember the first time I set down beside a white woman in a streetcar up North. I was setting there trembling and she didn't even look around."

"You feel funny as hell when you come North from the South."

"I use' to walk around all day feeling like I done forgot something."

"Yeah, every time I'd see a white man I'd feel like getting off the sidewalk to let 'im pass, like we had to do in the South."

"It took me a long time to get use' to feeling what freedom was like."

"Ain't it funny how some few folks is rich and just millions is poor?"

"And them few rich folks owns the whole world—"

"—and runs it like they please . . ."

". . . and the rest ain't got nothing?"

"Well, you know Gawd said the poor'll be with you always . . ."

"... and He was right, too."

"Some folks just ain't got no brains, that's all. If you divided up all the money in the world right now we'd be just where we is tomorrow."

"But don't you think all the white folks is smart. Some of 'em's crazy! I saw in the papers the other day where some old white woman over in Paris said a rose is a rose is a rose is a rose ... She wrote it in a book and when they asked her what it was she wouldn't tell ..."

"Wouldn't tell?"

"Wouldn't tell, man."

"Jeeesus, that sounds like old Cab Calloway."

"Aw, hell, he ain't never said nothing that crazy."

Lawd Today

Ralph Ellison

A brilliant, highly imaginative writer and critic, Ellison (1914–1994) to a large degree shared and articulated the surrealist point of view. Oklahoma-born and raised, he was educated as a musician at the Tuskegee Institute in the mid-1930s. A 1936 trip to New York, during which he visited Richard Wright, inspired his initial attempts as a fiction writer. His first novel, *Invisible Man*, received both the National Book Award and the Russwurm Award.

A prolific contributor to distinguished magazines and journals, Ellison taught at Bard College, the University of Chicago, Rutgers, and other leading universities. In 1964 he was appointed to the American Institute of Arts and Letters.

The texts published here are excerpted from *The Collected Essays of Ralph Ellison.*

THE POETRY OF IT

There is no place like a Negro barbershop for hearing what Negroes really think. There is more unself-conscious affirmation to be found here on a Saturday than you can find in a Negro college in a month, or so it seems to me.

I learned very early that in the realm of the imagination all people and their ambitions and interests could meet.

I read everything. I must have read fairy tales until I was 13, and I was always taken with the magical quality of writing, with the poetry of it.

I think that the mixture of the marvelous and the terrible is a basic condition of human life and that the persistence of human ideals represents the marvelous pulling itself up out of the chaos of the universe. In the fairy tale, beauty must be awakened by the beast; the beastly man can only regain his humanity through love. There are other terms for this but they come to much the same thing. Here the terrible represents all that hinders, all that opposes human aspiration, and the marvelous represents the triumph of the human spirit over chaos.

While the terms and the conditions are different and often change, our triumphs are few and thus must be recognized for what they are and preserved. Besides I would be hard put to say where the terrible could be localized in our national experience, for I see in so much of American life which lies beyond the Negro community the very essence of the terrible.

BEARDEN & THE DESTRUCTION OF THE ACCEPTED WORLD

Bearden seems to have told himself that in order to possess the meaning of his Southern childhood and Northern upbringing, and to keep his memories, dreams and values whole, he would have to re-create and humanize them by reducing them to artistic style. Thus in the poetic sense these works give plastic expression to a vision in which the socially grotesque conceals a tragic beauty, and they embody Bearden's interrogation of the empirical values of a society that mocks its own ideals through a blindness induced by its myth of race.

All this, ironically, by a man who visually, at least (he is light-skinned and perhaps more Russian than "black" in appearance), need never have been restricted to the social limitations imposed upon easily identified Negroes. Bearden's art is therefore not only an affirmation of his own freedom and responsibility as an individual and artist, but is an affirmation of the irrelevance of the notion of race as a limiting force in the arts. These are works of a man possessing a rare lucidity of vision.

Russell Atkins

The Cleveland-based musician and poet Russell Atkins (1926–) is best known as one of the most indefatigably experimentalist poets of the

1950s and 1960s. Around 1951 he gave his poetic and musical praxis the name Psychovisualism, basically a homegrown version of French Lettrism. His poems—many of them consisting primarily of scattered letters and random punctuation marks—prefigured the 1970s fad for concrete poetry.

Largely ignored and sometimes ridiculed for his eccentricity and what many readers called his incoherence, Atkins nonetheless had a small but devoted following. Encouraged by Langston Hughes, his *Free Lance* (1953-1976) became one of the livelier "little mags" of the time and was recognized as an especially important vehicle for young black poets. In recent years, Atkins' prolific and idiosyncratic work has begun to be discovered even by critics and scholars.

Never mentioned, however, is the curious fact that Atkins—long before Psychovisualism—published a poem (reprinted here) in the spring 1947 issue of the openly surrealist-oriented magazine *View*. Other contributors to that issue included surrealists Paul Nougé, Rufino Tamayo, David Hare, André Masson, Esteban Frances, and Joan Miró.

UPSTOOD UPSTAFFED

Upstood upstaffed passing sinuously away over airy arch
    streaming where all th' lustres (so splendid
    streaming an' sinuously shone
    bright where more sky
Upstood upstaffed) th' sumptuously ready
    flags full—
    th' shaded soothed an' blowing softly
    th' underlings smoothly
    with horses wavering with winds gently
    an' smooth th' men an' manners soft
    tangling with many manners thick
    gathering the steeds that
    forthwith
    up up
    Christophe
    appearing in th' imminent
    an' th' passion overjoying th' hour
    unfolding something splendidly
    had risen confused an' flamy
Highly th' imperial sign
    shone in his huger glory!

6. The 1950s Surrealist Underground in the United States

I. TED JOANS

> Jazz is my religion and surrealism is my point of view.
>
> —Ted Joans

In the face of systematic neglect and hostility, amounting to a kind of persecution, the unexpected, as so often happens, came to the rescue. Out of nowhere—or so it must have seemed—a veritable surrealist underground rose to the occasion. Its principal figures were not well known at the time, but they were highly skilled in the fine art of challenging the status quo, spreading the word, attracting attention, and finding reliable allies. Though limited in number, they spanned the continent, from New York to San Francisco. In contrast to the organizers of most surrealist groups in Europe and South America, these U.S. guerrilla poets were of impeccable working-class background. Both of them, moreover, were *black*.

Yes, the 1950s surrealist underground in the United States was started by an informal committee of two ("informal," because the two did not even know each other until much later in the decade.) The record, in any case, is plain. In the century's most ostentatiously antisurrealist decade, Ted Joans and Bob Kaufman—extraordinary characters by any standard—did more than anyone else to advance the cause of surrealist revolution in the United States.[1]

Joans started first. He was born in Cairo, Illinois, and discovered surrealism as a child. His mother was employed as a domestic by a wealthy white woman in or near Indianapolis (a friend of Nancy Cunard's). In that home he pored over copies of *Minotaure* and other French surrealist publications. A convinced surrealist at fourteen, Joans later studied painting at Indiana University, and he had a B.A. when in 1951 he took off for Greenwich Village and eventually became one of the first and for several years one of the best-known Beats. His surrealist costume balls, all-night parties, lively exhibition openings, and poetry readings were key events in the New York hip scene.

Joans in the 1950s had no communication with the surrealists in Paris (or elsewhere, for that matter). He did not know, for example, that Breton and his friends were part of the radical minority in France who defended the Mau-Mau rebellion, just as they later championed Lumumba's struggle in the Congo, and still later took up the cause of Black Power in the 1960s United States.

But Joans was on the same wavelength. One of the most memorable occasions was his 1953 surrealist Mau-Mau party, where Charlie "Bird" Parker appeared in a Mau-Mau costume.[2] The great alto saxophonist was one of Joans' closest New York friends and his roommate for a time. Many other jazz musicians, including Babs Gonzales and pianist Cecil Taylor, were also his good friends, along with numerous poets, artists, and revolutionaries such as Langston Hughes, Bob Thompson, and—a little later—Malcolm X.[3]

At Joans' parties, and also at his poetry readings around the Village and at colleges and universities all over the East Coast, he typically sounded off on his favorite subjects: the newest jazz (a.k.a. our own classical music); African independence; the black struggle for civil rights; surrealism; and rhinoceroses. Unquestionably, he helped put the names André Breton, Aimé Césaire, Wifredo Lam, and Benjamin Péret into wider U.S. circulation.

The abuse of the words "surrealism" and "surrealist" by the racist, reactionary former surrealist Dalí as well as by the commercial media irritated Joans to no end. Careful to point out that surrealism was far more than a way of writing and painting, he emphasized that its aims included not only the complete freedom of the imagination and radical social change, but also a far-reaching moral revolution.

Humor, then as always, was central to his message. His "It Is Time" manifesto—first published in *All of Ted Joans and No More* (1961), but clearly written in the mid-1950s—called for

—the President to study Dada and write a thesis on jazz and then apply for a Mau-Mau membership.
—jazz and more jazz and some more jazz and still more jazz.
—all workers to work only four hours a day, four days a week, and to be allowed to arrange that schedule themselves.
—rhinoceroses to roam the streets of Little Rock and spread joy.[4]

He especially urged students to read all the French Dada and Surrealist literature and the poetry of Langston Hughes. He freely offered a poet's advice:

Learn everything that you can in school, then come out and use it
   against them.
Dig all the old movies and applaud in wrong places in the new ones.
Love your life, and live by loving every minute in it.[5]

A good improviser in the black jazz tradition, he also had a surrealist's knack
for wordplay, and especially for subverting square song lyrics. With Ted Joans
holding forth, the corny pop song "I Saw Mama Kissing Santa Claus" suddenly
became "I saw Mau-Mau kicking Santa Claus."

Clearly, what Joans long afterward began to call his "Teducation" was already off to a good start.

His 1950s surrealist agitation, like Bob Kaufman's out in San Francisco, was
intimately allied with the then-growing ferment known as the Beat Generation.
Joans' 1958 reading at the Seven Arts Coffee Gallery, with Kerouac, Corso,
Ginsberg, and LeRoi Jones, made him a major player in the Beat game. As Jan
Carew remarked years later, Joans as a poet was essentially a *live act*, his poetry
at its best when he read it aloud. Hearing him read made people want to get his
books, and the books made them eager to go to his next reading.

As it turned out, his rapidly multiplying readings, combined with his other
events and art exhibits, added up to a highly popular one-man African American surrealist Beat Generation road show. It wasn't quite nonstop, but it kept
him on the move. Many of his appearances were arranged through the short-
lived but (while it lasted) very busy Rent-a-Beatnik Agency. Originally suggested by Village photographer Fred McDarrah as a joke, the agency not only
met a steady demand for "Beatniks" at parties, but also became a real source of
income for needy poets.

The Beat scene in the United States had other links to surrealism. According
to Diane diPrima, many people around the early Living Theatre in New York,
herself included, were strongly attracted by the surrealists' poetry, games, and
ideas.[6] Tom Postell, Amiri Baraka's friend, may not have considered himself a
surrealist, but his poems published in the little mag *Yugen* suggest that he was
definitely under the influence. Oliver Pitcher was also part of the scene. And
John Bracey recalls hearing Howard University's Percy Edward Johnston reading surrealist poetry—and getting arrested for it—at the Coffee & Confusion
coffeehouse in Baltimore, circa 1960.[7]

Postell, Pitcher, and Johnston are not well remembered today, and certainly
not as Beats, but back then they surely qualified as reinforcements for the Joans/
Kaufman surrealist underground.

Many years later, in his reminiscences of Charlie Parker, Joans looked back
on the Beats as "a swinging group of new people . . . intent on international

joy."[8] And he added: "We broke out of America's squareness just as Bird had done. We, as an unorganized movement of individuals, freed ourselves of the sickness of mass consumerism and pop culture conformity."

The Beat ethos figures prominently in his first books, *Funky Jazz Poems* (1959), *All of Ted Joans and No More*, and *The Hipsters* (1961). Today, some of this early work might seem a bit dated, especially the quaint and sometimes almost incomprehensible jargon of the time. But Joans' Beat shell contains many a surrealist kernel.

The Hipsters, a comic collage novel, is a good example of Joans' work as a visual artist. In word and image he satirizes such Village type as Jivey Leaguers, creepy creepniks, boring folkniks, and arrogant hipper-than-thou-niks. The book's four-and-a-half-page afterword, titled "L'Envoi," is an automatic text, opening with a militant rap on the rhinoceros and concluding with a quotation from André Breton.

In *The Beats* (1960), one of the first mass-market paperbacks on the subject, Seymour Krim offers this description: "Ted Joans is painter poet surrealist and gutsy outspoken Negro on the Greenwich Village scene. Has humor that can kill but is used for life; is a live wire a former trumpet-man, a graduate of the U. of Indiana, a lover of his favorite and mythical beast the rhinoceros, an American to his core, a bearded daddy who oozes creativity and jazz action the way squares breathe. A one-man movement who NEVER quits."[9]

II. BOB KAUFMAN

> People ask me, do I think surrealism will spread to Iowa.
> —Bob Kaufman

Exactly when Bob Kaufman began his own program of surrealist subversion is not known.[10] The rather muddled critical literature about him seems to agree that his earliest published work appeared in 1959, when *The Abomunist Manifesto* was serialized in the mimeographed Beat magazine, *Beatitude*, in San Francisco. According to his friends, however, Kaufman was a well-known participant in Bay Area poetry readings long before that—by 1956 if not earlier. In addition to these formal readings, Kaufman is also known to have read his poems and proclamations in the middle of the street, on street corners, and on the roofs of parked cars. At the Co-Existence Bagel Shop he frequently declaimed while standing on a table.

It seems plausible that a poet who took the trouble to read splendid poems on busy street corners and on tavern tables year after year might at least once in a while have run into someone who expressed interest in publishing a few of them. Mimeograph machines and small hand-set presses were still in wide use in the Fifties—the heyday of little mags—and it is not impossible that heretofore unknown poems or fragments by Kaufman appeared in one or more of them and may yet turn up.

For what it is worth, consider this anecdote from Franklin Rosemont:

> I recently had occasion to look through several issues of a little-known paper called *The Wasp*, a four-page hand-set and hand-printed weekly devoted to cultural affairs in and around Woodstock, New York, in the 1950s. My chief interest was not Woodstock but the anarchist couple who edited the paper: Holley Cantine and Dachine Rainer, better known as the editors of the influential anarchist journal *Retort*. Turning the pages, I found the following short notice under the title "New Band at Brattain's" (a local pub): "With the inauguration of a Modern Jazz policy, Brattain's brings to the community an art form sorely needed in these parts, for while our painting is abreast of the times, the only jazz available has been somewhat dated (circa 1922)! As to the group itself, its leader, who answers to the very common title Bobby, is quite an uncommon musician, an accomplished saxophonist, and consummate artist. He creates music for our time, and very well, too." This strong plug for the new jazz, signed "BOB KAUFMAN" (in capital letters), appeared in the issue for August 9, 1952.

Was the author *our* Bob Kaufman? Who can say for sure? But we do know this much: the poet Bob Kaufman was an ardent modern jazz enthusiast, indeed, a man deeply interested in all the arts, and in social radicalism, too, especially anarchism. From the late 1940s and for several years thereafter as a seaman, he is known to have divided his time between New York and San Francisco. Woodstock was then a flourishing leftist bohemian art center frequented by other anarchist-inclined West Coast poets, including Robert Duncan. A visit to Woodstock in 1952 would have been wholly in keeping with Kaufman's major interests in life at that time.

Sifting through the conflicting chronologies of Kaufman's life is no easy task. He did not date his poems, and evidently did not carry on any correspondence. It would be nice to know precisely when and where he made that bold and unequivocal affirmation: "I acknowledge the demands of surrealist realization"—but the chances of pinpointing it are slim indeed. Based on the recollections of friends, however, it seems safe to conclude that his passion for surrealist subversion—as exemplified by the *Abomunist Manifesto*—was well known, at least in the Bay Area, several years before the *Manifesto*'s publication in broadside form by City Lights in the fall of 1959.

ABoMUNIST MANIFESTo

BOB
KAUFMAN

Cover of Bob Kaufman's *The Abomunist Manifesto* (1959), a pamphlet/broadside and a classic of surrealist humor.

The *Manifesto* is an extraordinary document. Decades later Franklin Rosemont can still recall, vividly, reading it and then rereading it in the basement at City Lights Bookstore in September 1960:

> Although I had discovered surrealism only a year or so before, I knew
> enough to distinguish true surrealism from the many pseudo varieties
> and immediately recognized Kaufman's wonderful aphorisms ("Laugh-
> ter sounds orange at night") as the real thing—as good as any in the *152
> Proverbs* by Éluard and Péret. I also greatly appreciated the *Manifesto's*
> strong anarchism ("Abomunists vote against everyone by not voting
> for anyone"). But how disappointed I was when the folks at City Lights
> told me that Kaufman was not only out of town—but probably in New
> York!

Part manifesto, part parody, and part poem, the *Abomunist Manifesto* is all defiance, all humor. The word "Abomunism" is itself something of a conundrum, incorporating as it does the Abominable Snowman, Abolitionism, the A-Bomb, small-c communism, and even the author's own name (the *Manifesto* is signed "Bomkauf").

The text, subtly combining brilliant maxims worthy of La Rochefoucauld and Pascal, and hard-hitting shaggy-dog stories reminiscent of some of the lesser-known pages of Marx's *Capital*, differs radically—and immensely—from the work of other U.S. poets of the 1950s. In his *Manifesto*, Kaufman fearlessly embodies a no-holds-barred critique of the consumer society, government, militarism, Hollywood, law 'n' order, greed, bigotry, and other forms of authoritarianism and exploitation. In short, he issues an all-out challenge to white Christian-capitalist civilization. Instead of the tyranny and conformity of what he and his friends called "the square world," he urges nothing less than a truly free and poetic society: an anarchist, or surrealist world.

The *Manifesto's* openly revolutionary character reminds us that Kaufman was also very much an activist, a poet deeply involved in the struggle for civil rights and racial equality, and just as strongly against white supremacy, police brutality, the death penalty, nuclear weapons, and war. His activism, which sometimes assumed provocative forms, infuriated the blatantly racist San Francisco police. In one year Kaufman was arrested thirty-six times.[11] At a time when the word "poet" was increasingly synonymous with "academic," Kaufman adventurously took poetry to the streets.

Abomunism and social activism, Kaufman's preferred forms of surrealist action, set him far apart from the U.S. literary mainstream. Characteristically, he was also way to the left of the Beat scene. In his 1991 National Public Radio documentary on the poet, David Henderson quotes Kaufman's longtime friend

Jerry Stoll: "Bob was functioning as a critic of society in a much more social and political way than any of the other poets in North Beach. . . . It is really clear that people like Ginsberg and the rest of them, when they were political activists, were following Kaufman. They didn't lead Kaufman, he led them. He had the political consciousness."[12]

I would add that Kaufman also had a *poetic* consciousness. Indeed, with the exception of his good friend and fellow surrealist Philip Lamantia, many—perhaps most—of the North Beach poets and wannabes were more than a little jealous of Kaufman. (In France, he was celebrated as the Black Rimbaud.) The jealousy was in fact rather out in the open. Glaringly, for example, his work was not included either in the "San Francisco Renaissance" issue of *Evergreen Review* (1957) or in Donald Allen's anthology, *The New American Poets* (1960).

Such omissions cannot be considered innocent oversights. After all, what is most important about Kaufman is the fact that he was the author of some of the most beautiful, playful, and *effective* poetry of the last four hundred years. These are poems of a wildly unanticipated magic. Profoundly moving, Kaufman's poems of love, jazz, wonder, delirium, despair, and ecstasy remain his chief title to glory.

His altercations with cops, judges, and jailers are by no means negligible, but it was his magnificent poetry that did so much to keep the surrealist fires burning in repressive and gloomy times. Despite long years of dire poverty and illness, aggravated by heavy drinking, smoking, and drug use, he stubbornly held fast to a rigorous poetic praxis based on his own ready-or-not, no-compromise "surrealist realization." Dazzling examples of pure psychic automatism at its purest and most powerful, Kaufman's poetry has never ceased to resonate with the spirit of wholehearted revolt and the marvelous.

"When I die," he said, "I won't stay dead."[13] Over twenty years after his death from emphysema, his poetry is more alive, more contemporary, and more widely read than 95 percent of the work of the best-selling American poets of his time.

Notes

1. Most of the information in this section was supplied by Ted Joans— much of it in conversation, the rest from published writings and letters.

2. The postwar politics of the surrealist movement are detailed in Jean-Louis Bédouin, *Vingt ans du surréalisme;* Gérard Durozoi, *Histoire du mouvement surréaliste;* Joubert, *Le mouvement des surréalistes;* Penelope Rosemont, *Surrealist Women;* and Sakolsky, *Surrealist Subversions.*

3. The New York Mau-Mau party is described in Joans, "Bird and the Beats."

4. *All of Ted Joans and No More*, 51–53.

5. Ibid.; original emphasis. See also Joans, *The Hipsters.*

6. Diane diPrima, conversations with Franklin Rosemont, Chicago, April and May 2000.

7. John Bracey, telephone conversation with Franklin Rosemont, June 2006.

8. Joans, "Bird and the Beats."

9. Seymour Krim, ed., *The Beats*, 211.

10. Biographical data on Kaufman is scarce and undependable, but over the years Philip Lamantia, Cecil Taylor, Nancy Joyce Peters, Ted Joans, Diane diPrima, and Maynard Krasne have provided helpful details and reminiscences.

11. Raymond Foye, quoted in David Henderson's introduction to Kaufman's posthumous *Cranial Guitar*, 13.

12. Jerry Stoll, in ibid., 9–10.

13. Kaufman, *Solitudes Crowded with Loneliness*, 3.

Ted Joans

In the absence of an organized U.S. Surrealist Group in the 1950s, Ted
Joans (1928–2003) in New York and Bob Kaufman in San Francisco—
three thousand miles apart and at first unknown to each other—started
an authentically surrealist agitation of their own at the margins of the
Beat Generation.

Joans, born in Cairo, Illinois, discovered surrealism as a child, when
his mother, employed as a domestic in the house of a wealthy white
woman, showed him copies of *Minotaure* and other French surrealist
publications. A convinced surrealist at fourteen, he later studied painting at Indiana University, and he had a B.A. when in 1951 he took off for
Greenwich Village and became one of the first and for several years one
of the most celebrated Beats. His surrealist costume balls, lively exhibition openings, and poetry readings were key events in the New York hip
scene.

In the 1960s Joans left the United States for Africa, and he maintained a small house in Timbuktu for the rest of his life. Over the
years he traveled widely—all over Africa, Europe, the United States,
Mexico—with particularly long stays in Paris. He wrote to André Breton
and soon became his good friend. Active in the Paris Surrealist Group
for years, Joans also visited surrealists elsewhere. Indeed, his nomadic
ways made him a natural liaison between surrealists in other countries
and often an inspirer of international surrealist activities. A close collaborator and frequent guest of the Chicago Surrealist Group, he played
a decisive role in shaping the 1993 "Totems without Taboos" exhibition,
the first show in the United States devoted entirely to "exquisite corpse"
drawings, paintings, and collages.

Joans' impact on the surrealist movement, as poet and artist but also
as activist, was enormous and far-reaching, as in his efforts to change
the name of Lake Victoria to Lake Louis Armstrong (or Lake Satchmo,
for short), and his tireless campaign to save the rhinoceroses of the
world. He was also a crucial link between surrealism and the international Black Arts movement.

It is not easy to speak of him in the past tense, for Ted Joans' presence in world surrealism is still very much in evidence.

TED JOANS SPEAKS

Excerpts from Letters to André Breton

Who am I? I am Afro-American and my name is Ted Joans. Without surrealism, I would not have been able to survive the abject vicissitudes and acts of racist violence that the white man in the United States has constantly imposed on me. Surrealism became the weapon that I chose to defend myself, and it has been and always will be my own way of life.

I was born in 1928, the year of *Nadja, Treatise on Style,* and *The Spirit Against Reason.* For a time I lived in Kentucky, in a racially segregated city. I did not have the right to use the public library, and I was not allowed to attend the only local school that taught French.

In 1941 I met an admirer of Dalí who gave me the latter's address. I wrote to him for advice, and sent him some drawings. I also told this robber about my obsession: the rhinoceros. Neither he nor his representative sent me even a word of reply, but in 1951 Avida Dollars gave a conference at the Sorbonne, in which he proclaimed "his discovery of the rhinoceros." The rhinoceros is an African and Asian animal. I made my first drawing of a rhinoceros in 1939. I love rhinoceroses because they are rhinoceroses.

I moved to New York in 1951, after obtaining my diploma from the University of Indiana. In New York I encountered many isolated individuals who loved surrealism, but you and the other surrealists had already left the U.S.

Finally, I went to Europe in 1960, and I met you on June 6. I left for London the next day. My friend in London, Simon Watson Taylor, urged me not to become involved with the surrealists in Paris because, he said, most of them are Communists.

I left London for Nigeria, and later returned to America. I have read my surrealist poems with the protagonists of the Beat Generation. I have obtained much publicity among the Beatniks, so much so that I decided to exile myself from the America of the Beatniks and to go back to Africa. Africa is my mother country, and I have a small house in Timbuktu, in Mali. My plan is to write and paint in Africa until the U.S. rids itself of racist violence and moral poverty.

I was awakened today by the sun rising over the mountains of the Rif. I have just read seven strophes of *Les Chants de Maldoror* (as I do every day).

*   *   *

Perhaps you do not know exactly what a hipster is? Well, a hipster is a surrealist in both his internal and external activity. He is "in the current of things" (hip), and consequently nonconformist. The hipster dreams, but most of his time is spent in putting his dreams into reality. Sometimes he even creates the Marvelous without dreaming. Many of my Afro-American friends in the ghettoes of America are forced to lead a hipster's life out of simple necessity.

The white poets of the Beat Generation have borrowed the hipster attitude from black Americans. They have adopted their argot, comportment, and jazz music—all of which embody a surrealist point of view. The Beat Generation owes practically everything to surrealism. I have discussed this subject with Kerouac, Corso, and Ginsberg.

My dear friend, I am coming to Paris this summer to find a gallery to exhibit my paintings. But in autumn I shall return to Africa. I hope to see you—you and the other surrealists. This will be the realization of a dream for me. I am one of your most ardent disciples.

Bob Kaufman

In an excoriating 1976 critique of the so-called Post-Olson generation in U.S. poetry, and its "debasement of language," San Francisco surrealist Philip Lamantia acknowledged a very few exceptions to the prevailing reactionary conformity. His first exception, for reasons "both moral and poetical," was Bob Kaufman (1925–1986), whose no-holds-barred imagery exemplifies surrealism's unfettered imagination and "convulsive beauty" at their most daring and dazzling.

Kaufman's initial broadside, the *Abomunist Manifesto* (1959), is a marvelous mix of wild humor and revolutionary fervor, unlike anything else in the poetry of the time. Amiri Baraka said that Kaufman and his poetry were nothing less than a radical outsider force.

Kaufman was born in New Orleans, the son of an African American Jewish Pullman porter father and a black Martinican schoolteacher mother. Books were prized in the Kaufman family, and Bob—like his contemporary, Ted Joans—grew up a manic reader. A seaman in early manhood, he also took up radical politics, which eventually resolved into a kind of Buddhist-influenced surrealist anarchism. In his poetry as in his activism, he lived the life of a one-man surrealist insurrection. As with other outspoken defenders of free speech and subversive laughter, he often ran into trouble with the agencies of law 'n' order. During the Beat years in San Francisco's North Beach, he was routinely beaten and jailed by the white-supremacist police.

Two collections of his works, *Solitudes Crowded with Loneliness* (1965) and *Golden Sardine* (1967) have gone through many editions and brought Kaufman to wide attention.

ABOMUNIST MANIFESTO

ABOMUNISTS JOIN NOTHING BUT THEIR HANDS OR LEGS,
OR OTHER SAME.
ABOMUNISTS SPIT ANTI-POETRY FOR POETIC REASONS
AND FRINK.
ABOMUNISTS DO NOT LOOK AT PICTURES PAINTED
BY PRESIDENTS AND UNEMPLOYED PRIME MINISTERS.
IN TIMES OF NATIONAL PERIL, ABOMUNISTS, AS REALITY
AMERICANS, STAND READY TO DRINK THEMSELVES
TO DEATH FOR THEIR COUNTRY.
ABOMUNISTS DO NOT FEEL PAIN, NO MATTER HOW MUCH
IT HURTS.
ABOMUNISTS DO NOT USE THE WORD SQUARE EXCEPT WHEN
TALKING TO SQUARES.
ABOMUNISTS READ NEWSPAPERS ONLY TO ASCERTAIN THEIR
ABOMINUBILITY.
ABOMUNISTS NEVER CARRY MORE THAN FIFTY DOLLARS
IN DEBTS ON THEM.
ABOMUNISTS BELIEVE THAT THE SOLUTION OF PROBLEMS
OF RELIGIOUS BIGOTRY IS, TO HAVE A CATHOLIC
CANDIDATE FOR PRESIDENT AND A PROTESTANT
CANDIDATE FOR POPE.
ABOMUNISTS DO NOT WRITE FOR MONEY; THEY WRITE
THE MONEY ITSELF.
ABOMUNISTS BELIEVE ONLY WHAT THEY DREAM ONLY
AFTER IT COMES TRUE.
ABOMUNIST CHILDREN MUST BE REARED ABOMUNIBLY.
ABOMUNIST POETS, CONFIDENT THAT THE NEW LITERARY
FORM "FOOT-PRINTISM," HAS FREED THE ARTIST
OF OUTMODED RESTRICTIONS, SUCH AS: THE ABILITY TO
READ AND WRITE, OR THE DESIRE TO COMMUNICATE,
MUST BE PREPARED TO READ THEIR WORK AT DENTAL
COLLEGES, EMBALMING SCHOOLS, HOMES FOR UNWED
MOTHERS, HOMES FOR WED MOTHERS, INSANE ASYLUMS,
USO CANTEENS, KINDERGARTENS, AND COUNTY JAILS.
ABOMUNISTS NEVER COMPROMISE THEIR REJECTIONARY
PHILOSOPHY.
ABOMUNISTS REJECT EVERYTHING EXCEPT SNOWMEN.

Abomunist Manifesto

$$ ABOMUNUS CRAXIOMS $$

Egyptian mummies are lousy dancers.
Alcoholics cannot make it on root beer.
Jazz never made it back down the river.
Licking postage stamps depletes the body fluids.
Fat automobiles laugh more than others, and frink.
Men who die in wars become seagulls and fly.
Roaches have a rough time of it from birth.
People who read are not happy.
People who do not read are not happy.
People are not very happy.
These days people get sicker quicker.
The sky is less crowded in the West.
Psychiatrists pretend not to know everything.
Way out people know the way out.
Laughter sounds orange at night, because
reality is unrecognizable while it exists.
Abomunists knew it all along,
but couldn't get the butterscotch down.

Abomunist Manifesto

ABOMUNIST ELECTION MANIFESTO

1. Abomunists vote against everyone by not voting for anyone.
2. The only propositions Abomunists support are those made to members of the opposite sex.
3. Abomunists demand the abolition of Oakland.
4. Abomunists demand low-cost housing for homosexuals.
5. Abomunists demand suppression of illegal milk traffic.
6. Abomunists demand statehood for North Beach.
7. The only office Abomunists run for is the unemployment office.

Abomunist Manifesto

Tom Postell

In his 1984 autobiography, Amiri Baraka recalls Tom Postell (under the
name Tim Poston) as a wild character, a real poet, and, most enticingly,
influenced by surrealism. For a time, despite the fact that Postell was also
a heavy drinker and, indeed, a bottom-of-the-barrel bohemian, he was
one of Baraka's closest friends.

Frequenter of a milieu that included Billie Holiday, Archie Shepp,
Jack Kerouac, Diane diPrima, James Baldwin, Jack Micheline, Allen
Ginsberg, Gregory Corso, Frank O'Hara, Franz Kline, and many other
poets, artists, and musicians, Postell seems to have published very little,
and has been almost entirely ignored by literary historians, critics, and
memoirists.

The two poems reprinted here originally appeared in the little mag
Yugen (1958).

GERTRUDE STEIN RIDES THE TORN DOWN EL TO NYC

Then colors rose through the leaves in light
surprise.
The last peacock poised and sighed on the leaves
and rose.
Wonderful day careens while blighted riff-raff
children skate and
Laughingly dig the hole for the mid-western
bonfire.
Wrap honey in velvet air and hide it in October's
searching breath.
The bonfire dwindles as the circus leaves and
the animals roar.
It's only in the sun that madness splatters into
joy . . .
Cover down the moon for the night before you
lift the skirts of a cloud.
Love knocks on the inside of my skull and kicks
in my stomach.
A doe licks the gum from a tree and runs into
the woods.
She lets me govern her gaze when the parade

blares its colors.
Gertrude Stein is long dead but under cover rides
the torn-down El.

HARMONY

We, who stung stone know how our toil bathed us in ash, while lilies of the land covered their heads and shuttered. We had grass blades for legs and tree limbs for arms and our mouths were big black clouds, which at times would burst warnings to civilization.

We remember the times we were nearly human, and almost understood the caresses of fried fish laced around our groins by ambassador girl diplomats from the sorry state of God.

You and I were the wine glass tasting the wine but swallowing none. Sitting on the forgotten table of love. We looked in our own eyes and blinked stars the moons were jealous of.

I loved you under the crushing sledge of wrath, of morning's pressure on the heat of evening. Moons and secrets.

Percy Edward Johnston

A leading figure in the influential Howard University poets' group of the 1950s and 1960s, Johnston (1930–1993) published his work in such Black Arts "little mags" and compilations as *Dasein* and *Burning Spear.* Author of scholarly essays on the philosophy of Jupiter Hammon and a 1976 book, *Phenomenology of Space and Time*, he also wrote jazz-inspired poems. More than once, in those Beat times, his readings at Baltimore coffeehouses resulted in a night in jail. Rarely anthologized, Johnston's poetic work awaits rediscovery.

VARIATIONS ON A THEME

To you, Eileen, and to New England's
slaveship owners' sons, I confess:
I have a library card,
I wasted the GI bill on poetry.

I read the Bill of Rights,
I don't worship the white man's God,
I sleep where my caramel body is unwelcome,
I don't salute old glory!
I wept for Patrice Lumumba,
I respect Jomo Kenyatta!

LeRoi Jones, *Yugen* (1958)

Katherine Dunham, a University of Chicago Anthropology student, formed the first African American dance troupe. Her *Tropical Revue* performed in New York in 1944.

7. Surrealism, Black Power, Black Arts

We must find a way to overthrow the idea on this planet that whites
are superior beings.

—Larry Neal

The Sixties turned out to be the brightest, liveliest, and most hopeful decade in
a bloody and bewildering century. In the United States those ten frantic years
encompassed countless interconnected sagas. Inaugurated in part by a generation that considered itself Beat long before it finished high school, here all of
a sudden was a nationwide—and ultimately *worldwide*—anticonformist youth
movement that made the "roaring twenties" and swing-era Forties look tame
in comparison. Inspired by activist thinkers as different as Malcolm X, Martin
Luther King, Rosa Parks, James Forman, Robert F. Williams, Max Stanford, Ted
Joans, and Bob Kaufman, "hip" young people of all ages and colors were everywhere saying *no* to race discrimination, the Bomb, the House Un-American
Activities Committee, and the ludicrously square American way of life. But
they were also hollering *yes* to the new jazz, the civil rights struggle, African
independence, the Cuban Revolution, hitchhiking, and the four r's—revelry,
rebellion, revolt, and revolution—in all their myriad forms.[1]

Few historians have acknowledged the stimulating role of surrealism in the
new cultural and political atmosphere, but there is no getting around the fact
that the international surrealist movement flourished throughout the decade,
and well beyond it. Between 1958 and the mid-1970s new surrealist groups
were formed in Tokyo, Amsterdam, Milan, Caracas, Athens, Lisbon, São Paulo,
Chicago, and London. Surrealists in exile from various Arab countries—Algeria, Iraq, Lebanon, and Syria—organized a group in Paris. Nearly all of these
groups published journals; many also issued books, pamphlets, and tracts.

As the decade began, surrealism in the United States was still centered in
Ted Joans' Greenwich Village in New York and Bob Kaufman's North Beach in
San Francisco. Largely thanks to their efforts, however, a surrealist *spirit* was
soon making its presence felt just about everywhere. Distrust of authority, defiance of injustice, and a passionate yearning for *Freedom Now!* were in the wind,

along with a large-scale resurgence of poetry—not just reading it, but *living* it—and a firm determination to change the world and have a good time. Social transformations regarded as impossible just a few years earlier seemed now, in the wake of the overthrow of the Batista tyranny in Cuba, not only possible, but easy. Such old-fashioned terms as "mutual aid" and "direct action" were part of the vocabulary of many high schoolers. The very air seemed to tingle with a spirit of utopian vision, reckless daring, high humor, and—wonder of wonders—a new radical solidarity.

THE BLACK ARTS MOVEMENT AND SURREALISM

> Spirit is a weapon of defense.
> —Pierre Reverdy

Much of the historiography of the period has been obsessed with the white New Left, the white hippie scene, white rock stars, and such trivia as Pop Art. For many of us, however, it was clear then—and is even more obvious today— that the driving force of what was greatest and most enduring in the Sixties was the radical Civil Rights movement, its revolutionary successors, and, not least, its cultural affiliates and offshoots. Martha and the Vandellas' "Dancin' in the Streets" and James Brown's "Say It Loud—I'm Black and I'm Proud" were anthems of the age.

It was the age of Black Power. The term, as Ted Joans liked to point out, was coined in 1954 by Richard Wright, who used it as the title of his book on the African Revolution. Popularized in the latter days of SNCC (Student Non-violent Coordinating Committee) by Stokely Carmichael (Kwame Ture), who also used it as the title of his 1967 book coauthored with Charles Hamilton, it became one of the catchiest two-word slogans of that decade and the next. Like the ghetto riots during the long hot summers of those years, Black Power was suddenly here, there, and everywhere: in schools and colleges, in the workplace, in the unions, in wildcat strikes, in polling places, in sports, in the neighborhoods, and in the streets. As the older tactics of nonviolent civil disobedience gave way to self-defense and empowerment, a new and explicitly revolutionary spirit rose, so to speak, from the ashes. New groups emerged, including the Black Panther Party, the Republic of New Africa, and the League of Revolutionary Black Workers. Even the white left was affected. The liberal Students for a Democratic Society (SDS), which had long upheld such insipid slogans as "Part of the Way with LBJ," at last dared to come out against U.S. imperialism.

The age of Black Power was also the age of the Black Arts movement. Chronologically, in fact, Black Arts came first, but the attention it received from the media—particularly from the white media—was always much less than that paid to Black Power. Far greater was FBI and police attention. Never before or since in the United States have so many "officers of the law" devoted so much time to spying on and disrupting small collectives of poets and artists. Despite the conflicts that sometimes separated Black Arts and Black Power groups—to say nothing of the many police-instigated internal conflicts of each—the two currents by and large considered themselves part of the same struggle and concentrated on the essential: *black unity.*[2]

It was an exciting time. Rarely in the history of this country has there been so much serious coast-to-coast cultural ferment. Rarely, too, have the results been so impressive and enduring. The Black Arts movement embraced poets, painters, sculptors, novelists, actors, dancers, playwrights, a few filmmakers, and a powerful cohort of musicians. The marvelous black sounds of Thelonious Monk, Max Roach, Cecil Taylor, John Coltrane, Ornette Coleman, Charles Mingus, Eric Dolphy, Fred Anderson, Sun Ra, Pony Poindexter—and such younger cats as Joseph Jarman, Lester Bowie, Anthony Braxton, Roscoe Mitchell, and Henry Threadgill—did much to define the special magic of that decade. Nearly all their work is now recognized as classic.

The poets—and it is worth recalling that many of the musicians were also poets, and that poets and musicians had a way of flocking together in those years—were especially persistent and prolific; the sheer quantity of magazines they produced is dazzling. Here are the names of just a few: *Yugen, The Cricket,* and *Black Theatre* from New York; *Burning Spear* and *Dasein,* published by students from Howard University; *Ex Umbra,* another student publication, from Durham, North Carolina; *Soulbook* (closely linked to the Revolutionary Action movement, RAM) and *The Journal of Black Poetry* from San Francisco; and *Black Graphics International* from Detroit. Chicago's Association for the Advancement of Creative Musicians (AACM) also issued a magazine that included art and poetry. These publications, and many more like them, reflected diverse inspirations.

Surrealism, like poetry, politics, and adventure, appealed in various ways to Black Arts militants as different as Amiri Baraka, Larry Neal, Jayne Cortez, Cecil Taylor, A. B. Spellman, Ernest Allen, James G. Spady, Ishmael Reed, Aaron (Ibn Pori) Pitts, and no doubt many others. Although the word "surrealism" occurs only rarely in published discussions and debates on the black aesthetic and the new black poetry, it was nonetheless an important part of the mix.

Baraka, who as LeRoi Jones had acquired an international reputation as a Beat poet, was already one of the best-known poets in the United States in those days, and unquestionably *the* best-known *black* poet. His interest in Dada—and specifically a black Dada—was highly influential and much discussed. Less well known, but even more impactful in the long run, was his interest in surrealism, gleaned largely, as his 1984 *Autobiography* suggests, via his erratic and now scarcely remembered friend, the poet Tom Postell.[3] What intrigued Baraka about surrealism was not only its poetry, but also and above all its volatile blend of poetry and revolution, words that became, in effect, Baraka's lifelong motto.

Larry Neal was not only a cofounder of the Black Arts movement, but also one of its best theorists, a close friend of Baraka's, and the author of one of the movement's poetic masterpieces: *Hoodoo Hollerin' Bebop Ghosts* (1974). The essays collected in the 1989 posthumous volume *Visions of a Liberated Future*, with introductions by Jayne Cortez and others, are as fresh and vivid today as they were in the 1960s and 1970s. While they are not "about" surrealism, many of these essays reflect a surrealist sensibility, and we have it on the word of his friend and fellow Philadelphian James G. Spady that Neal in fact loved surrealism.

The essays resound with inspired provocations. A tribute to Malcolm X opens with the challenge: "What I liked most about Malcolm was his sense of poetry." And a splendid essay on Ralph Ellison—in large part a lyrical defense of the unfettered imagination—urges that we "consider . . . a system of politics and art that is as fluent, as functional, and as expansive as black music. No such system now exists; we're gonna have to build it. And when it is finally realized, it will be a conglomerate, gleaned from the *whole* of all our experiences."[4] Such dreams, with their boldness, beauty, and strongly implied action, are more than ever needed today. Anyone interested in surrealism, poetry, and revolution would do well to read and reflect on the writings of Larry Neal.

The Black Arts movement also stimulated the demand for translations of black and other revolutionary writings from abroad. Here, too, surrealism was a moving force. In the 1960s and 1970s, English translations of major works by André Breton, Aimé Césaire, Léon Damas, Joyce Mansour, and Tchicaya U Tam'si became readily available for the first time. The 1968 Présence Africaine bilingual edition of Césaire's classic *Return to My Native Land* had a significant impact on many in the Black Arts movement, as did the Grove Press paperback of his *A Season in the Congo* (a play about Lumumba) that same year. Césaire's scathing *Discourse on Colonialism*, published by Monthly Review Press in 1972, was another book high on Black Arts/Black Power reading lists. Edward A. Jones' 1971 anthology, *Voices of Negritude*—which includes poems by Césaire, Damas, David Diop, and others—was also influential.

Meanwhile, in Paris, books by Ted Joans and Bob Kaufman were translated into French and given considerable media attention.[5] Joans' poems and other writings also regularly appeared in the publications of the Surrealist Groups of Paris, Amsterdam, and Chicago.

Now and then a particularly bold periodical in the United States invited a mingling of Black Power, Black Arts, and surrealism. In 1970, for example, Paul Buhle's *Radical America*—the leading SDS journal—devoted a special issue to surrealism (with texts by André Breton, Robert Benayoun, Aimé Césaire, Ted Joans, Etienne Léro, Clément Magloire-Saint-Aude, Joyce Mansour, the Chicago Group, and many others, plus drawings by Wifredo Lam). The special issue concept caught on, and later issues included one on the work of C.L.R. James, and another on the League of Revolutionary Black Workers, edited by Eric Perkins, John Bracey, and John Higginson.

Another example was Lawrence Ferlinghetti's 1974 *City Lights Anthology*. Along with a fifty-two-page section entitled "The Surrealist Movement in the United States," this stunning compilation also includes a play by Ed Bullins; a lecture by Herbert Marcuse; poems by Huey Newton, Ericka Higgins, and Gary Snyder; and a tribute to Bob Kaufman by Kaye McDonough.

JAYNE CORTEZ: FREE SPIRIT AND FIRESPITTER

> I throw the flame, now catch it on the wing of my laughter.
> —Lucie Thésée

A later City Lights publication, the explicitly surrealist *Free Spirits: Annals of the Insurgent Imagination* (Jablonski, 1982), highlights Black Arts and Black Power concerns even more. A few excerpts from the *Free Spirits* opening minimanifesto will convey something of its exuberant character:

> *Free Spirits* desire the emancipation of all humankind.
> *Free Spirits* know that no revolution has gone far enough.
> *Free Spirits* reject cynicism and despair.
> *Free Spirits* resolve immobilizing antinomies.
> *Free Spirits* dream extravagantly.
> *Free Spirits* affirm the power of the imagination.
> *Free Spirits* reveal the poetry of life.
> *Free Spirits* find images to inspire action.
> *Free Spirits* evolve models of equality and freedom.
> *Free Spirits* exalt love.
> *Free Spirits* imagine possible futures.
> *Free Spirits* move to realize surreality.

Along with much else, its 224 large pages include articles by Bill Cole, Ornette Coleman, Mel Edwards, Wilson Harris, C.L.R. James, Ted Joans, James G. Spady, and Cheikh Tidiane Sylla. It also features poems by Amina Baraka, Dennis Brutus, Alexis de Veaux, and—of special importance in regard to surrealism—Jayne Cortez.

An inspiring presence and strong, clear voice in both the Black Arts and Black Power movements, Jayne Cortez was also coeditor of *Free Spirits*. She has

contributed prolifically to African American publications, and has also collaborated on every collective publication of the surrealist movement in the United
States since Ted Joans introduced her to the group in the mid-1970s. She is
widely and rightly recognized as one of the finest poets of our time, and, as is so
often true of first-rate poets, she is also a sharp thinker, a woman with audacious
and far-reaching ideas.

As is true of much of the work of Aimé Césaire and Benjamin Péret, Cortez'
risk-taking poetry is often political without ever being boringly propagandis-
tic. Bravely defying injustice and misery, her explosive turn-the-world-upside-
down imagery, in which surprise follows surprise, not only calls for a better,
more harmonious world, but also contributes to its realization. Profoundly
surrealist from cover to cover, her poetry broadcasts the language of high-
flying, no-compromise *freedom*, always wildly original and as fresh as a week
from tomorrow.[6]

Her public readings and her many recordings are memorable events in the
lives of those who are fortunate enough to hear her. Together with her many
books and chapbooks, her records and CDs add up to an indispensable body of
work—a library of the Marvelous at its most magical and revolutionary best.

A longtime friend of Ted Joans, Cortez since her teens has also been deeply
involved in the world of black music. Her good friends and codreamers include poets, writers, musicians, painters, surrealists, surrealist sympathizers, and
radical activists from all over the world. Through the years, however, her most
direct contact with ongoing surrealist activity has been with the globetrotting
Joans, the historian and social critic Robin D. G. Kelley, and the group in the
Windy City.

THE CHICAGO SURREALIST GROUP

> For all of us, the discovery of surrealism was much more than a turning
> point; it was a major *turn-on*, and really changed our lives.
> —Simone Collier

Surrealism in Chicago has a long history. Some of the first English translations
of surrealist writings appeared in the mid-1920s in Margaret Anderson's journal,
The Little Review, founded in Chicago. Marcel Duchamp had his first-ever U.S.
exhibition at the Chicago Arts Club in 1937. Elisa and André Breton spent a
few days in the city in 1945, on their way west. According to Elisa, they found
Chicago "far more interesting than New York," where they had lived during the
war. What interested André most in Chicago was the Oceanian art at the Field
Museum of Natural History.[7]

Several well-known surrealist painters enjoyed long stays in or near the city, most notably Wifredo Lam and Leonora Carrington. Chicago even had a couple of galleries friendly to surrealism: Katharine Kuh's in the 1940s and Richard Feigen's in the 1950s.

In the 1950s and early 1960s several artists with surrealist leanings were active in Chicago. The best known is Gertrude Abercrombie, whose house at 5728 Dorchester in Hyde Park—known simply as 5728 to the cognoscenti—was for years a hangout for all kinds of characters. An eccentric millionaire whose parents were opera stars, Abercrombie was the central figure of a group of surrealist-influenced artists, most of whom lived in Wisconsin. The group was all white, but Abercrombie herself had long-standing friendships with black jazz musicians, including Charlie Parker, Dizzy Gillespie, Max Roach, and many others. Gillespie wrote a delightful appreciation of her art, and Richie Powell, brother of pianist Bud Powell, dedicated a composition to her: "Gertrude's Bounce."[8]

At 5728 nonconformity was the rule. On a good evening one could meet—in addition to the greatest figures in modern jazz—poets Arna Bontemps and Aldine Gunn, novelists Nelson Algren and Jack Conroy, and even Bob Kaufman's Greenwich Village friend, Max Bodenheim, veteran of wild parties in Chicago dating back to the 1910s. Frequently present was African American anarchopacifist Joffre Stewart, who, after meeting Allen Ginsberg in San Francisco, found himself described in *Howl*.[9] In 1960 Stewart was the Beatnik Party's anticandidate for anti–vice president in a campaign sponsored by Slim Brundage's free-speech cabaret, the College of Complexes.[10]

Abercrombie's husband, Frank Sandiford, was something of a character himself: an ex-convict known to the press as the "Gentleman Burglar." To this day he is better known by his nom de plume, Paul Warren, author of the paperback *Next Time Is for Life* (1953). A hipster prison memoir, the book has interesting things to say about jazz, drugs, jails, and race relations behind bars.

Now and then the notorious Fallonites would show up—"Bud" Fallon and his band of rowdy proletarian quasi-Dadaists, acquaintances of Conroy's and Algren's from East St. Louis. An occasional guest was Abercrombie's neighbor, Leon Despres, who would later become the city's all-time greatest alderman, noted for his superb record on civil rights. In his earlier years, as a revolutionary socialist, Despres not only had served as one of Leon Trotsky's guards in Mexico, but also had escorted Frida Kahlo to the movies. In later years, he counted members of the Chicago Surrealist Group among his friends and even attended several of their public events.[11]

Abercrombie left a sizeable number of fine paintings, but her "circle" had only the vaguest connection with authentic surrealism. Closer to the true surrealist spirit was a young African American painter of real promise, Dino Campbell, who arrived in Chicago from San Francisco in 1959. Making a living as a cab driver and singer of songs, he took part in the local Beat scene and exhibited his work at outdoor art fairs. His paintings reflect the inspiration of Magritte and Clovis Trouille, but each one radiates his own distinctive humor and imagination. Sadly, Campbell died of cancer in the mid-1960s.

Very different, but also very much in surrealism's subversive spirit, was the work of Tristan Meinecke and Eve Garrison, who devoted themselves to the pursuit of a radical automatism in painting. Meinecke's drip paintings (starting around 1941) and Garrison's "sculptural relief oil painting" introduced audacity and provocation to a largely provincial art scene. Like Abercrombie, these artists of European descent were profoundly influenced by the new black music. Meinecke for years never missed a Chicago appearance of Charlie Parker, Dizzy Gillespie, or Bud Powell. And in a period of rampant McCarthyism and white liberal hypocrisy, he and his friends were actively antiracist. A pioneer of television music programming, Meinecke regularly played Charlie Parker and other bop records on a popular children's show hosted by his wife, Angel Casey, who, by the way, was a longtime close friend of jazz pianist Lil Hardin.[12]

Other radical arts groups active in Chicago in those years include the circle around noted printmaker Margaret Burroughs, cofounder of the DuSable Museum of Afro-American History; the Compass and Second City Players and other theater groups; Katherine Dunham's renowned Performance Arts Training Center; the Negro History Club, which sponsored a wide range of readings and lectures at Roosevelt University; and the Abraham Lincoln Center, an old Unitarian-supported settlement house that provided the fledgling AACM with rehearsal space.

In addition there were such long-standing open forums as the College of Complexes and Bughouse Square, numerous lively coffeehouses, and the beginnings of what became an extensive underground press. In two or three years, Chicago's nonconformist multiracial arts activists radically transformed the local cultural scene. In the changed milieu, Black Power and Black Arts were warmly welcomed.[13]

Encouraging as this was, however, it was a long way from organized surrealism. A few of the artists mentioned here may have thought of themselves as surrealists, others, decidedly not. Utterly lacking were a collective surrealist identity, a coherent theory and practice, basic agreement on aims, and a clear sense of surrealism as transformative and revolutionary.

And then, in 1966, like a bolt from the blue, the Chicago Surrealist Group was formed.

In February of that year in Paris, André Breton welcomed a young Chicago couple—the author of this introduction and his wife, Penelope—into the Paris Surrealist Group at the café La Promenade de Venus. At the group's daily meetings during the next few months, the situation of surrealism in the United

States, and the prospects of a group in Chicago, were much discussed. Without exception—as several individual and collective letters later confirmed—the Paris surrealists encouraged the Chicagoans to proceed with their plans, full speed ahead.

In his important study, *Le mouvement des surréalistes*, Alain Joubert, a leading figure in the Paris Surrealist Group from the mid-1950s on, summarizes the significance of the Chicago group:

> In addition to the small but active nuclei in Lisbon, London, Brussels
> and Madrid (among others), one could cite [in the late 1960s] four
> regularly functioning surrealist groups outside of France: in Brazil, Holland, the U.S., and Czechoslovakia. The most recent of these was the
> U.S. group, formed in 1966 by Franklin and Penelope Rosemont after
> their long sojourn in Paris and their meeting with André Breton. The
> Paris group had in fact been in correspondence with the Chicagoans
> for several years, and had addressed to them a collective message dated
> May First, 1967 (81st anniversary of the Chicago workers' uprising).
> And in October of that year, a communication from the Chicago group
> was translated and published in the Paris group's journal *L'Archibras*, tiled
> "Situation of Surrealism in the U.S.A."[14]

Concluding his summary, Joubert points out that, in the new millennium, the Chicago Group, along with the group in Prague, is "the most important surrealist group outside of France."[15]

The Chicago Group was the first surrealist group ever formed in North America. It was soon joined by numerous poets, writers, and artists who, ever since then, have conducted a genuine and forceful activity in favor of the surrealist project—via journals (*Arsenal*), books, translations, and international exhibitions. The group, moreover, has continued its activity to this day, without any interruption.

Formally organized in June 1966, the Chicago Surrealist Group announced its existence by distributing several thousand copies of its first tract, "The Forecast Is Hot!" at a huge downtown civil rights march led by Martin Luther King, Jr. A few weeks later it released its first pamphlet, *Surrealism & Revolution*. The fledgling group was soon recognized as one of the most active and innovative in the international movement, and as such, it was written up extensively in surrealist journals in Paris, Prague, and Amsterdam.[16] Articles also appeared in the Chicago dailies as well as numerous New Left, anarchist, and underground papers all over the country. The authoritative reference work *Dictionnaire général du surréalisme et de ses environs* (1982) describes the Chicago Group not only as "the first organized American surrealist group," but also as "one of the most active surrealist groups in the world."[17]

Of the many influences that shaped the character of Chicago surrealism, the meeting with Breton and the Paris Group was unquestionably most decisive. Other encounters, however—particularly with French poet Claude Tarnaud, Spanish painter and poet E. F. Granell, and Greek writer Nicolas Calas, all of whom were living in New York in the early 1960s—were also determining. Tarnaud, youngest of the three and one of postwar surrealism's finest poets, was the principal mentor of the nascent Chicago Group. His letters to us in the spring of 1963—the first of which reached me at the City Lights Bookstore in San Francisco—were followed by a weeklong visit with him and his wife, Gibbsy, a noted painter, at their Riverside Drive apartment. Our discussions, which lasted several hours each day, were a rich learning experience for us and, indeed, a major inspiration. Passionately committed to surrealism and its revolutionary goals, Tarnaud was also something of a hipster, in the best sense of the term, and very much in favor of devising and practicing "new forms of defiance."

An ardent admirer of Thelonious Monk, and of the new black music generally, Tarnaud emphasized the vitality, originality, and hopefulness of black culture in contrast to the cynical and complacent conformity of the dominant U.S. white middle class. In addition to his captivating commentaries on the near-mythic Monk, Tarnaud's illuminating discussions of the *Poèsies* of Isidore Ducasse (Lautréamont), Jacques Vaché's *War Letters*, Breton's *Arcane 17*, Simon Rodia's Watts Towers, the books of Charles Fort, and the work of Romanian surrealist Gherasim Luca also did much to shape Chicago Surrealist perspectives.

Correspondence played an important role. Letters, periodicals, books, and art sent to the Chicago Group from surrealist comrades in Paris, Brussels, Buenos Aires, London, Amsterdam, Prague, and many other places made it clear that the international surrealist movement was not only still on the go in the 1960s, but, indeed, very much in the forefront of that decade's revolutionary thought and action.

ST. CLAIR DRAKE AND BLACK ANTHROPOLOGY

> There is an impromptu ceremony always ready for every hour of life.
> No little moment passes unadorned.
> —Zora Neale Hurston

In addition to these specifically surrealist inspirations, the Chicago surrealists were also strongly influenced by Prof. St. Clair Drake at Roosevelt University, later known throughout the world as the father of black anthropology. Drake taught much more than the history, theory, and methods of the science of culture. His lectures on nineteenth-century slave revolts, Native American up-risings, May Day, the roots of the civil rights struggle, and the revolutionary ferment in Africa set forth the basics of an anti-imperialist and activist-oriented anthropology relevant to the times.

Sometimes, as in his discussions of Negritude and the Harlem Renaissance, Drake even touched on surrealism, thereby provoking a series of extended after-class chats on the subject. These informal sessions were always stimulating and productive. Drake's reflections on the possibilities of an urban anthropology, for example, led directly to the Chicago surrealists' conception of a vernacular surrealism, as manifested in popular culture and Outsider Art.[18]

Above all, St. Clair Drake made the emerging Chicago surrealists aware of the richness and urgency of black history, politics, and culture. His lectures on the varieties of African, Afro-Caribbean, and African American radicalism were especially moving. Thanks to Drake—and to his brilliant student John Bracey, cofounder of Roosevelt's Negro History Club—the Chicago surrealists were well versed in the works of such writers as Zora Neale Hurston, W.E.B. Du Bois, Richard Wright, George Padmore, C.L.R. James, Oliver C. Cox, Max Stanford of the RAM, and Drake's former student James Forman, who had since become head of SNCC and would later play important roles in other, even more radical, organizations.

Not too surprisingly, Drake was especially eloquent on the subject of his fellow anthropologist Zora Neale Hurston, whose combination of deeply felt, down-home fieldwork, attention to detail, and superb writing he greatly ad-mired. Hurston's books were not in fact easy to find in the early 1960s. Thanks to Drake's repeated recommendations, however, his students were out looking for them long before the 1970s Hurston revival.

Drake's lectures and Hurston's works also deepened the nascent surreal-ist group's awareness of the many and varied relationships between human societies and the natural world. As these ecological concerns expanded, Alain Joubert pointed out in a letter from Paris that the Chicagoans were helping develop a new language for surrealism—a language uninhibited by the old lan-guage of politics.

A VIBRANT, ENERGIZING FORCE

> The poet shocks those around him. He speaks openly of what authority has deemed unspeakable. He becomes the enemy of authority.
> While the poet lives, authority dies.
> —Bob Kaufman

At Roosevelt University in 1962–1963, several of the young poets who would later found the Surrealist Group formed the Anti-Poetry Club, expressly to ridicule the school's existing bourgeois Poetry Club. When Nelson Algren, the city's best-known novelist, read about the club's formation, he called it the best news he had heard in years.

The Anti-Poetry Club was only one of several interconnected and almost interchangeable anarchist- and surrealist-oriented groups. Another was the Roosevelt University Wobblies. Having learned that the old revolutionary labor union, the Industrial Workers of the World (IWW, or Wobblies), still maintained a hall in Chicago, several militants of the nascent Surrealist Group took out red IWW cards. As it turned out, the off-campus hangout of all these groups was the IWW's Solidarity Bookshop, which also served as the Surrealist Group's mailing address for several years. The Chicago IWW journal, more-over—*The Rebel Worker*—published a considerable quantity of surrealist material, mostly original, but also reprints of texts by Breton, Carrington, Péret, Mabille, and others. Years later, David Roediger, in *Encyclopedia of the American Left*, cited *The Rebel Worker* as "the first sustained U.S. surrealist-oriented publication."[19]

Noted especially for their large and youthful contingents at civil rights and antiwar demonstrations, these groups were truly a vibrant, energizing force in the new radicalism. Cynical remnants of the "Old" Left, however, as well as the more straitlaced adherents of the "New," objected to their playfulness, antiauthoritarianism, and hard-hitting humor, and tended to dismiss them as the left-wing of the Beat Generation.

Although most of these groups were ephemeral and have not been well remembered by historians, several people who took part in them became well known. Aside from Anti-Poetry Club member Scott Spencer, who became a best-selling novelist (*Endless Love, Men in Black*), these individuals were African American. John Bracey, Jr., who was Anti-Poetry Club main officer for a time, went on to become a noted historian and leading figure in African studies, author of many journal essays, and editor of such important works as *Black Nationalism in America* (1970) and an updated edition of C.L.R. James' *Facing Reality* (2006).

A trio of young women active in Solidarity Bookshop (and who also worked at the main post office, where Richard Wright had worked some thirty years earlier), went on to greater things: Charlotte Carter as a popular mystery writer; Simone Collier as a playwright; and Joan Smith as a psychologist.

The strongly multiracial dimension that characterized all these groups, together with their Far Left politics and emphasis on radical cultural activity, were key factors that distinguished them sharply from most Old and New Left sects. Influenced above all by surrealism and its revolutionary tradition, but also by Drake, John Bracey, Jr., the Negro History Club, folklorist Archie

Green—and the old-time Wobblies, whose reminiscences as hobo intellectuals and soapboxers were an education in itself—Chicago surrealism from its very beginnings maintained friendly relations with the most creative and uncompromising currents in African American radicalism, including the Revolutionary Action Movement, the Black Panther Party, and the later League of Revolutionary Black Workers.

Significantly—and highly revelatory of the dynamics of international surrealism—the Chicago surrealists' special attention to black radicalism also had a powerful impact on surrealist groups elsewhere, above all on the Paris Group. In January 1968, for example, the Chicagoans issued the first of a series of 17" × 22" wall posters titled *Surrealist Insurrection*, featuring the demand, "Free Huey Newton!" (the jailed cofounder of the Black Panther Party). Fully supporting this protest, the Paris surrealists sent in reply a letter of solidarity (with nineteen signatures), along with an international money order for the Huey Newton Defense Fund. The March issue of the Paris Group's journal, *L'Archibras*, features a striking Black Power cover and a two-page article on the subject by Ted Joans.[20]

In 1971 the Chicago Group sent out an inquiry to a couple of dozen individuals around the country who had indicated their desire to participate in collective surrealist activity. Twenty-two responded, spanning the continent from Nicolas Calas in New York to Marie Wilson in the San Francisco Bay Area. The responses were collated into a sixty-four-page compilation titled *Surrealism in 1971*. Among the respondents was Aaron (Ibn Pori) Pitts, a Detroit artist, musician, and writer, member of the League of Revolutionary Black Workers, and editor of the Black Arts magazine *Black Graphics International*. Noting that surrealism in the United States was impeded by "the refusal of Amerika to reveal the truth of the historical development of surrealism," Pitts urged that the best way to advance the surrealist cause was for surrealists "to do *more* of what they already are doing," and especially "to bring surrealist art to the people—by any means necessary." Later that year, in a lengthy discussion of surrealism in 1971 in the Paris Group's *Bulletin de Liaison Surréaliste*, Jean-Louis Bédouin himself drew particular attention to Pitts' insistence on the need to find "new ways of uniting art and politics" and his confidence that surrealism was itself a valuable contribution to "the unity of revolutionary theory and practice."[21]

In January 2007 Aaron Ibn Pori Pitts was saluted by the *Detroit Metro Times* as Artist of the Year.

Notes

1. The revolutionary imagination and activist innovation in the Sixties are the main themes of Franklin Rosemont and Charles Radcliffe, eds., *Dancin' in the Streets*.

2. James Edward Smethurst, *The Black Arts Movement.*

3. Postell's surrealist influence on Baraka is evident in Amiri Baraka, *The Autobiography of LeRoi Jones,* 131–133.

4. Larry Neal, *Visions of a Liberated Future,* 125 (Malcolm), 53–55 (Ellison).

5. Ted Joans' *Black Power Manifesto,* translated as *Proposition pour un manifeste Pouvoir Noir* by Jeannine Ciment and Robert Benayoun, was published by Eric Losfeld in 1969. Two collections of Bob Kaufman's poems (*Solitudes Crowded with Loneliness, Sardine Dorée*) have been translated by Mary Beach, Claude Pelieu, and others. Kaufman was also featured in the "Burroughs/ Pelieu/Kaufman" issue of the *Cahiers de l'Herne,* no. 9 (1967).

6. In addition to inclusion of her work in numerous anthologies, the growing critical literature on the poetry of Jayne Cortez includes "Jayne Cortez, Supersurrealist Vision," in D. H. Melham, *Heroism in the New Black Poetry;* Jon Woodson, "Jayne Cortez," 69–74; Aldon Lynn Nielsen, *Black Chant;* Karen Ford, "On Cortez's Poetry"; Kimberly N. Brown, "Of Poststructuralist Fallout, Scarification, and Blood Poems."

7. During a visit to the Bretons' studio at 42 rue Fontaine in early spring 1966, Penelope and I spoke at length with Elisa Breton about many things, including their brief 1940s stay in Chicago.

8. On Abercrombie, her milieu, and her interest in jazz, see the exhibition catalog *Gertrude Abercrombie and Friends* (Springfield: Illinois State Museum, 1983).

9. The lines described Joffre Stewart in *Howl* as in beards and shorts and passing out incomprehensible leaflets.

10. On the Beatnik Party and the 1960 elections, see Franklin Rosemont, *From Bughouse Square to the Beat Generation,* 30–34, 146–155.

11. The Fallonites and other characters at 5728 are described in the journal *New Letters* (Winter 1971), an issue that also contains an early sampling of Richard Wright's haikus. The Fallonites' East St. Louis background is detailed in Douglas Wixson, *Worker-Writer in America,* 429–438. At a surrealist lunch meeting, Leon Despres confided to Franklin Rosemont that the movie to which he escorted Kahlo was directed by Marc Alegret. Despres has published a memoir, *Challenging the Daley Machine.*

12. Surprisingly little has been written about Tristan Meinecke; I have relied here primarily on my many conversations with him and his wife,

Angel. Paul Buhle's *Cultural Correspondence,* no. 12–14 (1981), includes Meinecke's response to an inquiry on the future of surrealism, and several of his poems appear in *Arsenal/Surrealist Subversion,* no. 4 (1989). See also "A Fresh Breath of Habit-Breaking Unruliness: The Art of Tristan Meinecke," in Franklin Rosemont, *Revolution in the Service of the Marvelous,* 85–94.

13. Smethurst, *The Black Arts Movement.*

14. Joubert, *Le mouvement des surréalistes,* 84–85.

15. Ibid.

16. The Chicago surrealists' collaboration on the movement's publications abroad is noted in Sakolsky, *Surrealist Subversions,* 50–52. See also Rosemont et al., eds., *The Forecast Is Hot!*

17. Biro and Passeron, *Dictionnaire,* 34, 368.

18. The concept of vernacular surrealism was also inspired by folklorist Archie Green, who regularly sent copies of his articles to the Chicago IWW hall.

19. Mari Jo Buhle, *Encyclopedia of the American Left,* 761.

20. *L'Archibras,* no. 3 (1968), features Ted Joans' essay, "Black Flower" (pp. 10–11).

21. Aaron, from Bédouin's "News from the New World," appeared in French in the *Bulletin de Liaison Surréaliste,* no. 4 (December 1971). An English translation by Myrna Bell Rochester is included in Franklin Rosemont et al., *The Forecast Is Hot!,* 261–265.

Ted Joans

PROPOSITION FOR A BLACK POWER MANIFESTO

Black Power is the vanguard of the insurrection inside America today.

Black Power is that marvelous explosive mixture which has accumulated since the first Black slave uprising—Always the same motive: FREEDOM!

Black Power is dreams that are carried out into reality. Black Power has the real and beyond the real in which to move. Our African ancestry has enriched us with this marvelous surreality.

Black Power is not out to win the Civil Rights struggle, but to win the Human Rights struggle. Black Power is like jazz, it is based upon the freedom of the spirit.
    That spirit is black. Black people must never lose their freedom of spirit.

Black Power is fanatical for freedom.

Black Power is Black people charting their own destiny.

Black Power is marvelous and beautiful.

Black Power is a fierce black hope. Black Power is determined
    to surmount all obstacles.

Black Power is a black truth.

Black Power! Black Power!

Proposition pour un manifeste Pouvoir Noir

Hart Leroy Bibbs

Bibbs (1930–) was born in Kansas City, Kansas, and tried journalism as a young man. The new jazz led him straight into the far-reaching cultural rebellion of the late 1940s/early 1950s, and he became a vagabond, photographer, painter, sculptor, and poet above all. Seeking refuge from U.S. racism, he took off for Paris and made himself at home in Paris' flourishing African American jazz scene.

Unlike his longtime friend and fellow expatriate Ted Joans, Bibbs' formal association with the surrealist movement was tangential, but as Simon Njami points out, Bibbs' poetry is itself a form of surrealism. Several of his bitter and disorienting poems were recorded with music by Archie Shepp and Sonny Murray. For Bibbs, whose sense of urgency reaches fever pitch, the task of true poets is to ponder life's essentials.

The poems printed here appear in *Double Trouble* (1992), a joint production of Bibbs and Ted Joans, published in Paris.

HURRICANE

In a bed of rolling thunder
Trapped in pillows of rushing clouds
    White lightning flashing behind my red, swollen eyelids
And wild winds chasing dreams through my brain
It feels like I'm in a hurricane
It feels like I'm in a hurricane

BLACK SPRING

Be bleak spring but roll on northwards
with me through central park sign winding trail,
around the lake and reservoir,
through the hilly, singing, bird sanctuary
over the underpass of the horse;
the newly discovered path where a tale
was told but five minutes ago—
by one who had returned southward
of a sinister black bar

Jayne Cortez

Jayne Cortez was born in Arizona in 1936, grew up in California, and currently lives in New York City. She is the author of ten books of poems and performer of her poetry with music on nine recordings. Her voice is celebrated for its political, surrealistic, dynamic innovations, in lyricism, and visceral sound. Cortez has presented her work and ideas at universities, museums, and festivals in Africa, Asia, Europe, South America, the Caribbean, and the United States. Her poems have been translated into many languages and widely published in anthologies, journals, and magazines. She is the recipient of several awards, including Arts International, the National Endowment for the Arts, the International African Festival Award, the Langston Hughes Award, and the American Book Award. Her most recent books are *Jazz Fan Looks Back* (2002) and *Somewhere in Advance of Nowhere* (1996). Her latest CD recording with the Firespitter Band is *Taking the Blues Back Home,* produced by Bola Press. Cortez is director of the film *Yari Yari Pamberi: Black Women Writers Dissecting Globalization.* She is president of the Organization of Women Writers of Africa, Inc., and is on screen in the films *Women in Jazz* and *Poetry in Motion.*

NATIONAL SECURITY

If you take these capes
of wet sheets and broken glass
these torn hearts of mesh screens
these decorated screens of 2nd degree burns
and toilet tissue armbands
If you take these football helmets
towels and broom handle headdresses
these bullhorn mouths of mace
these spinning bullets full of navels and hostages
If you take these ornamental gifts
to the governor of shellshock
you will be rewarded
with the momentous eyes
of society's autopsy
attica

Scarifications

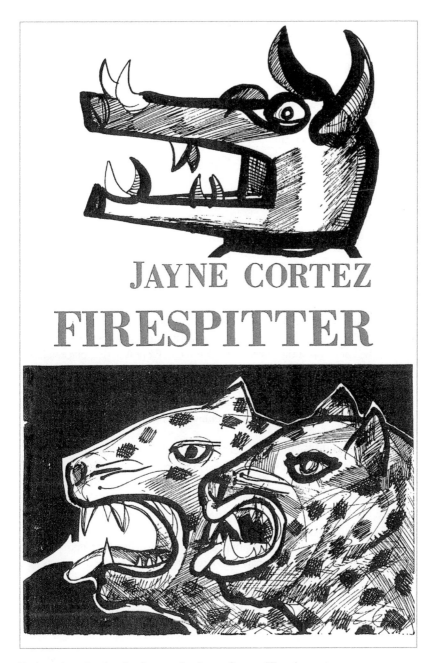

Firespitter (1982), a book of poems by Jayne Cortez. This dramatic cover was designed by sculptor Melvin Edwards.

MAKING IT

I know they want me to make it
to enter eye droppers and invade pills
turn around or get shot
I know they wanna vaccinate me with
the fear of myself
so I'll pull down my face and nod
I know they want me to make it
But I'm not in a hurry

Scarifications

St. Clair Drake

Frantz Fanon, in his most popular and influential book, *The Wretched of the Earth* (1961, p. 213), had occasion to insist that "the poets of negritude will not stop at the limits of the continent. From America, black voices will take up the hymn with fuller unison. The 'black world' will see the light and Busia from Ghana, Birago Diop from Senegal, Hampate Ba from the Sudan, and St. Clair Drake from Chicago will not hesitate to assert the existence of common ties and a motive power that is identical."

Coauthor with Horace Cayton of the classic *Black Metropolis* (1945)—for which Richard Wright wrote an important introduction—Drake (1911-1990) several decades later also wrote the magisterial two-volume *Black Folk Here and There* (1987-1990). In the meantime the "father of black anthropology" authored a veritable library of pamphlets, essays, speeches, reports, and reviews.

A wise, insightful, inspiring, and beloved teacher, his rapport with students was extraordinary. His after-class discussions were often as long as the class itself.

Drake's students at Chicago's Roosevelt University included Sterling Stuckey, John Bracey, Frank London Brown, James Forman, and nearly all of the young men and women who, a few years later, founded the Chicago Surrealist Group.

The text published here is excerpted from an essay originally written for Herbert Hill's *Soon, One Morning* (1968).

NEGRITUDE AND PAN-AFRICANISM

The end of the Second World War marked the beginning of the liberation of Africa and of racial integration in the United States. Although there is no causal connection between these two momentous developments, they are interrelated and they influence each other. That they occurred at approximately the same time has profound implications for Negro Americans, all of whom are aware that they are "of African descent." In America, this "African descent" is considered to be the only really socially relevant fact about Negroes, and some states actually define a Negro as "anyone with an ascertainable trace of Negro blood." Whether those who are defined as "American Negroes" like it or not, history and the peculiar evaluations of American society have linked them with the fate of Africa and its peoples. This is a reality to which Negroes in the United States have always had to adjust.

In 1925, the distinguished American Negro literary critic Alain Locke presented an anthology to the public which bore the title *The New Negro*. The poets, essayists, and writers of fiction whose works appeared in the volume were participants in what came to be called the Negro Renaissance, that remarkable outburst of literary creativity which followed the First World War. The dominant theme in the work of all these writers was the Negro experience. The intellectual vanguard of ten million Negro Americans was expressing the moods and wishes, the aspirations and frustrations, the joy as well as the anger, of their ethnic group. They were also revealing their own sensitive reactions to reality, and laying bare the distinctive configurations of ideas and emotions which each had elaborated in order to cope with reality. For some of them, Africa was a part of this reality.

Edward A. Jones

Mississippi-born, Edward A. Jones studied at Morehouse College in Atlanta, Georgia. After further studies at Middlebury College, Cornell University, and the Sorbonne in Paris, he returned to Morehouse as professor of French and chairman of the Department of Modern Foreign Languages. Over the years he contributed many articles and reviews to such publications as *South Atlantic Quarterly, Modern Language Journal, French Review,* and *The Journal of Negro History.*

The excerpts that follow are from his anthology *Voices of Negritude.* One of the earliest works on the subject in English, the book was a significant influence on the Black Arts movement.

THE BIRTH OF BLACK AWARENESS

The common denominator of all the Negritude writers is consciousness of color and racial pride, complemented by a deep conviction of solidarity among all blacks, both in and outside Africa, who share a common heritage of oppression, injustice, poverty, and economic ills resulting therefrom. The reaction of the various proponents of *Negritude* to the whites responsible for their plight runs the gamut from Senghor's humane forgiveness to the indignation and bitterness of Césaire *et al.* Their poems are veritable laments amounting to variations on a common theme: the suffering, insults, and humiliations resulting from racist attitudes and practices the world over. They all came to accept Senghor's concept of *Negritude* as an arm of deliverance, a tool for the liberation of blacks from their present-day serfdom, for without belief in one's own potential and pride in one's own past and ancestral culture, as well as group solidarity, blacks would lack the basic essentials for launching any kind of social revolution or for initiating any kind of movement for liberation that could possibly succeed [original emphasis].

* * *

Another factor in the birth of black awareness and solidarity among black expatriates in Paris in the decade 1925–1935 was their discovery of fellow black writers in the United States, such Afro-American literary pioneers of great talent as Alain Locke, an intellectual who interpreted to them the black experience in America and opened their eyes to the excellent writers of the Negro Renaissance, Charles W. Chestnut, W.E.B. Du Bois, Paul Lawrence Dunbar, Claude McKay, Countee Cullen, Langston Hughes, and Sterling A. Brown; novelists such as Jessie Fauset and Jean Toomer; painters Henry O. Tanner and William E. Scott; sculptors Meta Warrick Fuller, Mae Jackson, and Elizabeth Prophet. The meetings at Mlle. André Nardal's brought together blacks from two hemispheres and facilitated cross-fertilization of talent, unity of purpose, and color solidarity. Common ancestry and background, community in suffering, and long-pent-up resentments bridged the geographical distance separating these sons of Africa and endowed them with a *cause commune.* Indeed, the effect of Negro American intellectuals and writers on their African and West Indian counterparts was enormous.

Ishmael Reed

Born in Chattanooga, Tennessee, in 1938, Reed lived for several years in New York, where he coedited the *East Village Other* and contributed to many poetry, political, and underground magazines

He has taught at Yale, Dartmouth, and the University of California at Berkeley. His publications include several volumes of poetry, two plays, and a series of remarkable novels including the surrealist-from-cover-to-cover *Mumbo Jumbo*. His essays have been collected in *Shrovetide in Old New Orleans* and *Writin' Is Fightin'*. He has also directed two television productions: "Personal Problems" and "A Word in Edgewise."

Reed lives in Berkeley, California. The text published here appears as the opening chapter of *Writin' Is Fightin'*.

BOXING ON PAPER: THIRTY-SEVEN YEARS LATER

A black boxer's career is the perfect metaphor for the career of a black male. Every day is like being in the gym, sparring with impersonal opponents as one faces the rudeness and hostility that a black male must confront in the United States, where he is the object of both fear and fascination. My difficulty in communicating this point of view used to really bewilder me, but over the years I've learned that it takes an extraordinary amount of effort to understand someone from a background different from your own, especially when your life doesn't really depend upon it. And so, during this period, when black males seem to be on somebody's endangered-species list, I can understand why some readers and debating opponents might have problems appreciating where I'm coming from.

And so as long as I can be a professional like Larry Holmes, that is, have the ability to know my way around my craft, I'll probably still be controversial. Arguing on behalf of the homeless, but at the same time defending Atlanta's middle-class leadership against what I considered to be unfair charges made by the great writer James Baldwin (no relation). And as I continue to practice this sometimes uncanny and taxing profession, I hope to become humbler.

I've had a good shot. It's almost a miracle for a black male writer to last as long as I have, and though some may regard me as a "token," I'm fully aware that, regardless of how some critics protect their fragile egos by pretending that black talent is rare, black talent is bountiful. I've read and heard a lot of manuscripts authored by the fellas over the years. The late Hoyt Fuller was right when he said that for one published Ishmael Reed there are dozens of talented writers in the ghettos and elsewhere, who remain unpublished. And having lasted this long, I've been able to witness the sad demise of a lot of tokens who believed what their literary managers told them. Who believed that they were indeed unique and unusual.

Just think of all of the cocky boxers who got punched out by nobodies as they took on an unknown to warm up for their fight with the champion. In this business, spoilers are all over the place.

I was shocked to hear Secretary of State George Shultz acknowledge during the Iran-Contragate hearings what our cultural leadership, and "educational" defenders of Western civilization, fail to realize. That people are smart all over the world. I know that. I'm aware of the fellas, writing throughout the country in the back of beat-up trailers, in jails, on kitchen tables, at their busboy jobs, during the rest period on somebody's night shift, or in between term papers. All the guys burnt-out, busted, disillusioned, collecting their hundredth rejection slip being discouraged by people who say they'll never be a champion, or even a contender. This book is for them. Writin' is Fightin'.

Katherine Dunham

One of the central "founding mothers" of modern dance, Dunham (1909-2006) has long been celebrated as an outstanding dancer, choreographer, anthropologist, actress, writer, teacher, and activist in struggles against social injustice. Chicago-born, she was active as a young woman in the city's radical and Dadaesque free-speech forum, the Dil Pickle Club, noted for its controversial lectures and debates. Founder of the first African American dance company in Chicago, in 1931, her "Ballet Nègre" prefigured the Negritude movement. In her later dance troupes she not only developed new dance techniques, but also introduced Caribbean- and African-based dance into the modern dance repertoire, and in the process inspired several generations of dancers and actors to discover expressive movements of their own. Her students included Eartha Kitt, Ava Gardner, James Dean, and Marlon Brando.

As a University of Chicago anthropologist, Dunham made several field trips to the Caribbean, where she closely studied the wide variety of native dance and gesture. Her experience on the islands enabled her to incorporate elements of voodoo rituals into her dance long before the French surrealist dancer Hélène Vanel. Eventually Dunham claimed Haiti as her second home.

Her passion for social justice, meanwhile, was evident in her involvement in the Negro Federal Theatre Project (1938) and the New York Labor Stage (1939).

Her surrealist connections, rarely acknowledged by U.S. critics, are nonetheless memorable. The printed program for her troupe's performances in Paris during the late autumn of 1949 features an enthusiastic two-page tribute to Dunham by André Breton. On the same occasion, Roger Caillois wrote about her as well. She was also acquainted with Marcel Duchamp. According to African American scholar VeVe Clark, Dunham for years kept framed photographs of Breton and Duchamp on the mantle of her living room fireplace.

Reprinted here is an excerpt from an early article on her Ballet Nègre (*Abbott's Monthly*, 1931) and a summary of her views on dance as a major art.

BALLET NÈGRE

A Negro Ballet has to come. Periodically the Negro makes some startling innovation, some rich contribution to America's art. When freedom put a pen in the Negro's hand, he wrote a lyrical record, sometimes masked, sometimes pure in its racial expression. He found that those things which had belonged to his past, the workings of his mind, and even his daily life, were of great interest to the American public; and so he wrote them down, and as he wrote, he knew that only he could actually re-live that past.

The Negro sang, wrote, acted, and now he is about to dance. There will undoubtedly be some objection to the futurity expressed in this statement. There are those who will remind us that the Negro has been dancing since the dawn of history; but, perhaps unfortunately, civilization draws a sharp distinction between an uncurbed, purely racial expression—governed simply by rhythm and emotion—and the crystalline symphony of the traditional ballet.

Now the soul of the Negro Ballet has made itself articulate. We have discovered the *ésprit de ballet.*

NOTES ON THE DANCE

With Special Reference to the Island of Haiti

Dance is a rhythmic motion for one or more of a number of reasons: social cohesion, psychological or physiological catharsis, exhibitionism, auto-hypnosis, pleasure, ecstasy, sexual selection, play, recreation, development of artistic values, stimulus to action, aggressive or non-aggressive, extension and affirmation of social patterns and others.

I realize that this formula enters more into the terms of a description than a definition, which often occurs when, by a certain continuous extension of correlated characteristics, the only answers seem to be over-complexity or oversimplicity. Verbalization is apt to end in sterility, and the aesthetic experience such as makes up a large part of any art creation eludes explicitness with a tantalizing facility. (Even now I see, however, that I, like numerous other creative artists, have fallen into this pitfall and try to explain with many words an experience which is firmly rooted in man's essential being and may well be a key to his potentialities for personal and social integration.)

The universality of dance has for long been recognized by historians, philosophers, graphic and plastic artists, and of late has become a subject of interest to anthropologists, psychologists, and physiologists; there has begun to emerge in recent years a strong popular concern for this expression, not only from a theatrical or entertainment point of view, but in terms of its examination as a cultural trait, comparative analysis of its different forms and its significance, sociological, biological, and psychological. But as the cultural importance of the dance is brought to prominence by such media as the folklore theater, exploitation by camera, and the ever-growing library of descriptive travel-lore, there arises in modern society a dispute which has finalized itself in placing dance in that ambiguous position between science and art, between exposition and entertainment. This dichotomy seems to me to be a useless one, as the paths of art and scientific discovery too often cross, even merge, to allow for dispute. In primitive societies dance is an accepted functional element of both personal and community life, and for this reason the conflict of classification does not arise. The ecstasies, repressions, challenges, sorrows, and pleasures of peoples still living in a folkloric or primitive state find expression and are channeled, controlled, or released, as the case may be, by ritualized dance. And it is from a careful observation of the dance as a community expression that many useful hypotheses of culture type or pattern, psychology, and philosophy may be arrived at.

Alone or in concert man dances in his various selves and his emotions and his dance becomes a communication as clear as though it were written or spoken in an universal language.

Puma, ed., 7 *Arts*

Melvin Edwards

Edwards (1937–) was born and raised in Texas and studied art at the Los Angeles Art Institute and the University of Southern California in the 1960s. Well known as the most prolific African American sculptor in recent years and always politically active, he took part in the Civil Rights and Black Arts movements, and in the 1970s came into contact with the Chicago Surrealist Group. He has taught at the University of Connecticut, Rutgers University, Howard University, and other schools.

Regarding himself as the descendent of ancestral African metalworkers, Edwards has visited Africa many times and made a special study of the work of the brass casters of Benin. His own sculptures, embodying the most disparate found objects, including chains, hammers, and other tools, are among the most powerful and innovative artworks of our time. Widely exhibited in galleries and museums all over the United States as well as in Paris and many places in Africa, his work has also generated an impressive critical literature.

The text reprinted here appeared in the only issue of the surrealist journal *Free Spirits: Annals of the Insurgent Imagination*.

LYNCH FRAGMENTS

A lynching is a murder, a group murder. You take all of the energy of a lynching, all the hate and all the fear, and pile it on one human being. You tie that person to a tree and you slowly or fastly kill him. The Lynch Fragment series is a series of sculpture ideas. What I'm doing is taking fragments of the intensity of a lynching, turning it around, changing it into an object, and making that object something creative and positive. So the thing itself is not to look like it's been lynched, but to have that scale of intensity, and that kind of power.

I have developed suspended environmental works made of barbwire and of chains. I also make larger pieces, public sculpture meant to have a relationship with architecture and the general public. You can say that the Lynch Fragments are a private conversation. A one on one situation. The public works are meant to affect masses of people at once. The material used for the Lynch Fragments is steel. Sometimes a piece of brass or bronze or chrome is added but for the most part they are welded steel. Each Lynch Fragment is different from the other and each has an individual title. In that respect they are like traditional African sculpture. The idea of a lynching was bad luck, or bad fate, or a bad situation for African-American people in the United States. But the Lynch Fragment, the sculpture, is really a positive work. They are powerful and they are ours, and they are mine, if they are not made by our oppressor. They are made by us as a continuance of the resistance against oppression.

I started making them in 1963 during the period when the civil rights movement was in full force. It was my first experience with collective resistance. At that time I was teaching myself how to make sculpture and trying to find my own unique way of working. The Lynch Fragments come from family stories about lynchings. They come from my experiences of growing up in Houston, Texas, the black community in the fifth ward, the five years I lived in Dayton, Ohio, in the all-black Desoto-Bass housing project, and in the black neighborhoods in Los Angeles, California.

I intended for the Lynch Fragments to remind black people of what we have come out of. That's important because in the United States we're the only people to actually come out of the lynching experience. They lynched a few other people, but basically being lynched belonged to us. We were the only ones brought here to be slaves, and after slavery we were a people without rights. We were the only people who could be lynched with impunity. It's documented and it's not over yet. Making the Lynch Fragments is a strong way to work.

I'm a physical person. I believe in strong statements. I believe in a certain amount of significant directness. Within the visual arts, the abstract work is very much in the area of fiction and poetry. They're imaginary. You can put things together and in real life there would be no reason for them to be together, except in the reality of their being works of art. Once I have decided that my subject is lynching and Lynch Fragments, that calls into question the whole society. The whole of art, the whole of everything.

Joseph Jarman

Jarman was born in Pine Bluff, Arkansas, in 1937 and raised in Chicago. He learned drums in high school and took up the saxophone in the 1950s while in the army. Around 1961, at Wilson Junior College in Chicago, he met bassist Malachi Favors and three other saxmen—Roscoe Mitchell, Anthony Braxton, and Henry Threadgill—who shared his interest in the "new music" pioneered by Ornette Coleman, Cecil Taylor, and Albert Ayler. By 1962 Jarman and his young friends were taking part in the weekly sessions of Muhal Richard Abrams' Experimental Band, a wide-open group devoted to totally free improvisation.

The band, which met at the Abraham Lincoln Center (an old Chicago settlement house) and did not play in public, was in turn the nucleus of the new music's greatest co-op, the Association for the Advancement of Creative Musicians, which Abrams and Jarman and their aforementioned friends cofounded in 1965.

Within the AACM Jarman and Mitchell—with others (including Favors and newcomers Lester Bowie, trumpet, and Don Moye, drums), formed the Art Ensemble of Chicago, whose wildly theatrical concerts were often called "Dada" and "surrealist" by admirers and critics alike. The ensemble's sensational tours across the country and 'round the world soon made Chicago's new music and the AACM famous all over the planet.

In May 1986 Cecil Taylor attended the World Surrealist Exhibition in Chicago and urged Jarman and other AACM members not to miss it, and it was Jarman who introduced the surrealists to a sizeable group of AACM members. The long-range upshot was a whole series of events which brought the Surrealist Group and the AACM together.

One of the outstanding creative musicians of our time, Jarman is a man of many and wide-ranging interests. An accomplished poet, he is also a longtime student of Zen Buddhism and a teacher of the martial arts. He lives in Brooklyn, New York.

ODAWALLA

ODAWALLA came through the people of the Sun
into the grey haze of the ghost worlds
vanished legions, crowding bread lines—the people
of the Sun coated with green chalk
all kinds of warm light between them
destroyed for the silver queen of the ghost worlds
wild beast such as dogs gone mad and lechers—
the wanderers

ODAWALLA came through the people of the Sun
to warn them of the vanished legions
and to teach them how they may increase their bounty
through the practice of the drum and silent gong
(as taught by ODAWALLA) was realized

on seeing one another they transformed themselves into
one the hand the other the left big toe of KAW ZU PAM
(the one who creates the door through the passage on

the hill of
QUAN BU KA) their purpose
to guide the people of the Sun as they sought knowledge of
the door through the grey haze.

when SEKA saw the sound of the silent gong
SEKA sought to transform itself into the right hand
of ODAWALLA where COO BE SU rested while waiting
to move into the right big toe of KAW ZU PAM
(the one who creates the door through the passage on
the hill of
QUAN BU KA) their purpose
to guide the people of the Sun as they
seek to leave, seek to leave, seek to leave, seek to leave
the grey haze

only RIMUMBA remained to find the place of the
drum and silent gong
such knowledge would enable it to enter into the inner
organs of
KAW ZU PAM
(the one who creates the door through the passage on
the hill of
QUAN BU KA) their purpose
to guide the people of the SUN   the grey haze.
ODAWALLA vibrated the movement of CAM BE GILL
O POIU
causing the silent gong to sound silent, the body whole.

the grey haze

Sun people
drum
silent
gong—here now
here now
here now
here now—between us
grey haze Sun
people

Arsenal/Surrealist Subversion, no. 3 (1976)

Oliver Pitcher

Playwright, actor, and drama teacher by profession, Pitcher (1923–) was also a painter and a noted poet in the 1940s and 1950s underground. A contributor to periodicals as varied as the surrealist-oriented *Tiger's Eye*, the Paris-based *Présence Africaine*, *Negro Digest/Black World*, and the Beat *Yugen*, edited by Hettie and LeRoi Jones (Amiri Baraka), he was also active in the New York–based Umbra group of poets. He was born in Massachusetts and lived for extended periods in Pittsburgh, Atlanta, and New York before settling down in his later years in Palo Alto, California. Robert Hayden has hailed his offbeat and sardonic poetry, but Pitcher has published only one slim book, *Dust of Silence* (1958).

JEAN-JACQUES

Died August 23, 1946,
thumbing his nose
The sheets, spotted, a sad sea of Latin faces. Blood and
bone, grandmothers sitting, kneeling, knitting in a graveyard,
or doing their beads. And not a comptesse in the lot.
Jean-Jacques lies in an empty black room of the mind
where the face of the Angel of Death appears. . . .
"Take it on the lam, Angel with your twelve karat halo,
disrobed of personal feeling. Fat and beaming, or slick and
chi-chi, Angels of Death, all have smelly feet. . . ."
wet with tears. . . .
"Jean-Jacques. When you returned to yourself you were
dragging a carrion carcass behind you. Oh, Jean-Jacques."
"Shed your milky tears for the neon-world!"
"The door of entrances and exits has gone, Jean-Jacques.
Gone!" (Ave! Ave!)
A dark cloud of tragic laughter. All say goodbye. The
petrified sheet. Reflected on the half-lidded eyeball: the anxious gawk of a
    little black haired girl, half-hidden behind the
door. She shuts her eyes, and slams the door.
(Ave.
Ave.)

Tiger's Eye, no. 9 (October 15, 1949)

Frank London Brown

A truly great writer, Frank London Brown (1927–1962) has still not received the recognition his many-sided work deserves. To the extent that
he is acknowledged at all by mainstream critics it is for his first novel,
Trumbull Park (1959), a high-powered story based largely on his own experiences in the South Chicago racial battleground near the steel mills.
With its anger, humor, vivid detail, and radical insight, the book remains
a classic Chicago novel.

But as Sterling Stuckey emphasizes in one of the earliest and finest
essays on Brown's work, Brown always demanded more of himself. Both
before and after *Trumbull Park* he was at the same time an artist and a man
of action, and his writing boldly ventured into other dimensions. Brown
was also the first to read short stories (not poetry) to jazz accompani-
ment. Sadly, his admirable stories—scattered in various magazines—
have never been collected.

Brown's specifically surrealist affinities appear in his second and last
novel, *The Myth Maker* (1969). On one level it is the story of a group
of black youngsters trying to come to grips with early 1960s life, love,
and race politics, but it is also a weird and tragic tale of urban gothic
gloom: violence, nightmare, desperation, and death under the Southside
El tracks. Haunted by a phantomlike sage known only as the *monk*, the
book's tone and tempo lean toward the oneiric and even mythic, as the
title suggests. Defiance, delirium, and doom appear as driving forces.
And yet, challenging the horror and squalor, the sense of poetry and
wonder persist against all odds—a heightened awareness of the Marvelous inspired by nothing less than the magic of another monk, and the
impossible sounds that were realized by Thelonious Monk.

JAZZ

The chatter of the cymbals floored the high pitched introductory, gave it a base
from which to soar. And dew dropping off minor chords, shattering their reso-
nance with an even more contradictory high keyed set of notes, came Thelonious Monk. The bass started walking, booming like a strong man's healthy
heart beating beneath the drums, which beat beneath the piano, which chorded
beneath the tenor saxophone. The song built, throbbing while moving to the
height of the first chorus. Building, building, chugging now like a great steam
engine huffing uphill, clashing iron on the iron track, bells of piano ringing,
guiding the reverberation of sound from the walls of the booth's close tunnel.

Up the tenor went, repeating the melody, driving, chugging with the great train and box cars of bass, drums, and piano. The trumpet fell silent, and now the tenor pushed, bellowing and grunting, rough and beautiful in the nobility of coarseness, of mass trying to execute delicate gyrations. It was a big horn, not like Charlie Parker's or some light flute squawking pain and pity, hawking feelings thin and silver between and beneath great layers of muscle, guile and strength, but a big horn blowing, blowing the blues away. Blowing in news from Siam while the cymbals called out, called out to the world that the King was coming. Hail the king of life! Now the trumpet lay in wait, and the piano agitated the upward motion. The tenor said something, stated a phrase and the trumpet picked it up and the tenor eased into quiet.

Ernest listened to the music without patting his foot. He stood calmly. Listening to the sound turning into substance. Seeing a structure being built as surely as if it were brick, glass and steel. He saw the floor and the super structure and the places where the windows were to be, yet which Monk, the Master Architect, had purposely left out so that he, Ernest Day, could put them in.

Wong! went the piano, and now the Monk himself was taking a solo. He played in the low keys, and he played things that by passed the daily bread and the constant tick of the clock. Things that took time into another quarter, where it could not continue its constant repetition of the ancient archetype of beginning, middle and end; time of all times, blood of all bloods, image of all images. The thing done once, and no other thing again to be done. To Ernest, Monk moved history forward, took it from the cold grey grip of the eternal return, the repeating of things done and said, and hence the cyclic circularity of history, and of the future of man, and the end of the bad things, and the beginning of the good things. Forward! Monk's off chorded notes said. Never to come this way again! There are still secrets to be known. New secrets, not old regurgitated ones of crosses dark with the blood of too many saviors gone wrong.

Ernest laughed at the sounds, the impossible sounds that Thelonious Monk made possible. That was it! That was his appeal, his attraction. He was free, loose, weightless, yet not in need of wings! In need of nothing but his will to be free.

Frank London Brown, *Trumbull Park*

Pony Poindexter

Although he never quite hit the big time, Poindexter (1926–1988) was a superb alto and soprano sax player. New Orleans–born and widely known as "Little Pony"—he was a mainstay of the late 1950s/early 1960s San Francisco North Beach scene celebrated in the opening pages of Jack Kerouac's *The Dharma Bums.*

Soft-spoken, modest, with a lively critical intelligence and a good sense of humor, Poindexter also exemplified the new jazz as a moral force for a better world. His friends included Bob Kaufman, Philip Lamantia, Robert Stock, and other poets including Franklin Rosemont, who in 1959 was only sixteen, but very much involved not only in the Bay Area Beat and jazz scene, but also in the great Jazz Festival in Monterrey, where Ornette Coleman made one of his earliest public appearances before a large audience. Deeply interested in the New American poetry and in surrealism, these poets and artists frequented the Co-Existence Bagel Shop, the Coffee Gallery, and the Jazz Cellar, where Poindexter and his group often played.

A repeated victim of Bay Area police brutality, Poindexter moved to Paris in 1964, where he encountered many other black American musicians and—inevitably—globe-trotting poet Ted Joans. Shortly after his arrival in Paris, the interview excerpted here appeared in the leading French jazz journal.

JAZZ IS MORE FRENCH THAN AMERICAN

Why did you decide to settle in France?
I want to play every night. In Europe, I think I can do so.

You find the situation better?
There are too many musicians in America. For a small group, there are only a few places to work: New York (with three clubs), Philadelphia, Chicago, Pittsburgh, Los Angeles, San Francisco. And besides, in France, the public is much friendlier to jazz musicians. The whole ambiance is better.

Why do you think the situation is so bad in the U.S.?
Many musicians are very bitter, and their music sounds bitter. People want joy, they're looking for enthusiasm in music. Also, there is no real support for jazz in the U.S.; it is not written up in the newspapers, or featured on television. In America, people like jazz but they don't like those who play

it. I have some great projects in mind for jazz in France. I think there is every reason to expect jazz to expand all over Europe.

Why?

Jazz began with an African element, *rhythm* — and an occidental element, *harmony*. It was born in the U.S.A. in New Orleans, where the French influence was very strong. Believe me, jazz is more French than American. I want to recover that French ambiance.

But what, exactly, are you going to do?

First of all I'm going to play in my own style. I was born in New Orleans and I play a lively, high-spirited sound. I also want to play in schools; even to the very young. All people need is a little education. And that's what they *don't* get in the U.S.

Or here, it seems to me.

Don't be discouraged. The French are surely less narrow-minded than Americans. Hey, even French cops are sympathetic! In Pigalle, two of them stopped me to look at my "papers," and when they saw that I was born in New Orleans they said, "Ah, you're like Sidney Bichet! That's formidable!" In their honor I am composing a "Gendarme Blues." Listen, there's better music than rock 'n' roll. There's *good* music, that's all.

What are your greatest musical memories?

I have played with most of the best: Art Tatum, Max Roach, Lionel Hampton, but it's Charlie Parker who has affected me most, with his truly great virtuosity.

Do you have any friends here?

Yes — I've got the youngest impresario in France!

Jazz-Hot (October 1964)

Anthony Braxton

Chicago was a major center of the new revolutionary black music of the 1960s — the music influenced by John Coltrane, Cecil Taylor, Ornette Coleman, Eric Dolphy, and a few others — and it did not take long for Anthony Braxton (1945-) to become one of its central figures. Like Joseph Jarman, Leo Smith, Roscoe Mitchell, and Henry Threadgill, all

of whom he knew at Chicago's Wilson Junior College in the early years
of the decade, Braxton by late 1966 was one of the leading lights of the
cooperative AACM. A part-time librarian at Roosevelt University, he
also frequented the anarchist/surrealist Solidarity Bookshop.

This article appeared in the mimeographed single issue of the AACM
(Association for the Advancement of Creative Musicians) journal in
1968.

EARTH MUSIC

That the West is in the eleventh hour is now undebatable. We must redefine
every aspect of what we now call art. Steps should be taken to show that all art
is one (whether it be painting, writing, or running).

If I were to talk about my life (the part which the people of Earth call music)
I would say the essence of what I am doing is re-creating life. I would talk about
how amazed I am. All I know is that every day I wake up in this body and from
then on everything is in a constant state of flux. I have been told this is called
life. Since I really don't remember me before I was born, I find that something
is happening that I don't know about, and this is what I play and write about.

At this point in my music I find little use for harmony, time, development,
ideas, form, notes, technique, and sometimes sound — although some of the
nicest people I know feel differently.

[Until I played with the AACM] never could I have imagined creativity
on such a large scale. I am indeed fortunate to be able to work and exchange
ideas in what must be another important link in what will likely be called Earth
Music. The fact that we're being suppressed only gives us more time to explore
and perfect (walls are falling down, truths are emerging).

The music happening here in Chicago is the end-product of years of trying
to cooperate, help, and love each other, as well as an honest desire to participate in the cosmics.

Obviously, what is needed on this planet is some kind of understanding of
our lives. What people call art is, in fact, life.

There seems to be an unplanned movement in the air among the young
people with consciousness (I'll call them artists) toward unity. In Chicago, the
Association for the Advancement of Creative Musicians, the Afro-Arts Theater,
and COBRA are living proof that something is happening. In the last five years
the music here has advanced farther than I had ever dared to dream, and we are
only beginning.

There is a universal creative vibration in the air. The creativity here will undoubtedly play an important part when we gain more exposure (and when we do more exposing). More important, we are taking steps toward securing the development and understanding of art by teaching young people, and by becoming closer to our communities (knowing the self).

In the end, the destruction of art will lead to the rebirth of creativity, which is what is happening now.

Thelonious Monk

Maker of much of the most exciting, inspired, and inspiring music of the past century, Thelonious Sphere Monk (1920–1982) was always far more than what is commonly meant by the term "artist." His whole attitude set him apart: his wildly adventurous imagination; high-seasoned humor; electrifying intelligence; and carefree detachment from most of the world's busyness and boredom. In three words, his *unique poetic genius* qualified him early on as an exemplary figure. As far back as the 1940s, surrealists as different from each other as the Romanian Victor Brauner, the Chilean Roberto Matta, the French poet Claude Tarnaud, and the African American Ted Joans all regarded him as exceptional. Like Lautréamont and Jacques Vaché, two of surrealism's major precursors, Monk was recognized—*objectively*—as a thoroughgoing surrealist character. In the same way that André Breton once declared that Heraclitus was surrealist in dialectic, and Gustave Moreau in fascination, so too it is perfectly clear now that Thelonious Monk was surrealist in being Thelonious Monk.

This question-and-answer interview appeared in the jazz magazine *Metronome*.

THREE SCORE—A QUIZ FOR JAZZ MUSICIANS

(1) Whom do you consider one of the greatest Americans of the century?

(2) Excepting New York City and Los Angeles, where in the USA would you prefer to live? . . .

(6) Which classical musician, alive or dead, composer or performer, do you most enjoy? . . .

Thelonious Monk answers

(1) George Washington Carver.

(2) The moon. . . .

(6) Iturbi.

Cecil Taylor

One of the truly great pianists of our time, rightly celebrated for the profound originality and impassioned lyricism of his marvelous music, Taylor (1933?–) is also distinguished as poet, theorist, and choreographer. His interest in surrealism, dating from the 1950s, was inspired at least in part by Ted Joans and Bob Kaufman. In 1976 Taylor collaborated on the journal *Arsenal/Surrealist Subversion* and attended the huge World Surrealist Exhibition at Chicago's Gallery Black Swan. In 2004, with Jayne Cortez, Robin Kelley, and others, he played an important part in the memorial tribute to Ted Joans at New York University.

THE MUSICIAN

he pour'd floors talk
fly comment on latest views
arms moons ride fingers press inside
gallopin' galoshes shit ma points narrow'd in
torso wick torch   ease & confluent hips
silent upon open grass
voices float casts above
the own'd resolve
bronze suzy q'd sand spread
chapter behind raining lens
chatting arch'd contracting
parts travel   some sum's
speed deity alone fondles
like settin' almost dependable day
independent of time deliverance

spoken bitch workin' gospel
mean chants meant defy logics death
spies numerals rotating
all but the gentle lie buried there
you   see   come   heifer here
to   me   see
self forests chords calling solved goings
speech palms extends there many come
witness sword point yesterday sorrowing
now sparrow fly nut-spice beseeching
many new again grown to bring having
hyacinth seed by certain ides spring appear
knows inside whispers moves feeding
laughter swinging arms wait
pedigreed diameter bisected
brown body black being beside
behemoth poised to accede
Ring Dem Bells!
a head tone
phenomic color in
origin heated thoughts
cross & niger as
lines source contained
—within—
stamp stamp
dust mores
shadows float
Cire Perdue
process kept comin'
by out yet keepers
came
realms
all populate
even stride
bloodstain'd leer to catch
emperor's children
Muzimu   to
   heals   Oduduwa
secrets grown
protects   nature

projection   fast
  feed   becoming
Orisha
thru
gate

Arsenal, no. 3 (1976)

Ornette Coleman

A leading figure in the post-bop jazz revolution in the 1950s and 1960s, Ornette Coleman (1930-) radically transformed the way the world listened. While critics debated whether this was a blatant hoax, a new breakthrough in jazz, or something entirely new beyond jazz, young people all over the United States—and soon all over the world—were eagerly digging the new sound and relishing its beauty, delighted no end by Coleman's resolve to express more kinds of feeling than previously possible. His early albums, from *Something Else* (1958) to *Free Jazz* (1960) and beyond, were welcomed as harbingers of a sweeping social transformation, a new and marvelous freedom. This music dramatically changed people's lives.

Coleman is also a thinker, a theorist, a poet, and a teacher. A major inspirer of at least two generations of great musicians—including Albert Ayler, Eric Dolphy, John Coltrane, and the wonderful musician/magicians of Chicago's AACM—he is still, more than ever, inspiring up-and-coming young musicians.

Beyond the fact that surrealists—in the United States, Paris, Prague, and elsewhere—have long admired his music, Coleman's association with surrealism has been casual and occasional. In 1970 surrealist globe-trotter Ted Joans met him in Paris at an exhibition of the work of Romanian surrealist Victor Brauner, where Coleman told Joans that Brauner was in fact his favorite painter. Interestingly, too, his principal statement of his theory of Harmolodics—reprinted here—first appeared in the surrealist journal *Free Spirits: Annals of the Insurgent Imagination* (1982).

HARMOLODIC = HIGHEST INSTINCT

Something to Think About

When I speak of rhythm I'm speaking about the oxygen for the notes. The beat or the time is the constant format. It's the mechanical part of motion. Rhythm is the freest part of that motion. The beat is the cement for the road. It's the road that you're traveling on; the road doesn't necessarily ever change. Rhythm can be harmonic or melodic. Most listeners and players think of rhythm as the drums and think of non-rhythm as sound or words. To me they're the same. You can be moved rhythmically or non-rhythmically.

Improvising is a word used to express music that is not being written and calculated at the moment. Once I heard Eubie Blake say that when he was playing in black bands for white audiences, during the time when segregation was strong, that the musicians had to go on stage without any written music. The musicians would go backstage, look at the music, then leave the music there and go out and play it. He was saying that they had a more saleable appeal if they pretended to not know what they were doing. The white audience felt safer. If they had music in front of them, the audience would think that they were trying to be white. So that's what I think about the word improvising. It's outdated. The term doesn't describe the musician's individual struggle for expression. Usually the person improvising has to use some sort of vehicle to let you know he's doing that. It's a limited term. Memory has a lot to do with improvisation. People enjoy the music they've heard before, much more than the music they haven't heard. To me that's like memory. The same sensations that made them enjoy what they liked in the past, when it was the present, wasn't memory. That was an experience.

Sun Ra

Herman "Sonny" Blount (1914-1993), a member of Fletcher Henderson's orchestra in 1946-1947, adopted the name Sun Ra in the mid-1950s. He soon became one of the great iconoclasts of jazz, a man with a mission for whom music was a means of getting to know—and helping others know—the universe. Noted for his aggressive rejection of conventional melodic development, he and his band—the Intergalactic Research Arkestra—also elaborated their own uniquely uproarious and theatrical style of collective improvisation. Sun Ra's gigs were truly extraordinary multimedia events, complete with costumes, special lighting, dancing, film, and physical interaction with the audience, as he and his entourage snake-danced through the aisles, placing their hands on the shoulders of each and all while chanting, over and over, "The next stop is Jupiter!" or "Space is the Place!"

As suggested by the titles of his recordings—such as *Outer Planes of There*, *Secrets of the Sun*, and *The Heliocentric Worlds of Sun Ra* (in two volumes)—outer space clearly played a large role in Sun Ra's mythology. Deeply interested in cosmology and Egyptology, he was also a poet and agitator; in the 1960s he often soapboxed at Washington Square in Greenwich Village, together with surrealists, anarchists, and other revolutionaries and poets.

COSMIC EQUATION

Then another tomorrow
They never told me of
Came with the abruptness of a fiery dawn
And spoke of Cosmic Equations:
The equations of sight-similarity
The equations of sound-similarity
Subtle Living Equations
Clear only to those
Who wish to be attuned
To the vibrations of the Outer Cosmic Worlds.
Subtle living equations
of the outer-realms
Dear only to those
Who fervently wish the greater life

THE ENDLESS REALM

I have nothing
Nothing!
How really is I am. . . .
Nothing is mine.
How treasured rich am I
I have the treasure of nothing. . . .
Vast endless nothing

That branches out into realm beyond realm.
This and these are mine
Together they are nothing.

The idea of nothing
The notion of nations
Nation. . . . notion

I have the treasure of nothing
All of it is mine.
He who would build a magic world
Must seek my exchange bar
In order to partake of my endless
Treasure from my endless realm of nothing.

Babs Gonzales

No one knows whether Babs Gonzales (1919–1980) ever read any of
the surrealist manifestoes, but there is no getting around the fact that
he lived a surrealist life. Like many others who found imaginative ways
out of the daily grind—jazz people, circus folk, scholarly hoboes, and
street-corner soapboxers (the improv comics of their day)—the "king of
the bop poets" was street-smart to the point of street-genius and developed a hip version of vernacular surrealism that was all his own and
still capable today (on film, vinyl, and CD) of bringing down the house.
Humor, kicks, and good music were his game, and he played it with
uncompromising flamboyance. Cosmopolitan in the best sense, in his
English plaid coat, Mexican sombrero, and wooden shoes from Holland,
he enjoyed introducing musicians and songs in French, Danish, and
Swedish. His life story, *I Paid My Dues* (1967), is a book full of insight as
well as laughs.

For all his wordplay, gags, and funny stories, Babs Gonzales also had
a serious side. Highly critical of corruption in the music business, he
was fundamentally antiauthoritarian and an advocate of direct action to
solve problems that the "law" often prefers to ignore. Moreover, as the
excerpts reprinted here make clear, the maestro of "Three Bips and a
Bop" was by no means a moderate on race matters.

I PAID MY DUES

The street was really something in those days. The war was on and there were always loads of sailors and soldiers who wanted to and did fight every time they saw a Negro musician with a white girl. I'd seen a whore uptown beating her man with her shoe heel and him just holding his eyes screaming. When it was all over I asked her why the guy didn't fight back? She answered, "Just get a box of red pepper for a dime and throw it in his eyes and you'll win."

I took her advice and until today, I've never been without it.

*   *   *

Bird came by the theater on closing day and explained he'd just got in from Chicago, and didn't have a pad. I told him he could shack up with me for a couple of days so I took him home with me. The next morning I had an appointment with a shyster agent so I told Bird to "Lay Dead" until he got ready to split and to leave the key with the landlady.

When I got back that evening, Bird had departed with three of my suits. I wasn't worried because I knew he had to open up at the "Bopera" house in two weeks.

On his opening night, I walked in around midnight. He saw me and calmly walked down off the bandstand and went to the office in the rear. Ten minutes later he walked up to me and said, "Babs, baby, I know I downed your vines, so here's the tickets. They're in for five apiece. Here's twenty for the interest. Another five for cab fare and while you're here, have anything you want on me cause I love you." He just turned around and went back on the bandstand and played his ass off like nothing had happened. There are at least a thousand stories I can tell about Bird beating people out of something but in the ten years of our friendship, he always paid me back.

Gonzales, *I Paid My Dues*

A. B. Spellman

Poet, critic, and historian, Spellman (1935–) emceed the *Where It's At* jazz and ethnic music program in New York in the 1960s and contributed to magazines as different as *Metronome* and *The Liberator*. His *Four Lives in the Bebop Business* (1966) was one of the first in-depth appreciations of the new jazz.

THE NEW THING IN JAZZ: CULTIVATION OF THE MARVELOUS

Few people have been able to get next to Ornette Coleman's music in one hearing. There is just too much personality in his playing to relate its most salient sound to what even the most studiously prepared listener is accustomed to hearing, from any direction. Yet, everyone who attended the first press conference at the Five Spot came prepared to form a lasting opinion. Since then, some of those opinions have changed and some have not. But few of his original detractors consider Ornette a fake today, and this holds true even for those who still do not like his music.

At any rate, the original predictions that Ornette Coleman would change the direction of jazz proved to be completely true. Such modernists as John Coltrane and Jackie McLean admit that hearing Ornette has opened their own ears to new rhythmic possibilities in both group and solo playing. More important is the impact that Ornette's group has had on the younger generation of musicians who followed them. These younger musicians are overhauling jazz in much the same way the beboppers did, and they are just as controversial. There have been innumerable articles written pro and con on this new music, which was somewhat negatively named the "New Thing," as if it were a science fiction monster.

This impact, however, was not merely technical or, as LeRoi Jones wrote, "theoretical." . . . Ornette's confession that he doesn't "know how it's going to sound before I play it" [identifies his] true innovation. . . . That indefiniteness of not knowing how the music is going to sound before it is played . . . enhanced its emotional expression. Thus the new musician has been primarily involved in the cultivation of the Marvelous. And he judges his work more by the frequency with which the Marvelous occurs than by compositional values. It is therefore fair to say that Ornette Coleman's contribution to modern American music has been that he has opened up the way for the creation of situations wherein incredibly beautiful accidents occur.

Spellman, *Four Lives in the Bebop Business*

Dizzy Gillespie

One of the founding fathers of bebop, and the first person to try orchestrating the new sounds of Charlie Parker, Gillespie (1917–1993) remained throughout his life one of the major figures of twentieth-century music. His lively humor and repartee, together with his trademark beret and goatee, were well known all around the world.

Along with his passionate devotion to music, he maintained a deep interest in the other arts—especially painting. This touching tribute to his great Chicago friend, artist Gertrude Abercrombie, reflects this less-known aspect of his sensibility.

GERTRUDE ABERCROMBIE: BOP ARTIST

I would like to make an unequivocal statement: Gertrude Abercrombie is *the* bop artist, bop in the sense that she has taken the essence of our music and transported it into another art form. That is her main contribution, I think, because, in the future, the music that she loves will become *the* classical music. So we can say that the artistic career of Gertrude Abercrombie and the music of the 40s went hand in hand.

I have been following the career of Gertrude for many years. I have several of her paintings myself. I get great joy from them.

I remember an incident. I had a ring, an intaglio, and it was Minerva. I would wear this ring and when I would write somebody I would put some wax down and press it in and make a big impression on people. Well, I asked Gertrude to paint this ring. She looked at me and said, "Would I ask you, on one line of paper, to compose a symphony?"

Art and music are so closely related—we paint pictures too—we have to look to someone for inspiration. I know that Gertrude is versed in the fundamentals of her art. I can tell by the way she pushes her brush around. There are certain things that go with learning an art. Art is just an extension of the artist, but you know you are going in the right direction. First of all, you have to seek the truth in yourself and not what anyone else says about it and you just keep going and time will take care of it.

Exhibition catalog, Hyde Park Art Center, 1979

Amiri Baraka

Born in Newark, New Jersey, where he now makes his home, internationally renowned Amiri Baraka (1934–) published his first books as LeRoi Jones. His far-ranging influences as a poet and a revolutionary cannot be covered in this short note. It is impossible to list his numerous books and articles. (He is discussed elsewhere in this book.) Thus it was not possible to excerpt poetry, fiction, or theater, but following is a passage from his brilliant essay, "The Changing Same, R&B and the New Black Music."

THE CHANGING SAME

The content of the New Music, or The New Black Music, is toward change. It is change. It wants to change forms. From physical to physical (social to social) or from physical to mental, or from physical-mental to spiritual. Soon essences. Albert Ayler no longer wants notes. He says he wants sound. The total articulation. Ra's music changes places, like Duke's "jungle music." Duke took people to a spiritual past, Ra to a spiritual future (which also contains "Little Sally Walker . . . sitting in a saucer . . . what kind'a saucer? . . . a flying saucer").

African sounds, too: the beginnings of our sensibility. The new, the "primitive," meaning *first*, new. Just as Picasso's borrowings were Western avant-garde and "the new" from centuries ago, and Stravinsky's borrowings were new and "savage," centuries old and brand new.

The black musicians who know about the European tempered scale (Mind) no longer want it, if only just to be contemporary. That changed. The other black musicians never wanted it, anyway.

Change

Freedom

and finally Spirit. (But spirit makes the first two possible. A cycle again?)

What are the qualitative meanings and implications of these words?

There is the freedom to exist (and the change to) in the existing, or to re-emerge in a new thing.

Essence

How does this content differ from that of R&B?

Love, for R&B, is an absolute good. There is love but there is little of it, and it is a valuable possession. How Sweet It Is To Be Loved By You. But the practical love, like the practical church the R&B people left, a much more emotional church and spirit worship than most jazz people had, is a day-to-day physical, social, sensual love. Its presence making the other categories of human experience mesh favorably with beautiful conclusions. "Since I Lost My Baby" (or older) "When I Lost My Baby . . . I almost lost my mind." There is the *object* (even, the person). But what is the *object* of John Coltrane's "Love" . . . There is none. It is for the sake of Loving, Trane speaks of. As Ra's "When Angels Speak of Love."

Black Music

8. Toward the New Millennium:
The Mid-1970s through the 1990s

THE WORLD SURREALIST EXHIBITION, 1976

> Dreams have contributed greatly to humankind's culture and
> development.
>
> —Novalis

In her excellent biography of Joyce Mansour, Marie-Laure Missir emphasizes
that the surrealists in France, after a rancorous split in 1969 (which some people
naïvely mistook for the end of the movement) decided that an effective renewal of surrealist activity depended largely on the "international dimension."
As the ten issues of their *Bulletin de Liaison Surréaliste* demonstrate, Mansour and
her friends focused on the two most active surrealist centers: Prague, where
public surrealist manifestations were, unfortunately, forbidden; and Chicago,
where the group was not only youthful and prolific, but also closely in touch
with numerous collaborators throughout the country, and in other lands as
well. Prague and Chicago are similarly highlighted by French surrealist Alain
Joubert in his admirable critical history, *Le mouvement des surréalistes.*[1]

During the first half of the 1970s, the *Surrealist Insurrection* wall posters; the
surrealism issue of *Radical America;* the burgeoning Surrealist Research & De-
velopment Monograph Series from Black Swan Press; the surrealist section of
Lawrence Ferlinghetti's City Lights Anthology; the Chicago Group's journal,
Arsenal/Surrealist Subversion; the group's extensive correspondence with Herbert
Marcuse; and its comradely relations with the League of Revolutionary Black
Workers were all written up by Mansour, Vincent Bounoure and others in the
Bulletin de Liaison Surréaliste Group, as significant contributions to the movement's
international renewal.

The year 1976 heralded much more and was indeed a banner year for surrealism in Chicago. The ripple effect of the group's many actions spread across North America and 'round the world.

In January the magazine *Living Blues* ("A Journal of the Black American Blues Tradition") ran a special sixteen-page supplement titled "Surrealism & Blues," a collection of celebratory articles on the history, poetry, and politics of blues, edited by the Surrealist Group. A militant preface salutes "the blues' true source of inspiration, the black working-men and women of this country," and goes on to denounce "so-called 'white' blues" as a racist appropriation. The basic theme of the supplement is indicated in the opening lines: "Surrealism is the exaltation of freedom, revolt, imagination and love. The surrealists could hardly have failed to recognize aspects of their combat in blues (and in jazz), for freedom, revolt, imagination and love are the very hallmarks of all that is greatest in the great tradition of black music."

April brought the third issue of *Arsenal/Surrealist Subversion*—the largest issue yet (120 pages), with 30-plus articles, including one called "Black Music and Surrealist Revolution," a statement by Malcolm de Chazal (from Mauritius), some 50 reproductions, and poems by—among others—Jayne Cortez, Joseph Jarman, Cecil Taylor, Ted Joans, Clément Magloire-Saint-Aude, and Joyce Mansour.

And then came May Day, the opening of the World Surrealist Exhibition—"Marvelous Freedom/Vigilance of Desire"—at the Gallery Black Swan in Chicago.

Major international surrealist exhibitions had taken place in Paris, 1959; New York, 1960–1961; Milan, 1961; Amsterdam, 1961; Paris 1965–1966; and São Paulo, 1967. They varied widely. The Paris show, for example, featured 104 works by 75 artists from 19 countries, while the Milan show included only 24 works by 18 artists from 10 countries. Most of these shows were also organized with the assistance and support of a friendly gallery.

The 1976 Chicago exhibition was by far the biggest of all. With over 600 works by 150-plus artists from 31 countries, it was truly the largest exhibition in the movement's history. And with no friendly galleries at hand, the surrealists themselves had not only to find a space of their own, but also to secure the works, frame them, mount them on the walls, and—no small task—prepare the catalog, posters, and press releases.

Circumstances enabled them to fulfill a long-cherished dream: to defy and supersede gallery tradition by planning the show as an unrelentingly subversive manifestation. The space—named Gallery Black Swan for the occasion—was just the place to realize such a dream: a huge second-story car barn which, decades earlier, had housed trolleys and the horses that pulled them. The entrance was a wide ramp—no stairs. Nearly a half-block square, the sprawling cavernous chaos featured Eleven Domains of Surrealist Vigilance. Each was named for a mythic figure admired by surrealists, such as Alice in Wonderland, Bugs Bunny, Harpo Marx, T-Bone Slim, and Peetie Wheatstraw, the devil's son-in-law.

The arrangement was deliberately informal, with disquieting but playful installations at every turn (a forest of green gloves in the Robin Hood Domain; a six-foot-tall carrot in Bugs Bunny's bed). The overall effect was as unlike a museum as possible. Instead of an aesthetic spectacle, strollers encountered a series of poetic provocations. The large-format catalog included an architect's blueprint indicating the domains and such special features as the Corridor of the Forgotten Future, with Tristan Meinecke's twelve-foot-square three-dimensional paintings and Gerome Kamrowski's towering mobile, *Menagerie of Revolt*.

The *Chicago Tribune* critic likened the show to being at the scene of an explosion, but that did not seem to discourage the crowds that climbed the ramp day after day for two months.[2]

The Chicagoans did the organizing and the on-site work of setting up the show, but surrealists from out of state and overseas played key roles. Among the most helpful were Eugenio F. Granell (New York), Ted Joans (Paris, Timbuktu), Mário Cesariny (Lisbon), Édouard Jaguer (Paris), Conroy Maddox (London), Shuzo Takiguchi (Tokyo), and the Iraqi Abdul Kader El Janaby (Paris).

Thanks to Shuzo Takiguchi, well over two dozen works—including two of his own—arrived from Japan. Takiguchi, whose surrealist activity extended back to the 1920s, was a major figure in surrealism; his support, not only for the 1976 exhibition, but also for the Chicago Group's overall perspectives, meant a lot to the growing surrealist movement in the United States. Another Japanese exhibitor, Yoshie Yoshida, flew to Chicago for the opening with some additional works. After returning to Tokyo, he wrote a long and well-illustrated article on the exhibition for the November 1976 issue of Japan's leading art journal, *Mizué*.

Surrealist groups in Lisbon and Copenhagen sent crates of paintings. The Portuguese also sent pieces by Inácio Matsinhe from Mozambique and Malangatana Valente from Angola. Impressive packets also arrived from London, the *Bulletin de Liaison* Group in Paris, and the Arab Surrealist Movement in Exile. Édouard Jaguer—coorganizer of the 1960–1961 exhibition in New York—sent packets representing artists active in the *Phases* movement. Mimi Parent and many others sent their own works by airmail.

Others, including Jayne Cortez, Joyce Mansour, Philip Lamantia, Aurelien Dauguet, and Takasuke Shibusawa, participated by contributing poems to the catalog.

Special events gave the exhibition extra sparkle and sound. Opening night featured Alice Farley's *Surrealist Dance,* and later there was a showing of Fernando Arrabal's anti-Franco film, *Viva la muerte.* The June 5 "World Surrealist Exhibition Blues Show" highlighted the great acoustic blues guitarist and vocalist David "Honeyboy" Edwards, plus Eddie Shaw & the Howlin' Wolf Band. Edwards in later years played at other surrealist-related events; at least once a local newspaper identified him as an active member of the Surrealist Group.

The World Surrealist Exhibition also featured two stunning performances of "Great Black Music" by the Sun Song Ensemble, a free jazz group affiliated with Chicago's Association for the Advancement of Creative Musicians. The ensemble included Douglas Ewart (reeds), Hamid Drake (percussion), George Lewis (trombone), Gloria Brooks (vocalist), and Rrata Christine Jones (dancer). Emphasizing the unfettered imagination, improvisation, collective creation, and play, the AACM exemplified then, as it still does, an authentically surrealist spirit. The Sun Song recitals, combining music, song, dance, comedy, and costume, were not only a highlight of the exhibition but also a milepost of surrealist theater.

The participation of black artists in surrealist exhibitions had been steadily expanding over the years, but here too the 1976 Black Swan show was a landmark. In addition to individual pieces by Wifredo Lam and Malangatana Valente, there were multiple works by Ted Joans, Farid Lariby, Inácio Matsinhe, and Jacinto Minot, plus some thirty-odd paintings, watercolors, and metal sculptures by fifteen exhibitors from Haiti—artists still identified in those days as "naïves," many of whom (including Murat Brierre, George Liataud, and Gabriel Bien-Aimé) subsequently became well known. To the African American photographer Melody Rammel we owe much of the exhibition's best documentation.

In short, "Marvelous Freedom"—with its blues show, Sun Song concerts, and the many contributions to the catalog by black poets—added up not only to the biggest of all international surrealist exhibitions, but also the blackest. The *Tribune* critic notwithstanding, the show had an impact that is still reverberating. Few Chicago cultural events have received more international attention.

South African poet and antiapartheid activist Dennis Brutus, who was there at the opening, recalled years later that the 1976 exhibition was "the most stupendous and inspiring cultural event" of his first Chicago years, and went on to add that, during his many later years in the city, he had never seen anything better.

Pronouncing the show great and important, pianist and poet Cecil Taylor not only spent several hours taking it all in, but also took the trouble to phone musician friends all over Chicago, urging them to visit the Black Swan. Joseph Jarman and Henry Threadgill were just two of the many who followed his advice. Jarman went on to compose music titled "Marvelous Freedom/Vigilance of

Desire," and Threadgill composed music for Aimé Césaire's *Return to My Native Land.*

Gerome Kamrowski, seasoned veteran of art shows going back to the early 1940s, declared that the 1976 Chicago show was the largest completely unsubsidized art exhibition of all time. The *Dictionnaire du surréalisme et ses environs* sums it up as "an unprecedented panorama of *living* surrealism."[3]

A historical note: after June 1976 the Gallery Black Swan was not used again for exhibitions, surrealist or otherwise. Some twenty years later, the space was remodeled and renamed Michael Jordan's Restaurant.

SURREALISTS IN THE STREETS

> The main thing is to know and seize the critical moment.
>
> —Paul de Gondi, Cardinal de Retz

Even before the 1976 exhibition was over, the Chicago surrealists as a group had joined an activist coalition, Workers' Defense, and were soon involved in a vigorous campaign to support striking coal miners. Within a week, according to a Miners' Union official in Boonville, Indiana, the bumper sticker the group had designed was on every car in the mining region. A few weeks later surrealists were also active in a successful struggle against neo-Nazi racist terror in Chicago. "Thus," as French surrealist Guy Ducornet put it in a Paris-based magazine at the time, "surrealism in the U.S.A. is fulfilling its moral and political exigencies."[4]

Simple incidents of daily life are often highly revelatory. Like most artists, Jocelyn Koslofsky—a young woman of Lithuanian descent and active in the Chicago Surrealist Group in the 1970s—had to support herself with a day job. One afternoon an African American woman coworker told her that she was "the nicest white person I've ever known." And then another fellow worker, also black, said: "Hey, Jocelyn's not white—she's a *surrealist!*"

In 1978 the Surrealist Group disrupted the unveiling of Pop Artist Claes Oldenburg's *Batcolumn* statue (described in the surrealist leaflet as a hundred-foot-long billy-club). The Chicago *Sun-Times* declared: "As in all true Chicago cultural events, there were three arrests."[5]

NEWCOMERS

> It is not the technique of painting which is surrealist, it's the *painter*, and the painter's vision of life.
>
> —Joyce Mansour

The 1976 World Surrealist Exhibition was followed two years later by sizeable international shows in Milwaukee ("The 100ᵗʰ Anniversary of Hysteria") and London ("Surrealism Unlimited"), the latter organized principally by veteran British surrealist Conroy Maddox. The momentum persisted throughout the next decade and into the new millennium, with a multitude of smaller shows in places as varied as Paris, Lyon, Lisbon, Mexico City, Prague, Reykjavik, all over Chicago, and even in Gary, Indiana. Notable in the Gary show was the inclusion—for the first time anywhere—of four works by the then-unknown outsider artist Henry Darger.[6]

New surrealist exhibitions tend to involve new surrealists. The 1970s and 1980s brought forth the Milwaukee-based Senegalese painter, poet, and essayist Cheikh Tidiane Sylla and the Chicago-based Cuban painter Jacinto Minot. Other newcomers included three highly innovative African American artists whose work, like Sylla's and Minot's, has appeared in surrealist publications: Patrick Turner, a wildly imaginative collagist from Milwaukee; Chicagoan Norman Calmese, who later became well known as a cartoonist; and Tyree Guyton of Detroit.

Guyton's unique medium is collage on a grand scale. His collages consist of abandoned houses that he imaginatively embellishes with dolls, toys, bicycles, street signs, flat tires, pants, shoes, hubcaps, wheels, graffiti, and extravagant paint jobs often featuring large polka dots. His wife, Karen, his grandfather Sam Mackey, and many neighbors have helped on his projects. Here was a semislum, neglected by city officials, suddenly brightened up and given new life and beauty by a few imaginative residents. In *Surrealist Subversions* Ron Sakolsky commends Guyton for having "turned the flotsam and jetsam of urban debris into visual surrealist poetry inspired by an explicitly Afrocentric sensibility."[7] For Guyton's surrealist friends, the grandeur of these walk-in collages was enhanced by the fact that he preferred to work on them while listening to the recorded music of Thelonious Monk.

Guyton's amazing collaged houses, admired by many and detested by a few, soon became Detroit's top tourist attraction; large groups came from all over the world to see them. When the mayor and City Council announced their intention to destroy the buildings, the protest was immediate and enormous. The issue was even debated on the *Oprah Winfrey Show* (Oprah favored destruction). The surrealist movement in the United States promptly issued a poster and tract on the matter—a statement widely reprinted and eventually cosigned by surrealists and sympathizers in Paris, São Paulo, Madrid, and other cities. No collective declaration in the movement's history has included so many signatures.

Although Guyton lost his battle with Detroit's politicians, he nonetheless won renown as the city's most celebrated artist and, indeed, as one of the fore-most Outsider artists in the nation. With his community-backed collective art, moreover, Guyton also exemplified the truth of one of Malcolm X's most brilliant observations. At the founding meeting of the Organization of Afro-American Unity in June 1964, Malcolm argued that the black jazz musician's ability to improvise, to play "sounds that he never thought of before," should be regarded as the prefiguration of the black population's potential—when al-lowed to function in "an atmosphere of complete freedom"—to improvise *other* aspects of life as well: a new society, for example, a new philosophy, a new art and culture.[8]

A similar insight no doubt inspired French surrealist José Pierre's confi-dence that the work of sculptor Augustín Cárdenas and a few other poets and painters—he specifically named Aimé Césaire, Wifredo Lam, and Hector Hyp-polite—marks the beginning of a new civilization, free of all the old ethnic and aesthetic prejudices: a civilization, that is to say, founded on a new morality, a *surrealist* morality.[9]

A SURREALIST PUBLISHING BOOM

The unprecedented efflorescence of surrealism in the visual arts was only one aspect of the movement's large-scale ongoing resurgence internationally. From the spring of 1976 through the 1990s no fewer than thirty periodicals, in ten languages, were produced by surrealist groups around the world, and new groups sprouted up as never before. To help coordinate the activities of so many geographically scattered groups, several issues of the *International Surrealist Bulletin* appeared (in English, Swedish, Czech, French, Spanish, and Japanese).

For the always inspired and energetic Ted Joans, international surrealism's prime globe-trotter throughout this period and beyond, the 1980s and 1990s were as frantic and fulfilling as ever. His tours of North America included key stops in Chicago, Mexico City, and, later, Seattle and Vancouver. His Chicago visits were always momentous occasions. He took part in the 1985 "Free Nelson Mandela" antiapartheid demonstrations at Northwestern University. Joans also showed his Film Poems at the Occult Bookstore, lectured sagaciously on the rhinoceros as an endangered species, and arranged poetry readings at venues ranging from the downtown main library to black colleges.

It was Joans, too, who proposed the 1993 Exquisite Corpse exhibition, "Totems without Taboos," at the Heartland Café Gallery—the first U.S. show exclusively devoted to one of surrealism's earliest, best-loved, and most creative games.[10]

This was also a period rich in the publication of surrealist books. Joans brought out several new titles, as did Jayne Cortez, who also issued several new recordings. New Directions brought out the formerly uncollected poems of Bob Kaufman, *The Ancient Rain*. Anthony Joseph's *Teragaton* was published in London by Poison Engine Press.

The Éditions Surréalistes in Paris, Surrealist Editions in Chicago, and their equivalents in Prague, Stockholm, and elsewhere turned out volume after volume. Notable among the Stockholm publications was the pocket-sized anthology *Black Music and Surrealism*.

Larger publishers, too—commercial as well as academic—became increasingly interested in surrealism. In Paris, for example, Jean-Michel Place issued elegant reprints of such old and hard-to-find periodicals as *La Révolution Surréaliste*, *Le Surréalisme au Service de la Révolution*, *Légitime Défense*, and *Tropiques*. Robert Laffont published *Tracées*, a hefty selection of essays by René Ménil. Éditions Arabie-sur-Seine reissued Mary Low and Juan Breá's *La saison des flûtes*. Azul Editions brought out Aída Cartagena Portalatín's *Yania Tierra*. And Thunder's Mouth Press published a good-sized volume of Larry Neal's *Visions of a Liberated Future*.

Other publishers brought out the complete works of Joyce Mansour, André Breton, Claude Cahun, Jehan Mayoux, and Clément Magloire-Saint-Aude.

In Germany, Heribert Becker, with Édouard Jaguer in Paris and the Czech Petr Kral, edited *Das Surrealistische Gedicht*, the largest compilation of surrealist poetry in any language. The first edition (1985) ran to 1,475 pages; the 2005 edition was expanded to 1,888. German readers can now savor the poetry of Robert Benayoun, Juan Breá, Aimé Césaire, Jayne Cortez, Georges Henein, Ted Joans, Etienne Léro, Clément Magloire-Saint-Aude, Joyce Mansour, and scores of others.

Inevitably, the ongoing black surrealist renaissance has also inspired European and Euro-American surrealists. Guy Ducornet's *Ça va chauffer!*, the first French study of surrealism in the United States, details the American surrealists' passion for black music and includes a chapter on the critique of "whiteness." Interestingly, Ducornet in the 1950s was a student of the great Ralph Ellison and remained his friend and correspondent in later years.

In addition to the 1992 tract "For Tyree Guyton," important surrealist documents of the 1990s include an international tract against the procolonialist Columbus Quincentennial (1992), the widely translated "Three Days That Shook the New World Order: The Los Angeles Rebellion of 1992," and—voluminously circulated in the streets of Seattle in 1999—"Who Needs the WTO?"[11]

NEWS FROM CLAUDE TARNAUD

Claude Tarnaud's posthumously published *De* is a book in a category all by itself. Subtitled *The Hidden Face of an Afro-American Adventure* and written in the 1960s, slightly expanded in the 1970s, but not published until 2003, it was originally titled *The End of the World*, but Tarnaud—upon learning that the title had already been used—decided on the two-letter title, *de* being the end of the French word *monde* (world).

A new book by Tarnaud inevitably sparked a sensation in surrealist circles 'round the world, and especially in Chicago. His personal influence on the beginnings of Chicago surrealism—dating back to the spring of 1963—had been decisive to such a degree that the group regarded him as an honorary cofounder despite the fact that he was living in Switzerland at the time the group was actually formed. His letter on the Chicagoans, published in *La Brèche*, no. 5 (October 1963), was in fact the first public announcement of the Chicago group-to-be.

De is an apocalyptic, wildly humorous, and *noir* chronicle of adventures in New York City in the early and mid-1960s, during which Tarnaud frequented clubs featuring the finest jazz—Thelonious Monk above all, but also Max Roach, John Coltrane, Miles Davis, and Charles Mingus, as well as younger musicians, from Albert Ayler and Ornette Coleman to Pharoah Sanders and Archie Shepp. Centered around the rising Afro-American rebellion of that decade, the book abounds with references to Malcolm X, Patrice Lumumba, Black Power, Robert F. Williams, James Baldwin, Amiri Baraka, and Max Roach's *Freedom Now Suite*. It is also a hard-hitting critique of the lackluster monotony of Cold War white capitalist society, its hypercommercial and relentlessly *conditioned* consumerist pseudo-culture, and its nightmarish out-of-control "development."

Written at red heat in the brightest of bright moments, this dazzling and defiant book is a kind of spontaneous one-man surrealist insurrection.[12]

NEW APPROACHES TO THE WHITE PROBLEM

> Why are all blacklists white?
> —Bob Kaufman

In 1991 David Roediger, a historian who had long contributed to surrealist publications, brought out a new book, *The Wages of Whiteness: Race and the Making of the American Working Class*. Inspired by W.E.B. Du Bois' insight that low-paid white workers were compensated in part by a psychological wage, the book was an immediate sensation and a major influence on race studies. A few years later,

Noel Ignatiev's case study, *How the Irish Became White*, expanded the discussion. Not long afterward, Ignatiev and others started a lively journal, *Race Traitor*, centered on the white problem and what it is possible to do about it. The journal's motto was "Treason to whiteness is loyalty to humanity."

In 1998 *Race Traitor* devoted an entire issue to surrealism or, more precisely, to surrealist writings on various aspects of the "white mystique" and ways to overcome it. The issue's introduction states, in part: "This special issue of *Race Traitor* focuses on a particular group of race traitors—the world's first Surrealist Group in 1920s Paris, and its direct offshoot, the international (and multiracial) surrealist movement. With an unbroken continuity from 1924 down to the present day, the surrealist movement has helped develop not only a revolutionary critique of whiteness but also new forms of revolutionary action against it."

The volume's nearly two dozen articles add up to a sustained critique of "whiteness" in its various dimensions. Several articles examine the surrealists' "race politics" historically, among them a fourteen-page minianthology of texts titled "Surrealists on Whiteness, from 1925 to the Present"; David Roediger's "Plotting against Eurocentrism," on the 1929 Surrealist Map of the World; and Myrna Bell Rochester's "René Crevel: Critic of White Patriarchy."

Dennis Brutus contributed a vibrant, enthusiastic review essay on David Roediger's anthology, *Black on White: Black Writers on What It Means to Be White*. Others focus on more current issues: the Madrid Surrealist Group's "Beyond Anti-Racism: The Role of Poetic Thought in the Eradication of White Supremacy"; "Racist Cliches," by the Mexican/Native American poet Ronnie Burk; Charles Radcliffe's "Whitewashing the Blues"; and Australian surrealist Hilary Booth's "We're Sorry You're Not Sorry," on crimes against Aborigines Down Under.

Denounced by Rush Limbaugh, Communists, Nazis, the *New York Times*, liberals, and former New Leftists galore, *Race Traitor* proved very attractive to young anarchists. Like William Lloyd Garrison's *Liberator* 150 years earlier, it was also popular among black readers.

It is not easy to gauge the influence of a small radical journal, but *Race Traitor*—judging from its many letters to the editor—seems to have really got around and had more than a little impact. As it happened, the 1998 surrealist issue was something of a best seller and provoked more letters than ever. Burnham Ware, of Owenton, Kentucky—a longtime contributor to the journal *Living Blues*, called *Race Traitor* an excellent publication and added that "the Surrealists seem unafraid to align themselves with the black masses, and as a black male I appreciate that very much." Many others wrote in the same vein.

Darryl Lorenzo Wellington, a young black poet and reader of *Race Traitor*— which, by the way, he had purchased at a traveling circus!—not only praised the surrealist issue of *Race Traitor*, but also began a correspondence with the Chicago Surrealist Group. When he announced his plans to visit friends in Paris, the Chicagoans urged him to look up the Surrealist Group there and also to consider going to Prague, where an international surrealist conference, accompanied by an exhibition, was soon to be held. In short order Wellington was warmly welcomed by the Paris surrealists and was attending their meetings. He also made the trip to Prague, where he represented the surrealist movement in the United States. At the conference, he made a special presentation on the surrealist issue of *Race Traitor* and urged the delegates from European countries to establish solidarity with the oppressed Gypsies.

A second and larger special surrealist issue of *Race Traitor* (250 pages), edited by anarchist scholar Ron Sakolsky, appeared in summer 2001.[13] In addition to many of those mentioned in the immediately preceding paragraphs, its contributors included surrealists Gale Ahrens, Jayne Cortez, Brandon Freels, Jan Hathaway, Joseph Jablonski, Don LaCoss, Philip Lamantia, Mary Low, Anne Olson, and Nancy Joyce Peters.

SURREALISM AT THE BLACK RADICAL CONGRESS

The storms of youth precede brilliant days.

—Lautréamont

No doubt to the surprise of many, surrealism was a scheduled topic at the 1998 Black Radical Congress in Chicago. The speaker was the young New York–based black historian Robin D. G. Kelley, whose books (*Hammer and Hoe*, 1990; *Race Rebels*, 1994) surrealists in Chicago had read and admired. In a Chicago Surrealist Group discussion, the strong surrealist undercurrent in Kelley's writings was emphasized, a view amply confirmed by their reading of his *Yo' Mama's Disfunktional!* (1997), enthusiastically reviewed by Dave Roediger in the first surrealist issue of *Race Traitor*.

Kelley's talk at the congress brought forth a hearty response from Amiri Baraka, who commended the Chicago surrealists for, among other things, "restoring surrealism to its original revolutionary perspectives." A few years later, when Baraka was under attack by the Far Right, the surrealists—forty strong—issued a tract in his defense titled "Poetry Matters! On the Media Persecution of Amiri Baraka." A later edition included ninety-six additional signatures, among them John Bracey, Dennis Brutus, Diane diPrima, Martín Espada, Joseph Jarman, Utah Phillips, Archie Shepp, James Smethurst, and Gary Snyder.

After the Congress, Kelley began a series of essays about surrealism, or touching on it significantly. It was immediately evident—and not only to fellow surrealists—that he was one of the most insightful and innovative writers on the subject.

In a later talk to a large audience of black students in the South, he discussed the resplendent upheaval of black surrealism in the Caribbean during the 1940s. Relating the glory days of *Tropiques* to the new currents in African American youth culture in our own time, Kelley boldly predicted "a resurgence of surrealism beyond anything the world has ever seen."[14]

Notes

1. Missir, *Joyce Mansour,* 166; Joubert, *Le mouvement des surréalistes,* 85, 312.

2. *Chicago Tribune* (June 7, 1976).

3. Biro and Passeron, *Dictionnaire,* 368.

4. Guy Ducornet, "Introduction aux surréalisme actuel aux U.S.A.," *Phases,* New Series, no. 5 (November 1975), 67.

5. Roger Simon, "A Batty Welcome to Chicago," *Chicago Sun-Times* (April 15, 1977).

6. A paragraph in the Gary, Indiana, *Post-Tribune* (April 17, 1977, sect. D3), discusses the inclusion of Darger's work in the show.

7. Sakolsky, *Surrealist Subversions,* 95.

8. Malcolm X, *By Any Means Necessary,* 63–64.

9. José Pierre, "Cárdenas ou l'exigence et la grace," 133–136.

10. Originally planned as a one-month show, "Totems without Taboos" received considerable media attention and was extended for several weeks. Not long afterward, the Art Institute of Chicago exhibited a few *cadavres exquis* from Chicago collections.

11. "Who Needs the WTO?" was widely reprinted. The major book on the subject, Eddie Yuen et al., *The Battle of Seattle,* features the tract as its opening statement, right after the editors' introduction.

12. For further information on Tarnaud, see Sakolsky's *Surrealist Subversions,* and the short essay, "Claude Tarnaud and the Poetic Use of the Useless," in Franklin Rosemont, *Open Entrance to the Shut Palace of Wrong Numbers,* 46–49.

13. This second surrealist issue, titled "Surrealism in the U.S.A.," includes nearly fifty original texts by nearly as many writers, as well as twenty-five reproductions of artworks and a selection of documents from the 1960s through the 1990s.

14. Quoted in *Race Traitor*, no. 13–14 (Summer 2001), 63.

Aimé Césaire

MY JOYFUL ACCEPTANCE OF SURREALISM

I have never forgotten my meeting with André Breton in 1941. This meeting was such that it oriented my life in a decisive manner, and I must say that his image never has ceased to accompany me. Absent but familiar, and always there: Such was for me, and such is still for me the presence of André Breton: the very incarnation of purity, courage, and the noblest virtues of the mind.

I was ready to accept surrealism because I already had advanced on my own, using as my starting points the same authors that had influenced the surrealist poets. Their thinking and mine had common reference points. Surrealism provided me with what I had been confusedly searching for. I have accepted it joyfully because in it I have found more of a confirmation than a revelation. It was a weapon that exploded the French language. It shook up absolutely everything.

Surrealism interested me to the extent that it was a liberating factor. My thinking followed these lines: Well then, if I apply the surrealist approach to my particular situation, I can summon up these unconscious forces. This, for me, was a call to Africa. I said to myself: it's true that superficially we are French, we bear the marks of French customs, we have been branded by Cartesian philosophy, by French rhetoric; but if we break with all that, if we plumb the depths, then what we will find is fundamentally black. . . . A process of disalienation, that's how I interpreted surrealism. . . . A plunge into the depths. It was a plunge into Africa for me.

Interview with René Depestre, 1967; translated by Myrna Bell Rochester

Of course I am surrealist. I accept, absolutely, the surrealist teaching. For me, the surrealist teaching is an extremely precious thing. But I am *not* a Parisian surrealist. I have put surrealism in the service of something else.

Why did I affirm my complete agreement with surrealism? Because I recognized surrealism as the highest point of the European spirit, the point at which the European spirit harmonizes most with the spirit of the Far East and the spirit of the Black world. That is why I took part in surrealism.

Of course, my surrealism could not be the same as that of Breton, or the early Aragon. It is something different.

Interview with Michel Benamou, February 14, 1973; translated by Myrna Bell Rochester

I had read the *Surrealist Manifestoes*, a bit distractedly, but in the end I knew their content. I had read *Légitime Défense*, the journal of my Martinican surrealist friends—Léro, Monnerot, Ménil.

And then, I had already read the father of surrealism. Without truly being surrealist, I had the same ancestors that they had: Rimbaud, of course, Mallarmé, the symbolists. My own poetry, as a result, did not derive from the *Manifestoes*, but from the currents that had prepared the way for surrealism.

What did Breton bring us? He brought us *boldness*; he helped us take a strong stand. He cut short our hesitations and research. I realized that the majority of the problems I encountered had already been resolved by Breton and surrealism. I would say that my meeting with Breton was a confirmation of what I had already arrived at on my own. This saved us time; it let us go quicker, further. The encounter was *extraordinary*. I met him, and he literally *fascinated* me. This was a man of very great culture, with an *astonishing* sense of poetry. Truly a great man.

The encounter with Breton was *very important* for me. It was the end of hesitations.

Yes, I had read Lautréamont; but starting from the day that I met Breton I reread him *systematically*, with a different eye, a *new* eye, with the formidable illumination that Breton's presence had brought me.

Interview with Jacqueline Leiner, 1978; translated by Myrna Bell Rochester
(original emphasis)

HOMAGE TO FRANTZ FANON

Frantz Fanon is dead. We expected this for many months, but against all reason, we were hopeful. We knew him as such a determined person, capable of miracles, and as such a crucial figure on the horizon of men. We must accept the facts: Frantz Fanon is dead at age 37. A short life, but extraordinary. Brief, but bright, illuminating one of the most atrocious tragedies of the 20th century and detailing in an exemplary manner the human condition, the condition of modern man. If the word "commitment" has a meaning, then it is embodied in the person of Frantz Fanon. He was called "an advocate of violence, a terrorist." And it's true Fanon appointed himself the theoretician of violence, the sole weapon of the colonized against the barbarism of colonialism.

However odd it seems, his violence was non-violent; the violence of justice, of pureness, uncompromising. His revolt was ethical, his approach one of generosity. He did not simply join a cause. He gave himself to it. Wholly. Without reserve. Without measure. With unqualified passion.

A doctor, he knew human suffering. As a psychiatrist, he observed the impact on the human mind of traumatic events. Above all, as a "colonial" man he felt and understood what it was to be born and live in a colonial situation; he studied this situation scientifically, aided by introspection as much as observation.

His revolt was in this context. As a doctor in Algeria, he witnessed the unfolding of colonial atrocities, and this was what gave birth to rebellion. It wasn't enough for him to argue in defense of the Algerian people. He united himself with the oppressed, humiliated, tortured and beaten down Algerian. He became Algerian. Lived, fought and died Algerian. A theoretician of violence, doubtless, and yet more so of action. Because he had an aversion to mere talk. Because he had an aversion to compromise. Because he had an aversion to cowardice. No one was more respectful of ideas, more responsible to his own ideals, more exacting of life he imagined as a practical ideal.

It is thus that he became a combatant, and a writer, one of the most brilliant of his generation.

On colonialism, the human consequences of colonization and racism, the key text to read is *Black Skin, White Masks*. On decolonization, again by Fanon, *The Wretched of the Earth*.

Fanon died and one reflects on his life; his epic side as well as his tragic side. The epic side is that Fanon lived to the very end his destiny of a champion of liberty, mastering to the heights his sense of identity with humanity and that he died a fighter for Internationalism.

At the actual moment when he himself was entering the "great darkness," at the brink of which he was reeling, he understands: "Come Comrades, it is better to change our thinking. To shake off and leave behind the great darkness into which we have plunged. . . . It is necessary to invent, to discover . . . for Europe, for ourselves, and for mankind, . . . to develop a new way of thinking, to try to bring forth a new humankind."

I don't know of anything more moving or greater than this lesson of life coming from a deathbed.

Présence Africaine, no. 40 (1962); translated by Connie Rosemont

Jayne Cortez

THERE IT IS

There It Is: A collection of conscious/unconscious tonal attitudes, expressions, responses and rhythms poetry/music collaborations concerned with human need. The need for security, for education, for temporary migration or permanent immigration. Populations moving from one place to another out of necessity. This is a part of the content of "To a Gypsy Cab Man," a driver of an independent taxi service who generally services the Black and Hispanic communities. "Opening Act" opens with the band in a rapid intense free introduction that slows down into a good blues feeling. The poetry speaks of trials and problems connected with the presentation of creativity and the reality of continuing. The tone of the poem is defiance. "If the Drum Is a Woman," a short dialogue between the poet and the drums—a dialogue about human rights, equality and justice.

"U.S./Nigerian Relations," "There It Is" and "Blood Suckers" are poems commenting on big business, international trade and the dehumanization involved in the process. "Chano Pozo was the first conga player to play with a jazz band." I heard the famous Afro-Cuban drummer around 1948 at Wrigley Field in Los Angeles. He was playing with the Dizzy Gillespie band. I was very young but I remember being excited and impressed by his performance. I wrote the poem "I See Chano Pozo" for the Chano Pozo Music Festival at Dartmouth College in 1980. The poem speaks of the importance and significance of the drums. "You must come up for air."

In Denardo Coleman's instrumental composition "Skin Diver," the writing is harmolodically inspired and the playing is compositional improvisation.

And there it is, another example of what a poet does with music and what musicians do with poetry.

There It Is, album liner notes

WHAT'S UGLY

I learned very early about what's ugly, and racism is very ugly. . . .

We are waiting in the wings of a false democracy. People are inflamed. We have a growing community of homeless people. The wealthy are getting wealthier and more toxic-wasteful. Friends are dying. Folks are in a state of stagnation, a state of passivity, a state of frenzy. Areas of Los Angeles resemble areas of Beirut in conflict and solitude. Near Douglas, Arizona, you can't see the sky through the dense pollution. The nuclear industry is still in the business of producing man-made radiation. Television is still dominated by white men and their views of the world. U.S. policies concerning Third World countries are designed to destabilize—to cripple and destroy independence.

I'm opposed to these policies that promote death of people, death of land, death of a culture. I reject the notion that might is white, right, and supreme.

Interview with D. H. Melhem, *Heroism in the New Black Poetry*

POETRY MUSIC TECHNOLOGY

In a recording session or musical setting many important things just happen. Even though I have a certain amount of material prepared, the real structure is created while working. In performance I usually read from a manuscript, recite lines from memory and spontaneously compose on the spot. By using music and technology I'm trying to extend the poet's role, which means the poet in this situation becomes the band, the pen, paper, books, research, instruments, words and all the possibilities of the technology. The poet is in control. One of the highest compliments given in the arts is when an artistic work is said to be not only excellent but also has beautiful poetic qualities. This compliment usually suggests that the work is more sensitive, has more insight, and is at a higher level of expression. I am trying to move this combination of poetry, music, and technology to a higher poetic level. It's the poetic use of music, the poetic use of technology, the poetic orchestration of it all.

Poetic Magnetic

EVERYTHING CAN BE TRANSFORMED

I don't wait for inspiration. I write whenever I can.

*   *   *

I think of issues, I think of situations, I think of the future.

*   *   *

I'm concerned with reality, illusions, contradictions, transformations.

*   *   *

I use dreams, the subconscious, and the real objects, and I open up the body and use organs, and I sink them into words, and I ritualize them and fuse them into events. I guess the poetry is like a festival. Everything can be transformed.

The street becomes something else, the subway is something else, everything at a festival is disguised as something else. Everything changes: the look of the person changes, their intentions change, the attitudes are different, experiences are fiercer. Voices become other voices. So that's what I do in my poetry. I keep making connections. I try not to wade in the shallow water of shallowness and I try not to get stuck in the mud of art council standards and the spectators' demand for messages. It's called multiplication, subdivision, and subtraction.

*   *   *

The intellect and the intuition—that's all one thing. Can't be one without the other. I mean you select, and you think, you have an idea [*snaps fingers*], you reason and you don't reason. But it's all together; one reinforces the other. It's all one thing for me.

*   *   *

My role as a poet? I want to be creative, inventive, imaginative, free, secure, and make poetry.

I think that poets have the responsibility to be aware of the meaning of human rights, to be familiar with history, to point out distortions, and to bring their thinking and their writing to higher levels of illumination.

From an interview in D. H. Melhem, *Heroism in the New Black Poetry*

TAKING THE BLUES BACK HOME

This collaboration of poetry and music is focused on the basic progressive aspects of the blues in the deepest sense.

Taking the Blues Back Home means being progressive. I am using elements of my personal history and the history of my people in all of its spirit, conditions, and experience, and taking it forward. The blues talks about and has respect for the struggles of the past and is definitely concerned with the present and the future. It talks about Black culture and reinvestigates the African experience as encountered all over the world. We are piecing together our story, recombining different African literary and musical forms and experimenting.

Taking the Blues Back Home is, itself, the subject, the information, the Angola one step, deep ocean currents, African ancestors, and the miracle of survival.

Taking the Blues Back Home, CD liner notes, introduction

LÉON DAMAS: HUMAN WRITES POETRY

Léon-Gontran Damas is the poet who reminds us what growing up in French Guiana meant and what he observed and experienced while living in Martinique and Paris. In his poetry he speaks of the suppression of feelings, the repression of life, humiliation, and human rights. He said: "I always feel about to foam with rage against what surrounds me, against what prevents me from being a man." "There are nights with no moon when clammy suffocation nearly overwhelms me, the acrid smell of blood spewing from every muted trumpet and my childhood returns in a rousing fit of hiccups."

Damas was like his poems: quick, precise, sharp, ironic, intense, humorous, confrontational, nonconforming, on the edge, not for commercial use, and not for sale. He reminded me of myself and other poets of the 1960s whose need for self-expression had exploded into poetry, into the black is beautiful, militant revolutionary, poetic movement within the Civil Rights movement, which moved into the streets, into the homes and minds of black people and was a peoples movement for justice and freedom. . . .

We read his work in English translation on paper. He read our work in French translation on paper. We spoke to each other in broken English, broken French, and in the other voice, the voice of laughter, songs, jokes, complaints, predictions, disappointments, the voice with African, Creole, and Ebonic words and phrases. The voice poets use when they really want to communicate and pass the torch on, as he did, right in the middle of the belly of the beast . . .

Damas was a progressive political thinker, a poetic person who did not have "the frenzy of eyes, the frenzy of feet." His eyes were focused on the future, his feet were pointed toward Africa. His conversations were about creativity and how to create and move forward. . . . His message was clear. He felt abused, overused, overly Frenchified, and toxic. He rejected the atmosphere of exclusion, he rejected "white European civilization" with its violence, oppression, and white superiority complex. His staccato style is not static. His song is a protest against all forms of discrimination. His poetic vision is held together by his love of life, love of the earth, love of nature, love of human capacity and possibilities. He asserted his blackness, his desire to be independent, to set himself free. We encountered him as Negritude in motion. . . .

He created his language from the natural tones of black French Guiana, black Paris. His message concerned with the experience of the black world is condensed into a high voltage of metaphors, connotations, imagery, irony, and allusions. The subject is language, his own poetic identity. He interconnected inflections of his voice into his own written drum language. . . . He developed his own spontaneous form of rhythmic patterns and accents. He taught us the art of sound repetition, the variations on a theme, the magic of words and imagination. He was a universe of universal expressions. His poems remind us of African American blues: blunt, direct, indirect, coded, and complex. They are like jazz in their feeling of swing and improvisation. . . .

Through these encounters I understood the concept of Negritude to be broad and subject to many interpretations and applications and to vary from place to place because the African Diaspora is large, broad, complicated, and crosses many cultures, many languages, many national borders, and a multitude of circumstances. If the problems can be identified in the realm of Negritude, the solutions to the problems can be found in the realm of Negritude. Damas used to say: "Negritude has many fathers but only one mother." His confidence, solidarity, Pan-Africanism meant Negritude. Negritude as a force that exists to help forge a new world. Negritude as a step used in literature to fight the slave master, to defend oneself against negative images, distorted information, cultural and spiritual imperialism. . . . Negritude as black life, black thought, black attitude and multiculturalism. Negritude as a link between the past, present, and future. Damas could see that the planet was in trouble, that resources were limited, that the atmosphere was polluted, that the ecological system had already been affected by industrial technology. That's why *"Human Writes Poetry"* and Damas was Damas. Good news for poetry, bad news for those who have established a system of domination.

For the Léon-Gontran Damas Symposium, Cayenne, French Guiana, October
    1998

MAINSTREAM STATEMENT

I had a real problem writing a statement for this forum because I needed to know the [conference] organizer's definition of mainstream. Now the Mississippi River is the largest river in the United States. It is the middle of the country, has a Native American name, and is a mainstream watershed. In the United States there are about three million miles of streams. Based on numbers mainstream literature is the literature that's not published. The minority stream is what's published. Commercial publishers are not publishing from all streams. The record of the American publishing industry is much worse than the segregated school system of the Deep South in the 1960s and is in need of a Civil Rights movement to put it on a more sharing and more democratic course. The use and invention of the term "mainstream" is another colonial device, this time applied to literature.

Mainstream is a metaphor for whitestream, a stream set up with standards to exclude other streams. It means cultural, political, economic domination. There is a real need to develop a publishing industry and distribution network which would include the cultural experiences and language of all the people in the United States. I cannot tell you why this writer or that artist considers herself or himself mainstream. I can only speak for myself. I am my own mainstream. I absorb moisture from different soils, infiltrate other streams, emerge as precipitation in the air, mix with additional components, transport my zone of saturation into new zones, and move through life in a natural turbulent way.

For the Bumbershoot Forum, Seattle, Washington, September 2, 1990

LARRY'S TIME

It's good to have the opportunity to take a closer look at the poetry of Larry Neal. Great to see the porkpie hat, the pegged legged boys with polished saxophones, the ears flying into space, distant orishas, the sun sperms exploding and hear the thick thudding sounds and the juju wonder songs of his world again. Larry Neal jumped into the middle of the whirlpool of cultural activity in the early 1960s and 70s. A young man. A young poet/writer/activist, with friends and associates who together doo wopped, finger popped, name dropped, orally bounced information off each other, offered social and political comments to audiences, and produced books, magazines and articles that gave voice to unheard voices of alternative attitudes and viewpoints. Larry Neal, smack dab in the center of the swirl of events, teaching, writing, linking his poetry to the black struggle for liberation, stood in the front row of the march for civil rights, the literary part of the need for revolution. He wrote about Malcolm X, Frantz Fanon, the Watts & Newark rebellions, historical African roots, and the current affairs affecting people in his community. Neal, an urban poet, syncopating and mixing dissonant levels of insults, mythologies, ideologies, appropriations, clichés and rhetoric as poetic combinations, was still evolving, still in the first draft of his research when "touched by death's whisper." Now we can examine some of the aspects of his poetic experience.

Larry Neal, *Visions of a Liberated Future*

James G. Spady

Economist and historian, James G. Spady has long been associated with the Black History Museum in Philadelphia. His books include "Negritude, PanBaNegritude and the Diopan Philosophy of History"; *Sterling A. Brown: A UMUM Tribute;* and more recently, studies of hip-hop.

LARRY NEAL NEVER FORGOT PHILLY

He was not only a famed son of Philadelphia (recipient of a Guggenheim fellowship, a Yale fellowship, a man listed in *Contemporary Poets*, and a *New York Times* film and drama critic), but he used this city as a constant motif in his artistic expressions. His *oeuvre* is deft testimony against the many jokes we have all heard about this being an urban wasteland, a city that becomes doomstown as the evening sun sets. Larry elevated the folk expressions of the people to an art form.

North Philly, for him, was a place to conjure with — the deep and heavy seat of the cool ones. At night, it became a place of fear, but also of electrifying possibilities. Barbershops were places where old and young men twisted their dreams and shaped new worlds from lean fables.

North Philadelphia, where garment factories bent low to hear the seething saxophone sound of John Coltrane. Is this not the building where the great tragedian Edward Forrest lived?

The great mansions of North Philly's past had been turned into apartments and life bubbled within them anew, spilling onto the streets and into the Uptown Theater.

That was a part of Larry Neal's world of reality, his artistic landscape. He was a great knower of folk traditions. Reaching constantly for the coefficients necessary to complete those equations. Ever in search of the marvelous. His name never will be known in the streets, and he was given a quiet funeral.

Larry Neal — the Great Knower of Black arts of language as art, carrier of the "Phillystyle" tradition to worlds beyond us.

Philadelphia Enquirer (February 9, 1981)

Charlotte Carter

A one-time Chicago postal worker, Charlotte Carter in the 1960s was
active in a rebellious youth milieu that included Roosevelt University
and the Civil Rights movement as well as the nascent Chicago Surrealist
Group and its favorite hangout, Solidarity Bookshop. Carter went on to
become a popular writer of mystery novels, among them several featuring an African American street musician with a knack for solving crimes.
She has lived in France, North Africa, and Canada and currently lives in
New York. The text printed here—a reverie on the magic of movies—is
excerpted from her unpublished 1974 manuscript.

ON FILM

There's nothing like a good movie. Film. Basically everyone in the country is
a star. The Japanese photographer said it: If you're not news, you're nothing.
I can't believe there is a single living human being who does not live with the
same camera setup, or some variation on it, as I do. I can't imagine anyone not
knowing what it's like to live with the monitor.

Degrees of schizophrenia, degrees of genius, degrees of disconnectedness—
measured by how many monitors there are. You can live in a space where you're
constantly aware of the monitor. In a space where you're constantly aware of
a monitor monitoring a monitor. Aware of a monitor monitoring a monitor
monitoring a monitor—and so on.

Film. Cinema. Pictures. The movies. The kinnies. The bios. Part of my consciousness—like people I have become. In some sense I suppose it's impossible to have a favorite film. It's all the same. 400 Blows—5 times/Jules and Jim
5 times/Morocco/Rebel without a Cause/Now Voyager/Casablanca 7 times/
Maltese Falcon 12 times/Deception/Lolita/The Organizer 5 times/The Lady
Vanishes/Los Olvidados/L'Aventura.

There are key words in movie language. Words like Paris. He has instructed
Sam not to play the song. Not ever again. Though Ingrid calls him the boy at
the piano, she is reduced to catching peanuts like a trained seal in the Paris
zoo—for him—You Know Who. Screw the husband, Streetfighter, Anti-Nazi
Counterfeit bedroom eyes, Concentration camp victim.

Claude Rains. Peter Lorre. Sydney Greenstreet. You're going over for it,
Sweetheart. Miles was my partner. Smiles of a Summer Night/Mr. Deeds Goes
to Town/Breathless.

Let's get out of here, boss.

Robin D. G. Kelley

Born in New York, Kelley (1962–) grew up in Harlem, Seattle, and Pasadena. His New York boyhood was especially exhilarating, for 1960s Harlem was a community strongly influenced by civil rights agitation and Black Nationalism. As a youngster, Kelley took part in the Black Panther Party's free breakfast program. At his elementary school, students sang "Lift Every Voice and Sing" instead of the "Star-Spangled Banner," and the colors of the school flag were red, black, and green, symbolizing black liberation.

A precocious lad, Kelley did exceptionally well at all the schools he attended, and as a university student rapidly secured degree after degree. At the age of thirty-two he was hailed as one of the youngest full professors in the country. He has taught at the University of Michigan in Ann Arbor, New York University, Columbia, and, most recently, the University of Southern California in Los Angeles.

In a 1998 interview at Stanford University, he summed up his political outlook as "Marxist Surrealist Feminist: not just anti-something but pro-emancipation, pro-liberation. Marxist is anti-capitalist, feminism is anti-patriarchy. But it's also about re-envisioning our lives in this world."

Among his books are *Hammer and Hoe; Race Rebels; Yo Mama's Disfunktional!;* and *Freedom Dreams*, which includes a detailed chapter on surrealism titled "Keeping It (Sur)real: Dreams of the Marvelous."

REFLECTIONS ON MALCOLM X: IN A BLUE HAZE OF INSPIRATION . . .

Recalling his appearance as a teenager in the 1940s, Malcolm dismissively observed, "I was really a clown, but my ignorance made me think I was 'sharp'" (*Autobiography*, 78). Forgetting for the moment the integrationist dilemmas of the black bourgeoisie, Malcolm could reflect: "I don't know which kind of self-defacing conk is the greater shame—the one you'll see on the heads of the black so-called 'middle-class' and 'upper class,' who ought to know better, or the one you'll see on the heads of the poorest, most downtrodden, ignorant black men. I mean the legal-minimum-wage ghetto-dwelling kind of Negro, as I was when I got my first one" (*Autobiography*, 55). Despite Malcolm's sincere efforts to grapple with the meaning(s) of "ghetto" subculture, to comprehend the logic behind the conk, the reat pleat, and the lindy hop, he ultimately failed to solve Ralph Ellison's riddle. In some ways this is surprising, for who is better suited to solve the riddle than a former zoot suiter and brilliant organic intellectual who rose to become one of America's most insightful social critics of the century?

When it came to thinking about the significance of *his own* life, the astute critic tended to reduce a panoply of discursive practices and cultural forms to dichotomous categories—militancy versus self-degradation, consciousness versus unconsciousness. The sort of narrow, rigid criteria Malcolm used to judge the political meaning of his life left him ill-equipped to capture the significance of his youthful struggles to carve out more time for leisure and pleasure, free himself from alienating wage labor, survive and transcend the racial and economic boundaries he confronted in everyday life. Instead, "Detroit Red" in Malcolm's narrative is a lost soul devoid of an identity, numbed to the beauty and complexity of lived experience, unable to see beyond the dominant culture he mimics.

What Malcolm's narrative shows us (unintentionally, at least) is the power of cultural politics, particularly for African-American urban working-class youth, to both contest dominant meanings ascribed to their experiences and seize spaces for leisure, pleasure, and recuperation. Intellectuals and political leaders who continue to see empowerment solely in terms of "black" control over political and economic institutions, belittle or ignore class distinctions within black communities, and insist on trying to find ways to quantify oppression need to confront Ellison's riddle of the zoot suit. Once we situate Malcolm Little's teenage years squarely within the context of wartime cultural politics, it is hard to ignore the sense of empowerment and even freedom thousands of black youth discovered when they stepped onto the dance floor at the Savoy or Roseland ballrooms, or the pleasure young working-class black men experienced when they were "togged to the bricks" in their wild zoot suits, strolling down the avenue "doin' the streets up brown."

But "collapsing" the divisions Malcolm erected to separate his enlightened years from his preprison "ignorance" also compels us to see him as the product of a *totality of lived experiences.* As I have tried to suggest, aspects of Malcolm's politics must be sought in the riddle of the zoot suit, in the style politics of the 1940s that he himself later dismissed as stupidity and self-degradation. This realization is crucial for our own understanding of the current crisis of black working-class youth in urban America. For if we look deep into the interstices of the postindustrial city, we are bound to find millions of Malcolm Littles, male and female, whose social locations have allowed them to demystify aspects of the hegemonic ideology while reinforcing their ties to it. But to understand the elusive cultural politics of contemporary black urban America requires that we return to Ellison's riddle posed a half century ago and search for meaning in the language, dress, music, and dance styles rising out of today's ghettoes, as well as the social and economic context in which styles are created, contested, and reaccented. Once we abandon decontextualized labels such as "nihilism" or "outlaw culture," we might discover a lot more *Malcolm Xes*—indeed, more El-Hajj Malik El-Shabazzes—hiding beneath hoods and baggy pants, Dolphin earrings and heavy lipstick, Raiders caps and biker shorts, than we might have ever imagined.

Norman Calmese

Chicagoan Norman Calmese, as he explains in the statement published here, first discovered his surrealist affinities while still a grade-school student in the city's Hyde Park area. His meeting with the Chicago surrealists a few years later soon led to his participation in the international exhibition "Surrealism in 1978: 100th Anniversary of Hysteria" (in Milwaukee), and other local shows, as well as his collaboration on the journal *Arsenal/Surrealist Subversion*. His work is also represented in Ron Sakolsky's anthology, *Surrealist Subversions*.

MY DISCOVERY OF SURREALISM

As far back as I can remember I have loved to draw. As a kid I was always drawing, even during class in grade school, when I was supposed to be doing something else. Sometimes the teacher would grab one of my drawings and say, "What's this got to do with today's lesson?"

In high school everybody who saw my drawings said, "you're a surrealist." This disturbed me at first; I had never heard of surrealism and had no idea of what a surrealist was. But I looked it up in the encyclopedia and was fascinated by what I read—about André Breton and the Surrealist Manifesto; that surrealism was an international movement; that it was based on brilliant ideas— pure psychic automatism; freeing the imagination repairing the break between dream and reality. What it said about surrealist poetry and art I found very exciting. The more I read, the more I thought: "This is me—this is who I am: a surrealist."

But at the end of the article in the encyclopedia, it said that the Surrealist movement fell apart around 1940 and didn't exist anymore. I almost cried. I couldn't believe it. In fact, I *refused* to believe it. I thought: if surrealism is dead, then I must be dead, too—and since I'm still alive, then surrealism is still alive, too!

For a long time I thought I was probably the only surrealist alive in the world. Needless to say, I kept right on drawing.

I tried to find more out about surrealism at the library. It didn't have much, but I loved the reproductions of surrealist paintings by Yves Tanguy, Victor Brauner, René Magritte and all the rest.

And then one say at the food store checkout counter, I saw a headline in the neighborhood newspaper, the *Hyde Park Herald*. It announced that surrealists—I could hardly believe my eyes!—were having an exhibition right there in Hyde Park, and opening that very day!

Of course I rushed straight over there . . .

Unpublished manuscript

Ted Joans

KAUFMAN IS A BIRD CALLED BOB

Bob Kaufman has said, "I acknowledge the demands of surrealist realization," and his great dazzling poem, "Song of the Broken Giraffe," is an affirmation of his surrealization. Kaufman is one of *true* poets that became known during the Beat Generation. His images are more magical and humorous than those of his contemporaries. Immersed in the Marvelous, Kaufman confronts the human condition directly in all its tragic facets. Yet he giggles while struggling. He is one of the greatest poets on this planet Earth.

Kaufman is like Bird—he too has always been "High on Life." He is the man that walks down crowded streets talking aloud to himself in spite of many (too many) unhip people running in the opposite direction, instead of toward him. Kaufman is a Bird (of the poetic word) called Bob. His *Solitudes* give us all a chance to share his poetry with the international multitudes.

Dig him!

Ted Joans Papers, University of California-Berkeley

COGOLLO: AFRICAN ARTIST FROM COLOMBIA

In the world of music—that is, folk and jazz music—the Black creators have always been the innovators. Even in the world of sports the Black athlete has added a certain style to the game and is more often the "star." But in the field

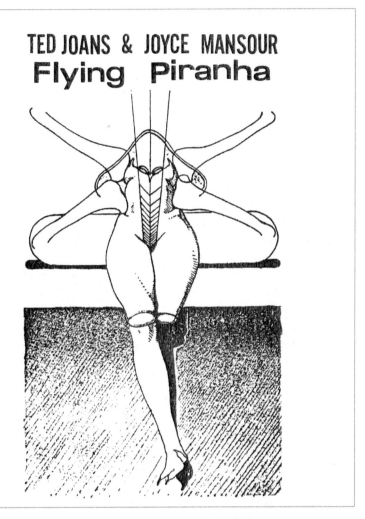

Flying Piranha (1978), a book of poems by Ted Joans and Joyce Mansour, who felt a special affinity as surrealists since Joyce was from Cairo, Egypt, and Ted Joans from Cairo, Illinois. The drawing is by Heriberto Cogollo, a surrealist born in Colombia, making this a truly international collaboration spanning oceans, cultures, and continents the way only surrealism can. The flying piranha was a canary who always defended Elisa Breton.

of creative painting (Fine Arts), especially the so-called avant garde, the Black painter or sculptor has not been recognized as the innovator. Where are the painters who can honestly say that their bit is on par (creatively and original) with such Black musicians as Louis Armstrong, Duke Ellington, Dizzy Gillespie, Charlie Parker, Bud Powell, John Coltrane, Coleman Hawkins, Lester Young, or Bessie Smith? What sculptor is continuing the great African tradition of sculpture, who can say that his work is as important to humanity as those works created by our ancestors?

Now to hit closer to home. Where is Afroamerica's Ray Charles in oils, or Miles Davis of sculpturing, or even the equals of Albert Ayler and Sunny Murray in modern art? Where are they? We do have some mighty powerful swingers in paint and sculpture who now are getting their thing (which is OUR thang) together. One of the brothers is Cogollo. He is one of our naturals, and is on par with his musical brethren in the U.S.

Cogollo was born in the Republic of Colombia, in so-called Latin America South. He attended all the usual academies there and in Europe. Cogollo went back to his roots, which he had never left spiritually. He was born in 1945 at Cartagena, a town where the European slave ships used to dock. Cogollo is a direct descendant of those Africans who were brought there. Cogollo continues the African tradition by remaining in contact with his descendants, thus allowing them to "direct and dictate" that which he paints. Cogollo is a man possessed.

Cogollo's thought hinges on the healthy idea of fertility, a celebration of the organic life on earth, including spectrophilia. This is very evident in many of his works, especially in the large oil titled *Jeux de Jeunes Filles*. In the works of Cogollo, a genuine link with Africa's faith in its positive black magic and with its spiritual vision, proper to all of West Africa, survives. He has learned the Euro tribal techniques, the perfect use of their tools, but has avoided being led into their "integrated," Art-For-Arts-Sake popular swamps. Perhaps Cogollo has learned from the great Afro-Chinese-Cuban painter Wifredo Lam that a non-white artist must swim with his own original strokes to avoid drowning in the polluted "art," undercurrents. Cogollo's and Lam's works are totally different, as different as Ornette Coleman and John Coltrane soloing. But their works are just as vital to the revolutionary cause of emancipation of humankind's mind. Their works reveal the African old and new; their works are neither dreams nor reality, but the natural (for them) fusion of both. Thus, before the creations of these men one stands at the threshold of the marvelous. Cogollo is a young creative Black master painter; let us thank our ancestors for him.

Joans, *Complete Works*

9. Looking Ahead: Surrealism Today and Tomorrow

> A gathering of peoples at the crossroads . . . an' reports are still comin' in
> —Anthony Joseph

It is surely a sign of the times—and a heartening sign—that one of the most influential books pertaining to surrealism since 1990 is Robin D. G. Kelley's *Freedom Dreams: The Black Radical Imagination* (2002). Other writers have tried, with varied success, to approach surrealism from different angles, but Kelley has convincingly provoked entirely new ways of regarding the movement and its far-reaching project, from the 1920s to our own time.

Freedom Dreams is not only the first book to relate surrealism to the long and eventful history of black radicalism, but also—and more precisely—the first to compare surrealist ideas to the thought of such great black dreamers, theorists, and activists as Anna Julia Cooper, Ida B. Wells, W.E.B. Du Bois, C.L.R. James, Amiri Baraka, Malcolm X, and James Forman. Kelley's discussion of black surrealism—from Etienne Léro and the *Légitime Défense* Group of the 1930s through the Césaires, *Tropiques*, and Wifredo Lam to Ted Joans, Bob Kaufman, Jayne Cortez, and others in more recent years—is by far the most illuminating summary in English. Impressive, too, is his perceptiveness in recognizing the surrealist qualities in artists not usually considered surrealist, such as Richard Wright, Frank London Brown, and Thelonious Monk.

In a similar vein, he suggests that women surrealists in Europe in the 1920s and 1930s—Toyen, Valentine Penrose, Leonora Carrington, Meret Oppenheim, Claude Cahun, Mary Low, and others—would have benefited from hearing the songs of such women blues artists as Bessie Smith, Ma Rainey, Alberta Hunter, Memphis Minnie, Lucille Bogan, and Ida Cox. The language barrier blocked that possibility back then, but Kelley argues that such lost connections still have a place in freedom dreams today.

Deeply rooted in surrealism's high priorities—poetry, freedom, love, and the unfettered imagination—*Freedom Dreams* is also a superb critique of the same old protest politics and a splendid example of that rarity of rarities: a history directed toward the future. It is no wonder that the book has had, and continues to have, a strong impact—not only in the United States and the rest of the English-speaking world, but also in other lands, and not only among surrealists and people interested in surrealism, but also among a wide readership looking for ways out of today's massive misery and miserabilism.

Ayana Karanja's *Zora Neale Hurston* is a very different book, but it shares much of Kelley's poetry-inspired radicalism and exhilaration. This wide-ranging, innovative study is first of all a searching reassessment of a great ethnographer, folklorist, novelist, and playwright. But it is also much more. Deftly combining black feminist social criticism, utopian reverie, and an acute awareness of the politics of language, Karanja reflects on every page an ardent respect not only for oral literature but also for the dream experience as a source of knowledge. Indeed, her own dreams and her interpretations of them are a crucial part of this deeply moving narrative, which is further enhanced by her poems and photographs.

Impassioned throughout, Karanja's vivid appreciation of Hurston exemplifies a free-spirited reconceptualization of ethnography as an imaginative, creative, and playful activity, in other words, a *surrealist* activity.

These two books alone would suffice to place black writers in the forefront of surrealism today, but they are only part of the story. Just about every surrealist group in the world today maintains a Web site, but the surrealist book publishing boom begun in the 1990s not only has continued, but has greatly expanded in the 2000s. Books by and about black surrealists and their allies are clearly in demand. In 2000 Monthly Review Press brought out a handsome new edition of Aimé Césaire's *Discourse on Colonialism*, with a new introduction by Robin Kelley. A 2005 Charles H. Kerr edition of C.L.R. James' *A History of Pan-African Revolt* also has a preface by Kelley. Richard Wright's *Twelve Million Black Voices* has been reissued with a new introduction by Noel Ignatiev. Haymarket Books has brought out an excellent collection of Dennis Brutus' poems and essays under the title *Poetry and Protest* (2006).

To Paris publishers we owe Marie-Laure Missir's lavishly illustrated biography of Joyce Mansour and the complete works of Georges Henein, a volume of 1,062 pages. In São Paulo two beautiful little books—one on the singer Elsie Houston, the other on pioneer Brazilian jazz orchestra leader Abigail Moura (both with CDs)—were issued in connection with the large 2003 "Negras Memórias, Memórias de Negros" exhibition in São Paulo.

This short list—many more titles could in fact be added—suffices to indicate that the work of black surrealists, heretofore snubbed by more than a few pompous white critics, is not only becoming more and more visible to an ever-increasing audience, but also more and more studied and appreciated. No doubt about it, in many and diverse realms of research, criticism, creativity, and action, surrealists black, brown, and beige are clearly leading the way.

Take poetry, for example. Ted Joans—one of the movement's most tireless public figures for half a century—was still cogitating and agitating as surrealist poet, mage, and sage until, as Robin D. G. Kelley puts it, he "joined the ancestors" in May 2003. Several dozen legends in his own time, Joans influenced and inspired countless young poets of all ages and colors, and from all over the world. His last books—*Okapi Passion*, the voluminous *Teducation*, illustrated by Cogollo; *Wow* and *Our Thang*, both with drawings by his companion, Laura Corsiglia—include much of his finest work.

A poet first and last, Joans was also noted for his lectures on many topics, from jazz history to the struggle against South African apartheid. He enjoyed addressing black students on such outstanding figures—and friends of his—as Langston Hughes, Charlie Parker, and Malcolm X. On several occasions he intervened in academic conferences on the "Beat Generation," bringing his personal experience, truth, and clarity to an otherwise all-too-mystified subject.

The best friend the rhinoceros ever had, Joans spoke eloquently and often on this endangered species, and more generally identified himself with wilderness preservation and animal rights.

Many important facets of Joans' work have been overlooked by commentators: his film-poems, for example, above all his lovely tribute to the Facteur Cheval's "Ideal Palace" (accompanied by the bop sounds of Charlie Parker). His paintings, drawings, and collages—especially the splendid "Alphabet Surreal" series—also deserve far more attention than they have received, and ditto for his "Outagraphs"—photographs in which one or more images have been cut out and replaced by other images.

In addition to his prolific poetry and work in the visual arts, Joans left a large and impressive critical literature. His many jazz reviews in *Coda* magazine surely merit publication in book form, as do his scattered contributions to such surrealist journals as *La Brèche, Brumes Blondes, L'Archibras, Arsenal, Free Spirits*, the surrealism issues of *Race Traitor*, and the hefty one-shot *Dies und Das* that Joans coedited with poet Richard Anders in Berlin in 1984.

Ted Joans' surrealist legacy is rich, diverse, still very much in the wind, and—like the well-attended memorial for him at New York University in 2003—full of hipness, humor, revolt, the Marvelous, and the everlasting joy of jazz. Al Young signaled Joans as the wandering grandfather of today's Spoken Word poetry.

Fortunately, the voice of Ted Joans continues to reach new ears, for many of his readings, lectures, and impromptu talks were recorded. More than a few of these recordings marked truly memorable occasions. His fabulous joint reading with Jayne Cortez, for example, at the 2002 Printers' Row Book Fair in Chicago, attracted far and away the largest crowd ever for a poetry event at the city's annual outdoor book expo. No one who was there will ever forget it.

Cortez herself, one of contemporary poetry's international treasures, remains as active as ever, on tour in the United States and 'round the world, on CD, and in print. Her influence on the new generation of poets has been great and is certainly growing. Her *Jazz Fan Looks Back*, with its cover by Melvin Edwards, is a veritable classic—an all-day, all-night celebration of the best in black music from its African roots through blues and bebop to free jazz. With her many and diverse African, Caribbean, South American, and other connections, and an activist background that includes civil rights agitation and union organizing, Jayne Cortez is truly a world force—for poetry and the Marvelous, ecology and women's emancipation, and freedom struggles everywhere.

Many of the younger black surrealist poets coming up probably do not even know each other yet. Together, however, each in his or her own way, they exemplify an audacious return to the deepest, most radical automatism. As it turns out, what André Breton called pure psychic automatism was not only surrealism's bold starting point, way back in 1919, but has also served as a port of call for the movement's poets and artists ever since.

Anthony Joseph, a Trinidadian active in the Surrealist Group in London; Deusdedit de Morais, of the Surrealist Group Decollage in São Paulo; Gérard Janvier, from Haiti but currently living in Chicago; and Ron Allen, of Detroit and Los Angeles—a poet also noted for his dynamite plays—are some of the truest and livest "live wires" of today's ongoing surrealist generation. These are poets who, to paraphrase an observation John Coltrane once made about Albert Ayler, are moving poetry to even higher frequencies.

In the introduction to his sensational book of poems, *Teragaton* (1997), Anthony Joseph outlines his method: "I had to locate myself in a parallel present, unravel my tongue, reclaim all headspace, disengage critical analysis—to find the core object lost in Simulacra, until the text became a mind map and if possible, a transliteration before it is censored by consciousness. Essentially I had to write until I wrote without writing, accessing the unconscious by using its language."

This is the very voice of surrealism today—the revolutionary poetic spirit at its most daring and defiant. At fever pitch, the freedom of dreams leads straight to the realization of the age-old but always up-to-the-minute dreams of freedom.

Or as the South African Dennis Brutus puts it, poetry and revolt automatically go hand in hand with freedom, love, and changing the world. In the discussion following his April 2006 lecture at Northwestern University, Brutus emphasized the strong solidarity and affection he felt for those brave spirits who, during reactionary periods, had been unafraid to defend surrealism and its goals. For surrealists and their allies, Brutus went on to affirm, revolutionary politics, the practice of poetry, cultural liberation, and radical ecology are fundamentally one and the same struggle for true freedom and a good life for all.

Now as always, poetry—language as a way to infinite imaginary combinations, according to Philip Lamantia—remains surrealism's heart and nervous system, but it is important to keep in mind that surrealist poetic practice embraces *all* forms of human expression. It is not surprising, therefore, that in the visual and performance arts, too, black surrealists are increasingly in the forefront throughout the world.

Surrealism in music, for example—a topic that most academic works on surrealism do not even mention—is more than ever in the air today. In Chicago the magician musicians of the Great Black Music AACM are still going strong after their fortieth anniversary in 2005. Hamid Drake, widely and without exaggeration renowned as the world's greatest living drummer, and the redoubtable reed man from Jamaica, Douglas Ewart—both of whom have played at many surrealist events over the years—continue to bring us the liberating sounds we need to realize the new society humankind has long been dreaming about. And now they have been joined by a new AACM generation that includes tenor sax tornado David Boykin and one of the all-time greatest jazz flutists, Nicole Mitchell. To Mitchell the world is indebted for some of the most entrancingly initiatory music of our time: music that truly opens the doors of the Marvelous. She is also a highly original thinker and brilliant writer, with a profound sense of poetry at its emancipatory best, as evidenced in the splendid liner notes to her *Vision Quest, Afrika Rising,* and other CDs.[1]

TOMORROW IS THE QUESTION

> The street has become another, more ancient; the lights in the
> window are turned off: it's tomorrow already.
>
> —Joyce Mansour

Globally and locally, surrealism today is a far-reaching panorama, an open-ended, free-spirited example of unity and solidarity in an incredibly dynamic diversity. Vastly exceeding its numerical strength, its influence, now as in the past, is especially evident among various sectors of young people and the oppressed, who, despite the discouraging temper of today's mainstream dominant authoritarian politics and culture, have not abandoned the dream of transforming the world and changing life.

Today as in the past, surrealism rejects commercial dabblers, poseurs, and other pseudo-surrealists such as the moronic imitators of Dalí who clutter up the Internet. The movement remains resolutely nonsectarian, however, and is by no means unfriendly to the many scattered individuals who—for whatever reason—have chosen not to identify themselves with organized surrealism, but have followed a parallel path.[2]

Now as always, what interests surrealists above all is not establishment art or the literary scene, or any particular genre, or any other kind of specialization, but, rather, human expression in all its forms, the becoming of freedom, objective chance, the realization of poetry in everyday life. Jacques Brunius' ambitious 1945 proposal, that surrealism's practice of collective research should be extended to every field of knowledge—has by no means been exhausted and is not likely to be exhausted in the near future. It is obvious, however, that the movement's fields of inquiry, creativity, critique, and discovery in recent years have been enormously broadened and deepened and are still expanding in all directions.

Obvious, too—a few bigoted art critics notwithstanding—is the fact that black surrealists have been a major force in this continuing expansion. As for the future, the possibilities are infinite.

A marvelous mix of poetics and politics, surrealism exemplifies activism as its best and brightest. In April 2008, the "All Power to the Imagination" conference took place at the New College in Sarasota, Florida. The explicitly anarchist gathering was organized and conducted not by professors but almost entirely by young African American students. A featured speaker, Ashanti—an anarchist who had been a member of the Black Panther Party—spoke enthusiastically of Robin Kelley's work and also noted that his own writing involved the connections between jazz improvisation and anarchy.

As Dennis Brutus has put it, there is every reason to expect that the international surrealist movement will continue to pursue its revolutionary poetic imperatives and *"keep soaring!"*[3]

This much is certain: black surrealism is here and everywhere—and on the move!

Notes

1. For background on the AACM, see John Litweiler, *The Freedom Principle*, 172–199. A tribute to its fortieth anniversary, and to Nicole Mitchell, appears in Franklin Rosemont, *Revolution in the Service of the Marvelous*, 127–129.

2. I am thinking particularly of such poets as T. J. Anderson III, Will Alexander, Regie Gibson, and the Milwaukee-based hip-hop-oriented Black-Surreal band.

3. Dennis Brutus, conversation with Franklin Rosemont, Chicago, April 2006.

Ted Joans was famous for his letters and mailings to friends coming from all over the world—Timbuktu to Portland, Oregon. He was especially fond of enclosing tickets, collages, and photos.

Aimé Césaire

On December 5, 2005, for the first time in his long career as mayor of Fort-de-France, Martinique, Aimé Césaire, at ninety-two, refused to see a visitor—France's interior minister, Nicolas Sarkozy, who had come with the specific plan to convince the Martinican government to soften up the contents of the island's textbooks, particularly in regard to such matters as slavery and colonialism. Here is Césaire's response.

I DO NOT AGREE TO RECEIVE THE MINISTER

I do not agree to receive the Minister of the Interior, Nicolas Sarkozy, for two reasons: 1) Personal reasons, and 2) Because, as the author of the *Discourse on Colonialism*, I remain faithful to my doctrine, and continue to be a resolute anticolonialist.

Robin D. G. Kelley

SURREALISM: THINKING ABOUT FREEDOM IN NEW WAYS

Surrealism opens an avenue to try to talk about redemptive politics, but specifically to think about freedom in new ways that are non-religious. That might get me into some trouble, but I don't think that's necessarily an antithesis of what Dr. King was saying. I don't really have an answer for this. I love reading the surrealists like Suzanne Césaire and Aimé Césaire, even Richard Wright's surrealism, because it seems to me to break with the old language. We need a new language of struggle, a new language of hope and possibility. I don't think we even have the language to talk about what kind of world we want to create. In some ways, poetry is the quest to explode language as we know it, to open it up.

I feel like I'm caught between a lot of different movements. I feel like I'm still somewhat of a Marxist, but that Marxism is too little. I feel like my roots are in Black Nationalism, as critical as I am of nationalism and of nations. The core of that movement, that attracted me in the first place, was the idea of building a sense of humanity. Black Nationalism allowed ordinary black people to stake a claim to history, to say that we're contributing to the world. That sense of pride is something that I'm still very much connected to, as much as I'm anti-nationalist.

And then there's the sense of emergency. I too get caught up in the immediate moment and the need to solve immediate problems, whether it's to keep the U.S. out of the war or to save battered children. Whatever it is, I will continue and many people will continue to fight those battles on a day-to-day basis. I'm simply saying that, as we fight these battles, they should be opportunities to produce new visions of the future.

I honestly, to this day, cannot map out that new vision. One of the main points of *Freedom Dreams* is to say that one doesn't map out a new future by simply "dreaming." I don't know what the future of politics will look like. I think that we are in a tremendous ideological transformation, but, if I believe my own argument, I can't know what that is because part of knowing is learning in the process of struggle, in a collective movement. In other words, no one can see it. That's the New Age, where you meditate, or you're in a steam room, and all of a sudden you're able to see and envision it. No, it's on the picket lines; it's in the streets; it's in study groups; it's participation in social movements. Even the failures are very, very important, for they provide very important lessons for thinking about the future. But it requires work, it requires organizing, it requires study, to read, to think, to debate.

The sense of the future and what's possible is in all my books. It's in *Hammer and Hoe*, it's in my other books, that you can win, that the next generation will take us there.

If you think of something like the end of slavery as one of the most revolutionary moments in U.S. history, in 1854—a decade before the end of slavery—none of those people thought slavery would end. It wasn't even in the cards. Imagine if we write history not from the perspective of the victors or even in hindsight—by that I mean standing in the present, turning back and trying to explain how we got here. But if you stand in 1854, what you see ahead is not the end of slavery. You don't see any of that.

Too often we're told that, if you're a real radical, you're not supposed to be optimistic. That's the culture we grew up in. But the radicals I wrote about, they're all optimistic. Just imagine what it meant in the middle of the Depression in 1934 to join a movement where they were going to inherit the earth, "a better world's in birth." The future was theirs and they knew it. That's why they fought every day.

It's always the work of struggle, the thing that transforms the conditions in which we operate, that makes things possible. You cannot dream your way out of your situation. You dream to imagine where you're going to go next, but without social movement, without struggle, you're stuck.

Unpublished manuscript

Ayana Karanja

Born and raised in Chicago, Ayana Karanja is director of black world studies and teaches in the Department of Sociology and Anthropology at Loyola University. Poet, photographer, and filmmaker, deeply interested in the poetics of black women's life narratives, she is noted especially for her innovative study *Zora Neale Hurston*.

Long familiar with the writings of André Breton, Aimé Césaire, and other surrealists, Karanja was also impressed by the long chapter on surrealism in Robin D. G. Kelley's *Freedom Dreams*. Not long after reading Kelley's book she encountered the Chicago surrealists, and her friendly association with the group continues to this day.

CONTEMPLATION

(A Lighted Candle)

Ancient mother of the seas,
   your womb, a vessel of sacred blood.
You make mountains with your wings and
   stars fall from your mouth.
   Pierce the night with mystic eyes.
Ride the spray of my breath, the sound of my voice
   to the cusp of yesterday.
Hear the sound of my words playing on the wind.
   Wrap my voice in your hair;
   awaken the daughter/spirit in your bosom-nest.
   Sing the song of her primeval name.
   Ride the breath of my voice.
     Ride the breath of the wind.
   Ride the breath of my voice.
     Ride the breath of the wind.

Hear the breath of her voice on the sound of the wind.
  Voices moving . . . mooooving . . . moooooooving.
Nyazema breathes; her voice sings re/memberings.
  Hear the breath of my voice.
  Hear the breath of the wind.
     Feel the spray of her voice.
     Feel the spray of her words.
  Our voices soar on the edge of the wind.

In *Zora Neal Hurston*

Melvin Edwards

THINKING ABOUT SURREALISM

By the time I was eighteen in 1955 Haitian Art had already hit the art world. I started seeing it in the late 50s and by the mid 60s I had seen plenty of it. And by then I had also heard of Wifredo Lam. I hadn't seen too much of his work but I heard of him and knew him to be an important Afro-Cuban-Chinese painter related to the upper crust international modern art world. He was an important intellectual black figure and considered a surrealist. I did not know a lot about surrealism at the time, but I knew enough to know that surrealism fit within a kind of free approach to developing images in visual art.

Instead of surrealists going to the geometry, they went to the subject, the subject inside reality, the subject in imagination and the subject in dream and combined them in new different ways. For black artists in the United States there's not much record of them in that period (1920-1940). Among those who started a little later would have been Norman Lewis who had been through some surrealist ideas, but I don't think you could call Norman a surrealist. Also there was the painter Eldzier Cortor who often uses the female figure in a surreal interior and exterior environment. Of course, the epitome for creativity in Western art was the female nude, the nude being transformed. Transformation as a process is essential to surrealism. Surrealism is never alone. One important thing about surrealism is that there are many styles. Surrealists are individualistic.

In my sculpture experiment was based on a free approach. By the time (1963) I entered the general art world as a sculptor I could use any approach to putting forms together. I'm curious about many ways of making art. I've chosen assemblage, metal fabrication and industrial welding as a primary way of working. I combine many ideas, cut old, used, new and found forms and shapes, then feel free to distort, twist, forge or do anything I want to them. My way of conceiving, making, and presenting my sculpture is comfortable in the open space of surrealism. But not limited to that universe. My most direct contact with surrealism was knowing Léon-Gontran Damas from 1969 to 1978. He was the strongly political co-father of Negritude from French Guiana. We met in New York City and became family friends. He was a real example of the committed politically aware active creative writer. I made the sculpture "Homage to the Poet" dedicated to his memory and the continuing struggle inspired by his poetry philosophy and participatory experience in the esthetics of the freedom struggle for Pan African liberation and independence. He spoke of artists he knew in France: Arp & Duchamp etc.

Surrealism comes out of colonialism and international trade. Information and ideas were showing up in Europe from many cultures around the world. Artists had access and were sensitive and using what they saw and heard. Our generation was a generation that studied art which started from the cave to the renaissance and from the renaissance to yesterday afternoon. So we were potentially affected by anything from anywhere, we were everywhere in art. Some were in New York City like Emilio Cruz in the 1950s and 60s.

With existentialism, the beat generation, with Norman Lewis, and Ed Clark in abstract expression, and surrealism very much a part of that. What I'm saying is a person, black and coming from the black community but his or her black input is coming from many experiences. There are two generations of artists and I'm talking about the Emilio Cruzes the Bob Thompsons, the Wifredo Lams, the Romare Beardens.

Those are artists who have been to art school and whose works were headed for the museum art world and collections. They use culture from their own community but in their studios they were putting their own ideas together and creatively trying to make art develop in the most unique forms that they could come up with. They always go home to the black community for information, luckily in New York City black music is there, present and experimental and black visual artists think they are also experimental, use black stuff with the most avant garde ideas like the musicians.

I'm talking about people trying to be original and be honest about how they actually got to it and that they didn't necessarily learn all those things from home or from their neighborhoods. But you have to always remember when someone says abstraction and cubism that traditions of African art are folded in that. People are paying attention to traditional African art and it varies from person to person.

In contemporary African art many artists can be discussed as having surrealistic imagery. Malangatana Ngwenya from Mozambique is celebrated for his fantastic compositions of humans, animals, plants and complex environments. Compositions alive with their own natural surreal dynamic at home in African art imagination. There are many other artists in Africa who move artistically beyond classification. The black artists who appeared since 1940 and who are most often called surrealists came from the French African Caribbean country of Haiti and the Haitians artists are unique, but I don't want to call them surrealists because maybe they call themselves something else.

They make use of voudou combinations, political imagination, history, religion, the underworld, other worlds, and this world at the same time. The same is true of the Zimbabwe stone sculptors who also have surrealist tendencies but they are not called surrealists even though their realism is fantastic unique art. Artists like Joram Mariga, John Takawira, Locadia Ndandarika and Tapfuma Gutsa are artists whose imaginative stone carvings from traditional myths and modern themes are transformed beyond ordinary reality. The painter Heriberto Cogollo, who lives in France is a fantastic realist and magical surrealist academy trained painter who extends the early dynamics of surrealism. In his work there are the things that could be and the things that are. The smoke coming from the flesh of a horse's butt looks like smoke and veils the truth. He takes realism to the realm of the new fantastic. Cogollo is like the pre-industrial poet who is a surrealist and being a modern Afro-Colombian he has Afro-Colombian imagery and mysticism in his work.

Surrealism was a set of ways of inventing and from surrealism other ways evolved that have new qualities. It sometimes takes the reader a long time to catch up with the writer and it's the same thing with the visual artists and the viewer.

Unpublished manuscript

T. J. Anderson III

T. J. Anderson (1958–) is the author of *At Last Roundup* and *Notes to Make the Sound Come Right: Four Innovators of Jazz Poetry* and has published both poetry and poem translations. His research interests include jazz poetry, African American literature, and the work of Aimé Césaire.

AT LAST ROUNDUP

I want to clear the table
a train language speeding on tracks
with sidewinder skulls in midland dust
a weed star called dandelion
draining its filament
in a full smoke gallop.

The eye arrives a top hat mandrake
vein hood insides squared off and drowsing.

But there is something riding
high on tear foam
too many blotches of air wrapped caracaras
too many soldiers shaking on their watch
too many shamans making strange uses of rain.

The real furnace is the blistering mouth
thrashing like a cylindrical fish.

Be plaintive my pig headed dinosaur
melting in the gold rim haze
of a paleontologist's spectacles.

Everywhere we are wrong.

I unbutton my sleeve
bare my arm
In the streets imbeciles are melting
in the juice of their wits.

At Last Roundup

VAUDEVILLE 1951

A weighs the tear suspended
on the eye's scaffold
minstrelled under top hat accordion
le blanc glove splay
solar parasol five fingers to shine
where the spotlight
plays furnace to night's easel

a thigh to tuxedo romp
here's looking at tree swing
beef shank in transit
erector leg launch
crossroads familial catacomb

snake stick hard
cold glimmer tiger smock
the false drape dribble
where zoot suits illumine
a mirror's shadowed conversion.

At Last Roundup

Michael Stone-Richards

Born and raised in Britain, Stone-Richards' introduction to surrealism was a volume of poems by Ted Joans given to him as a graduation present by his father. He has gone on to become a leading scholar of international surrealism, with a special interest in the groups in Paris and Prague. His articles on various aspects of surrealism—in poetry, painting, politics, and life—have appeared in journals as varied as *Pleine Marge, Art History, Race Traitor,* and *Equinoxe.* His essay "The Political in the Culture of Surrealism" is one of the richest contributions to surrealist studies in recent years.

Stone-Richards has taught at Northwestern University and other schools. At the time of this writing he was associate professor in the Department of Liberal Arts, College for Creative Studies, Detroit, Michigan.

The text published here originally appeared in the "Surrealism in the U.S.A." issue of *Race Traitor* (Summer 2001).

SURREALIST SUBVERSION IN EVERYDAY LIFE

We are struck, have always been and will always be, by a fact of particular singularity: that of all the avant-garde movements with any claims to historical importance for the first third of the last century, Surrealism alone, in any significant way, held within its fold women and people of color, and that one cannot

RACE TRAITOR

SPECIAL ISSUE

SURREALISM: REVOLUTION AGAINST WHITENESS

summer 1998   number 9 $5

TREASON TO WHITENESS IS LOYALTY TO HUMANITY

Race Traitor was founded by Noel Ignatiev. This special 1998 issue was edited by the Surrealist Group in Chicago.

imagine Surrealism without their presence. What is it, then, that Surrealism made possible for them, that no other movement could even approximate? It is clear, astoundingly clear, that Surrealism alone found a way of translating into practice certain of the ethical insights from the generation of the great Symbolists Huysmans, Mallarmé, of Igitur in which the question was not first and foremost the displacement of one political party or order by another, but the far more basic question of a new form of thinking in which the erotic and the feminine would be allowed to structure perception and action.

What is it in Surrealist experience—its conception of love, its deep thinking of friendship that bewilders and unsettles patriarchy and masculine sensemaking if not the passage a l'act of a mode of feeling and responsiveness based upon reciprocity (to and from the world, to and from the desired subject), a mode of thinking which, long before the Lacanians of the 1960s, uncovered the ethics of desire and long before the tedium of talk about performativity, realized the radical contingency of the subject in the movement of desire? If, as Breton says in *Les vases communicants*, a work that speaks of desire and not mere pleasure, desire, if it is real, refuses itself nothing, it also remains, hence the importance of reciprocity and reversibility for Breton, that desire must renew itself and everything in relation to itself.

An ethic of desire is not, indeed, about mere satisfaction; patriarchy, based upon suppression and the manipulation of commodified desire, cannot allow for reciprocity and thus has need of a politics of mere satisfaction and reification. The challenge posed by Surrealism, historically, is to think from the position of the third, of the other which is to say, from the position of radical liberty. We are far from exhausting, still less realizing the implications of this thinking.

Is it possible, any longer, to think of chance, coincidence, strangeness and encounters in everyday life without doing so in terms that bespeak a demotic Surrealism? We think not. It is, though, more difficult to link these experiences to a sense of the liberation from the constraints of everyday life, the shared tedium of humdrum life, of routine, of crushing habit, all the more so as the forces of technological modernity impose by ever more successful ruses a deathly uniformity. And yet, faced with the vogue of Existentialism upon his return to Paris from America in 1945, Breton rejected Existentialism with the declaration," Away with Miserabilism!" whilst in the same breath, and in agreement with Bataille, he rejected Stalinism with the unanswerable truth that it was "moral extermination." This is a rejection of the politics of order in favor of an ethics of liberty; henceforth, as was clear from the disaster of the Stalinization of the Party in the 1930s, politics could only be an infrapolitics.

Can Surrealism, undoubtedly correct in its diagnosis of the misery of modernity, still have something to offer? That depends very much upon what it is that one might be expecting. Certainly there is no formula, no blueprint that kind of politics is for the bureaucratic mind and the reconstructed Stalinists with their boy-scout view of history. What remains is the insistence on liberty and recognition (of the other), the refusal of work, the constant effort of renewal (in the words of Sade, "Cosmopolites de tous les pays, encore un effort!").

In the context of a discussion on Surrealism, internationalism and the Caribbean in June 1999, Franklin Rosemont made a comment of startling limpidity that made me think of something obvious: he spoke of the American contribution to Surrealism as being largely a demotic Surrealism. Looking through any of the classic Surrealist reviews, alongside the discovery of the everyday, the recognition of such forms as Le Palais ideal of the Facteur Cheval, there is, noticeably, a constant, if critical engagement, with what can only be called the remnants, avatars of high culture. To look through the American Surrealist journals from the 1960s onward, is to see the prevalence of the demotic—the Watts Tower, for example, the American lawn ("What's wrong with it? Everything!") side by side with a commitment to anarchist and workingclass politics, a politics of the specific unlike anything to be found in French or European or Japanese Surrealism. Has this commitment to infrapolitics as a distinctive commitment of American Surrealism been sufficiently noted?

As with the case of the role and significance of women in the articulation of Surreality, likewise the presence of people of color in the articulation of Surrealism from *Légitime Défense* to *Tropiques* and beyond bears witness to the range, depth and singularity of the Surrealist vision: the questions of gender, sexuality, race and the post-colonial so much a part of our contemporaneity can be seen to have informed the distinctive definition of Surrealism from the moment of its response to French military adventurism in the Riff to its denunciation of the colonial exhibition in 1931. It is also telling that when one looks at Surrealism internationally, it is almost impossible to confound its manifestations in Hungary or France with the Antilles/Caribbean, for Surrealism avails itself, as Aimé Césaire realized, of the fauna and flora of the local imaginary; thus when Breton, with Pierre Mabille, assisted at Voudoun ceremonies in Haiti he could acknowledge that there was no question of bringing Surrealism to Haiti, it was already present.

Magloire-Saint-Aude is a poet who could not but be Surrealist. Surrealism, inconceivable without its desire to re-think alterity, as witnessed in its Map of the World (1929) which put into practice Valéry's insight that "L'Europe est finie," presented for people of color a means of articulating the local in relationship to the universal. When Césaire left the Party he declared that Party-Communism could not address the particularities of Black experience, whilst the glorious Suzanne Césaire could write in "Le Surréalisme et nous" in *Tropiques*: "Surrealism tightrope of our hope."

After the Second World War, the most significant, the most urgent develop-ments in Surrealism passed through women (Joyce Mansour, Annie Le Brun) and people of color: the French Caribbean and Francophone Africa. Every-thing that Surrealism understood concerning the relationship between the freedom of the imagination and liberty found a new voice of passionate refusal in anti-colonialism and the dream of liberty of the civil rights movement: The power implicit in the experience "I have a dream" was the color of a time long awaited. It is the color of a time still to come.

With Julien Lenoir

Ron Allen

Poet, playwright, and apostle of "weightless language," Ron Allen was a dynamic force in the Motown arts scene for two decades or more before his resettlement in southern California. Deeply influenced by Buddhism as well as post-bop jazz, he remains a vehement word consciousness ex-plorer whose ecosphere insurgency aims at nothing less than the poetic transformation of the world and the realization of the Marvelous.

REVELATION

open
the
head
walk
up
the
neck
look
in
the
cortex
read
the
bones
fly

Unpublished

Detroit poet and playwright Ron Allen's *Neon Jawbone Riot* appeared in *Race Traitor*, no. 9 (Summer 1998), with the cover by Shaqe Kalaj.

CONVERSATION BETWEEN EYE AND MOUTH

MOUTH: the first official act was the mouth, the taste of cucumber . . .
It drained the rosemary in us. It was thyme, the eye of the
rosewood.

EYE: the first official act was the eye, a griddlecake of history,
juniper, paper onions, of deliberate corruption. It was rancid—
foiled sheep, and deep wounds of game.

MOUTH: the first official act was tomato, a core of myopia, a balm, a
weaving tongue text of urgency, a happening. It was sweet, a
conflict, sweet tunnel of muck, an evening, a night shade.

EYE: a vinegar of dried wombs, coarse rhubarb in the wheat-
malted crud of black.

MOUTH: it tasted of camphor and chamomile, frankincense and
sandalwood, fish baked in the sun with plum pits, orange
blossom, and salt, sour milk and fetid gas, sweat and syrup of
hung bergamot, hair fried mud pie and vapors.

EYE: the first official act was a resin of trash bags and machine
grinding life, pit bull in desiccated shit, musk and twisted
peels of lime and rosewater, a red image of pomades and rats

MOUTH: a turnstile of a cavity sickly sweet as whores' wine, a medicine
in the gut, castor and cinnamon, grease, mildew, chard,
cheese and blood.

EYE: a priest, nipple, sachet of cork, the candy of reubens and vanilla.

MOUTH: soggy mattresses and sage in the blunt end of the mouth.

EYE: ash penicillin in the dumpster of the eye.

MOUTH: dried fruits, lamp oil, cow tongue in smokey brine.

EYE: caskets and mace roaches, and us.

MOUTH: in the wine cellar, twisted dreams of wigs, dollar faxed copper and myrrh.

EYE: a slow rush of maple, tar, onyx, and cocoa.

MOUTH: crushed fruit rinds of saltpeter tincture, and us.

EYE: coffee and prisons, and us.

MOUTH: spoons, melons, and us.

EYE: the first official act was . . .

MOUTH: the first official act was . . .

EYE: murder.

"Eye Mouth Graffiti Body Shop"

Anthony Joseph

Born and raised in Trinidad, Joseph moved to London in 1989. He was a longtime friend of poet and publisher John La Rose and surrealist globetrotter Ted Joans, and in the 2000s has become active in the London Surrealist Group. His publications include *Desfinado, Teragaton,* and the CD *Liquid Textology—Readings from the African Origins of UFOs.* Still a resident of the United Kingdom, Joseph has traveled and lectured widely in Europe and the United States.

HOW SURREALISM FOUND ME

My interest/evolution in surrealism was a gradual realization. I had been writing since childhood but around 1994 I began a search for what I called "the core text." I was interested in speed, a way of bypassing the conscious. I realized that the poetry I enjoyed writing, the poems that resonated most, were the ones I wrote in an out-of-body moment, the ones that were "abstract" or "cryptic," and seemed to leap off the page: texts of transcendence.

And so I became obsessed with the idea of the unconscious and with ways of accessing it. I believed that, as Madan Sarap wrote, "the true speech, the unconscious, breaks through usually in a veiled and incomprehensible form." Around this time I was introduced to the work of Ted Joans, André Breton and Aimé Césaire, and the musicians Albert Ayler, Charles Mingus, John Coltrane, Pharaoh Sanders, Ornette Coleman.

In surrealism I finally found what I had been searching for—the release of the unconscious ego, a way of writing swiftly from some internal space. Like a jazz musician reaching for the point where notes didn't matter, where what mattered was the purity of intent, the core, the truth. And it was almost as if in my dislocation from home and culture, I was trying to find within the text, or at least to record the memory of Trinidad. At this point the whole modus of my writing seemed to congeal into surrealism. I had found a name for the things I had been doing. All those years in Trinidad, going to the Baptist church with my grandparents, seeing the spirit possessions and hearing the glossolalia, dancing in the streets at the annual carnival, bathing in mud and white paint, riots of noise and color, the way we speak in Trinidad; breaking language into morsels of liquid text—all these informed the surreal for me.

So in a way surrealism found me!

Unpublished manuscript

EXTENDING OUT TO BRIGHTNESS

this floating island spun centre of the earth as an epicentre of all things sensual. here we measure time by temperature. distance by breath, prefer death by fire. revellers, we as dense as wet gravel down henry, george and charlotte street, all the way down to the jetty in a vast and surging kaleidoscope of blazing fire mas.

wire frames support rabelaisian disguises, meticulous sequins and fetish figures of startling silver worn swinging with the hip shake/my chest gone tight as a warm drum, niggerman, make the snare pop! sweet socalypso man chanting till him heart bust an' big big arse rolling 'pon truck top. grind mama grind and shake the firmament—o gorm—no man can brace when the tempo
   drop.

it what make moko jumbie come down from the st ann's hills—ten leg long, look! a shit hound hoppin' through a bush of masquerade boots—'e tongue heng slack like the red bandana roun' he neck and he sniff and lickin' snowcone syrup, lickin' rum spit dried crisp on the hot so hot heels leave holes in bitumen and sweat salt collects in the gutters to dissolve woe within the flux of blood and spum and bile and funk piss grieving through muck and breastmilk like kingfish liver oil. immortelles are in bloom of electric orange in memorial square. and on this festival road, every flag that slap my face is a blessing for exile. then a chantwell come his come from up duke street, strumming bones on a bamboo saxophone, leading a mud mas band and 10,000 watts of wild island jazz on a mack truck back. down in the engine room the bass man start pump an' the drummer knock claves and the horns leggo bop and the whole band ketch a vaps and start churn a revel rhythm/congas run amok like footsteps of runaway slaves.

well saturnalian ointment began to bead like salt butter saliva—and a river of arms rise up when the singer chants. his voice moves like mad bull kite in dry season. much like syrup dripping from a guava tree, such like thick black love dripping like the blood of Gabriel into an old man's eye as he reclines—hung over the door for good luck but blinds him cold
when it
    drop.
and the brass band begin to push past the park for the big yard stage.
but some of us are shaking and some of us are waiting
for the fruit to fall.

Unpublished manuscript

Patrick Turner

The work of Patrick Turner (1953–), one of the quickening forces in imaginative collage in recent years, is profoundly influenced by black music and has been widely shown in outdoor art fairs throughout the country. It has been reproduced in surrealist publications, including *Arsenal.*

Milwaukee-based, Turner is also a noted blues musician. His thoughtful statement, reprinted here from Ron Sakolsky's *Surrealist Subversions,* is excerpted from Turner's exhibition catalogs.

UNRESTRICTED IMAGES: A CONTINUOUS FLOW OF ENERGY

The mind has to think in terms of unlimited possibilities when working in collage. A common ground is established between time and space.

There is a continuous search for that harmonic relationship that is in tune with the universal beat. There are secrets to be discovered among the shuffled shadows that move within the jungles of a transient playground.

Moments for a private ecstasy will burst forward from an earthly wilderness.

On the road of life there will be many twists, turns, and detours. The deviation of a unsuspecting glance is now challenged to unbridle the penetrating mysteries that stretch our dimensions beyond the horizon.

The silence of a night saturates a void. Astral prophecies remain dormant. The anatomy of a conversation stubbornly bends into the concentration of an exhaustive intellect. The essence of a thought is now weighed for its true wisdom.

The final expression created in a work of art should be a *surprise* to the artist and the viewer.

I like to think of myself not only as an artist in a broad sense, but as a *visual poet*.

Adrienne Kennedy

Born in Pittsburgh, Pennsylvania, as Adrienne Hawkins (1931–), Kennedy's first play, *Funnyhouse of a Negro,* was produced by Edward Albee in New York. Since then she has written and had produced numerous plays that draw on myth, history, and the American experience. See the discussion in the afterword by Robin D. G. Kelley.

PEOPLE WHO LED ME TO MY PLAYS

People on Old Maid cards: (1936, age five):
Through make-believe one could control people on a small scale.

Paper dolls:
You could invent enchantment with paper.

..E BIRD (1940 movie):

...mewhere, if I could find them, there were some steps, many, many steps, that led to the Blue Bird of Happiness. But I would have to climb them and they sort of sat just in the middle of the sky. It would be worth it, though. I wondered if they were in another city. What city?

Jack and Jill:
Went up a hill to fetch a pail of water. Jack fell down and broke his crown and Jill came tumbling after. What's a crown? I asked my mother. His *head,* she said. [Original emphasis]

Blondine:
A heroine in a fairy tale who went through trials and hectic adventures to find happiness, until she befriended a tortoise who helped her destroy her nemesis, a wicked king. I had never seen a tortoise and didn't know anyone who had one. I wondered if I had to confront an evil king who would help me?

Elves:
I asked my mother, could we leave milk for the elves that came out at night.

People my mother dreamed about:
In the morning I could hardly wait to hear about them. The stories she told of them were as exciting as the movies of Frankenstein and Dracula that I saw at the Waldorf.

These people my mother dreamed about continued to grow in my imagination. Like the people in the red scrapbook, they often knew each other and had known my parents when they were young.

I would list them in my mind as I sat on the front steps of our house (the steps that faced the orange tower).

Her mother who died when she was three.

Her stepfather who was killed walking across an electrified railroad track.

Her Aunt Hattie who died when my mother was pregnant with me.

When my mother was making oatmeal on winter mornings as I sat waiting with my bowl at the kitchen table, I secretly yearned that my mother would talk more about people she had dreamed about. There is no doubt that a person talking about people in his or her dreams became an archetype for people in my monologues, plays and stories.

People Who Led Me to My Plays

Tyree Guyton

THERE IS A TRUE MAGIC HERE

On the Heidelberg Project in Detroit: Interview by Maurice Greenia (October 10, 1991)

Looking at the art world today, I feel that a lot of artists have deviated. They're not painting from the heart. They're caught up in the fame or prestige or the money factor. But going out there and saying "I'm going to try something new," or "I'm going to take a chance"—I don't meet many artists saying that or doing that today.

I'll tell you what I found to be incredible. I never visualized, that I was going to have people from all over the world coming here to see the project. I just went out there and I just wanted to say something. I had this problem. The house was *begging* for someone to put life back into it. And me being an artist, it spoke to me. I connected with that house. And I just had to put life back into it. And I was shocked to find out that this work of art was going to speak to so many people. I grew up on this street—Heidelberg Street. I remember starting school from here. My great-grandmother and great-grandfather came here and moved into this house in 1947.

I was always painting [as a kid]. I always had some kind of watercolor paint set. The painting I was doing was sometimes rather weird stuff. Grandpa was a house painter and he would take me with him, teaching me how to mix colors and explaining about direction and contrast, light and dark.

Then I heard about Charles McGee. He was teaching a master's residency program at Eastern University, and he was also teaching a course over at Northern High School. He was teaching a philosophy, and he would play music—I would hear jazz playing all the time. He was listening to people like Thelonious Monk. He even told me to go out and buy some albums—to buy some of the music and study it. He felt I needed to know about this person. He really talked a lot about Thelonious Monk. And I began to listen—to Monk, and to McGee talking about Monk and his unique style.

I think the art world needs a lot of changing, I think the world of capitalism plays a big part in it now. People really get caught up in that fame. They get caught up in that power syndrome. Having somebody from *Art News* coming to do a story—they get caught up in that. I try to stay away from it myself. I see the system as being very out of order.

How did I get started on the Heidelberg Project? A lot of the paintings I was working on were too large to do inside—and some of the sculpture pieces, too. I started working with fifty gallon drums—some of that stuff got too large. So right next door we had a vacant lot here. The house that had been there was not up to city code and the city came out and condemned it. That was the first house we started on. It was called "Fun House." I was just visualizing doing something on that house—just doing something with it.

Every day when I first started it was like something so magical, something so beautiful. Once I started, I couldn't stop. Driving around the city looking—inside buildings and junk yards and rummage sales and flea markets, looking for stuff—like stopping on the expressway picking up hubcaps.

When I began transforming and repainting houses, there was a lot of mixed emotion. Some of the neighbors thought I was kinda crazy. They felt, "this guy's gotta be totally out of his head to be doing that kind of stuff." And then there were people that would come over and you just couldn't get them off, they were so excited—so thrilled about the fact of there being art [on Heidelberg Street]. And the kids *loved* it—loved the art. They came down here, and came back, and looked, and shared things with us.

I'm a radical artist myself. And I find myself looking real, real deep into life. There is a true magic here. I feel personally that we were put here on this planet to do something extraordinary—to do something great. And I believe that the Heidelberg Project is not dead. I believe it's going to revive. I believe that something greater will truly manifest from all this chaos that has happened. I keep hearing something—and it keeps telling me to look beyond. And already I've begun to think of new ideas—new things I want to do. Another project must come out of it—something great.

Henry Dumas

Poet and teacher Henry Dumas (1934-1968) was active in the Civil Rights and Black Power movements. His works have been published thanks to his friend Eugene Redmond. Notable are poetry collections *Play Ebony: Play Ivory* (1974), *Knees of a Natural Man* (1989), and fiction works *Ark of Bones* (1974) and *Jonoah and the Green Stone* (1976). See the discussion of his life by Robin D. G. Kelley in the afterword.

WILL THE CIRCLE BE UNBROKEN?

Probe was deep into a rear-action sax monologue. The whole circle now, like a bracelet of many colored lights, gyrated under Probe's wisdom. Probe was a thoughtful, full-headed black man with narrow eyes and a large nose. His lips swelled over the reed and each note fell into the circle like an acrobat on a tight rope stretched radially across the center of the universe.

He heard the whistle of the wind. Three ghosts, like chaff blown from a wasteland, clung to the wall. . . . He tightened the circle. Movement began from within it, shaking without breaking balance. He had to prepare the womb for the afro-horn. Its vibrations were beyond his mental frequencies unless he got deeper into motives. He sent out his call for motives. . . .

The blanket of the bass rippled and the fierce wind in all their minds blew the blanket back, and there sat the city of Samson. The white pillars imposing . . . but how easy it is to tear the building down with motives. Here they come. Probe, healed of his blindness, born anew of spirit, sealed his reed with pure air. He moved to the edge of the circle, rested his sax, and lifted his axe . . .

There are only three afro-horns in the world. They were forged from a rare metal found only in Africa and South America. No one knows who forged the horns, but the general opinion among musicologists is that it was the Egyptians. One European museum guards an afro-horn. The other is supposed to be somewhere on the West Coast of Mexico, among a tribe of Indians. Probe grew into his room a black peddler who claimed to have traveled a thousand miles just to give it to his son. From that day on, Probe's sax handled like a child, a child waiting for itself to grow out of itself.

Inside the center of the gyrations is an atom stripped of time, black. The gathering of the hunters, deeper. Coming, laced in the energy of the sun. He is blowing. Magwa's hands. Reverence of skin. Under the single voices is the child of a woman, black. They are building back the wall, crumbling under the disturbance.

In the rear room, Jan did not hear the volt, nor did he see the mystery behind Probe's first statement on the afro-horn. He had closed his eyes, trying to capture or elude the panthers of the music, but he had no eyes. He did not feel Ron slump against him. Strands of Tasha's hair were matted on a button of Ron's jacket, but she did not move when he slumped. Something was hitting them like waves, like shock waves. . . .

The musicians stood. The horn and Probe drew up the shadows now from the audience. A child climbed upon the chords of sound, growing out of the circle of the womb, searching with fingers and then with motive, and as the volume of the music increased penetrating the thick callousness of the Irishan twirling his stick outside of black flesh, the musicians walked off, one by one, linked to Probe's respectful nod at each and his quiet pronouncement of their names. He mopped his faced with a blue cloth.

"What's the matter here?"

"Step aside, folks!"

"These people are unconscious!"

"Look at their faces!"

"They're dead."

"Dead?"

"What happened?"

"Dead?"

"It's true then. It's true. . . ."

Echo Tree: The Collected Short Fiction of Henry Dumas

Deusdedit de Morais

The young Afro-Brazilian poet who calls himself Deusdedit is a co-founder and member of the Surrealist Group in São Paulo in 2006—a group that has adopted the name Decollage.

In addition to his specifically surrealist activity, Deusdedit and his wife also operate what is widely regarded as the single best bookstore in São Paulo.

CAFÉ DE CHERBOURG (AUTOMATIC WRITING)

The living room is a chaos of immense universes and noises—the air oily and dizzy. Touch the switch and the pallid lamp under the lampshade illuminates a tight room in protest. My soul is a window near the wall of this unfinished house in this dense parade of opaque lights which border the avenue almost devoid of cars.

I see myself in silence and pain, and a long rainbow escapes from me, from deep in my eyes, invading the living room, the furniture, the floor (bright and full of termites), throwing me, in less than a second, into the immensity of the rain and the emptiness.

Clusters of car drones bluster at remote intervals, a crazy beggar curses the gods under the rain, a melancholic cab driver is immobilized in a suspended animation.

Askia the Great walks in beauty and ferocity under the rain. Aimé Césaire is my neighbor. Out of vague territory comes an immense continent, ready to cross the earth, from north to south, and the volcanic blue of the cafe in "Les Parapluies de Cherbourg"—I wish it were my soul.

Unpublished manuscript; translated by Marcus Salgado

Jayne Cortez

POETRY COMING AS BLUES AND BLUES COMING AS POETRY

Blues singer John Lee Hooker once said: "I was born with the blues, I eat with the blues, I sleep with the blues because the blues comes from way way back." Leadbelly said: "It's that old feeling." Lightnin' Hopkins said: "It's real to my way of knowin'." And for me that feelin', that knowin', that way way back is the Angola one step, deep ocean currents, African ancestors, Black struggle and the miracle of survival.

The poetry coming as blues and the blues coming as poetry is filled with the smell of fish fluid and leopard musk, the taste of volcanic rocks and cemetery head stones. It is marked by black snakebites and is jammed with sermons at the crossroads, shipwrecks at the temptation club, conversations with invisible forces, competitive triangles, self-centered fixations, the aftermath of rebellious gestures and the meanness of madness smoldering and pacing in a circle of 4/4 time. It is the feeling behind the feeling. And like the Bouki character of black folktales, the blues makes and solves its own contradictions. "It carries its own mind away."

It's the search, the heat, and the showdown, the call, repeat, and response device. It is stripped to the bone of revolt and loneliness and is mystified in apprehension, masqueraded with tragedy, stuffed with exile, and vitalized with humour. It is "pulled out of the sky" and is a force that hears itself saying: "I love you baby, ain't gonna tell you no lie, but the day you quit me that's the day you die." It is dotted with protest: "We got so much trouble at home, we don't need to go to Vietnam." It is the story of poetic verse.

The story of performers/composers like Big Bill Broonzy, Bessie Smith,

Charlie Patton, Howlin' Wolf, J. B. Lenoir, Son House, Robert Johnson, Memphis Minnie, Muddy Waters, Big Mama Thornton and others pushing the poetic fission of blues beyond repetition, stock phrases and structural limitations and into spontaneous intense vocaltudes. The blues is like a skeleton key opening the door to the cockpits, to the chaotic tornadoes, to the swaying chain gangs, to the stagnant ponds of racism, to the love potions, to sexual escapades, to the "drinkin' and not thinkin'," to "blues falling down like hail" and "hell hound on my trail," to the bluntness "you're like an old horseshoe that has had its day," lines of resentment, "will I be called a man or do I have to wait till I'm 93."

It is riddled with the lack of opportunity and money problems, "You can't spend what you ain't got, you can't lose what you ain't never had." It's about "bad luck at your door" and "blues please turn your train around." It's about instruments imitating the human voice and the human voice imitating machines, imitating the howling of coyotes, and musicians fixing the form into a 12 measure structure. But the soul, the poetic fission of the blues can't be fixed.

It is unruly, uncompromising and persistent. It is matted down in black cultural matters when agitated it speaks like a whirlwind, stings like a bolt of lightning, tears a guitar to pieces, melts harmonicas, and pulverizes piano keys.

For the Bouki Blues Festival, January 10, 2002, St. Louis, Senegal

FREE TIME FRICTION

For Ted Joans (2003)

I heard that
A zillion mosquitoes
     rode a million human ankles into
           the twilight of madness
and even mudfish cults
          took off their helmets as
crickets wailing like uncontrollable sirens
 lifted you into
 baritone fire of the eclipse

and night surfaced with ghosts from Katanga
with lava from city of Goma
with Ouagadougou dust on words flying on
         flying piranhas
       back through
    crevices of Timbuktu

                  as you
entered yourself
drinking black stout
chewing kola nut
and riff-raffin' like the great djali you were
with your inflamed spirit lungs
spotted okapi legs
and overheated bongo lips beating in
            free-time-friction
very conflictive
very defensive
very Ted-u-nomadically
  camel walking forward
  & sand-dancing sideways into
        a song swallowing its tooth on
                        a proverb that says:
        "The fly has nobody to advise"
        & it was
another dawn rising with murmuring roosters
another dump smoking through used wallets
another octopus throbbing between zoot-suited penguins
another prostate full of untamed windstorms
another ear of canned laughter embedded with
                butcher rhythms backed by
                horns turning corny lyrics into
                beautiful instrumental music
        & it was like
another sanctified shrine chalked in gun powder
another mask of assertive razors hanging in hallways
another agitated banjo drunk on crocodile tears sold
                    in plastic bottles to
other civilizations in the mirror of
other planets disappearing with
        burros painted like zebras
        flamboyant monkeys swinging on
        rubber tires in medicine stalls
        & the freeze dried bottom of Mars
re-entering steel-purifying-processes in
competition with blow-torch blow of
the trillion trilling tonalities assembled like jackals under

purple postal pulp of your tongue as you yelled
        "Tell the Tuaregs I'm on my way"

And it was another pipeline in the treaty
another muted cornet call under
                        off shore drilling rigs
another bundle of bank notes smiling at
another shitty border dispute
        & the battle for who you are
        and what you feel
        was saying that
"joy is more transient than grief"
        & there are
all kinds of uninhabited areas
all sorts of extractions and precipitations
        oozing from
sweet surreal marshes of your body splashing into
  intersection for irresistible insurrections where
        you sit like
  an autographed picture that says:
  the poet was what he was
        and what he was looking for
        and deeper than that is not deep
        "Tell the Tuaregs I'm on my way"

Jayne Cortez

Surrealism and the Creation of a Desirable Future

Robin D. G. Kelley

I discovered surrealism buried under the rich, black soil of Afro-diasporic culture. In it I found a most miraculous weapon with no birthdate, no expiration date, no trademark. I traced it from the ancient practices of Maroon societies and shamanism back to the future, in the metropoles of Europe, and forward into the colonial world. I came to Breton through Césaire, came to Péret through Richard Wright, came to Leiris through Jayne Cortez, traveled to Toyen through Wifredo Lam's jungle on the backs of one of Ted Joans' rhinos. Although I'm still just a neophyte to this expansive, revolutionary thought and practice and I have much to figure out, surrealism has provided me with a clear and wide open window onto what freedom is all about.

My coeditor, Franklin Rosemont in Chicago provided me with a treasure map. And this book in many ways represents the fullest and richest articulation of the surrealist vision I have yet encountered. It's fitting that my initial meeting with Franklin and Penelope Rosemont took place at the inaugural Black Radical Congress in 1998, when revolutionaries and progressives from around the country and parts of the world converged on Chicago to figure out a way forward. As a committed Marxist among Marxists, I felt stuck. I knew all the "antis," but the "pros" seemed less clear, aside from a vague understanding of what a socialist society might look like. But even that vision was mechanical, utilitarian, functional. It didn't address feeling or the psyche, spirit or soul, or desire. In my own sort of halting, confused way, I tried to speak to what I believed was a failure to grasp desire in our efforts to imagine a revolutionary future. I suggested the surrealists might have something to offer, but I just was not sure what.

I had an inspiration, though, thanks to a chance encounter with the late, great poet Ted Joans, who, along with his wife, Laura Corsiglia, sat me down at an Indian restaurant in Greenwich Village and proceeded to give me a "Teducation." He taught me that we must learn how to turn our mental chains into instruments of freedom—sax, trumpet, claves, drums, paint brushes, chisels—weapons for beauty-making, not just retaliation or self-defense. From Ted I learned what it meant to be hip, to be cool, to possess the power to pull the marvelous out of a pot, a sweet potato pie, a champagne glass, a sliver of garlic, an abandoned piece of wood, a tattered roll of paper, a memory, a story, a song . . . laughter. A homeboy of Cairo, Illinois, Joans came into the world on July 4, 1928, but he was not born on a riverboat as legend would have it. He studied trumpet, sang bebop, and earned a bachelor's degree in fine arts from Indiana University before moving to Greenwich Village in 1951. He was one of the original Beat poets, though you wouldn't know it from most Beat anthologies. Joans was the granddaddy of bringing jazz and "spoken word" together on the bandstand. When his former roommate, the great saxophonist Charlie Parker, passed away in 1955, it was Joans who began scrawling "Bird Lives!" all over lower Manhattan.[1]

A well-known black expatriate, in the early 1960s Joans initially bypassed Europe and went straight to Africa, making Timbuktu his home base while he traveled throughout the continent and much of the world, reading poetry, making love, writing jazz criticism, creating "happenings" before that term became popular, and turning a life into an adventure. He exchanged ideas with the leading figures of Surrealism, hung out with Jack Kerouac, met an admiring Malcolm X, broke bread with Afro-Cuban painter Wifredo Lam, shared bread with African American painter Bob Thompson, exchanged bread stories with singer and hustler "Babs" Gonzalez, and played invisible man when invitations came with . . . no bread.

While André Breton himself acknowledged Joans as the only African American surrealist he had ever met, Joans' main man was Langston Hughes. One hears echoes of Hughes in Joans' poems as well as in his performance style. Author of over thirty books of poetry, prose, and collage, including *Black Pow-Wow, All of Ted Joans and No More, Afrodisia, Double Trouble,* and *Teducation,*[2] Joans' best-known statement is a poem titled "The Truth." He warns us not to fear the poets, for they speak the truth; they are our seers, clairvoyants, visionaries. Joans knew that speaking truth was a dangerous thing, which is why he called one series of poems "hand grenades" since they were intended to "explode on the enemy and the unhip." While his topics ranged from love, poverty and Africa to the blues and rhinos, all of his writing, like his life, was a relentless revolt. In 1968, Joans dispatched his nearly-forgotten "Black Flower" statement, a surrealist manifesto that envisioned a movement of black people in the U.S. bringing down American imperialism from within with the weapon of poetic imagery, "black flowers" sprouting all over the land.[3] While some of his poems blow up like a bomb, others spring to life like a fake snake in a can. His imagery is rich with humor, joy, and sensuality, evident in poems like the "Flying Rats of Paris" or the darkly humorous "Deadnik."

As Ted put it succinctly: "Jazz is my religion, surrealism my way of life."

A way of life?

So I stood there before my black radical comrades and quoted Ted and talked about creating "a way of life." And Amiri Baraka laughed and nodded. I think he was the only one. At the time I was woefully ignorant of his insightful and critical essay on Aimé Césaire, published in his *Daggers and Javelins: Essays, 1974-1979.*[4] And I remembered he once ran with Ted Joans back in the day. Afterward, I ran into Rosemont, a long-time mover of Charles Kerr publishers whose work I had been referencing just minutes earlier. I gained an even deeper appreciation for those four little words.

And thus was born nearly a decade-long correspondence and a confirmation that the distance between socialism and surrealism is not so great. After all, surrealists have consistently opposed capitalism, promoted internationalism, and have been strongly influenced by Marx and Freud in their efforts to bridge the gap between dream and action. Indeed, they continue to demand the overthrow of bourgeois culture and insist that proletarian revolution is one of their "First Principles." In other respects, surrealism is night to socialism's day: it breaks the chains of social realism and rationality, turning to poetry as a revolutionary mode of thought and practice. I learned this from Aimé Césaire's great essay "Poetry and Cognition," first published in 1945.[5]

Opening with the simple but provocative proposition that "Poetic knowledge is born in the great silence of scientific knowledge," he then attempts to demonstrate why poetry is the only way to achieve the kind of knowledge we need to move beyond the world's crises. "What presides over the poem," he writes, "is not the most lucid intelligence, the sharpest sensibility or the subtlest feelings, but experience as a whole." This means everything—every history, every future, every dream, every life form from plant to animal, every creative impulse—plumbed from the depths of the unconscious. Poetry, therefore, is not what we simply recognize as the formal "poem," but a revolt: a scream in the night, an emancipation from old ways of thinking—an emancipation of *language.*

Consider Césaire's third proposition regarding poetic knowledge: "Poetic knowledge is that in which man spatters the object with all of his mobilized riches." Surrealism, in other words, is not an ideology but a state of mind, a "permanent readiness for the Marvelous," as the late Suzanne Césaire once put it. To embrace Surrealism is not a simple matter of reading a manifesto and signing a card; it requires a freeing of the mind, a willingness to enter the domain of the strange, the marvelous and the fantastic, a domain scorned by people of certain inclinations. Here is the freed image, dazzling and beautiful, with a beauty that could not be more unexpected and overwhelming. Here are the poet, the painter and the artist, presiding over the metamorphoses and the inversions of the world under the sign of hallucination and madness . . . Here at last the world of nature and things makes direct contact with the human being who is again in the fullest sense spontaneous and natural. Here at last is the true communion and the true knowledge, chance mastered and recognized, the mystery now a friend and helpful.[6]

Suzanne Césaire's words were like a birth canal for me. They left me wet and vulnerable and curious about the world I thought I knew. She gave me new eyes and replaced all my nerve endings. The Afro-Cuban painter Wifredo Lam, another surrealist of the African diaspora, also taught me how to see anew. Lam's childhood in "black Cuba" actually prepared him for surrealism, exposing him to African culture as well as revolt. His godmother, Mantonica Wilson, was a practitioner of Santeria, and was consulted far and wide for remedies for physical and spiritual afflictions. Lam studied art in Madrid and stayed long enough to participate in the defense of Republican Spain during the Civil War and, partly through Picasso, studied African sculpture while in Paris. As Lam embraced the marvelous, his work became more totem-like, less androcentric. "The Jungle," one of his greatest paintings, offers one of the most powerful representations of Surrealist revolution. We are confronted with four monster-like creatures of enormous feet and masks, surrounded by powerful spirits he knew from childhood—the *orishas* of his godmother's religious practices. Lam himself thought of it as a representation of revolt but from the depth of the unconscious. "My idea was to represent the spirit of the Negroes in the situation in which they were then. I have used poetry to show the reality of acceptance and protest."[7]

Lam rejected social realism at a time when most politically radical artists believed it was the only path to revolutionary art. Instead, he sought to express "the Negro spirit, the beauty of the plastic art of the blacks. In this way I could act as a Trojan horse that would spew forth hallucinating figures with the power to surprise, to disturb the dreams of the exploiters. I knew I was running the risk of not being understood either by the man in the street or by the others. But a true picture has the power to set the imagination to work, even if it takes time."[8]

Richard Wright tried to achieve with his writing what Lam was attempting to do with his painting. Like Lam, Wright did not have to travel too far to find

Surrealism; he was surrounded by it in the lives of black working people. Indeed, his 1941 text, *Twelve Million Black Voices*, captures the surrealist character of black life and turns to poetry as a means to elucidate alienation and its impact on the psyche. "The noise of our living," he writes, "boxed in stone and steel, is so loud that even a pistol shot is smothered."[9] What a remarkable text! *Twelve Million Black Voices* is in many ways a History that, in Baudelaire's words, attempts to "plunge to the bottom of the abyss, Hell or Heaven . . . to the bottom of the Unknown in order to find the new!"[10]

For Wright, plumbing the depths is not only an investigation into the unconscious but a plunge into the world of which history is often unconscious, where the actors/creators have no names, no faces. He is uninterested in the middle class, the success stories who are "like single fishes that leap and flash for a split second above the surface of the sea." Instead, he focuses on the "tragic school that swims below in the depths, against the current, silently and heavily, struggling against the waves of vicissitudes that spell a common fate."[11]

The hell, the tragic, the abyss. It is the dark-side of Surrealism that is, more often than not, the purview of black surrealists who understand that emancipation begins by knowing the mind and understanding what black existential reality does to the psyche. We must then reckon with the work of Adrienne Kennedy, Henry Dumas, Amiri Baraka, in addition to Wright and Ellison and many others. In my book *Freedom Dreams*, I failed to reckon with this side of Surrealism because I was so set on discovering the Marvelous, on finding roads to emancipation. I did not come to terms with the multiplicities of Madness, the nightmares, the terrifying hallucinations embedded in the collective black unconscious.

My *mea culpa* is sincere, but so is my peculiar journey to Surrealism. I focused on Afro-diasporic artists not only because their work brought me to Surrealism, but because they each suggest that a thorough understanding and embrace of the Marvelous existed in the lives of Blacks and non-Western peoples, particularly in music, dance, speech, the plastic arts, and above all philosophy. Perhaps my own dissatisfaction with "proletarian realism" has to do with the suppression of key elements of black culture that Surrealism embraced: the unconscious, the spirit, desire, magic, and love.

BARAKA, DUMAS, KENNEDY—ORIGINALS!

Adrienne Kennedy's play, "The Ohio State Murders," opens with playwright Suzanne Alexander (her fictional alter ego) explaining to a college lecture hall why there is so much violent imagery in her work. She answers the question by telling the story of her college experience—a harrowing tale of racism, murder, and betrayal. Violent imagery erupts in her imagination because violence constitutes the context for black people's lives in America. Her plays focus on what the physical and psychological violence of racism and colonialism do to the psyche.

Surrealist imagery dominates her work, which plumb the depths of the unconscious through dreamlike, hallucinatory flights of terror.[12] Her characters and the spaces they occupy are rendered surrealistically—like the "pale Negro children" who are half human, half rat in "A Rat's Mass" (1966), or her hallucinatory conversations/monologues in works like "Funnyhouse of a Negro," (1964), "The Owl Answers," (1965), "She Talks to Beethoven" (1989), and "Sleep Deprivation Chamber" (1996).[13] Although hallucinations are sometimes the path to clairvoyance, the outcomes are tragic because her dreams are nightmares—much like the reality of black life.

In "Funnyhouse of a Negro," for example, Sarah's hallucinations, which transform her room into a "funnyhouse" replete with a hall of mirrors and two sinister clowns mocking her, leads her to suicide. In her unconscious state, her identity is fragmented into four selves: Queen Victoria, the Duchess of Hapsburg, Patrice Lumumba, and Jesus Christ. It is an extreme manifestation of DuBois' "double-consciousness" as multiple personality disorder. Victoria and the Duchess not only represent Sarah's "European" side but Empire writ large—the empire that not only swept "Africa" into modernity, but was brought to modernity *by* Africa. Lumumba, bloodied is her African side, but more specifically her revolutionary opposition to racism and Empire. And Jesus Christ, played as a yellow dwarf dressed in rags, is distorted, disfigured, and poor—symbolic of the distorted, corrupt and racist theology imposed on colonial subjects. In the age of decolonization, she underscores DuBois' famous characterization of double-consciousness as "two warring ideals in one dark body, whose dogged strength alone keeps it from being torn asunder."[14] And yet, while her dark (or rather mulatto) body is ultimately turn asunder, her warring identities are virtually identical, in that they repeat the same lines, sometimes in unison. The play speaks to her own sense of isolation—as a foreigner (she wrote much of "Funnyhouse" in Ghana and Rome), a wife of a frequently absent husband, a new mother, a black person in Europe, an African American in Africa, and as a lover of British literature in an age of anticolonialism. By plumbing the unconscious to give voice to her own alienation, she speaks to the very collective and multilayered alienations that Frantz Fanon explores in *Black Skin, White Masks* (1952) and *The Wretched of the Earth* (1961).

Born in Pittsburgh in 1931, Kennedy grew up in Cleveland in a black middle-class family. She was surrounded by fairy tales, and classic European literature, as well as black oral tradition, her father's stories of racial uplift, and her mother's dreams of death, suffering, and memory. Rather than excerpt a passage from her plays, which is difficult to do out of context, we included a short section from her autobiographical, stream-of-consciousness compendium of influences on her work, *People Who Led to My Plays* (1987). The book essentially is a response to two simple questions: "Who influenced you to write in such a nonlinear way? Who are your favorite playwrights?" It provides a lens into what led Kennedy to surrealism.

Henry Dumas understood that part of what rendered black life surreal was the frequent confrontation with violence and death. The African American was a modern subject, born of slavery, Jim Crow, lynching, and police brutality. He/she lived in brutal contradiction, offering America a vision of hope, freedom, and democracy, while every day confronting the possibility of violent death.

Dumas' short stories and poems illuminated this contradiction, and he experienced it firsthand. On May 23, 1968, a white transit cop fatally shot Henry Dumas in a subway station at 125th Street in Harlem. His crime? Singing out loud and putting his hands in his pockets when the cop approached him. In the dystopia known as black reality, this simple gesture rendered him a suspect. He was thirty-three years old. For the Black Arts Movement of which he was a beloved part, it felt like an assassination. After all, Dumas was known for creating characters that used music and poetry as weapons against The Man. As his friend and collaborator, poet Eugene B. Redmond, put it, "one needed very little imagination or coaxing to conclude that Dumas' awesome abilities as a seer/sorcerer had been deemed dangerous enough to destroy."[15]

With characteristic insight, Amiri Baraka declared Dumas an "Afro-Surreal Expressionist,"[16] a phrase he coined that could apply to any number of thinkers included in this text. In the tradition of black surrealists, freedom was Dumas' obsession and black music was its highest form of expression. Yet, while black music gives voice to the Marvelous, for Dumas it also narrates the pain and violence of black existence; it is a lethal weapon in struggle, and a sigh of the spirit. And like Wifredo Lam, Richard Wright, and others, Dumas found his surrealist imagery in black folk culture, particularly the realm of the spirit world. The Arkansas-born, New York-bred writer absorbed the prophetic teachings of the Bible as well as the world of hoodoo, spirit possession, ghosts, ancestor divination, Sufism, Buddhism, Hinduism, and Islam. He found in the churched and unchurched sacred world the mythic, magical, and imagistic elements that made up his brilliant short stories such as "Ark of Bones," "Goodbye, Sweetwater," "Fon" and "Rope of Wind."[17] Black sacred expressions—whether in the form of music, chants, sermons, prayer—spoke of death as a journey "home"; heaven as the reward for one's labors, where there is no more labor, no more suffering, only pure love; a world where people can fly, speak all manner of languages, engage spirits and angels, and can perform acts of physical transformation. In many ways, Dumas' writing paralleled the musical explorations of John Coltrane and Albert Ayler (in my mind, the musical equivalent to Dumas who also died a violent death in New York City at age 34), whose passage to the so-called "avant-garde" required a deep exploration of black sacred music. And it is no accident that just before his tragic murder, he was studying with composer/pianist/visionary Sun Ra.

The excerpt is from his short story "Will the Circle Be Unbroken?" included in this volume. The story might read as a dark, violent tale, but it's about black liberation and the lethal power of black liberation arts. Dumas tells the story of Probe, a musician whose magical "Afro-horn" kills three whites (one a cop) who force their way into a black club despite warnings. The point here is that the "New Thing," the avant-garde, the music associated with Coltrane, Ayler, Sun Ra and Archie Shepp, is lethal.

Poet, playwright, essayist, propagandist, revolutionary, teacher, scholar, music critic, musician, Amiri Baraka has been one of the most prolific and influential artists of the last half century. Despite a very long, critical engagement with Surrealism and Dadaism, going back at least to the publication of his poem "Black Dada Nihilismus" (1964)[18] and his novel, *The System of Dante's Hell* (1965),[19] few critics have associated Baraka with surrealists. On the one hand, despite the surrealistic character of much of his writing—poetry and prose—he has leveled a very sharp critique of Surrealism as political practice from a Marxist-Leninist position. In his often ignored essay on Aimé Césaire, Baraka acknowledges Surrealism's powerful critique of bourgeois society, but suggests that in its disillusionment with Western humanism it has erred in the direction of "exoticism and primitivism." Moreover, Surrealism simply doesn't go far enough: "Surrealism calls for a disordering finally of the bourgeois world, but even that is momentary, and it does not really call for its destruction."[20]

On the other hand, where surrealism is revolutionary is in its insistent reordering of reality and hence the imagination. For Baraka (and André Breton), the juxtaposition of different elements in real life produce new associations, new meanings, and thus new possibilities. But he warns that the "rearrangement of reality" alone is not the point, but rather "the creation of a new reality after the destruction of the old."[21] While Baraka acknowledges the Paris Surrealist Group's short-lived decision to join the Communist Party as an action intended to create a new reality, in his view the Surrealists have done more rearranging than changing. Of course, given the history of activism among surrealist Groups worldwide, Baraka's critique is a bit premature.

Nevertheless, Baraka's own commitment to creating a new reality is unassailable. For nearly five decades, he has been continually active in movements for change, from Black Nationalist formations to Marxist-Leninist-Maoist groups to community-based cultural forums. However he positions himself vis-à-vis Surrealism, Baraka is nonetheless responsible for some of the most forceful and revolutionary poetry to come out of the United States. What makes his poetry forceful is not just words but the "sound" and the effect. As critic/poet Sherry Brennan wrote, for Baraka the poem must act and have effect in the world. "It does so directly, by taking up the activity and energy of a people, the history, economy, and struggle of a people, directly into the sound and force of the poem. To write such poetry is to proceed by something other than linguistic sense. Is to proceed by the spirit and material force that carries revolution itself. This force is the sound of poetry. . . . It is a black sound, and this black sound is a social body. It is an active body, a living justice, or the sound of justice carried under and through the language, which animates that language and speaks it as black as a black sound, as a black social body."[22]

The poem as an emancipation of language, a freeing of the imagination, a radical act. Here we hear Baraka's surrealism as revolutionary music. It should not surprise us, then, that some of his most powerful surrealist expressions erupt when he is exploring the emancipatory potential of black music.

DIALECTICAL METHOD

That most black radicals did not jump on the Surrealist bandwagon, ironically, might have something to do with its very familiarity; its revolutionary core was recognized as having always existed in black life. Throughout the African diaspora, one can plainly see the practice of Surrealism in everyday life—cultures that, for the most part, value imagination, improvisation, and verbal agility, from storytelling, preaching, singing, to toasting and the dozens. The emphasis on turning all expressions, practices, and communications into art coincides with Lautréamont's injunction that "Poetry must be made by all."[23] As early as 1792, Olaudah Equiano described the world from which he was stolen as "a nation of dancers, musicians, and poets."[24]

Surrealism has not only compelled me to think differently about Afrodiasporic culture, about art and imagination, about ancient practices and the power of spirituality, it has also compelled me to think differently about Marxism. As hard as it is for me to admit, I believe Marxism has failed to comprehend this elusive thing we call consciousness, despite wonderful efforts to incorporate psychoanalysis by Wilhelm Reich and Eric Fromm,[25] writings on spirituality by Ernest Bloch and Cornel West, and cultural insights of Georg Lukacs and Herbert Marcuse. (Marcuse, of course, drew a great deal from Surrealist writings in his own reassessments of Marxist philosophy late in his life.) Surrealists took up the revolutionary implications of Freud and psychoanalysis even before Reich, and retained a very strong dialectical method in their thinking. Yet, they have always pushed further, resisting notions of "progress" seen as so essential to modernity on both sides of the ideological spectrum; drawn on "primitive" ideas of dreams, magic, social organization; explored the explosive emotional realms of Love and Madness.

Conscious or not, Surrealist injunctions have been present in contemporary anti-racist, feminist, gay and lesbian, indigenous, reparations, and environmental justice movements. The very contexts of globalization and the latest manifestation of U.S. empire have generated new, expanded visions of what a "desirable future" might be. And steps toward realizing that vision is not dependent upon seizing state power. The Zapatistas and Autonomista movements in Argentina, for example, question whether the goal of revolution is simply taking institutional power (state). Instead, they are creating spaces for prefiguring or modeling the world they want to create; to transform social relations and build a new society in these liberated zones. Hakim Bey calls these Temporary Autonomous Zones—and we see them popping up in Latin America and I believe here in the U.S.[26]

The combination of the history of Third World liberation movements, anti-racist struggles, the notion of Temporary Autonomous Zones, radical feminism (especially as defined by women of color), and the challenge of U.S. militarism, neoliberalism, and globalization, has inspired many youth organizations to develop new visions of a desirable future right here in the United States. One of the most Surrealist of the new movements is the Sista II Sista Collective, a Brooklyn-wide community-based organization located in Bushwick. They describe themselves as "a collective of working class young and adult Black and Latina women building together to model a society based on liberation and love. Our organization is dedicated to working with young women to develop personal, spiritual and collective power. We are committed to fighting for justice and creating alternatives to the systems we live in by making social and political change."[27] They insist that internal, spiritual, and emotional transformation is essential to social transformation, and vice versa. Survival, in other words, is not simply making it alive to the next day. It is about crafting a sustainable life, a loving life, a joyous life, a life worth living.

As the texts gathered here demonstrate, Surrealism is not some lost, esoteric body of thought longing for academic recognition. It is a living practice and it will continue to live as long as we dream. For me at least, it takes us to places where Marxism and other "isms" in the name of revolution have yet to fully tread. Surrealism recognizes the decadence of Western civilization but doesn't fall into the trap of cynicism or technotopias or fatalism and false prophets. Nor is it some atavistic romanticization of the past. It considers, above all, love and poetry and the imagination as powerful social and revolutionary forces, not as a *replacement* for organized protest, for marches and sit-ins, for strikes and slow-downs, for matches and spray paint. Surrealism recognizes that any revolution must begin with thought, with how we imagine a New World, with how we reconstruct our relationships with each other, with unleashing our desire and building a new future on the basis of love and creativity rather than rationality (which is the same word they use for improving capitalist production and limit-ing peoples' needs—rationalize/ration, etc.)

There is no doubt that we need more bread, better homes, better schools, more time, better air to breathe and land on which to live. That goes without saying. But to stop there, to accept the rule of some bogus notion of pragma-tism, to not even delve into the question of Freedom seems so defeating. If we cannot articulate our dreams without being accused of being utopian and un-realistic, then we might as well submit to the current order and open up more soup kitchens.

Notes

1. Ted Joans interview with author, December 15, 1995; Ted Joans, "Je Me Vois (I See Myself)," *Contemporary Authors Autobiography Series*, vol. 25 (Detroit: Gale Research, 1996).

2. Ted Joans, *A black manifesto in jazz poetry and prose* (London: Calder and Boyars, 1971); *Black Pow-Wow: Jazz Poems* (New York: Hill and Wang, 1969); *All of Ted Joans and no more, poems and collages* (New York, Excelsior-Press Publishers, 1961); Ted Joans and Hart Leroy Bibbs, *Double trouble: Poems* (Paris: Revue Noire, Editions Bleu Outremer, 1992); *Teducation: selected poems 1949-1999* (Minneapolis, MN: St Paul, MN: Coffee House Press, 1999).

3. Ted Joans, "Black Flower" *L'Archibras* 3 (March 1968), 10-11.

4. Amiri Baraka, *Daggers and Javelins: Essays, 1974-1979* (New York: Williams Morrow, 1984).

5. Aimé Césaire, "Poesie et Connaissance," Tropique 12 (January 1945), translated and reprinted as "Poetry and Knowledge" in *Refusal of the Shadow: Surrealism and the Caribbean*, trans. by Michael Richardson and Krzysztof Fijalkowski (London: Verso, 1996), 134-145.

6. Suzanne Césaire, "Domain of the Marvelous," in Penelope Rosemont, ed., *Surrealist Women: An International Anthology* (Austin: University of Texas Press, 1998), 137.

7. Lam quoted in Lowery Stokes Sims, *Wifredo Lam and the International Avant-Garde, 1923–1982* (Austin, Tex: University of Texas Press, 2002), 63; see also, Max-Pol Fouchet, *Wifredo Lam* (Barcelona: Ediciones Polgrafa, S.A., 1989 [2nd ed.]).

8. Lam quoted in Sims, *Wifredo Lam and the International Avant-Garde*, 62.

9. Richard Wright, *Twelve Million Black Voices* (New York:Thunder's Mouth Press, 2003 [orig. 1941]), 108.

10. This line comes from Charles Baudelaire's celebrated poem, "Le Voyage," quoted in Charles Baudelaire, *Flowers of Evil and Other Works*, edited and translated by Wallace Fowlie (Mineola, NY: Dover Pub., 1992), 103.

11. Both quotes from Wright's preface to, *Twelve Million Black Voices*, p. xx.

12. On Kennedy's surrealism see, Paul Bryant-Jackson, "Intersecting Boundaries: The Surrealist Theatre of Poet/Playwright Adrienne Kennedy," *African American Review* 27, no. 3 (1993 Fall), 495–500 [reprinted in Robert Scanlan, "Surrealism as Mimesis: A Director's Guide to Adrienne Kennedy's *Funnyhouse of a Negro*," in Paul K. Bryant-Jackson and Lois More Overbecke, eds., *Intersecting Boundaries: The Theatre of Adrienne Kennedy* (Minneapolis: University of Minnesota Press, 1992)], 93–109; Philip C. Kolin, *Understanding Adrienne Kennedy* (Columbia, SC: University of South Carolina Press, 2005).

13. All published in Adrienne Kennedy, *The Adrienne Kennedy Reader* (Minneapolis: University of Minnesota Press, 2001).

14. W. E. B. DuBois, *The Souls of Black Folk* (Chicago: A. C. McClurg and Co., 1903), 3.

15. Eugene B. Redmond, "Introduction: The Ancient and Recent Voices Within Henry Dumas," *Black American Literature Forum* 22, no. 2 (Summer 1988), 144.

16. Amiri Baraka, "Henry Dumas: Afro-Surreal Expressionist," *Black American Literature Forum* 22, no. 2 (Summer 1988), 164–166.

17. See Dumas, *Echo Tree: The Collected Short Fiction of Henry Dumas* (Minneapolis, MN: Coffee House Press, 2003), and his *Play Ebony Play Ivory*, ed. Eugene B. Redmond (New York: Random House, 1974), both published posthumously.

18. Reprinted in William J. Harris, ed., *The LeRoi Jones/Amiri Baraka Reader* (New York: Thunder's Mouth Press, 1991), 71–72.

19. Amiri Baraka, *The System of Dante's Hell* (New York: Grove Press, 1965).

20. Amiri Baraka, "Aimé Césaire," in William J. Harris, ed., *The LeRoi Jones/ Amiri Baraka Reader,* 325–326. The essay originally appeared in Amiri Baraka, *Daggers and Javelins: Essays, 1974–1979* (New York: Morrow, 1984), 189–200.

21. Ibid., 332. As critic Maurice Lee observed, "To Breton, this perspective is the fusion of the waking and sleeping (dream) state, the unconscious with the conscious. To Baraka this perspective is the fusion of the social with the individual, the existential self, that self that does not conform. Since, however, the societal self for the Black man is also nonconformist and alienated, in image, language, and reality, his world is always fragmented. Duality, therefore, a double consciousness, or in a physical sense, 'schizophrenia,' is a healthy state in a Barakian character. And, to Baraka, 'healthy' does not mean physically well so much as it means spiritually functioning." [Maurice Lee, *The Aesthetics of LeRoi Jones/Amiri Baraka: The Rebel* (Valencia: Universitat de Valencia, 2004), 31.] Here is where Baraka meets Adrienne Kennedy meets Henry Dumas. Although Kennedy's fragmented identities signal a spiritual dis-ease, both agree that it is the existential reality of the modern black subject. And all three writers, if not virtually everyone gathered together in this book, regard the healthy functioning of the spirit as an essential precondition for emancipation.

22. Sherry Brennan, "On the Sound of Water: Amiri Baraka's 'Black Art,'" *African American Review* 37, nos. 2/3 (Summer–Autumn, 2003), 309–310.

23. Comte de Lautréamont, *Maldoror and Poems,* transl. by Paul Knight (New York: Penguin Books, 1978), 252.

24. Olaudah Equiano, *The Interesting Narrative and Other Writings* (New York: Penguin, 1995), 34.

25. Robert S. Corrington, *Wilhelm Reich: Psychoanalyst and Radical Naturalist* (New York: Farrar, Straus and Giroux, 2003); Eric Fromm, *The Art of Loving* (London: Thorsons, 1957); *Psychoanalysis and Religion* (New Haven: Yale University Press, 1950); *Marx's Concept of Man* (New York: Frederick Ungar, 1961); *The Crisis of Psychoanalysis. Essays on Freud, Marx, and Social Psychology* (New York: Holt, Rinehart and Winston, 1970).

26. Hakim Bey, *The Temporary Autonomous Zone: Ontological Anarchy, Poetic Terrorism* (Brooklyn, NY: Autonomedia, 1991).

27. "Sista II Sista: Hermana a Hermana," http://www.sistaiisista.org/main.html.

Bibliography

Adandé, A. *Haiti, poètes noirs*. Présence Africane 12. Paris: Du Seuil, 1951.

Ahmad, Muhammad (a.k.a. Maxwell Stanford, Jr.). *We Will Return in the Whirlwind: Black Radical Organizations, 1960-1975*. Introduction by John Bracey. Chicago: Charles H. Kerr, 2007.

Alexander, Will. *The Stratospheric Canticles*. Berkeley, Calif.: Pantograph Press, 1995.

Alexandrian, Sarane. *Georges Henein*. Paris: Seghers, 1981.

———. *Histoire de la philosophie occulte*. Paris: Éditions Seghers, 1994.

Allen, Ron. "Eye Mouth Graffiti Body Shop." Unpublished play.

———. *Neon Jawbone Riot*. Detroit, Mich.: Weightless Language Press, 2000.

Almeida, Fernando Mendes de. *Phantom Carrousel*. São Paulo: Editora SPES, 1937.

Anderson, T. J., III. *At Last Round Up*. Somerville, Mass.: Lift Books, 1996.

———. *Notes to Make the Sound Come Right: Four Innovators of Jazz Poetry*. Fayetteville: University of Arkansas Press, 2004.

Andrews, Wayne. *The Surrealist Parade*. New York: New Directions, 1977.

Antoine, Régis. *Les ecrivains français et les Antilles*. Paris: Maisoneuve et Larose, 1997.

Aragon, Louis. *Les cloches de bâle*. Paris: Denoël, 1960 (1934).

———. "Fragments d'une conférence." *La Revolution Surréaliste*, no. 4 (July 15, 1925): 23-25.

Araujo, Emanoel, ed. *Abigail Moura: A Orquesta Afro-Brasileira*. São Paulo: Negras Memórias, Memórias Negros, 2003.

———. *Elsie Houston: A feminilidade do canto*. São Paulo: Negras Memórias, Memórias Negros, 2003.

Arnold, A. James. *Modernism and Negritude: The Poetry and Poetics of Aimé Césaire*. Cambridge, Mass.: Harvard University Press, 1981.

Artaud, Antonin. *A la grand nuit ou le bluff surréaliste. Oeuvres complètes*, vol. 1. Paris: Gallimard, 1956.

Atkinson, J. Edward. *Black Dimensions in Contemporary American Art*. New York: New American Library, 1971.

Baeza Flores, Alberto. *La poesía dominicana en el siglo XX: Historia, crítica, estudio comparativo y estilístico*. 4 vols. Santiago: Universidad Católica Madre y Maestra, 1976-1986.

Baker, Houston A., Jr. *Blues, Ideology, and Afro-American Literature: A Vernacular Theory.* Chicago: University of Chicago Press, 1984.

Balakian, Anna. *Surrealism: Road to the Absolute.* New York: Dutton, 1959; revised 1970.

Baldwin, James. *No Name in the Street.* New York: Dell, 1972.

Baragaño, J. A. *Wifredo Lam.* Havana, 1958.

Baraka, Amiri. *The Autobiography of LeRoi Jones.* New York: Freundlich Books, 1984.

————. *Black Music.* New York: Da Capo Press, 1998.

————. *Daggers and Javelins: Essays, 1974–1979.* New York: Morrow, 1984.

————. "Henry Dumas: Afro-Surreal Expressionist." *Black American Literature Forum* 22, no. 2 (Summer 1988).

————. *The System of Dante's Hell.* New York: Grove Press, 1965.

Bearden, Romare, and Harry Henderson. *A History of African American Artists.* New York: Pantheon, 1993.

Becker, Heribert, Edouard Jaguer, and Petr Kral. *Das Surrealistiche Gedicht.* Frankfort: Museum Bochum, 1985.

Bédouin, Jean-Louis. *Vingt ans du surréalisme.* Paris: Denoël, 1961.

Bélance, René. *Épaule d'ombre.* Port-au-Prince: Imprimerie de l'État, 1945.

————. *Luminaires.* Port-au-Prince, Haiti: Morissett, 1941.

Benayoun, Robert. *Anthologie du nonsense.* Paris: J. J. Pauvert, 1959.

————. *Erotique du surréalisme.* Paris: J. J. Pauvert, 1965.

————. *Le rire des surréalistes.* Paris: La Bougie de Sapeur, 1988.

Berry, Faith. *Langston Hughes: Before and Beyond Harlem.* New York: Citadel Press, 1992.

————. *Légitime Défense before and beyond Harlem.* New York: Citadel, 1982.

Biro, Adam, and René Passeron. *Dictionnaire général du surréalisme et ses environs.* Paris: Universitaires de France, 1982.

Bounoure, Vincent. *La civilisation surréaliste.* Paris: Payot, 1976.

————. *Moments du surréalisme.* Introduction by Michael Löwy. Paris: L'Harmattan, 1999.

Bracey, John, Jr. *Black Nationalism in America.* Indianapolis, Ind.: Bobbs-Merrill, 1970.

————, August Meier, and Elliott Rudwick. *Black Nationalism in America.* Indianapolis, Ind.: Bobbs-Merrill, 1970.

Brandon, Ruth. *Surreal Lives: The Surrealists, 1917–1945.* New York: Grove Press, 1990.

Breá, Juan, and Mary Low. *Red Spanish Notebook: The First Six Months of the Revolution and the Civil War.* Introduction by C.L.R. James. London: Martin Secker and Warburg, 1937.

————. *La verdad contemporánea.* Havana: Privately printed, 1943.

Breton, André. *L'Amour fou.* Paris: Gallimard, 1937.

————. *Arcane 17.* New York: Brentano, 1944.

————. *L'Art magique.* Paris: Club Français du Livre, 1957.

————. "Away with Miserabilism!" In *Surrealism and Painting.* New York: Harper & Row, 1956.

————. *La clé des champs.* Paris: Pauvert, 1967.

————. *Communicating Vessels.* Translated by Mary Ann Caws. Lincoln: University of Nebraska Press, 1990.

————. "Distances." In André Breton, *Les pas perdus.* Paris: Nouvelle Revue Français, 1924.

————. *Entrétiens.* Paris: NRF, 1969.

————. *Fata morgana.* Buenos Aires: Éditions des Lettres Françaises, Sur, 1942.

————. *Fata Morgana.* Translated by Clark Mills. Chicago: Black Swan Press, 1969.

————. "Le jeu de Marseilles." In André Breton, *La clé deschamps.* Paris: Pauvert, 1967.

————. *Martinique: Snake Charmer.* Translated by David W. Seaman; introduction by Franklin Rosemont. Austin: University of Texas Press, 2008.

————. *Nadja.* Paris: Gallimard, 1928.

————. *Oeuvres complètes.* Edited by Marguerite Bonnet et al. 3 vols. Paris: Gallimard, 1988–1999.

————. "Prolegomena to a Third Manifesto of Surrealism or Not." In *What Is Surrealism: Selected Writings.* New York: Pathfinder, 2000.

————. "Revolution Now and Forever." In *What Is Surrealism? Selected Writings.* New York: Pathfinder, 2000.

————. *Martinique, charmeuse de serpents.* Paris: Sagittaire, 1948.

————. *Situation du surréalisme entre les deux guerres.* Paris: Éditions de la Revue Fontaine, 1945.

————. "Sur l'échec du front populaire." In Marguerite Bonnet et al., eds. *Oeuvres complètes,* vol. 2. Paris: Gallimard, 1992.

————. *Surrealism and Painting.* Translated by Simon Watson Taylor. New York: Harper & Row, 1972.

————. *Le surréalisme et la peinture.* Paris: Gallimard, 1965.

————. *What Is Surrealism? Selected Writings.* New York: Pathfinder, 2000.

————. *Young Cherry Trees Secured against Hares.* Translated by Edouard Roditi. New York: View Editions, 1946.

————, ed. *This Quarter: Surrealist Number.* New York: Arno Press, 1969.

————, and Édouard Glissant. *Cárdenas.* Translated by John Ashbery. Chicago: Richard Feigen Gallery, 1961.

Breton, André, and Gérard Legrand. *L'Art magique.* Paris: Éditions Phebus, 1991.

Breton, André, and Benjamin Péret. "Revue de la presse." *Le Surréalisme au Service de la Révolution,* no. 5 (May 15, 1933).

Bricktop, with James Haskins. *Bricktop.* New York: Atheneum, 1983.

Brown, Fahamisha Patricia. *Performing the Word: African American Poetry as Vernacular Culture.* New Brunswick, N.J.: Rutgers University Press, 1999.

Brown, Frank London. *The Myth Maker: A Novel.* Chicago: Path Press, 1969.

————. *Trumbull Park.* Chicago: Regnery, 1959.

Brown, Kimberly N. "Of Poststructuralist Fallout, Scarification, and Blood Poems: The Revolutionary Ideology behind the Poetry of Jayne Cortez." In Kimberly N.

Brown, *Other Sisterhoods: Literary Theory and U.S. Women of Color.* Urbana: University of Illinois Press, 1998.

Brown, Sterling A. *The Collected Poems of Sterling A. Brown.* Edited by Michael S. Harper. Chicago: TriQuarterly Books, 1980.

————. *The Negro Caravan.* New York: Arno Press, 1970 (1941).

————. *Southern Road.* New York: Harcourt, Brace, 1932.

Brutus, Dennis. *Poetry and Protest: A Dennis Brutus Reader.* Edited by Lee Sustar and Aisha Karim. Chicago: Haymarket Books, 2006.

————. *Stubborn Hope.* Washington, D.C.: Three Continents Press, 1978.

Bryant-Jackson, Paul. "Intersecting Boundaries: The Surrealist Theatre of Poet/Playwright Adrienne Kennedy." *African American Review* 27, no. 3 (Fall 1993).

Buhle, Mari Jo. *Encyclopedia of the American Left.* Oxford: Oxford University Press, 1998.

Buhle, Paul, et al., *Free Spirits: Annals of the Insurgent Imagination.* San Francisco: City Lights, 1982.

Buñuel, Luis. *My Last Sigh.* New York: Knopf, 1983.

Cabral, Amílcar. *Revolution in Guinea: An African People's Struggle.* London: Stage 1, 1969.

————. *Unity and Struggle: Speeches and Writings of Amílcar Cabral.* Introduction by Basil Davidson. Biographical notes by Mário de Andrade. New York: Monthly Review Press, 1979.

Calas, Nicolas. *Confound the Wise.* New York: Arrow Editions, 1942.

Camacho, Jorge. *Le mythe d'Isis et d'Osiris.* Paris: La Table d'Emeraude, 1995.

Cardinal, Roger, and Robert Short, eds. *Surrealism: Permanent Revelation.* New York: Dutton, 1970.

Caws, Mary Ann. *The Poetry of Dada and Surrealism.* Princeton, N.J.: Princeton University Press, 1970.

Césaire, Aimé. *Aimé Césaire: Écrivain martiniquais.* Edited by S. Battestini. Littérature Africaine 9. Paris: Fernand Nathan, 1967.

————. *Les armes miraculeuses.* Paris: Gallimard, 1946.

————. *Cadastre.* New York: Third Press, 1973 (1961).

————. *The Collected Poetry.* Edited and introduced by Clayton Eshleman and Annette Smith. Berkeley & Los Angeles: University of California Press, 1983.

————. *Discourse on Colonialism.* Introduction by Robin D. G. Kelley. Translated by Joan Pinkham. New York: Monthly Review Press, 2000 (1955).

————. *Et les chiens se taisaient.* Paris: Présence Africaine. 1956.

————. *Letter to Maurice Thorez.* Paris: Présence Africaine, 1956.

————. *Lyric and Dramatic Poetry, 1956–1982.* Charlottesville: University Press of Virginia, 1990.

————. *Poètes d'aujourd'hui.* Paris: Pierre Seghers, 1962.

————. *Return to My Native Land (Cahier d'un retour au pays natal).* Translated by Emil Snyders. Paris: Présence Africaine, 1968.

————. *A Season in the Congo.* New York: Grove Press, 1968.

————. *A Tempest: Based on Shakespeare's* The Tempest: *Adaptation for a Black Theatre.*

Ubu Repertory Theater Publications, 0738-4009: 14. New York: G. Borchardt, 1985 (1969).

———. *The Tragedy of King Christophe*. New York: Grove Press, 1969.

Chapman, Abraham, ed. *New Black Voices: An Anthology of Contemporary Afro-American Literature*. New York: New American Library, 1972.

Charpier, Jacques. *Lam*. Paris: Le Musée de Poche, 1960.

Clarke, John Henrik, ed. *Harlem, U.S.A.* New York: Collier Books, 1971.

Cogollo, Heriberto. *Cogollo: Le monde d'un Nobor*. Exhibition catalog. Paris: Galerie Suzanne Visat, 1973.

Cole, Bill. *John Coltrane*. New York: Da Capo Press, 1993.

Colquhoun, Ithell. *Goose of Hermogenes*. London: Peter Owen, 1961.

Coombs, Orde, comp. *Is Massa Day Dead? Black Moods in the Caribbean*. Garden City, N.Y.: Anchor Books, 1974.

Cooper, Anna Julia. *A Voice from the South*. New York: Oxford University Press, 1988 (1892).

Cooper, Wayne F. *Claude McKay: Rebel Sojourner in the Harlem Renaissance*. Baton Rouge: Louisiana State University Press, 1987.

Cortez, Jayne. *The Beautiful Book*. New York: Bola Press, 2007.

———. *Firespitter*. San Francisco: City Lights, 1982.

———. *Jazz Fan Looks Back*. Brooklyn, N.Y.: Hanging Loose Press, 2002.

———. *Mouth on Paper*. New York: Bola Press, 1977.

———. *Poetic Magnetic*. New York: Bola Press, 1991.

———. *Scarifications*. New York: Bola Press, 1973, 1978.

———. *Somewhere in Advance of Nowhere*. New York: Serpent's Tail, 1996.

Cossery, Albert. *The House of Certain Death*. New York: New Directions, 1949.

———. *The Lazy Ones*. Translated by Willia Goyen. Norfolk, Conn.: New Directions, 1949.

———. *Men God Forgot*. Translated by H.E. Berkeley, Calif.: G. Leite, 1946.

Costa, Sosígenes. *Morro do desterro*. São Paulo: Editora Cultrix, 1979.

Cripps, Louise. *C.L.R. James: Memories and Commentaries*. New York: Cornwall, 1997.

———. *Puerto Rico: The Case for Independence*. Dorado, P.R.: Borinquen Books, 1993.

Crowder, Henry, with Hugo Speck. *As Wonderful As All That?* Introduction by Robert L. Allen. Navarro: Wild Trees Press, 1987.

Cruz è Souza, João da. *Evocações*. Rio de Janeiro: Typographia Aldina, 1898.

Cunard, Nancy, ed. *Negro Anthology*. London: Wishart & Co., 1934.

Damas, Léon-Gontran. *African Songs of Love, War, Grief, and Abuse*. Ibadan, Nigeria: Mbari Publications, 1961.

———. "A Caribbean View on Sterling A. Brown." In *Sterling A. Brown: A UMUM Tribute*. Philadelphia: Black History Museum UMUM Publishers, 1976.

———. *Pigments*. Paris: GLM, 1937.

———. *Névralgies*. Paris: Présence Africaine, 1972.

———. *Poètes d'expression française (d'Afrique Noire, Madagascar, Réunion, Guadeloupe, Martinique, Indochine, Guyane) 1900-1945*. Paris: Éditions du Seuil, 1947.

———. *Veillées noires*. Ottawa: Éditions Leméac, 1972 (1943).

Davidson, Basil. *The Liberation of Guiné*. Middlesex, Eng.: Penguin Books, 1969.

de Andrade, Mário. *Será o Benedito!* São Paulo: Pontifícia Universidade Católica, 1992.

———, and Aimé Césaire. *Modernisme brésilien et négritude antillaise*. Paris: Harmattan, 1999 (1957).

Despres, Leon. *Challenging the Daley Machine*. Evanston, Ill.: Northwestern University Press, 2005.

Deveney, John Patrick. *Paschal Beverly Randolph: A Nineteenth Century Black American Spiritualist, Rosicrucian, and Sex Magician*. (Albany: State University of New York Press, 1997.

Documents 34. Reprinted in *L'Arc 37*. Paris: N.d.

Drake, St. Clair. *The American Dream and the Negro: 100 Years of Freedom?* Chicago: Roosevelt University, 1964.

———. *Black Folk Here and There: An Essay in History and Anthropology*. 2 vols. Los Angeles: Center for Afro-American Studies, University of California, 1987–1990.

———. *The Redemption of Africa and Black Religion*. Chicago: Third World Press, 1991 (1970).

———, and Horace R. Cayton. *Black Metropolis: A Study of Negro Life in a Northern City*. Introduction by Richard Wright. 2 vols. New York: Harper Torchbooks, 1962 (1945).

Ducornet, Guy. *Ça va chauffer! Situation du surréalisme aux U.S.A., 1966–2001*. Mons: Talus d'Approche, 2001.

———. *Le punching-ball & la vache lait: La critique universitaire nord-américaine face au surréalisme*. Paris: Actual/Deléatur, 1992.

Dumas, Henry. *Ark of Bones and Other Stories*. Edited by Eugene B. Redmond. New York: Random House, 1974.

———. *Echo Tree: The Collected Short Fiction of Henry Dumas*. Minneapolis, Minn.: Coffee House Press, 2003.

———. *Jonoah and the Green Stone*. New York: Random House, 1976.

———. *Knees of a Natural Man: Poetry*. New York: Thunder's Mouth Press, 1989.

———. *Play Ebony: Play Ivory*. Edited by Eugene B. Redmond. New York: Random House, 1974.

Durozoi, Gérard. *Histoire du mouvement surréaliste*. Paris: Hazan, 1997.

Edwards, Melvin, and Jayne Cortez. *Fragments*. New York: Bola Press, 1994.

El Alailly, Ikbal. *Vertu de l'Allemagne*. Cairo: Éditions Masses, 1945.

El Janabi, Abdul Kader. *Horizon vertical*. Translated by Charles Illouz and Mona Huerta. Arles, France: Actes Sud, 1998.

Ellison, Ralph. *The Collected Essays of Ralph Ellison*. Edited by John F. Callahan. Preface by Saul Bellow. New York: Modern Library, 1995.

———. *Invisible Man*. New York: Signet, 1952 (1947).

———. *Shadow and Act*. New York: Vintage Books, 1972 (1953).

Éluard, Paul. *Selected Writings*. Norfolk, Conn.: New Directions, n.d.

———. "La suppression de l'esclavage." *La Révolution Surréaliste*, no. 3 (1925).

Equiano, Olaudah. *The Interesting Narrative and Other Writings*. New York: Anchor Books, 1995 (1789).

Esenwein, George. "Testament of a Revolution." *Arsenal/Surrealist Subversion*, no. 4 (1989).

Eshleman, Clayton, and Annette Smith, trans. *Aimé Césaire: The Collected Poetry*. Berkeley & Los Angeles: University of California Press, 1983.

Fabre, Michel. *The Unfinished Quest of Richard Wright*. Urbana: University of Illinois Press, 1993.

————, et al., eds. *The French Critical Reception of African-American Literature: From the Beginnings to 1970*. Westport, Conn.: Greenwood Press, 1995.

————. *From Harlem to Paris: Black American Writers in France, 1840–1980*. Urbana: University of Illinois Press, 1991.

Fabre d'Olivet, Antoine. *Miscellanea Fabre d'Olivet*. Nice: Claude Boumendil, 2000.

Fanon, Frantz. *Black Skin, White Masks*. New York: Grove Press, 1968.

————. *The Wretched of the Earth*. New York: Grove Press, 1963 (1961).

Ferlinghetti, Lawrence, ed. *City Lights Anthology*. San Francisco: City Lights Books, 1974.

Flamand, Élie-Charles. "Introduction." *Les oeuvres de Nicolas Flamel*. Paris: Éditions Pierre Belfond, 1973.

Ford, Karen. "On Cortez's Poetry." In Karen Ford, *Gender and the Poetics of Excess*. Oxford: University Press of Mississippi, 1997.

Fouchet, Max-Pol. *Wifredo Lam*. Paris: Éditions Cercle d'art, 1976.

Fowlie, Wallace. *Age of Surrealism*. Bloomington: Indiana University Press, 1960.

Frutkin, Susan. *Aimé Césaire: Black between Worlds*. Miami, Fla.: University of Miami Press, 1973.

Fry, Varian. *Surrender on Demand*. Boulder, Colo.: Johnson Books, 1997 (1945).

Fusco, Rosário. *O agressor: Romance*. Rio de Janeiro: J. Olympio, 1943.

————. *Poemas cronológicos*. Rio de Janeiro: José Olympio, 1940.

Garon, Paul. *Blues and the Poetic Spirit*. San Francisco: City Lights, 1996.

————. *The Devil's Son-in-Law: The Story of Peetie Wheatstraw and His Songs*. London: Studio Vista, 1971.

————. *What's the Use of Walking If There's a Freight Train Going Your Way? Black Hoboes and Their Songs*. Chicago: Charles H. Kerr, 2006.

————, and Beth Garon. *Woman with Guitar: Memphis Minnie's Blues*. New York: Da Capo Press, 1992.

Gascoyne, David. *A Short Survey of Surrealism*. San Francisco: City Lights, 1982.

Gaudibert, Pierre, and Jacques Leenhardt. *Wifredo Lam: Oeuvres de Cuba*. Paris: Librairie Séguier, 1989.

Gayle, Addison, Jr., ed. *The Black Aesthetic*. New York: Anchor Books, 1972.

Gershman, Herbert. *The Surrealist Revolution in France*. Ann Arbor: University of Michigan Press, 1969.

Gertrude Abercrombie and Friends. Exhibition catalog. Springfield: Illinois State Museum, 1983.

Gillespie, Dizzy. *Gertrude Abercrombie.* Chicago: Hyde Park Art Center, 1977.

Gonzales, Babs. *I Paid My Dues: Good Times—No Bread.* East Orange, N.J.: Expubidence Publishing, 1967.

Granell, E. F. "La aventura surrealista en las Antilles." In *El surrealismo entre viejo y nuevo mundo.* Exhibition catalog. Gran Canaria: Centro Atlántico de Arte Moderno, 1989–1990.

Gysin, Brion. *To Master—A Long Goodnight: The Story of Uncle Tom.* New York: Creative Age Press, 1946.

Harrington, Oliver W. *Why I Left America and Other Essays.* Jackson: University Press of Mississippi, 1993.

Harris, Wilson. *Eternity to Season.* London: New Beacon, 1978.

———. *Palace of the Peacock.* London: Faber & Faber, 1960.

———. *Tradition: The Writer and Society.* Port of Spain: New Beacon, 1967.

Henein, Georges. *Oeuvres.* Paris: Denoël, 2006.

Hellwig, David J., ed. *African-American Reflections on Brazil's Racial Paradise.* Philadelphia: Temple University Press, 1992.

Henderson, Stephen. *Understanding the New Black Poetry: Black Speech and Black Music as Poetic References.* New York: William Morrow, 1973.

Henein, Georges. *De la liberté comme nostalgie et comme projet.* Paris: Arabie-sur-Seine, 1984.

———. *Déraisons d'être.* Paris: Éditions de la Géhenne, 1999.

———. *L'esprit frappeur (Carnets 1940–1973).* Paris: Encre Éditions, 1980.

———. *La force de saluer.* Paris: Éditions de la Différence, 1978.

———. *Notes sur un pays inutile.* Paris: Puyraimond, 1977.

———. *Pour une conscience sacrilège.* Cairo: Éditions Masses. 1944.

———. *Qui est Monsieur Aragon?* Cairo: Éditions Masses, 1945.

———. *Le signe le plus obscur.* Paris: Puyraimond, 1977.

Henry, Marjorie Louise. *Stuart Merrill: La contribution d'un Américain au symbolisme français.* Paris: Éditions Champion, 1927.

Henry, Paget, and Paul Buhle, eds. *C.L.R. James's Caribbean.* Durham, N.C.: Duke University Press, 1992.

Herriman, George. *Krazy Kat.* New York: H. Holt, 1946.

Hill, Herbert. *Soon, One Morning: New Writing by American Negros, 1940–1962.* New York: Knopf, 1968.

Huddleston, Sisley. *Paris Salons, Cafes, Studios.* New York: Blue Ribbon Books, 1928.

Hurston, Zora Neale. *Dust Tracks on a Road: An Autobiography.* Philadelphia: J. B. Lippincott, 1942.

———. *Mules and Men.* Philadelphia: J. B. Lippincott, 1935.

———. *Tell My Horse.* Philadelphia: J. B. Lippincott, 1938.

Ignatiev, Noel. *How the Irish Became White.* New York: Routledge, 1995.

Jablonski, Joseph. "Millennial Soundings." In Paul Buhle et al., *Free Spirits: Annals of the Insurgent Imagination.* San Francisco: City Lights, 1982.

Jahn, Janheinz. *Muntu: African Culture and the Western World.* Introduction by Calvin C. Hernton. New York: Grove Weidenfeld, 1990 (1961).

————. *Neo-African Literature: A History of Black Writing.* New York: Grove Press, 1968.

James, C.L.R. *The Black Jacobins: Toussaint L'Ouverture and the San Domingo Revolution.* New York: Vintage Books, 1963.

————. *Facing Reality: The New Society: Where to Look for It & How to Bring It Closer.* With the collaboration of Cornelius Castoriadis; new introduction by John H. Bracey. Chicago: Charles H. Kerr, 2006.

————. *A History of Pan-African Revolt.* Introduction by Robin D. G. Kelley. Chicago: Charles H. Kerr, 2005 (1938).

————. *Minty Alley.* London: M. Secker & Warburg, 1936.

————, and Grace C. Lee. *Facing Reality.* Chicago: Charles H. Kerr, 2006.

James, Winston. *A Fierce Hatred of Injustice: Claude McKay's Jamaica and His Poetry of Rebellion.* London & New York: Verso, 2000.

Joans, Ted. *Afrodisia: New Poems.* New York: Hill & Wang, 1970.

————. *All of Ted Joans and No More: Poems and Collages.* New York: Excelsior Press, 1961.

————. "Bird and the Beats." *Coda,* no. 181 (1981).

————. *Black Power Manifesto. Arsenal: Surrealist Subversions,* no. 2.

————. *Black Pow-Wow: Jazz Poems.* New York: Hill & Wang, 1969.

————. *Funky Jazz Poems.* New York: Rhino Review, 1959.

————. *The Hipsters.* New York: Corinth Books, 1961.

————. *Okapi Passion.* Berkeley, Calif.: Ishmael Reed, 1994.

————. *Our Thang: Several Poems, Several Drawings.* Illustrations by Laura Corsiglia. Victoria, B.C.: Ekstasis Editions Canada, 2001.

————. *Proposition pour un manifeste Pouvoir Noir.* Translated by Jeannine Ciment and Robert Benayoun. Paris: Eric Losfeld, 1969.

————. *Sure, Really I Is.* Harpford, Sidmouth, Devon: Transformaction, 1982.

————. *Teduction: Selected Poems 1949–1999.* Minneapolis, Minn.: Coffee House Press, 1999.

————. *WOW.* Illustrated by Laura Corsiglia. Mulkiteo, Wash.: Quartermoon Press, 1999.

————, and Hart Leroy Bibbs. *Double Trouble.* Paris: Éditions Bleu Outremer, 1992.

Joans, Ted, and Joyce Mansour. *Flying Piranha.* New York: Bola Press, 1978.

Joans, Ted, et al., eds. *Dies und Das.* Berlin: Dies und Das, 1984.

Johnson, Fenton. *A Little Dreaming.* College Park, Md.: McGrath, 1969 (1913).

————. *Songs of the Soil.* New York: F.J., 1916.

————. *Tales of Darkest America.* Freeport, N.Y.: Books for Libraries Press, 1971 (1920).

————. *Visions of the Dusk.* New York: F.J., 1915.

Johnston, Percy Edward. *Phenomenology of Space and Time.* New York: Dasein, 1976.

Jolas, Eugene, ed. *Transition Workshop.* New York: Vanguard Press, 1949.

Jones, Edward A. *Voices of Negritude: The Expression of Black Experience in the Poetry of Senghor, Césaire and Damas.* Valley Forge, Penn.: Judson Press, 1971.

Jones, LeRoi. *Blues People: Negro Music in White America.* New York: William Morrow, 1963.

Joseph, Anthony. *Teragaton.* London: Poison Engine Press, 1997.

Josephson, Matthew. *Life among the Surrealists.* New York: Holt, Rinehart, 1962.

Joubert, Alain. *Le mouvement des surréalistes ou le fin mot de l'histoire: Mort d'un groupe — naissance d'un mythe.* Paris: Maurice Nadeau, 2001.

Karanja, Ayana I. *Zora Neale Hurston: The Breath of Her Voice.* New York: Peter Lang, 1999.

Kaufman, Bob. *The Abomunist Manifesto.* San Francisco: City Lights, 1959.

———. *The Ancient Rain: Poems 1956–1978.* Edited by Raymond Foye. New York: New Directions, 1981.

———. *Cranial Guitar.* Minneapolis, Minn.: Coffee House Press, 1996.

———. *Golden Sardine.* San Francisco: City Lights, 1967.

———. *Solitudes Crowded with Loneliness.* New York: New Directions, 1965.

Kelley, Robin D. G. *Freedom Dreams: The Black Radical Imagination.* Boston: Beacon Press, 2002.

———. *Hammer and Hoe: Alabama Communists during the Great Depression.* Chapel Hill: University of North Carolina Press, 1990.

———. *Race Rebels: Culture, Politics, and the Black Working Class.* New York: Free Press, 1994.

———. *Yo' Mama's Disfunktional! Fighting the Culture Wars in Urban America.* Boston: Beacon Press, 1997.

———, and Earl Lewis, eds. *To Make Our World Anew: A History of African Americans.* Oxford: Oxford University Press, 2000.

Kennedy, Adrienne. *People Who Led Me to My Plays.* New York: Theatre Communications Group, 1987.

Kerouac, Jack. *The Dharma Bums.* New York: Viking Press, 1971 (1958).

Kesteloot, Lilyan. *Les écrivains noirs de langue française: Naissance d'une littérature.* Brussels: Université Libre de Bruxelles, 1965.

———. *Poètes d'aujourd'hui: Aimé Césaire.* Paris: Éditions Pierre Seghers, 1962.

Kober, Marc, ed., with Iréne Fenoglio and Daniel Lançone. *Entre nil et sable: Écrivains d'Égypte d'expression française (1920–1960).* Paris: Centre National de Documentation Pédagogique, 1999.

Kréa, Henri. *Revolution and Poetry Are One and the Same Thing.* Paris, 1960.

———. *La révolution et la poésie.* Paris: M. J. Minard, 1965.

Krim, Seymour, ed. *The Beats: A Gold Medal Anthology.* New York: Gold Medal, 1960.

Kuhn, Reinhard. *The Return to Reality: A Study of Francis Viélé-Griffin.* Geneva: A Droz, 1962.

Laâbi, Abdellatif. *Rue du Retour.* London: Readers International, 1989 (1982).

LaCoss, Don. *Surrealism in '68: Paris, Prague, Chicago.* Chicago: Surrealist Research & Development Monograph Series, 2008.

Lam, Wifredo. *Wifredo Lam: Figures cara bes.* Exhibition catalog. Preface by Édouard Jaguer. Paris: Galerie Thessa Herold, 2002.

Lamantia, Philip. *Bed of Sphinxes.* San Francisco: City Lights, 1997.

Lariby, Farid. *Hater l'exigence*. Paris: Hourglass Editions, 1990.

———. *Homage a Farid Lariby*. Paris: Hourglass Editions, 1990.

La Rose, John. *Foundations: A Book of Poems*. Port of Spain: New Beacon Publications, 1966.

Lautréamont, Comte de (Isidore Ducasse). *Les chants de Maldoror*. Paris: Éditions de la Renaissance, 1967 (1869).

———. *Poèsies*. London: Allison & Busby, 1978.

Lebel, J.-J., and Tristan Sauvage. *Front unique*. Milan, 1959.

Lebovics, Herman. *True France: The Wars over Cultural Identity, 1900–1945*. Ithaca, N.Y.: Cornell University Press, 1992.

Lecherbonnier, Bernard. *Surréalisme et Francophonie; la chair du verbe: Histoire et poétique des surréalismes de langue française*. Montreal: Éditions Publisud, 1992.

Legrand, Gérard. *Preface au système de l'eternité*. Paris: Losfeld, 1971.

———. *Puissances du jazz*. Paris: Arcanes, 1953.

Leiner, Jacqueline, ed. *Soleil éclaté: Mélanges offerts à Aimé Césaire à l'occasion de son soixante-dixième anniversaire / par une équipe internationale d'artistes et de chercheurs*. Tübingen: G. Narr, 1984.

Leiris, Michel. *Wifredo Lam*. New York: Abrams, 1972.

Lemaitre, Georges. *From Cubism to Surrealism in French Literature*. Cambridge, Mass.: Harvard University Press, 1945.

Leperlier, François. "La solution poétique." In André Breton, *Oeuvres complètes*, edited by Marguerite Bonnet et al. Vol. 3. Paris: Gallimard, 1998.

Léro, Etienne, et al. *Légitime défense*. Translated by Alex Wilder. *Arsenal: Surrealist Subversion*, no. 2 (1973).

Léro, Yva. *Peau d'ébène: Poèmes*. Martinique: Copyrapid Carbet, 1979.

Lima, Jorge de. *Invenção de Orfeu*. Rio de Janeiro: Livros de Portugal, 1952.

———. *A pintura em pânico*. Rio de Janeiro: J. de Lima; Tip. Luso-Brasileira, 1943.

Lima, Sérgio. *A aventura surrealista*. 4 vols. Campinas, S.P., Brazil: Editora de Universidade Estadual de Campinas; São Paulo, S.P, Brazil: Fundação para o Desenvolvimento da UNESP: Editora UNESP; Petrópolis, R.J., Brazil: Editora Vozes, 1995–.

———. *O corpo significa*. São Paulo: EDART, 1976.

Lippard, Lucy, ed. *Surrealists on Art*. Englewood Cliffs, N.J.: Prentice-Hall, 1970.

Litweiler, John. *The Freedom Principle: Jazz after 1958*. New York: William Morrow, 1984.

———. *Ornette Coleman: A Harmolodic Life*. New York: Da Capo Press, 1994.

Lomax, Alan, and Raoul Adbul, eds. *3000 Years of Black Poetry*. New York: Dodd, Mead, 1984.

Low, Mary, and Juan Breá. *La saison des flûtes*. Paris: Arabie-sur-Seine, 1987.

Mabille, Pierre. *Egrégores, ou la vie des civilisations*. Paris: Jean Flory, 1938.

———. *Le miroir du merveilleux*. Paris: Les Éditions du Minuit, 1962.

Magloire-Saint-Aude, Clément. *Dialogue de mes lampes et autres textes*. Paris: Jean Michel Place, 1998.

Maisonet, Luis A. *Arte para la escuela elemental*. San Juan, P.R.: Editorial del Departamento de Instrucción Pública, Estado Libre Asociado de Puerto Rico, 1955.

Malcolm X. *The Autobiography of Malcolm X*. New York: Ballantine Books, 1973.

———. *By Any Means Necessary*. Edited by George Breitman. New York: Pathfinder, 1970.

Mansour, Joyce. *Le bleu des fonds*. Paris: Le Soleil Noir, 1968.

———. *Ça*. Paris: Le Soleil Noir, 1970.

———. *Carré blanc*. Paris: Le Soleil Noir, 1965.

———. *Flash Card*. Cambridge, Mass.: Cherry Valley Editions, 1978.

———. *Les gisants satisfaits*. Paris: Société des Éditions Jean-Jacques Pauvert, 1958.

———. *Histoires nocives: Jules César îles flottantes*. Paris: Gallimard, 1973.

———. *Jules César*. Paris: Pierre Seghers, 1958.

———. *Phallus et Momies*. Paris: Daily-Bul, 1970.

———. *Prose and Poésie*. Paris: Actes Sud, 1991.

———. *Rapaces*. Paris: Pierre Seghers, 1960.

———. *Screams*. Sausalito, Calif.: Post-Apollo Press, 1995.

Marat, Jean-Paul. "Du droit qu'ont nos colonies de secouer le joug tyranique de la metropole." *Front Unique* 1 (1959).

Masson, André. *Anatomy of My Universe*. New York: C. Valentin, 1943.

———. *Nocturnal Notebook*. New York: C. Valentin, 1944.

Matthews, Marcia M. *Henry Ossawa Tanner: American Artist*. Chicago: University of Chicago Press, 1969.

McCulloch, Jock. *In the Twilight of Revolution: The Political Theory of Amílcar Cabral*. London: Routledge & Kegan Paul, 1983.

McKay, Claude. *Banjo: A Story without a Plot*. New York: Harper & Brothers, 1929.

———. *A Long Way from Home: An Autobiography*. Introduction by St. Clair Drake. New York: Harcourt, Brace & World, 1970 (1937).

Melham, D. H. *Heroism in the New Black Poetry: Introductions & Interviews*. Lexington: University Press of Kentucky, 1990.

Mendes de Almeida, Fernando. *Carrussel fantasma*. São Paulo: Editora Spes, 1937.

Ménil, René. *Tracées: Identité, négritude, esthétique aux Antilles*. Paris: Robert Laffont, 1981.

Meyrelles, Isabel, et al. *Inácio Matsinhe: Transformei-me em tartaruga para resistir*. Colecção Artistas de Moçambique. Lisbon: Casa Viva, 1974.

Michel, Jean-Claude. *Les ecrivains noirs et le surréalisme*. Sherbrooke, Qué., Canada: Naaman, 1982.

Michel, Jean-Paul. *Mohammed Khaïr-Eddine (1941–1995)*. Bordeaux: William Blake, 1995.

Miller, Eugene E. *Voice of a Native Son: The Poetics of Richard Wright*. Jackson: University Press of Mississippi, 1990.

Millette, James. "The Black Revolution in the Caribbean." In *Is Massa Day Dead? Black Moods in the Caribbean*, Orde Coombs, comp. Garden City, N.Y.: Anchor, 1974.

Miner, Luke. *Jazz in Paris*. New York: The Little Bookroom, 2005.

Missir, Marie-Laure. *Joyce Mansour, une étrange demoiselle.* Paris: Jean-Michel Place, 2005.

Monnerot, Jules. *Les faits sociaux ne sont pas de choses.* Paris: Gallimard, 1946.

———. *Inquisitions.* Paris: Librairie José Corti, 1974.

———. *La poésie moderne et la sacré.* Paris: Gallimard, 1945.

———. *Sociology of Communism.* Translated by Jane Degras and Richard Rees. Westport, Conn.: Greenwood Press, 1976 (1949).

Mudimbe, V. Y., ed. *The Surreptitious Speech: Présence Africaine and the Politics of Otherness, 1947-1987.* Chicago: University of Chicago Press, 1992.

Nadeau, Maurice. *The History of Surrealism.* New York: Macmillan, 1965.

Ndiaye, Jean-Pierre. *La jeunesse africaine face l'impérialisme.* Paris: François Maspero, 1971.

Neal, Larry. *Hoodoo Hollerin' Bebop Ghosts.* Washington, D.C.: Howard University Press, 1974.

———. *Visions of a Liberated Future: Black Arts Movement Writing: Poetry and Prose.* Edited by Michael Schwartz. New York: Thunder's Mouth Press, 1989.

Nichols, Grace. *I Is a Long Memoried Woman.* London: Karnak House, 1983.

Nielsen, Aldon Lynn. *Black Chant: Languages of African American Postmodernism.* Cambridge: Cambridge University Press, 1997.

———, and Lauri Ramey, eds. *Every Goodbye Ain't Gone: An Anthology of Innovative Poetry by African Americans.* Tuscaloosa: University of Alabama Press, 2006.

Noel, Bernard. *Marseilles/New York: A Surrealist Liaison.* Marseilles: André Dimanche, 1985.

Okeke, Uche. *Drawings.* Ibadan, Nigeria: Mbari Publications, 1961.

Orsenna, Erik. *L'Exposition coloniale.* Paris: Éditions du Seuil, 1988.

Ortiz, Fernando. *Wifredo Lam y su obra.* Havana: Publicigraf, 1993.

Pastoureau, Henri. *Ma vie surréaliste.* Paris: Maurice Nadeau, 1992.

Paulino, Ana Maria. *Jorge de Lima.* São Paulo: Universidade de São Paulo, 1995.

Peters, Nancy J. "Philip Lamantia." In Ann Charters, ed., *The Beats: Literary Bohemians in Postwar America.* Detroit, Mich.: Gale Research; Bruccoli Clark, 1983.

Pierre, José. "Cárdenas ou l'exigence et la grace." In José Pierre, *L'Abécedaire.* Paris: Losfeld, 1971.

———. *Cogollo: Le monde d'un Nobor.* Paris: Éditions Georges Visat, 1973.

———, ed. *Tracts surréalistes et declarations collectives (1922-1939).* Paris: Losfeld, 1980.

Pitcher, Oliver. *Dust of Silence.* New York: Troubadour Press, 1958.

Portalatín, Aída Cartagena. *Culturas africanas: Rebeldes con causa.* Santo Domingo, Dom. Rep.: Taller, 1986.

———. *Yania Tierra: Poema documento—Document Poem.* Translated by M. J. Fenwick and Rosabelle White. Washington, D.C.: Azul Editions, 1995.

Puma, Fernando, ed. *7 Arts.* Garden City, N.Y.: Permabooks, 1954.

Rabéarivelo, Jean-Joseph. *24 Poems.* Ibadan, Nigeria: Mbari Publications, 1962.

Racine, Daniel. *Léon-Gontran Damas: L'Homme et l'oeuvre.* Paris: Agence de Coopération Culturelle et Technique, 1970.

Ragon, Michel. *Atlan*. Copenhagen: Éditions Ejnar Munksgaard, 1950.

Randolph, Pascal Beverly. *After Death: The Disembodiment of Man*. Boston: Randolph & Company, 1870.

Redmond, Eugene B. "Introduction: The Ancient and Recent Voices within Henry Dumas." *Black American Literature Forum* 22, no. 2 (Summer 1988).

Redpath, James. *Echoes of Harper's Ferry*. Boston: Thayer and Eldridge, 1860.

Reed, Ishmael. *Mumbo Jumbo*. New York: Avon Books, 1978.

———. *Shrovetide in Old New Orleans*. Garden City, N.Y.: Doubleday, 1978.

———. *Writin' Is Fightin': Thirty-Seven Years of Boxing on Paper*. New York: Atheneum, 1990.

Renton, David. "Georges Henein: Surrealism and Socialism." In *Dissident Marxism: Past Voices for Present Times*. London: Zed Books, 2004.

Richardson, Michael. *Refusal of the Shadow: Surrealism and the Caribbean*. Translated by Michael Richardson and Krzysztof Fija Kowski. London: Verso, 1996.

Robinson, Jontyle Theresa, and Wendy Greenhouse. *The Art of Archibald J. Motley, Jr.* Chicago: Chicago Historical Society, 1991.

Rochester, Myrna Bell. "René Crevel: Critic of White Patriarchy." *Race Traitor* 9 (1998).

Rodney, Walter. *The Groundings with My Brothers*. London: Bogle-L'Ouverture Publications, 1969.

———. *How Europe Underdeveloped Africa*. Washington, D.C.: Howard University Press, 1974.

Roediger, David R. *Black on White: Black Writers On What It Means to Be White*. New York: Schocken Books, 1998.

———. *Colored White: Transcending the Racial Past*. Berkeley & Los Angeles: University of California Press, 2002.

———. *History against Misery*. Chicago: Charles H. Kerr, 2006.

———. *How Race Survived US History: From Settlement and Slavery to the Obama Phenomenon*. London: Verso, 2008.

———. "Plotting against Eurocentrism: The 1929 Surrealist Map of the World." In *Colored White: Transcending the Racial Past*. Berkeley & Los Angeles, University of California Press, 2002.

———. *Revolution in the Service of the Marvelous: Surrealist Contributions to the Critique of Miserabilism*. Chicago: Charles H. Kerr, 2004.

———. "Three Days that Shook the New World Order: The Los Angeles Rebellion of 1992." *Race Traitor*, no. 2 (Winter 1993).

———. *The Wages of Whiteness: Race and the Making of the American Working Class*. New York: Verso, 1991.

———. *Working toward Whiteness: How America's Immigrants Became White*. New York: Basic Books, 2005.

Roger, Bernard. *A la découverte de l'alchimie*. Paris: Éditions Dangles, 1988.

Rosemont, Franklin. *From Bughouse Square to the Beat Generation: Selected Ravings of Slim Brundage*. Chicago: Charles H. Kerr, 1997.

————. "George Herriman (Krazy Kat)." In Franklin Rosemont, ed., *Surrealism & Its Popular Accomplices.* San Francisco: City Lights, 1980.

————. *Jacques Vache and the Roots of Surrealism.* Chicago: Charles H. Kerr, 2008.

————. *Open Entrance to the Shut Palace of Wrong Numbers.* Chicago: Surrealist Editions, 2003.

————. *Revolution in the Service of the Marvelous.* Chicago: Charles H. Kerr, 2004.

————. "Surrealist, Anarchist, Afrocentrist: Philip Lamantia Before and After the Beat Generation." In Jennifer Guglielmo and Salvatore Salerno, eds., *Are Italians White? How Race Is Made in America.* New York: Routledge, 2003.

————, ed. "Surrealism: Revolution against Whiteness." *Race Traitor* 9 (Summer 1998), special issue.

————, and Charles Radcliffe, eds. *Dancin' in the Streets: Anarchists, IWWs, Surrealists, Situationists and Provos in the 1960s, As Recorded in* The Rebel Worker *and* Heatwave. Chicago: Charles H. Kerr, 2005.

Rosemont, Franklin, with Penelope Rosemont and Paul Garon, eds. *The Forecast Is Hot! Tracts and Other Declarations of the Surrealist Movement in the United States, 1966–1976.* Chicago: Black Swan Press, 1997.

Rosemont, Penelope. *Dreams and Everyday Life: André Breton, Surrealism, Rebel Worker, SDS and the Seven Cities of Cibola.* Chicago: Charles H. Kerr, 2008.

————. *Surrealist Experiences: 1001 Dawns, 221 Midnights.* Foreword by Rikki Ducornet. Chicago: Black Swan Press, 2000.

————, ed. *Surrealist Women: An International Anthology.* Austin: University of Texas Press, 1998.

Roumain, Jacques. *Masters of the Dew.* Translated by Langston Hughes and Mercer Cook. New York: Reynal and Hitchcock, 1947.

————. *When the Tom-Tom Beats: Selected Prose and Poetry.* Translated by Joanne Fungaroli and Ronald Sauer. Washington, D.C.: Azul Editions, 1995.

Sakolsky, Ron. "Jayne Cortez." In Ron Sakolsky, ed., *My Revolution in the Service of the Marvelous.* Chicago: Charles H. Kerr, 2004.

————. "Jayne Cortez: The Language of Freedom." In Ron Sakolsky, ed., *My Revolution in the Service of the Marvelous.* Chicago: Charles H. Kerr, 2004.

————, ed. "Surrealism in the USA." *Race Traitor* 13/14 (Summer 2001), special issue.

————. *Surrealist Subversions: Rants, Writings and Images by the Surrealist Movement in the United States.* Foreword by Franklin Rosemont. New York: Autonomedia, 2002.

Saunders, Frances Stonor. *Who Paid the Piper? The CIA and the Cultural Cold War.* London: Granta Books, 1999.

Schwarz, Arturo. *I surrealisti.* Milan: Mazzotta, 1989.

Schwarz, Dieter. *Sonja Sekula, 1918–1963.* New York: The Swiss Institute, 1996.

Seligmann, Kurt. *The History of Magic.* New York: Pantheon, 1948.

Senghor, Léopold Sédar. *Anthologie de la nouvelle poésie nègre et malgache de langue française.* Paris: Presses Universitaires de France, 1969.

Shapiro, Norman R., ed. and trans. *Négritude: Black Poetry from Africa and the Caribbean.* New York: October House, 1970.

Sherman, Joan R. *Invisible Poets: Afro-Americans of the Nineteenth Century.* Chicago: University of Illinois Press, 1989.

Short, Robert Stuart. "Contre-attaque." In Ferdinand Alquié, *Entrétiens sur le surréalisme.* Paris: Mouton, 1968.

———. "The Politics of Surrealism." In Raymond Spiteri and Donald LaCoss, eds., *Surrealism, Politics and Culture.* Burlington, Vt.: Ashgate, 2003.

Sidran, Ben. *Black Talk.* Foreword by Archie Shepp. New York: Da Capo, 1983.

Simon, François-René. *John Coltrane.* Paris: Vade Retro, 1996.

Smethurst, James Edward. *The Black Arts Movement: Literary Nationalism in the 1960s and 1970s.* Chapel Hill: University of North Carolina Press, 2005.

Spady, James G. "The Interstellar Connection." *Free Spirits* (1983).

———. "Negritude, PanBaNegritude, and the Diopian Philosophy of African History." *Current Bibliography of African Affairs,* 5, no. 1 (January 1972).

———. *Sterling A. Brown: A UMUM Tribute.* Introduction by Dr. Albert Huff Fauset. Philadelphia: Black History Museum, UMUM Publishers, 1976.

———. "Surrealism and the Marvelous Black Plunge in Search of Yemanga and the Human Condition." *Cultural Correspondence,* nos. 12-14 (Summer 1981).

Spector, Jack J. *Surrealist Art & Writing, 1919-1939.* Cambridge: Cambridge University Press, 1997.

Spellman, A. B. *Black Music.* New York: Schocken Books, 1970.

———. *Black Music, Four Lives.* New York: Schocken Books, 1970.

———. *Four Lives in the Bebop Business.* New York: Pantheon, 1966.

Stephens, Ruth, and John Stephens, eds. *The Tiger's Eye: On Arts and Letters (1940-1949).* Westport, Conn.: 1940-1949.

Stich, Sidra. *Anxious Visions: Surrealist Art.* Berkeley, Calif.: University Art Museum, 1990.

Stone-Richards, Michael. "The Political in the Culture of Surrealism." In Raymond Spiteri and Donald LaCoss, eds., *Surrealism, Politics and Culture.* Burlington, Vt.: Ashgate, 2003.

Stovall, Tyler. *Paris Noir: African Americans in the City of Light.* Boston: Houghton Mifflin, 1996.

Suleiman, Susan. *Subversive Intent.* Cambridge, Mass.: Harvard University Press, 1990.

Surya, Michel. *Georges Bataille: An Intellectual Biography.* London: Verso, 2002.

Sylla, Cheikh Tidiane. "Surrealism and Black African Art." *Arsenal/Surrealist Subversion,* no. 4 (1989).

———. "Symposium on the Future of Surrealism." *Cultural Correspondence,* nos. 12-14 (1981).

Tarnaud, Claude. *De . . . la face cachée d'un aventure afro-américaine.* Paris: L'Écart Absolu, 2003.

———. *De: The Hidden Face of an Afro-American Adventure.* Paris: L'Écart Absolu, 2003.

Tashjian, Dickran. *A Boatload of Madmen: Surrealism and the American Avant-Garde.* New York: Thames & Hudson, 1995.

Thirion, André. *Revolutionaries without Revolution.* New York: Macmillan, 1975.

Tengour, Habib. "Maghrebian Surrealism." *Peuples Méditerranéens,* no. 17 (1981).

Thirion, André. *Revolutionaries without Revolution.* New York: Macmillan, 1975.

Thomas, Darryl C., ed. "Race and Class: Cedric Robinson and the Philosophy of Black Resistance," *Race and Class,* 47, no. 2 (October–December 2005).

Thomas, John Jacob. *Froudacity: West Indian Fables Explained.* Introduction by C.L.R. James. London: New Beacon, 1969 (1889).

———. *The Theory and Practice of Creole Grammar.* Port-of-Spain, Trin.: Chronicle Publishing Office, 1869.

Tomich, Dale. "Aimé Césaire and Negritude." In Ron Sakolsky, ed., *Surrealist Subversions: Rants, Writings and Images by the Surrealist Movement in the United States.* Foreword by Franklin Rosemont. New York: Autonomedia, 2002.

———. *Slavery in the Circuit of Sugar: Martinique and the World Economy, 1830–1848.* Baltimore, Md.: Johns Hopkins University Press, 1990.

———. *Through the Prism of Slavery: Labor, Economy and World Economy.* Oxford: Rowman & Littlefield, 2004.

Toomer, Jean. *Cane.* New York: Boni & Liveright, 1975.

———. *Essentials.* Chicago: Lakeside Press, 1931.

Tropiques: Collections complètes. Paris: Éditions Jean-Michel Place, 1978.

Tutuola, Amos. *The Palm-Wine Drinkard and His Dead Palm-Wine Tapster in the Dead's Town.* New York: Grove Press, 1953.

U'Tamsi [U Tam'si], Felix Tchicaya. *Brush Fire.* Ibadan, Nigeria: Mbari Publications, 1964.

———. *Le mauvais sang.* Honfleur, France: P. J. Oswald, 1970 (1955).

———. *Selected Poems.* Translated by Gerald Moor. London: Heinemann, 1970.

Valorbe, François. *Carte noire.* Paris: Éditions Arcanes, 1953.

Van DeBurg, William. *New Day in Babylon: The Black Power Movement and American Culture, 1965–1975.* Chicago: University of Chicago Press, 1992.

Vidales, Luis. *Suenan timbres.* Bogotá: Editorial Minerva, 1926.

Viot, Jacques. *Poèmes de guerre.* Paris: Jean-Michel Place, 1994.

Waldberg, Patrick. *Surrealism.* Skira, 1962.

Warlick, M. E. *Max Ernst and Alchemy.* Austin: University of Texas Press, 2001.

Warner, Keith Q. *Critical Perspectives on Léon-Gontran Damas.* Washington, D.C.: Three Continents Press, 1988.

Warren, Paul. *Next Time Is for Life.* New York: Dell, 1953.

Wixson, Douglas. *Worker-Writer in America: Jack Conroy and the Traditions of Midwestern Literary Radicalism, 1898–1990.* Urbana: University of Illinois Press, 1994.

Woodson, Jon. "Jayne Cortez." In *Dictionary of Literary Biography,* vol. 41. Detroit, Mich.: Gale Research, 1985.

Woolman, David S. *Rebels in the Rif.* Stanford, Calif.: Stanford University Press, 1968.

Wright, Richard. *Black Power.* New York: Harper & Brothers, 1954.

———. *Eight Men.* New York: Avon, 1961.

————. *Lawd Today.* New York: Avon, 1963.

————. *The Long Dream.* Garden City, N.Y.: Doubleday, 1958.

————. *Twelve Million Black Voices: A Folk History of the Negro in the United States.* New York: Viking Press, 1941.

Yuen, Eddie, Daniel Burton Rose, and George Katsiaficas, eds. *The Battle of Seattle: The New Challenge to Capitalist Globalization.* New York: Soft Skull Press, 2001.

Zangana, Haifa. *Through the Vast Halls of Memory.* Paris: Hourglass, 1991.

Index

9 780292 725812